SCBCD Exam Study Kit

SCBCD
Exam Study Kit

JAVA BUSINESS COMPONENT DEVELOPER CERTIFICATION FOR EJB

PAUL SANGHERA

MANNING

Greenwich
(74° w. long.)

For online information and ordering of this and other Manning books, please go to www.manning.com. The publisher offers discounts on this book when ordered in quantity. For more information, please contact:

Special Sales Department
Manning Publications Co.
209 Bruce Park Avenue   Fax: (203) 661-9018
Greenwich, CT 06830   email: orders@manning.com

Manning Publications Co.   Copyeditor: Linda Recktenwald
209 Bruce Park Avenue   Typesetter: D. Dalinnik
Greenwich, CT 06830   Cover designer: Leslie Haimes

ISBN 1-932394-40-0
Printed in the United States of America
1 2 3 4 5 6 7 8 9 10 – VHG – 09 08 07 06 05

*To my parents, Parkash Kaur Sanghera and Nazar Singh Sanghera,
who gave me the things I needed to grow up—and wings to fly.*

*To my son, Adam Sanghera, and my wife, Renee Sanghera,
who give me everything every day that a being needs for living.*

brief contents

contents

Part 2   Session beans   55

3   Client view of a session bean   57

Part 4   Message-driven beans   245

11   Message-driven beans   247

Part 5   EJB services   265

12   EJB transactions   267

preface

It's a good thing, perhaps, to write for the amusement of the public, but it is a far higher and nobler thing to write for their instruction, their profit, their actual and tangible benefit.

— Mark Twain, "Curing a Cold"

This book is for Java programmers and students who know basic Java and want to prepare for the SCBCD exam, CX-310-090. Since the book has a laser-sharp focus on the exam objectives, expert EJB developers who want to pass the exam can use this book to ensure that they do not overlook any objective. Yet, it is not just an exam-cram book. The chapters and the sections within each chapter are presented in a logical learning sequence: every new chapter builds upon knowledge acquired in previous chapters, and there is no hopping from topic to topic. The concepts and topics, both simple and complex, are explained in a concise yet comprehensive fashion. This facilitates stepwise learning and prevents confusion—and makes this book also useful for beginners who want to get up to speed quickly, even if they are new to EJB technology. You will find yourself returning to this book as a handy reference even after you have taken and passed the exam.

How this book is organized

This book has five parts:

Part	Topic	Chapters
1	Enterprise JavaBeans	1 through 2
2	Session beans	3 through 5
3	Entity beans	6 through 10
4	Message-driven beans	11
5	EJB services	12 through 14

How each chapter is organized

With the exception of chapter 1 on J2EE, each chapter begins with a list of those exam objectives on which the chapter focuses. We follow the order of the objectives as published by Sun for the most part, but we do deviate from the published sequence in a few places in order to keep the topics and the subject matter in line with sequential learning and to avoid hopping from topic to topic.

The first section in each chapter is the Introduction, in which we establish the concepts or topics that will be explored in the chapter. As you read through a chapter, you will find Notes to emphasize important concepts or information and Alerts to point out information that may be contrary to your expectations depending on your level of experience with the technology. Both Notes and Alerts are important from the point of view of the exam. The Summary section of each chapter provides the big picture and reviews the important concepts in the chapter.

The Exam's-Eye View section highlights the important points in the chapter from the perspective of the exam: the information that you must comprehend, the things that you should watch out for because they might not seem to fit in with the ordinary order of things, and the facts that you should memorize for the exam.

Each chapter ends with review questions. This section has a two-fold purpose: to help you test your knowledge about the material presented in the chapter and to help you evaluate your ability to answer the exam questions based on the exam objectives covered in the chapter. The answers to the review questions are presented in appendix D.

This book and the exam are based on the EJB 2.0 specification, which you can download from the Sun web site http://www.sun.com/documentation

Conventions used in this book

Some of the conventions used in this book are described below:

- Methods are referred to as follows:

  - When a method name ends with (...), it means the method has one or more arguments.

  - When a method name ends with (), it means the method may or may not have one or more arguments.

  - When a method name does not end with (), it means we are referring to any method that belongs to a group of methods starting with this name; for example, a create method could be `create()`, `create(...)`, `createDiscount()`, and so on.

- The term "bean type" refers to a bean of a specific class, for example, a CustomerBean. A bean type may have multiple instances.

- The term "bean flavor" refers to three kinds of beans: session beans, entity beans, and message-driven beans. There are only these three flavors of beans.

Downloads

Source code for the programming example in appendix A is available for download from the publisher's web site at http://www.manning.com/sanghera.

You will also be able to download the abridged version of Whizlabs SCBCD Exam Simulator with practice exam questions from the same web site. More information on the exam simulator is available on page xxvii.

Author Online

Purchase of the *SCBCD Exam Study Kit* includes free access to Author Online, a private web forum run by Manning Publications, where you can make comments about the book, ask technical questions, and receive help from the author and from your fellow users. To subscribe to the forum, point your browser to http://www.manning.com/sanghera. This page gives you the necessary information on how to access the forum once you are registered, what kind of help is available, and the rules of conduct on the forum.

Manning's commitment to our readers is to provide a venue where a meaningful dialogue among individual readers and between the readers and the authors can take place. It is not a commitment to any specific amount of participation on the part of the authors, whose contribution to the AO is voluntary and unpaid.

The AO forum and the archives of the previous discussions will be accessible from the publisher's web site as long as the book is in print.

You can also reach the author through his web site at http://www.paulsanghera.com or via email at paul_s_sanghera@yahoo.com.

About the author

Dr. Paul Sanghera is an educator, technologist, and entrepreneur living in Silicon Valley, California. An expert in Java technologies and TCP/IP networking, Paul has ten years' programming and substantial teaching experience in Java. He has taught Java and other technologies at San Jose State University, Brooks College, CSU Hayward, and Golden Gate University. Having contributed to the development of technologies such as Netscape Browser and Novell's NDS, he has earned several industry certifications, including Sun Certified Business Component Developer, Sun Certified Java Programmer, CompTIA Project+, CompTIA Network+, and CompTIA Linux+. As a senior software engineer and an engineering manager, Paul has been at the ground floor of several successful startups such as WebOrder and mp3.com. With a master's degree in computer science from Cornell University and a PhD in physics from Carleton University, he has authored and co-authored more than 100 technical papers published in well-reputed European and American research journals. He has also presented talks by invitation at several international scientific conferences.

acknowledgments

As they say (well, if they don't anymore, they should), first things first. Let me begin by thanking Marjan Bace, publisher of Manning Publications, for opening the door for me to the world of technical book writing. With two thumbs up, thanks to Jackie Carter, the development editor for this book, for her patience, perseverance, professionalism, and above all for the trust she put in me during this turbulent and wonderful ride.

My first lesson in book writing is that it takes a team to transform an idea into a finished book. It is my great pleasure to acknowledge the hard work of the Manning team that made it happen. Here are only a few names I'd like to mention: Karen Tegtmeyer for managing the reviews, Iain Shigeoka for providing web support, Mary Piergies for managing the production process, Dottie Marsico for editing the design, and Denis Dalinnik for typesetting the manuscript. My special thanks to Linda Recktenwald for copyediting, Liz Welch for proofreading, and Jonathan Esterhazy for tech editing.

For offering constructive criticism and useful suggestions, my thanks to all the reviewers of the manuscript: Mahender Akula, Muhammad Ashikuzzaman, Vincenzo Baglio, Saikat Goswami, Mark Monster, Deiveehan Nallazhagappan, Debankur Naskar, Anil Punjabi, Paul Risenhoover, and Severin Stöckli.

In some ways, writing this book became an expression of the technologist and educator inside me. I thank my fellow technologists who guided me at various places during my journey in the computer industry from Novell to Dream Logic: Chuck Castleton at Novell, Delon Dotson at Netscape and MP3.com, Derrick Oien at MP3.com, Kate Peterson at WebOrder, and Dr. John Serri at Dream Logic.

I also thank my colleagues and seniors in the field of education for helping me in so many ways to become a better educator. Here are a few to mention: Dr. Gerald Pauler (Brooks College), Professor David Hayes (San Jose State University), Professor Michael Burke (San Jose State University), Dr. John Serri (University of Phoenix), Tim Heath (Embry-Riddle University), and Dr. Gary Tombleson (Embry-Riddle University).

Friends always lend a helping hand, in many visible and invisible ways, in almost anything important we do in our lives. Without them, the world would be a very boring and uncreative place. With that in mind, here are a few I'd like to mention: Stanley Huang, Patrick Smith, Kulwinder, Major Bhupinder Singh Daler, Deborah Critten, Ruth Gordon, Srilatha Moturi, and the Kandola family (Gurmail and Sukhwinder).

about the exam

With the popularity of J2EE in the enterprise, SCBCD certification is an important credential for an EJB developer to earn. SCBCD has Sun Certified Java Programmer (SCJP) certification as a prerequisite, and it is part of a spectrum of Java certification exams available from Sun.

The Java certification exams from Sun

The Java platform comes in three flavors: Java 2 Standard Edition (J2SE), Java 2 Enterprise Edition (J2EE), and Java 2 Micro Edition (J2ME). The certification paths based on these platforms include exams for the following certifications: Sun Certified Java Programmer (SCJP), Sun Certified Java Developer (SCJD), Sun Certified Web Component Developer (SCWCD), Sun Certified Business Component Developer (SCBCD), Sun Certified Developer for Java Web Services (SCDJWS), and Sun Certified Mobile Application Developer (SCMAD).

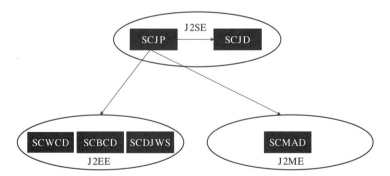

Certification paths based on the J2SE, J2EE, and J2ME platforms. SCJP certification is a prerequisite for SCBCD and all other certifications.

Preparing for the SCBCD exam

The Sun Certified Business Component Developer (SCBCD) for the Java 2 Platform, Enterprise Edition (J2EE) 1.3 exam is for programmers and developers who are responsible for designing, developing, testing, deploying, and integrating Enterprise JavaBeans (EJB) applications. If you are a beginner, you will learn EJB technology while preparing for the exam because this book is not a mere exam-cram. Even an expert may fail the exam if not prepared for it properly. From the exam point of view, pay special attention to the following items while preparing for the exam:

1 Carefully read the exam objectives in the beginning of each chapter.

2 Make sure you understand the Notes and Alerts in each chapter.

3 Study the review questions at the end of each chapter.

4 Review the Exam's-Eye View sections and Quick Prep in appendix E, during the last hours of your preparation.

Taking the SCBCD exam

The SCBCD certification consists of one exam available at authorized Prometric Testing Centers throughout the world. Following are some important details of the SCBCD exam:

- Exam ID: CX-310-090

- Prerequisite: SCJP certification

- Cost: $150 (The cost may vary by country and also if you have discount coupons.)

- Number of questions: 70

- Pass score: 64 percent; that is, answer 45 questions correctly out of 70

- Maximum time allowed: 120 minutes

The exam is available in the following languages: English, Simplified Chinese, Traditional Chinese, Japanese, Korean, and German. The question types are multiple choice, including drag and drop. In most of the questions, you are asked to select the correct answers from multiple answers presented for a question. The number of correct answers is given. Pay attention to the Exhibit button if it appears in a question. You click it to get the required information for the question. In some questions, you are asked to drag and drop options to the right place. According to many exam takers, there are hardly any questions with true/false answers, a lot of questions with two (or sometimes three) correct answers, and quite a few questions with radio button answers. Some questions will have very small code fragments. If you can't make up your mind about the answer to a question, you can skip it and come back to it later.

Like other Sun exams, the SCBCD exam starts with a survey that asks you questions regarding your level of knowledge and experience with different topics on EJB technology. Please don't get confused or panic; rest assured that this is not part of the actual exam.

Following are the main steps in the process of taking the exam:

1 You should purchase an exam voucher from your local Sun Education Services Office. You can also purchase the voucher online by going to http://suned.sun.com/US/certification/register/index.html.

2 The exams are conducted by Prometric all across the world, but you need to schedule your exam with them. After you have purchased the exam voucher, contact an authorized Prometric Testing Center near you. You can get the information regarding this from http://www.prometric.com.

3 Reach the testing center at least 15 minutes before the test start time, and be prepared to show two forms of identification, one of which should be a photo ID.

4 After you finish the test, the computer screen will display your result (whether you have passed or not). You will also receive a printed copy of the detailed results.

5 Within a month or so, you will receive your certificate from Sun in the mail if you passed the exam. For the current and complete information, you can visit the Sun exam site:

http://www.sun.com/training/certification/

Best wishes for the exam. Go for it!

about the exam simulator

The *SCBCD Exam Study Kit* offers you further resources to facilitate your preparation for the SCBCD exam including free access to the Whizlabs Exam Simulator available online and the Quick Prep Notes that you will find in appendix E, both provided courtesy of Whizlabs Software Pvt. Ltd.

Whizlabs SCBCD Exam Simulator

The abridged version of Whizlabs SCBCD Exam Simulator contains the following:

- 1 complete mock exam replicating the actual exam environment
- Quick Revision Notes (abridged version)
- Tips N Tricks
- Interactive Quiz (30 questions)

To download the software and information about system requirements, installation, activation, and usage please go to http://www.manning.com/sanghera.

Readers can also enjoy an exclusive 20% discount from Whizlabs on the full version of the SCBCD Exam Simulator. This version is more comprehensive and provides a total of 504 challenging questions spread across 5 Mock Exams (350 questions) and Quiz (154 questions). It additionally includes features like Quick Revision Notes, Tips N Tricks, Exhaustive Explanations, Comprehensive Reports, Customizable Exams & Quiz, Adaptive testing and 150% Test Pass Guarantee, all in a single package.

Whizlabs offers a special 10% discount for the readers of this book on all its Java-related instructor-led online trainings (SCJP 1.4, SCBCD, and SCWCD 1.4 trainings). Conducted over the Internet, by certified and expert instructors, Whizlabs Instructor-led Online Trainings are an effective technique of certification exam preparation.

NOTE Details about the offers mentioned above can be obtained by sending an email to manning_scbcd@whizlabs.com. Be sure to include the license number (2462952541) of the Whizlabs SCBCD abridged version. Or you can visit their web site at http://www.whizlabs.com.

Quick Preparation Notes

The Quick Preparation Notes cover important concepts and exam tips for the SCBCD exam, courtesy Whizlabs Software Pvt. Ltd. Developed comprehensively they will help you to revise the concepts taught in each chapter. Brushing through key areas in one go provides ease of learning and better retention of information for the exam. You can find these Quick Prep Notes in appendix E.

about the cover illustration

The figure on the cover of *SCBCD Exam Study Kit* is a "Turco del Asia," a Turk of Asia. The Turkic people are defined as those who speak languages in the Turkic family. They number close to 150 million in population and are the diverse descendants of large groups of tribespeople who originated in Central Asia, living today not only in Turkey, but also in the Balkans, Greece, Russia, the Middle East, and even in China. The illustration is taken from a Spanish compendium of regional dress customs first published in Madrid in 1799. The book's title page states:

> *Coleccion general de los Trages que usan actualmente todas las Nacionas del Mundo desubierto, dibujados y grabados con la mayor exactitud por R.M.V.A.R. Obra muy util y en special para los que tienen la del viajero universal*

which we translate, as literally as possible, thus:

> *General collection of costumes currently used in the nations of the known world, designed and printed with great exactitude by R.M.V.A.R. This work is very useful especially for those who hold themselves to be universal travelers*

Although nothing is known of the designers, engravers, and workers who colored this illustration by hand, the "exactitude" of their execution is evident in this drawing. The "Turco del Asia" is just one of many figures in this colorful collection. Their diversity speaks vividly of the uniqueness and individuality of the world's towns and regions just 200 years ago. This was a time when the dress codes of two regions separated by a few dozen miles identified people uniquely as belonging to one or the other. The collection brings to life a sense of isolation and distance of that period—and of every other historic period except our own hyperkinetic present.

Dress codes have changed since then and the diversity by region, so rich at the time, has faded away. It is now often hard to tell the inhabitant of one continent from another. Perhaps, trying to view it optimistically, we have traded a cultural and visual diversity for a more varied personal life. Or a more varied and interesting intellectual and technical life.

We at Manning celebrate the inventiveness, the initiative, and, yes, the fun of the computer business with book covers based on the rich diversity of regional life of two centuries ago, brought back to life by the pictures from this collection.

Enterprise JavaBeans

In this part of the book, you'll learn about Enterprise JavaBeans (EJB): session beans, which represent the processes; entity beans, which represent the data; and message-driven beans, which handle the messages. We'll examine the roles of the container provider, the application assembler, the deployer, and the system administrator—as well as your role as the bean provider, or bean developer.

In each chapter, we'll explore three avenues in search of the "prize": the certificate from Sun and a five-letter designation attached to your name, SCBCD (or Sun Certified Business Component Developer), that will bring you illumination.

To begin, let's take a bird's-eye view of Java 2 Enterprise Edition (J2EE) and then the part of it that we're interested in exploring: EJB. If you're already familiar with J2EE, you can start directly with the EJB part.

C H A P T E R 1

Introduction to J2EE

LEARNING OBJECTIVES

- The main features of the J2EE architecture
- J2EE containers
- Technologies used to develop, deploy, and execute a J2EE application
- Services offered by the J2EE platform
- Multiple roles in the process of developing, deploying, and executing J2EE applications
- The relationship between the J2EE and Enterprise JavaBeans (EJB) versions

INTRODUCTION

Enterprise JavaBeans (EJB) is a part of the Java 2 Platform Enterprise Edition (J2EE), a Java-based platform that offers a multitier integrated environment for developing, deploying, and executing enterprise applications. Because J2EE itself is not part of the SCBCD exam, no exam objectives are listed in this chapter. To enable you to comprehend EJB in the context of the big picture, we present a bird's-eye view of J2EE by exploring three avenues: the J2EE architecture, the technologies used to develop and support J2EE applications, and the multiple roles that transform the idea of the J2EE platform and the applications into reality. If you are already familiar with J2EE, you can skip this chapter.

3

1.1   *THE J2EE ARCHITECTURE*

The Java 2 Enterprise Edition (J2EE) platform standardizes the development of a distributed enterprise application. It is a component-based distributed architecture that introduces two server-side containers in which the components are deployed and executed.

A *component* is a reusable unit of software with well-defined interfaces and dependencies. Java servlets, JavaServer Pages (JSP), and JavaBeans are some examples of components. The presentation logic is implemented in components such as servlets and JSP that live in the web container, and the business logic is implemented in components called enterprise beans that live in the Enterprise JavaBeans (EJB) container, which is sandwiched between the web container and the database server.

The web and EJB containers are both parts of the J2EE architecture explored in the next section. Let's begin with a high-level view of the J2EE architecture in terms of tiers.

1.1.1   Bird's-eye view of the J2EE architecture

The J2EE architecture is defined in the J2EE specifications, which are developed under the control of Sun Microsystems through the Java community process, which is an organization of developers and industry partners. Let's explore the various aspects of the J2EE architecture. It offers a multitier distributed environment to develop, deploy, and execute enterprise applications. Figure 1.1 presents the J2EE architecture at the tier level.

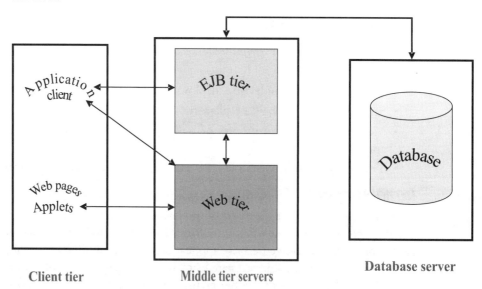

Figure 1.1   The multitier J2EE architecture. The business logic in the EJB tier and the presentation logic in the web tier are well separated from each other. The database part is sometimes called the Enterprise Information System (EIS) tier.

The client, the presentation logic, and the business logic are implemented in three separate tiers called the client tier, the web tier, and the EJB tier, respectively. For the storage of the application data, the J2EE standard requires a database accessible through the Java Database Connectivity (JDBC) API.

Now that you have a bird's-eye view of the J2EE architecture, let's explore its characteristics.

1.1.2 Characteristics of the J2EE architecture

To understand and appreciate the J2EE architecture, you must comprehend its core characteristics discussed in this section.

Multitier architecture

A *tier* is a layer that groups the software components to offer a specific kind of functionality or service. The multitier feature forms the basis for the J2EE architecture. This allows the software components to be distributed across different machines, which in turn facilitates scalability, security, and division of responsibility during development, deployment, and execution. The arrows in figure 1.1 represent tier-to-tier access. Depending on the application, a client may access the EJB tier directly or only through the web tier. In principle, any client (other than an applet) may access the database directly, but that defeats the whole purpose of J2EE. Similarly, an element in the web tier may access the database directly or only through the EJB tier, again depending on the application design. This flexibility in the architecture leaves room for varieties of applications of various sizes and with varied degrees of complexity. The web tier is also called the presentation tier because its function is to handle user input and present the results to the client. Similarly, the EJB tier is sometimes also called the business tier because this is where the business logic of the application is implemented. The database part is sometimes called the Enterprise Information System (EIS) tier in the literature.

The distributed environment

The distributed environment of the J2EE architecture allows the components of a system running on different machines to accomplish a common task. The multitiered nature of the J2EE architecture supports the distributed environment for the application. For example, while the components belonging to different tiers can run on different machines, they can run on the same machine as well. So, there is a lot of flexibility here. You can run components belonging to all the tiers on just one machine. However, this is a very trivial and perhaps impractical scenario. A practical yet simple scenario is for the client, the middle tier server, and the database server to be running on three different machines. To add sophistication to this case, you can replace the middle tier server with a cluster of servers, and of course there may be (and often are) multiple client machines.

Portability

Portability, in general, refers to the ability of an application to run on any platform. The motto of the Java language is "write once, run anywhere." That means an application written in Java can run on any operating system (OS). In other words, Java offers OS independence. J2EE offers two-dimensional portability: OS independence and vendor independence. OS independence is the result of J2EE being a Java-based platform, while vendor independence refers to the ability of a J2EE application to be deployed and run on different implementations of the J2EE platform by different vendors. Although J2EE supports portability, you, the developer, still have to take precautions while writing code to keep your application portable. You will learn more about it in the next chapter; for now, just trust me.

Interoperability

Interoperability refers to the ability of the software components written in one language and running in one environment (say J2EE) to communicate with the software components written in another language and running in a different environment (say Microsoft's .NET). This is important because enterprises end up using multiple platforms (environments) to meet their diverse needs. Interoperability between multiple platforms is vital to keep the enterprise systems integrated, and it is achieved through widely supported standards. J2EE supports interoperability with other platforms such as Common Object Request Broker Architecture (CORBA) and .NET. The interoperability of J2EE with non-Java platforms emerges from its support of the standard Internet communication protocols such as TCP/IP, HTTP, HTTPS, and XML.

Scalability

This property refers to the capability of a system to serve an increasing number of users without degrading its reliability and performance. Also, it means that if there is a huge increase in the number of users of the system, you need only make relatively small additions to the system to meet increased user demand. Because J2EE is a distributed architecture, it allows for scalability. For example, you could implement a cluster of J2EE servers to meet the needs of an increasing number of clients.

High availability and high performance

The multitier and distributed architecture of J2EE also supports high availability and high performance. These features can be implemented through clusters and load balancing. Servers can be added dynamically to meet the demands of increased load, and single points of failure can be eliminated by applying redundancy. Recall that J2EE is a software system, and therefore the high availability and high performance in this context are software (and not hardware) attributes.

Simplicity

Simplicity makes its way into the complexity of the J2EE architecture. By moving the task of implementing the infrastructure-level services to the J2EE server, the J2EE architecture greatly simplifies the process of developing, deploying, and executing enterprise applications. Developers now can focus on implementing the business logic without worrying about writing the code for the underlying infrastructure-level services.

> **NOTE** J2EE enables enterprise applications to follow both principles: write once, run anywhere, and write once, deploy anywhere, that is, OS independence and J2EE server independence.

The J2EE architecture comprises multiple tiers, and each tier contains software components and containers. Let's take a look at the containers.

1.1.3 J2EE platform containers

Before a component can be executed, it must be assembled into a J2EE application and deployed into its container. In other words, a J2EE application component can be executed only in a container and not without it. A J2EE container holds one kind of J2EE application components and provides them runtime support in the form of various services. For example, an application client container contains the client components, the web container contains the web tier components, and the EJB container contains the EJB tier components. Figure 1.2 shows the containers in the J2EE architecture.

Note that the application client, typically a Java program, is packaged in an application client container, and it can communicate directly with the EJB container or the

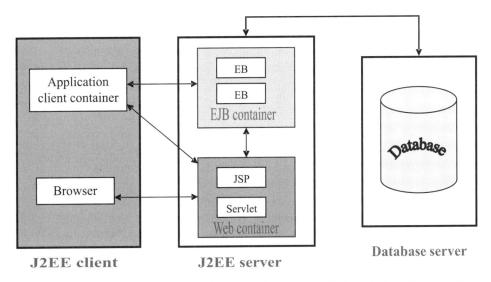

Figure 1.2 J2EE containers contain and manage the components in their tiers. For example, the EJB container contains the enterprise beans.

web container. The web client, which uses HTTP to communicate, communicates exclusively with the web container. The client could also be a Java applet, which typically executes in a web browser. The web container and the EJB container are implemented by the J2EE product vendor in the J2EE server.

Some of the functions that the containers perform are listed here:

- They provide methods for the application components to interact with each other, that is, they mediate the interactions.
- The container providers provide APIs to support a Java-compatible runtime environment. For example, J2EE 1.3 containers are required to provide the runtime environment of Java 2 Platform Standard Edition (J2SE) version 1.3.
- The containers offer services to the components such as transaction management, security, naming and lookup, and remote connectivity.

Implementing the infrastructure-level functionality such as remote connectivity common to all J2EE applications makes the application development task much simpler and easier. J2EE application developers now can focus on the presentation and business logic.

> **NOTE** A J2EE application component can be executed only in a container. It needs a container to be deployed in, to get runtime services, and to be executed at an appropriate time.

The J2EE architecture presents an integrated environment encompassing all the parts of an enterprise application from the client to the database. An application on the J2EE platform would in general be a distributed application system of software components working together to accomplish a common task.

1.2 J2EE APPLICATION SYSTEM

The J2EE platform offers support for end-to-end applications that extend all the way from the client to the database. As an example, consider an application that would present an amazon.com-like online bookstore. J2EE applications are generally complex and sophisticated. However, a J2EE server based on the multitier distributed architecture simplifies application development, deployment, and execution. WebSphere from IBM and WebLogic from BEA Systems are examples of J2EE servers. Because these servers from different vendors are based on the same standard specifications, an application written once can be deployed and executed on a J2EE server from any vendor, a principle called "write once, deploy anywhere."

Not to anyone's surprise, it takes a multitude of technologies to put together an application system of this magnitude in size and scope. We list those technologies in the next section.

1.2.1 Using J2EE technologies for application development

Because J2EE applications are end-to-end, sophisticated, and distributed systems, you need a variety of technologies to develop them. J2EE supports a number of technologies that you can use to develop software components for the different tiers. Some of these technologies are discussed here.

Client technologies

A J2EE client is a software component in the client tier. Two kinds of J2EE clients are

- *Application client*—An application client can communicate directly with a software component in the EJB tier or with a component in the web tier using HTTP. An application client can have a command-line interface or a graphical user interface (GUI). Application clients are developed using the Java language.
- *Web client*—A web client is a software component in the client tier that uses HTTP to communicate with the components in the web tier. It may be a Java program that opens an HTTP connection, or a web browser. The HTTP response from the web tier may have a Java applet embedded in the HTML page. The applet is a small Java program that would be executed in the Java Virtual Machine (JVM) installed in the web browser.

On the server side, we need presentation technologies to write the components for the web tier.

Presentation technologies

These are the technologies that are used to develop software components for the presentation layer, that is, the web tier. These components receive the request from the client and communicate with the components in the EJB tier, or they can directly interact with the database in the EIS tier to compile a response. They present the response, for example, in a web page, and send it to the web client. You develop these software components using Java servlets or JSP technologies. Java servlets are HTTP-aware Java classes. A JSP is a script-like document that is translated into a Java servlet by the JSP engine and is dynamically compiled and executed. You can use servlets, JSP, or both. You may also develop JavaBeans for the web tier that could be used by a servlet (or a JSP) to communicate with the EJB tier or the EIS tier. JavaBeans are the Java classes written according to certain rules. They are different from EJBs.

Before the presentation layer can present the response, the response needs to be figured out and compiled using business logic. So, we need technologies to implement the business logic of the application.

Business logic technologies

These technologies are used to develop the software components for the business layer, that is, the EJB tier. The components built using these technologies implement the business logic of the application. In J2EE, these business components are developed using the component technology called Enterprise JavaBeans.

> **NOTE** JavaBeans and Enterprise JavaBeans are two different Java technologies. While JavaBeans are standard Java classes written according to some rules and executed in a JVM, Enterprise JavaBeans are the components that need a container for runtime support and can be executed only inside the container. Also, they are generally more sophisticated in their functionality than JavaBeans.

The last tier in the J2EE system is the EIS tier, and J2EE supports some technologies to connect to this tier.

Database API technologies

The software components in the web tier or in the EJB tier (and possibly in the client tier as well) use a database API if they want to communicate directly with the database tier. The J2EE platform requires the use of the JDBC API (a set of Java classes and interfaces) for communicating with the database.

The technologies discussed in this section are used to develop the software components for various layers. These components are executed in their containers, which provide the runtime support for them. The containers are implemented in the J2EE platform provided by the J2EE product vendors.

Now you can ask questions such as "How do the components in different tiers and possibly on different machines communicate with one another?" and "How does the container implement the services that it offers?" Let's reduce your questions, for now, to a less-ambitious question: "What are the technologies used for supporting the J2EE applications?"

1.2.2 J2EE platform support for applications

The J2EE specification requires a set of standard services that a J2EE product vendor must implement. These services are used to support the J2EE application. Some of these services are discussed here.

Naming service

Because the J2EE platform offers a distributed environment, the components and services can reside on multiple machines. Consequently, a naming and lookup mechanism is required to locate the components and services. The Java Naming and Directory Interface (JNDI) provides this mechanism. For example, a client program would use JNDI to find a service on another machine.

Transaction service

Managing the transactions for the application components is an important task. This task is accomplished in a platform-independent way using the Java Transaction API

(JTA). For example, consider multiple clients accessing the database concurrently. The JTA would help maintain correctness and consistency during these concurrent database operations. Transactions in EJB are discussed in detail in chapter 12.

Message service

Enterprise applications need to exchange messages such as notifications and invoices with one another. The Java Message Service (JMS) API facilitates messaging in both models: point to point and publish-subscribe. In the point-to-point model, a message sent by a sender is consumed by only one receiver, while in the publish-subscribe model, a message sent by a sender may be consumed by multiple receivers called subscribers.

Mail service

Enterprise applications may require the ability to send and receive email messages. The Java Mail API implements this functionality.

Remote access service

In a distributed environment, a component on one machine may need to invoke a method of a component on another machine: the remote invocation. The Java Remote Method Invocation (RMI) standard hides the network details by providing "seamless remote invocation on objects in different virtual machines."

XML processing service

Extended Markup Language (XML) is an integral part of J2EE applications. Java API for XML (JAXP) is used for writing and parsing XML files. JAXP provides support for XML tools such as Simple API for XML Parsing (SAX), Document Object Model (DOM), and XML Stylesheet Language for Transformations (XSLT). XML provides an open standard for exchanging data between applications over the Internet. It's also useful for writing configuration files in text format for the applications running on the local machine. Appendix B presents a brief introduction to XML.

Security service

The security in an enterprise application is usually enforced by controlling user authentication and access authorization to this application. The Java Authentication and Authorization Service (JAAS) provides this security by offering a mechanism for authenticating users or a group of users who want to run the application. Security in EJB is explored in chapter 14.

In table 1.1, we present a list of the J2EE technologies discussed on these pages.

Table 1.1 J2EE 1.3 technologies. This is not a complete list.

Technology	Popular Name/Acronym	Version
Enterprise JavaBeans	EJB	2.0
Extensible Markup Language	XML	1.0
Java API for XML Parsing	JAXP	1.1
Java Authorization and Authentication Service	JAAS	1.0
Java Mail	JavaMail	1.2
Java Message Service	JMS	1.0
Java Database Connectivity API	JDBC API	2.0
Java Naming and Directory Interface	JNDI	1.2
JavaServer Pages	JSP	1.2
Java Servlets	Servlets	2.3
Java Transaction API	JTA	1.0

Developing a multitier distributed J2EE system (application and platform) is a monumental task. The good news is that we have a standard specification to follow, and J2EE is a distributed architecture. This allows the possibility of splitting this task into multiple subtasks that will be performed by different parties.

1.3   THE J2EE IMPLEMENTATION

The J2EE implementation involves developing applications and the platform to support the applications. Depending on the business requirements, an application could be anywhere on the spectrum from a very simple application running on one machine to a very complex application running on several machines. Because the J2EE architecture is based on tiers and components, it allows multiple parties (individuals or organizations) to implement different parts of the J2EE system. The responsibility of each party in implementing the J2EE system is called an *implementation role*.

1.3.1   J2EE implementation roles

To implement the end-to-end J2EE system, we meet the diverse skill requirements by defining multiple roles in the implementation process starting from developing the J2EE platform to administering the running J2EE application. These roles are discussed in the following sections.

J2EE product provider

This is the vendor that develops and markets the J2EE platform with all the containers and services required by the specifications. This vendor also supplies the deployment and management tools.

Tool provider

A tool provider develops and markets tools for the development, packaging, deployment, management, and monitoring of applications. The J2EE product providers usually also provide the tools.

Now we need someone to write the software components.

Application component provider

This is a developer (a person or a company) who develops the components for the web container or the EJB container:

- *Web component developer*—The responsibility of a web component developer is to implement the client side (presentation) logic in the following components: JSP, servlet, HTML, graphics, and Java files, including JavaBeans. The web component developer also writes the deployment descriptor files and bundles the .class, .jsp, .html, and descriptor files into the Web Archive (WAR) file.

- *EJB component developer*—The responsibility of an EJB component developer (a person or a company) is to develop Enterprise JavaBeans, write the deployment descriptor, and bundle the .class files and the deployment descriptor into a Java Archive (JAR) file, called an ejb-jar file.

Who will put these components together to compose an application?

Application assembler

The responsibility of an application assembler is to assemble the components (the web components and the EJB components) into a full J2EE application. This involves packaging the WAR file and the ejb-jar file into an enterprise archive (ear) file. In order to accomplish this task, the assembler typically uses the tools supplied by the application product provider or the tool provider.

Now, somebody has to deploy the application into the real operational environment.

Application deployer

After the application has been assembled, it needs to be deployed into a specific operational environment before it can go live. The deployer accomplishes this task by taking the following steps:

1. *Installation*—Move the application package (ear file) to the J2EE server.
2. *Configuration*—Configure the application for the operational environment at hand by modifying the deployment descriptor.
3. *Execution*—Start the application.

Now, we want to make sure the application keeps running.

Application administrator

An application administrator is usually the system administrator responsible for the application server and the underlying infrastructure. Therefore, the responsibility of an application administrator is to monitor and manage the deployed application and its environment, the application server, the machine, and the network.

Vendors such as IBM and BEA Systems develop commercial versions of the J2EE platform. In this book, we will use the reference implementation by Sun Microsystems.

1.3.2 The J2EE reference implementation

The J2EE reference implementation (RI) is a noncommercial product available from Sun Microsystems free of charge. This package includes a J2EE server, a web server, a relational database called Cloudscape, and a set of development and deployment tools. You can download the J2EE Software Development Kit (SDK) from http://java.sun.com/j2ee/download.html#sdk.

A comprehensive guide on installing the SDK and setting up the development environment on your machine is presented in appendix A.

1.4 THE J2EE AND EJB VERSIONS

EJBs are a part of J2EE. When you download the J2EE Software Development Kit (SDK), EJB is included with it. This book is based on EJB version 2.0. The version numbers of J2EE and EJB are different from each other in the same package. To avoid any confusion about versions, we present the EJB versions corresponding to the different J2EE versions in table 1.2.

Table 1.2   Versions of EJB and J2EE

EJB Version	Corresponding J2EE Version	Main New EJB Features	Status
EJB 2.0	J2EE 1.3	Message-driven beans, local interfaces, EJB query language, and more interoperability features	In wide use.
EJB 2.1	J2EE 1.4	Support for web services, container-managed timer service, enhancements to EJB QL	The industry has not yet made the complete transition to this version.
EJB 3.0	J2EE 1.5	Simplifies the process of development and deployment	Work in progress at the time of writing this book.

In the exercise presented in appendix A, you will be using version 1.3 of J2EE, which contains version 2.0 of EJB.

1.5 SUMMARY

The Java 2 Enterprise Edition (J2EE) architecture offers a multitier and distributed environment for developing, deploying, and executing enterprise applications. The three main tiers are the client tier, the web tier, and the Enterprise JavaBeans (EJB) tier. In addition to these tiers, J2EE supports connection to the Enterprise Information Systems (EIS) tier that contains the database. J2EE is a component-based architecture. Each tier is composed of a container that holds the software components. The components can run only in the containers, which manage the components by offering infrastructure-level services.

From the development viewpoint, a J2EE system has two parts: the application and the platform, which offers the runtime environment for the application. The platform is provided by server vendors that implement the container services and other system-level services. The J2EE applications are end-to-end solutions extending from the client side all the way to the database. Therefore, multiple roles are involved in the process of developing, deploying, and executing these applications.

The middle tier of J2EE contains the web tier and the EJB tier. The presentation logic of the application is implemented in the web tier, while the business logic is implemented in the EJB tier. The EJB tier, the subject of this book, contains Enterprise JavaBeans as its software components. In the next chapter, we present an overview of EJB.

C H A P T E R 2

Overview of Enterprise JavaBeans

EXAM OBJECTIVES

1.1 Identify the use, benefits, and characteristics of Enterprise JavaBeans technology, for version 2.0 of the EJB specification.

1.2 Identify EJB 2.0 container requirements.

1.3 Identify correct and incorrect statements or examples about EJB programming restrictions.

1.4 Match EJB roles with the corresponding description of the role's responsibilities, where the description may include deployment descriptor information.

1.5 Given a list, identify which are requirements for an ejb-jar file.

13.1 Identify correct and incorrect statements or examples about an enterprise bean's environment JNDI naming.

13.2 Identify correct and incorrect statements about the purpose and/or use of the deployment descriptor elements for environment entries, ejb references, and resource manager connection factory references, including whether a given code listing is appropriate and correct with respect to a particular deployment descriptor element.

13.3 Given a list of responsibilities, identify which belong to the deployer, bean provider, application assembler, container provider, system administrator, or any combination.

INTRODUCTION

In the previous chapter, you took a quick tour of the distributed J2EE architecture, which supports the development, deployment, and execution of enterprise applications. The J2EE architecture is composed of multiple tiers, including the web and business tiers. The business tier of the J2EE platform, used to implement the business logic of an application, is defined in the Enterprise JavaBeans (EJB) specification. EJB is a component-based, server-side, and distributed architecture that standardizes the development, deployment, and execution of enterprise applications that are scalable, secure, and transactional and that support multiple users concurrently. Furthermore, EJB facilitates the development of applications that are portable across multiple J2EE-compliant application servers and also are interoperable with platforms other than J2EE, such as .NET.

The EJB architecture is composed of two main parts: EJB components (enterprise beans) and the EJB container. The complex distributed nature of the EJB architecture requires multiple distinct roles in the lifecycle of an enterprise application: the bean provider, application assembler, deployer, system administrator, and container provider.

In this chapter, we will provide a bird's-eye view of the EJB landscape. Our goal is two-pronged: show you the big picture, and provoke you to ask questions about the details that will be answered throughout the book. The three avenues you will explore are enterprise beans, the environment in which they live and die, and the players of EJB land who run the show, such as the bean provider and the container provider.

2.1   UNDERSTANDING THE EJB ARCHITECTURE

EJB is a component-based architecture that specifies the business tier of the J2EE platform. It supports the development of distributed and portable enterprise applications with automated security and transaction management. The EJB architecture contains the EJB components, that is, the enterprise beans, which run inside the EJB container. To explore the EJB architecture, consider the following questions:

- What are the pieces of the EJB architecture?
- How are the pieces related to each other?
- How do the pieces work together in the big picture of J2EE?

This section is an answer to these questions. Let's begin with an overview of the EJB architecture: the different pieces of the architecture and how they work together.

2.1.1 EJB architecture: The big picture

A high-level view of the EJB architecture is presented in figure 2.1, which shows different components of the architecture and displays several possible scenarios about how the different components interact with each other. We will discuss these scenarios in this section.

Pieces of the EJB architecture

The EJB architecture has three main pieces:

- The software components: the Enterprise JavaBeans, which we will also refer to as enterprise beans or just beans
- The EJB container that contains and manages the beans and offers them run-time services
- The EJB server that contains the EJB container and offers system-level services

Currently, the EJB specifications do not draw a clear line between the EJB container and the EJB server. The J2EE server acts as the EJB server.

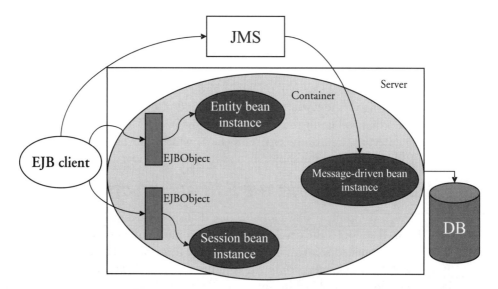

Figure 2.1   The EJB architecture. A client does not have direct access to the beans. It communicates with beans through mediators: an EJBObject or JMS. The client may be a message producer for the JMS server, a client for a session bean instance, or a client for an entity bean instance. Each bean instance has its own EJBObject.

There are three kinds of enterprise beans:

- Session beans, which represent a process; for example, there could be a session bean to implement the shopping cart for an online store.
- Entity beans, which represent an entity in the database; for example, there could be an entity bean to represent a customer in the database.
- Message-driven beans, which handle messages from the Java Messaging Service (JMS); for example, there could be a message-driven bean to send a newsletter when it's published to the users who subscribed to it.

Later in this chapter, we will discuss these pieces further. Now, let's see how these pieces work together.

EJB pieces working together

The job of a bean is to service the client call by executing an appropriate bean method. The client of a bean could be a simple Java program or another bean. However, a client cannot call the bean methods directly; the call will get to the bean only through mediators. The mediators are the JMS in the case of a message-driven bean and interfaces in the case of a session bean and an entity bean. The interfaces expose some methods implemented in the bean class. The container provides classes that implement the bean's interfaces, which fall into two categories: component interfaces and home interfaces. An instance of the class that implements the component interface is called an *EJBObject*.

An EJB client cannot call the bean methods directly, but it can invoke them through an EJBObject. What makes the EJBObject? The container constructs an EJBObject by instantiating the class that implements the component interface. Then the container uses the EJBObject to intercept the calls from the client to the bean instance. In other words, the client cannot have direct access to the bean instance; the client call is interrupted by the EJBObject associated with the bean instance and is routed to the bean instance by the container. So, when an EJB client is communicating with an entity bean or a session bean, there are two players in the middle of the client and the bean instance, and the client call goes to the bean instance through these two players: an EJBObject and the container.

The calls from the client to the message-driven bean are routed through the JMS. In other words, no EJBObject is involved in the case of a message-driven bean. The bean instance and the container collaborate to interact with the database in the Enterprise Information Systems (EIS) tier.

> **NOTE** In the case of a session bean and an entity bean, the bean client communicates with the bean instance through an EJBObject associated with the bean instance and the container. The communication between a client and a message-driven bean is mediated by the JMS.

The container provides the low-level services for the beans. We discuss the services required of the container by the EJB specification in the next section.

2.1.2   Defining container requirements

You have seen in the previous section that the bean and the container implement the interfaces and use them to interrupt the client calls to the bean and route the calls to the bean instance. It is clear by now that the container mediates the client calls to a bean instance. You may wonder what else the container does for the bean. The relationship between the container and the bean is defined by the EJB specification by specifying a contract (API) between the enterprise beans and the container. This enables the beans to run in any container that meets the EJB specification. The container provides the runtime support for the beans by offering a set of services. From the developer's viewpoint, this simplifies the application development process. Now the developers don't need to write the code in each application to implement these services. We list here the main services offered by the container.

Transaction management

The business applications often require handling a *transaction,* which is a set of operations, generally on a database, that are treated as an atomic unit. The EJB platform supports both kinds of transactions: local and distributed. A *local* transaction usually involves a single database, while a *distributed* transaction may involve multiple databases on several machines. To offer a transaction management service, the container uses the Java Transaction API (JTA) to apply the Java Transaction Service (JTS). The EJB transactions are covered in chapter 12.

Security management

The container offers authentication and access rights services. These services may be invoked by defining appropriate elements in the deployment descriptor file. EJB security is covered in chapter 14.

State management

The container offers the state management service to manage the state of the bean instances. For example, it will save the bean's state between two consecutive method calls to a stateful bean.

Lifecycle management

To manage the lifecycle of a bean, the container provides services such as object activation, thread management, resource allocation, and object destruction. We will explore the lifecycle of a session bean, an entity bean, and a message-driven bean in chapters 5, 8, and 11, respectively.

Persistence management

The container takes care of when and how to store and retrieve persistent object data. Persistence management is done for the beans that represent in memory the entities in persistent storage. You will learn more about persistence management in chapters 7 and 9.

Location transparency

The container provides this service by transparently handling network communication. This enables the client to communicate with the bean without having to make a distinction between a local and a remote call. Therefore, the clients that use the remote interfaces to communicate with a bean instance may be deployed within the same Java Virtual Machine (JVM) as the bean or within a different JVM on a different machine; that is, the remote clients are not aware of the location. This is not true for the local clients; a client that uses a local interface to communicate with a bean instance must be deployed within the same JVM as the bean.

Support for multiple types of clients

The bean developer does not have to deal with the issue of what type of client would access this bean. The container provides support for multiple types of clients, such as a component from the web container, an HTTP client, or another enterprise bean.

> **NOTE** The remote client of an EJB bean may be deployed within the same JVM where the bean is deployed or within a different JVM on a remote machine, while a local client must be deployed within the same JVM where the bean is deployed.

In the upcoming chapters, you will learn in greater detail about all the services required from the container. For now, simply note that the beans live inside the container that offers them the runtime services. In the next section, we will take a closer look at Enterprise JavaBeans, the software components of the EJB architecture.

2.2 UNDERSTANDING THE EJB COMPONENTS

EJB is one of several popular component-based architectures in which a *component* refers to a reusable piece of application code that was written according to a standard and that may be customized at deployment time. Components in other architectures are written in various languages such as Visual Basic and C++.

In EJB, enterprise beans are the software components written in Java, and they are used to implement the business logic of an enterprise application. They are the heart of the EJB architecture. To clarify what we mean when we refer to the EJB architecture and enterprise beans, let's get some terminology straight. Strictly speaking, enterprise beans and Enterprise JavaBeans (EJB) do not mean the same thing. *Enterprise JavaBeans* (EJB) refers to the architecture of the business tier in the J2EE, and *enterprise beans* are the components in this architecture. Having clarified this, we will follow the conventional terminology throughout this book; from now on whenever we use the term *enterprise bean*, *bean*, or EJB, we mean enterprise bean unless stated otherwise.

Enterprise beans are the components that are used to implement the business logic of an enterprise application, while Enterprise JavaBeans (EJB) is an architecture to which the enterprise beans conform.

Even if you have not used enterprise beans, you may have heard of or used JavaBeans, which we also refer to as ordinary Java beans or plain Java beans in this book. In the following section, we will discuss the characteristics of enterprise beans (or Enterprise JavaBeans) and what makes them different from the ordinary Java beans (or JavaBeans).

2.2.1 Characteristics of enterprise beans

To truly understand and appreciate all the characteristics of enterprise beans, you need to read through this whole book. So, to build your appetite for this journey, we are singling out some essential characteristics to list here.

Dynamic

Enterprise beans are dynamic in two ways: they can be customized at deployment time, and their instances are created at runtime by the container. This means you can change the behavior of an enterprise bean by modifying the parameters in a file called a *deployment descriptor*, and you do not need to change the code and recompile it. This allows a developer to write flexible beans that can be used by various applications and customized to fulfill the varying needs of the same or different applications.

Container controlled

An enterprise bean is created, managed, and served by the EJB container. It cannot run without the container. In other words, it has no `main()` method of its own. Furthermore, the container acts as a mediator between the bean and its client. The container also provides system-level services such as transaction management and security. Keeping these services separate from the bean allows the service information to be managed by tools during application assembly and deployment as opposed to coding it into the bean. This helps to make the bean more dynamic, customizable, and portable.

Write once, deploy anywhere

Because they are written in Java, enterprise beans obviously inherit the operating system independence of Java: "write once, run anywhere." However, the EJB platform takes you one step further on the road to independence. Because both the beans and the container/server in which the beans execute are written in compliance with the EJB specification, you can deploy your bean into an EJB container/server from any EJB-compliant vendor. This property of enterprise beans is called "write once, deploy anywhere." Note that this is true only if the bean uses only the services defined by the EJB specification. The vendors usually implement additional services in the container—what the vendors call "value-added services." If a bean depends on one of these value-added services, it can be deployed only in another container that offers that service as well. So, a value-added service can reduce the portability of your bean.

Reusability

An enterprise bean, once written, can be used in multiple applications without having to make any changes in the source code and hence without having to recompile. Those applications may be running on different platforms, on J2EE servers from different vendors, and may need to use the bean in different ways. This capability follows from the platform independence (write once, run anywhere), server independence (write once, deploy anywhere), and customization capability of an enterprise bean.

NOTE Enterprise beans follow the two important principles of the J2EE world: "write once, run anywhere" and "write once, deploy anywhere."

Did anybody say business logic? Yes, the core functionality of enterprise beans is to encapsulate the business logic of an application. Repeat...

If you have developed or used ordinary Java beans, you will realize that the characteristics discussed above take Java bean technology to a whole new level. This is also apparent from the following section where we compare ordinary Java beans with enterprise beans.

2.2.2 JavaBeans and Enterprise JavaBeans

The odds are pretty good that you knew JavaBeans (the ordinary Java beans) before you bumped into Enterprise JavaBeans. The common term *JavaBeans* shared by the two may create confusion for a beginner. Therefore, it is important to understand the differences between them. Although both JavaBeans and Enterprise JavaBeans are written in Java, they are two different beasts. The differences between JavaBeans and Enterprise JavaBeans are listed here:

- JavaBeans run in the JVM, while Enterprise JavaBeans run in an EJB-compliant container and use the low-level services provided by the container and the server.
- Both JavaBeans and Enterprise JavaBeans are written in Java. However, enterprise beans take the meaning of reusability to a new level. The behavior of the enterprise beans may be changed without ever changing the code and recompiling it, for example, with the use of deployment descriptors.
- JavaBeans are much simpler, while enterprise beans can be much more sophisticated and designed to implement often-complex server-side business logic.
- JavaBeans are often used in the presentation tier, for example, to build a GUI component, while Enterprise JavaBeans are used in the business tier to implement business logic.

All of these distinguishing features of Enterprise JavaBeans simplify the development of distributed, transactional, secure, and portable enterprise applications. Note that JavaBeans and Enterprise JavaBeans are not alternatives to each other. JavaBeans generally serve the presentation tier, and Enterprise JavaBeans serve the business tier. Therefore, even though JavaBeans and EJB are both written in Java, EJB is a different technology with a bigger scope. In the next section, we will discuss some of the benefits of this technology.

2.3 BENEFITS OF EJB TECHNOLOGY

One of the exam objectives expects you to identify the benefits of Enterprise Java-Beans technology. This rather vague objective actually refers to the business benefits. If you, the developer, are aware of the business benefits of EJB technology, this knowledge can help you to convince the decision makers in your organization (or a client of your organization) to use EJB technology for the project under consideration. Also as a developer, you would be apt to keep things in perspective if you knew the business benefits of the technology you develop. Therefore, in this section, we will venture toward the junction of marketing and technology.

It's important to understand that scalability, versatility, maintainability, and round-the-clock availability have become not just desired but required features of the commerce systems in the economy of the Internet age. EJB technology holds the promise of meeting these requirements by offering the benefits discussed in the following sections.

2.3.1 Reduced time to market

The following features of EJB technology contribute to making development faster and thereby reducing the time to market:

- Multiple vendors implement the infrastructure-level services such as security, transaction management, state management, and connection pooling required by the EJB specification in an application server. Therefore, developers needn't develop these services as part of their applications. They can focus on implementing business logic in the beans that would run in the server environment.

- Enterprise beans, once written, can be used in multiple applications without having to change the code or recompile. This reusability feature allows you to purchase off-the-shelf beans and deploy them in your application.

Reducing the time to market gives a vendor a competitive advantage and indirectly contributes to cost effectiveness.

2.3.2 Cost effectiveness

The following features of EJB technology help reduce the development cost:

- Because EJB is a Java-based technology, it inherits portability from Java. Applications, once written, may be run on a wide spectrum of operating system platforms. This reduces the cost because, in general, corporations have multiple operating system environments.

- Because the server vendors build the services in compliance with the same EJB specification, enterprise beans, once written, can be deployed to any EJB-compliant server. This greatly reduces the cost by freeing corporations from vendor lock-in.

Development cost is only part of the overall project cost. Other features such as reliability and robustness help reduce the overall cost as well.

2.3.3   Reliability and robustness

The following features of EJB technology contribute to building reliable and robust applications:

- Because the infrastructure-level services are offered by well-tested commercial application servers, the applications become more robust and reliable.
- EJB technology, by providing a distributed environment, facilitates the implementation of fault tolerance by replication and hence promotes reliability.

Although load balancing and fault tolerance are not mandated by the EJB specification, the distributed nature of EJB technology allows for multiple servers that can offer load balancing and fault tolerance. Such a system is scalable in the sense that adding one more server into the system can satisfy the demand put on the system by a significant increase in the number of clients. The system is fault tolerant because if one server goes down, another server in the cluster can take over. This also ensures round-the-clock availability.

There is another benefit of EJB technology from the application viewpoint: it covers a comprehensive scope for developing solutions to business problems. To handle the business logic of a broad spectrum of enterprise applications, EJB architecture offers three types of beans; we introduce these in the next section.

2.4   *THREE FLAVORS OF ENTERPRISE BEANS*

When a client invokes a method on the bean, it may be looked upon as a communication between the client and the bean because the data is generally exchanged in method calls. Clients communicate with enterprise beans through the EJB container. The communication generally may be one of two kinds: synchronous or asynchronous. The communication is called *synchronous* when the communicating entities have to be present on both ends at the same time. A telephone conversation is an example of synchronous communication. In *asynchronous* communication, the two communicating entities don't have to be present on both ends at the same time. Email is an example of asynchronous communication. EJB supports both kinds of communication by offering three kinds of beans: entity beans, session beans, and message-driven beans.

2.4.1 Beans that handle synchronous communication: Entity beans and session beans

Synchronous communication is needed for interactive applications. EJB offers two kinds of beans to support synchronous communication: entity beans and session beans. The applications are written to solve real-world problems. The real world consists of things and the interactions between the things. In EJB, things are represented by entity beans, and interactions (processes) by session beans.

Entity beans

Entity beans are used to represent entities such as students, employees, managers, and invoices. When you think of an entity bean, think of a noun. An instance of an entity bean would hold in memory a record about the corresponding entity from the data table in the database. For example, an instance of the Student bean may hold (name=Gurmail, ID=101, GPA=4.0), while another instance of the same entity bean may hold (name=Dan, ID=420, GPA=2.0). Entity beans also implement data access logic. In short, entity beans encapsulate the logic for accessing and manipulating the entities stored in persistent storage.

Session beans

While entity beans deal with business data, session beans encapsulate the logic for a business process and business rules. Defining session beans separately from entity beans allows you to change the business rules (or a process) without changing the business data. A session bean serves a single client and performs operations such as verifying credit card info. When you think of a session bean, think of a verb. There are two variations of session beans: stateful session beans and stateless session beans. A *stateful* session bean maintains the conversation state with a client for multiple method invocations from the same client. An instance of a stateful session bean serves only one client and exists only for the lifetime of the session with that client. In contrast, a *stateless* session bean does not maintain the conversational state with a client. The container can create a number of instances of a stateless session bean and put them into a pool. A method call on a stateless session bean can be serviced by any of these instances, and after servicing the call, the instance goes back to the pool. Because stateless session bean instances do not maintain the conversational state with the client, method calls from the same client can be serviced by different instances.

> **NOTE** A stateful session bean instance serves only a single client and is destroyed at the end of the session. A stateless session bean instance serves only one client at a time and after serving a method call goes back to the pool.

A comparison of entity beans and session beans is presented in table 2.1.

Table 2.1 Comparison between an entity bean and a session bean

Characteristic	Stateful Session Bean	Stateless Session Bean	Entity Bean
Identity	Represents a process. Performs a task for only one client during its full lifecycle.	Represents a process. May serve several clients during its lifecycle but only one client at a time.	Represents a business entity in persistent storage. Holds a data record for that entity from persistent storage.
Access	One client, one instance.	One client, one instance at a time.	Multiple clients, one instance. Concurrent access by multiple clients allowed.
Persistence	When the client terminates the session, the corresponding bean instance is destroyed.	Goes back to the pool after serving a method call.	Even when the server stops or crashes, the entity state represented by a bean instance persists in the database. This state can be represented by another instance when the server is restarted.

In a nutshell, a business problem solved by an application generally contains business processes and business data. Business processes are handled by session beans, while business data is handled by entity beans. The existence of two bean flavors, session and entity, allows us to separate the process from the data.

After making a method call to a session bean or an entity bean, the client is stuck right there waiting for the call to return, because it's synchronous communication. Let's now take a look at how asynchronous communication is handled in EJB.

2.4.2 Beans that handle asynchronous communication: Message-driven beans

Communication between a client and an enterprise bean in a noninteractive application is asynchronous and is supported by message-driven beans (MDB), introduced to the EJB architecture in version 2.0. An MDB instance handles only one client message at a time and is relatively short lived. The message from the client arrives through the JMS and is handed by the container to the MDB instance. The JMS server provides message services such as storing messages, routing messages, and transferring messages in one-to-one or one-to-many models. The JMS server separates the client from the message bean and hence facilitates asynchronous communication.

As an example, consider an application that allows customers to subscribe to an email newsletter. The client sends the newsletter to the JMS server. Upon arrival of the message, the container invokes the message bean, which in turn executes the business logic and sends the newsletter to each subscriber.

You write these beans following the EJB spec and without making any assumptions about a specific container from a specific vendor in which the beans would run. Note that keeping the container separate from the bean is a natural consequence of the component-based architecture approach. You would like to be able to take your bean to different containers and different applications without changing the code.

This is what "write once, deploy anywhere" means. Furthermore, this approach creates room for distinct roles and responsibilities in the process of developing, deploying, and executing sophisticated enterprise applications.

2.5 SPECIFYING EJB ROLES AND RESPONSIBILITIES

The EJB architecture provides the basis for a distributed enterprise application. One advantage of a distributed system with a component-based architecture is the distribution of responsibilities; its parts can be built and managed independently of one another by different individuals or organizations. The EJB specification clearly defines six distinct roles in the lifecycle of an EJB application. Although depending on the size of a given project some of these roles may be performed by the same party, it is important to understand the six roles in their distinct forms. To ensure the compatibility between the pieces delivered by the six roles, the EJB architecture specifies sets of requirements called *contracts*. You will be learning about these requirements throughout the book.

The six distinct roles defined by the EJB architecture are as follows:

- Enterprise bean provider
- Application assembler
- Bean deployer
- EJB server provider
- EJB container provider
- System administrator

We describe these roles in the following sections.

2.5.1 Enterprise bean provider

The life story of an enterprise bean starts with you writing the code for the bean. You, the developer, play the role of an enterprise bean provider. The bean provider develops enterprise beans to implement the business logic of an enterprise application. Because the system-level services are provided by the container/server, the developer does not have to know system programming but must understand the application's business logic. To be specific, the bean provider is responsible for delivering the following:

- The Java classes for the bean that contain the business methods
- The Java interfaces that the client will use to interact with the bean
- The deployment descriptor (an XML file) that holds customizable information about the bean, which will be used by some other roles such as the assembler and the deployer

An enterprise bean's external dependencies, such as database connections, are declared in the deployment descriptor file. The bean provider generally packs these files in a JAR file, called an ejb-jar file. An ejb-jar file can be given any name and may contain more than one bean but only one deployment descriptor. The deployment descriptor file must be named ejb-jar.xml and must exist in a directory named META-INF. Note here that the file named ejb-jar.xml is not a JAR file; it is an XML file—one of several files in the ejb-jar file.

> **NOTE** You may put more than one bean into an ejb-jar file but only one deployment descriptor file whose name must be ejb-jar.xml, and it must reside in a directory named META-INF.

The ejb-jar file contains one or more beans and a deployment descriptor file that contains information about the beans. Think of this JAR file as an EJB module that could possibly be deployed standalone, or it could be assembled into a bigger J2EE application.

2.5.2 Application assembler

Enterprise beans are independent, reusable components. They can be assembled into an application in order to use them. For example, a bean representing a shopping cart from one bean provider and a bean representing a credit card verifier from another bean provider may be assembled into an e-commerce application. Assume that the application assembler received these two beans in two separate ejb-jar files from the same or different bean providers. The application assembler, in this example, may leave the beans in separate ejb-jar files or may decide to create a single ejb-jar file that will contain all the beans being assembled. The decision is generally driven by how the application will be deployed. During this process, the application assembler adds the application assembly instructions into the deployment descriptor files. In addition, the application assembler needs to understand the functionality provided by the enterprise beans' interfaces and may be required to combine enterprise beans with other components, possibly from other tiers such as JavaServer Pages (JSP). Therefore, the assembler needs to be an application domain expert.

Application assembly typically happens before deployment. However, the EJB specifications do not rule out the possibility of full or partial deployment happening before assembly. Remember, a bean (the ejb-jar file) is a component that can be independently deployed. The possibility of changing some application assembly instructions after the bean is deployed provides flexibility in deployment and assembly tools.

Given the nature and size of the project, the same person can play the roles of bean provider and application assembler.

Before the beans can be executed, they need to be deployed.

2.5.3 Bean deployer

Enterprise beans can run only in an operational environment, a specific EJB container. The bean deployer obtains the beans in the form of ejb-jar files from the application assembler or the bean provider and deploys them into a specific operational environment. The deployer first must do the following:

1 Resolve the external dependencies declared in the deployment descriptor files from the bean provider, for example, making sure the database server is available and binding the logical database name used in the bean to the real name.

2 Follow the application assembly instructions in the deployment descriptor files entered by the application assembler.

To actually deploy the beans, the deployer executes the following two steps:

1 Using the vendor tools, generates the container-specific classes and interfaces. These are the classes that the container uses to manage the beans at runtime.

2 Installs the JAR and other files at the correct place in the server environment.

The deployer may need to customize the business logic implemented in the beans. This may involve writing simple code, typically by using the tools, that wraps around the bean's business methods. The deployer is an expert in a specific operational environment. To accomplish the deployment tasks, the deployer generally uses the tools provided by the EJB server provider.

By now, you must be ready to ask the question "What is the difference between a server and a container?"

2.5.4 EJB server provider and container provider

The EJB server provides the environment in which the container runs, and the container in turn provides the environment in which the beans run. The EJB specification assumes that the same vendor generally performs both roles: the EJB server provider and the EJB container provider.

EJB server provider

The EJB server provides an environment in which the container runs. For example, the server may provide system-level services such as multiple processing and load balancing. The vendors usually implement their proprietary services in the server. The current EJB architecture assumes that the same vendor would perform the server provider and container provider roles. Furthermore, the architecture does not define any interface between the EJB server and the EJB container. Therefore, the vendor is free to determine which service will be implemented in the server and which in the container.

EJB container provider

The responsibility of this role is to implement runtime support for the enterprise beans and to provide the deployment and other tools. The runtime support may include services such as management of transactions, security, and resources. The expertise required for this role is system-level programming and some knowledge of the application domain.

The deliverable from the container provider is a secure, scalable, and transaction-enabled container that is integrated with the server. Following the principle of "write once, deploy anywhere," the beans should not depend on the specifics of the container/server.

The server offers infrastructure-level system services such as thread management, load balancing, and other (possibly vendor proprietary) services, while the container offers services immediately related to the enterprise beans, such as maintaining the pool of bean instances, bean security management, bean transaction management, and bean deployment tools.

Since the EJB specification makes no clear distinction between the container and the server, the division between the two is only at the conceptual level. What you buy in the market is a server, for example, WebLogic and WebSphere. At this point, it is perfectly valid to think of the container as an abstract architectural element and the server as its implementation. From this point on, we will use *container* and *server* interchangeably to refer to the same component: the container and server combined.

The container/server provider also supplies the tools for the assembler, the deployer, and the system administrator.

2.5.5   System administrator

Once the beans have been developed, assembled into an application, and deployed into a container, you need to have the application executed and monitored. This responsibility is handled by the system administrator, who is generally also responsible for the configuration and administration of the enterprise computing and network infrastructure, including the EJB container. The system administrator configures the EJB server to make it available to other network services and to handle the user load and also ensures that the server is running correctly.

2.5.6   Overlap of roles

Depending on the size of the project and the organization, there could be an overlap of EJB roles. You should note the following role overlaps:

- The same programmer may perform the roles of bean provider and application assembler.

- The same vendor may (and usually does) perform the roles of server provider and container provider. There is no clear distinction marked by an API between the server and the container.

- The deployer role overlaps somewhat with the bean provider role in the areas of customizing the bean's business logic and generating container-specific classes. Generally, however, the deployer would generate the classes using vendor tools.

The EJB roles and responsibilities are summarized in table 2.2.

Table 2.2   EJB roles and responsibilities

Role	Deliverables	Characteristics
Enterprise bean provider	One or more ejb-jar files that include the following: Classes for one or more beans Interfaces Deployment descriptor	Java developer, application domain expert, who understands the business logic
Application assembler	One or more ejb-jar files that include beans and application assembly instructions	Application domain expert
Bean deployer	Beans (or an application containing beans) customized and installed in a specific server environment	Expert in a specific operational environment
EJB container/ server provider	EJB server compliant with the EJB specification to provide runtime support for beans and tools	System-level programmer
System administrator	Configuration and monitoring of the EJB server	System and network administrator

This is enough theory for now. It's time to see how the beans are actually programmed in practice.

2.6   PROGRAMMING THE BEANS

An enterprise bean is composed of several pieces. In this section, we present a simple session bean, the FortuneBean, which has one class and two interfaces. The class is used to implement the business logic, and the bean clients use the interfaces to access the bean instances. When a client calls the bean, the bean returns a fortune statement for the client.

2.6.1   Coding the bean class

You implement the business logic in a method of the bean class. In this example, the bean class is named `FortuneBean`. The word *Bean* in the name is not mandatory but is just a matter of convenience. The code for the class is presented in listing 2.1.

Listing 2.1   Code for FortuneBean.java

```java
import javax.ejb.*;

public class FortuneBean implements SessionBean {

private String[] yourFortune = {"Fortune and glory, kid. Fortune and glory",
"You're gonna get killed chasing after your damn fortune and glory!", "Feels
like I stepped on a fortune cookie!", "The fortune cookie will slip right
through your fingers!", "It's not a cookie, it's a bug!", "It is your time
to do research and dig up the treasure!","It is your year!", "While looking
for a fortune cookie, hold on to your potatoes!", "You are in a position
unsuitable to give orders!"};

    public void ejbActivate(){
        System.out.println("From ejbActivate()");
    }
```

```
    public void ejbPassivate(){
        System.out.println("From ejbPassivate()");
    }

    public void ejbRemove(){
        System.out.println("From ejbRemove()");
    }

    public void setSessionContext(SessionContext ctx){
        System.out.println("From setSessionContext()");
    }

    public String getNextFortune() {
        System.out.println("From getNextFortune(): ");
        int randomNum = (int) (Math.random() * yourFortune.length);
        return yourFortune[randomNum];

    }

    public void ejbCreate(){
        System.out.println("From ejbCreate()");
    }
}
```

The business logic is implemented in the method `getNextFortune()`. The business logic here is very simple: select the next fortune statement at random and return it. In a real-world application, the business logic would be based on a more involved technique. The other four methods are from the interface `SessionBean`. As the class definition shows, `FortuneBean` implements the `SessionBean` interface; that's what makes this bean the session bean. Therefore, you have to implement the methods of the `SessionBean` interface in the `FortuneBean` class. You will learn more about these methods in chapters 4 and 5.

2.6.2 Coding the bean interfaces

The bean client uses the bean interfaces to gain access to the bean. The client uses the home interface that implements the `EJBHome` interface to get a reference to the component interface that extends the `EJBObject` interface. The component interface is used to invoke business methods on the bean, because the bean exposes its business methods in the component interface.

Component interface

In the component interface, you define the business method `getNextFortune()`, which you implemented in the bean class. By defining this method here, you make it accessible to the client. For our example, we name the component interface `Fortune`, and its code is presented in listing 2.2.

Listing 2.2   Code for Fortune.java

```
import javax.ejb.*;
import java.rmi.RemoteException;

public interface Fortune extends EJBObject {

  public String getNextFortune() throws RemoteException;

}
```

Note that the `Fortune` interface extends the `EJBObject` interface. The container implements the `Fortune` interface in a class and instantiates that class when needed, and we will call that instance the EJB Object, or EJBObject. The EJBObject will mediate any communication from the client with the bean through the component interface. Following the standard convention in the literature we will be using EJBObject for both the `EJBObject` interface and the instance that implements the component interface. You can make distinction from the context.

The `EJBObject` interface is a remote interface, so the `Fortune` interface that extends it is also remote by inheritance. The client uses remote method invocation (RMI) to communicate with the `EJBObject`. Each method of the `Fortune` interface must declare that it throws `RemoteException`. You will learn all the details about it in chapter 3.

Home interface

The client uses the home interface to create, find, or delete references to the bean—actually to the EJBObject. This is the starting point for the client in gaining access to the bean. The source code for the home interface, `FortuneHome`, in our example is presented in listing 2.3.

Listing 2.3   Code for FortuneHome.java

```
import javax.ejb.*;
import java.rmi.RemoteException;

public interface FortuneHome extends EJBHome {

  public Fortune create() throws CreateException, RemoteException;

}
```

This code defines a single method, `create()`. Note that the `create()` method returns the component interface type, `Fortune`. That means the client would use the home interface to get a reference to the component interface. `FortuneHome`, like any other remote home interface, extends the `EJBHome` interface. The container implements the `FortuneHome` interface in a class and instantiates that class when needed, and we will call that instance the EJB Home, or EJBHome. Following the standard convention in the literature we will be using EJBHome for both the EJBHome interface and the instance that implements the remote home interface. Again, you can make the distinction from the context.

Note that the names `Fortune` and `FortuneHome` are not mandatory; you can give the interfaces any legal Java names.

Bean client

The bean may be accessed by several types of clients, such as an HTTP client, a Java applet, or a simple Java program. For this example, we use a simple Java program as a client. In the client you need to implement the following three steps:

1 Locate the home interface for the bean.

2 Get a reference to the component interface from the home interface.

3 Use the component interface to call the business method of the bean.

The source code for the client FortuneClient in our example is presented in listing 2.4.

Listing 2.4   Code for FortuneClient.java

```java
import javax.naming.Context;
import javax.naming.InitialContext;
import javax.rmi.PortableRemoteObject;
import java.math.BigDecimal;

public class FortuneClient {

    public static void main(String[] args) {
        try {
            Context ictx = new InitialContext();
            Object objref =                     Set up and use initial context for JNDI lookup
                ictx.lookup("java:comp/env/ejb/FortuneSelector");

            FortuneHome home =                                              Narrow
                (FortuneHome)PortableRemoteObject.narrow(objref,           before
                                       FortuneHome.class);                 casting
            Fortune fortuner = home.create();

            System.out.println(fortuner.getNextFortune());
                                    Use the component interface to
            System.exit(0);            invoke the business method

        } catch (Exception ex) {
            System.err.println("Caught an exception!");
            ex.printStackTrace();
        }
    }
}
```

The client uses the Java Naming and Directory Interface (JNDI) to look up the bean's home interface. In listing 2.4, we enter the JNDI by creating the initial context, and then we look for the bean using the JNDI name (`FortuneSelector`) that the deployer provided during deployment. The home reference returned by the lookup may be in a more general form to make it interoperable, so it must be narrowed before casting it to the home interface.

Now that we have written the bean class and interfaces, the next step is to write the deployment descriptor.

2.6.3 Writing the deployment descriptor

The deployment descriptor describes the bean to the server, that is, how the bean is structured and how it should be managed. It can be written manually or created using a deployment tool. Listing 2.5 presents a very simple deployment descriptor, ejb-jar.xml, for the enterprise bean in our example. However, in the lab exercise presented in appendix A, you will be building the deployment descriptor using the deployment tool.

Listing 2.5   Code for ejb-jar.xml

```
<?xml version="1.0" encoding="UTF-8"?>
<!DOCTYPE ejb-jar PUBLIC '-//SUN MICROSYSTEMS, Inc. // DTD Enterprise Java
  Beans 2.0//EN'   'http://java.sun.com/dtd/ejb-jar_2_0.dtd'>
<ejb-jar>
 <display-name> FortuneBean </display-name>
<enterprise-beans>
 <session>
       <display-name>FortuneBean</display-name>
       <ejb-name>FortuneCookieBean</ejb-name>
       <home>FortuneHome</home>          <─── Assigns home interface name
       <remote>Fortune</remote>          <─── Assigns component interface name
       <ejb-class>FortuneBean</ejb-class>   <─── Assigns bean class name
       <session-type>Stateless</session-type>   <─┐ Declares
       <transaction-type>Bean</transaction-type>   │ session bean as
       <security-identity>                         │ stateless
          <description> </description>
          <use-caller-identity>  </use-caller-identity>
       </security-identity></session>
</enterprise-beans>
</ejb-jar>
```

The deployment descriptor specifies the name of the bean class, the name of the home and component (remote) interfaces, and so forth. The goal here is just to introduce you to the concept of a deployment descriptor; you will be learning the details later in the book (for example, you will learn more about security tags in chapter 14). The deployment descriptor file is written using XML. The exam does not expect you to know XML. However, a brief tutorial on XML is presented in appendix B.

Note that whether a session bean is stateful or stateless is declared in the deployment. You cannot tell it from the bean class definition because in both cases the class extends the `SessionBean` interface. There is no such interface as `Stateful-SessionBean` or `StatelessSessionBean`.

> **NOTE** A session bean is declared stateful or stateless at deployment time and not in the definition of the bean class. However, you will obviously be aware of whether you are writing a stateless or a stateful bean.

Enterprise beans are portable; in other words, a bean, once written, may be deployed into an EJB-compliant server from any vendor. The EJB spec provides some programming restrictions that you must follow to keep the beans portable.

2.6.4   Programming restrictions

If you want your beans to be true to the principle of "write once, deploy anywhere," as advertised, you (the bean provider) must follow the programming restrictions required by the EJB spec. These restrictions apply to the business methods in the enterprise bean class.

Thou shalt respect the distributed environment

If you are using static variables in a bean, make sure they are read-only and not read/write. You can ensure this by declaring all static variables in a bean as final. Not following this rule may result in creating inconsistencies among several instances of a bean running on different machines (that is, in multiple JVMs) in a distributed environment.

Also, do not use the thread synchronization primitives inside a bean as an attempt to synchronize the execution of multiple bean instances. The synchronization would not function properly when the multiple instances are distributed over multiple JVMs.

Thou shalt not violate security

By practicing the following restrictions, you can avoid creating security holes in the application:

- From inside the bean, do not directly read or write a file descriptor.
- From inside the bean, never try to obtain the security policy information about a code source.
- From inside the bean, never use the object substitution or subclass features of the Java Serialization Protocol.
- Inside the bean, never try to pass `this` as an argument of a method or a result from a method. Instead, you can pass the result of the appropriate object method call, such as `SessionContext.getEJBObject()`, `Session-Context.getEJBLocalObject()`, `EntityContext.getEJBObject()`, or `EntityContext.getEJBLocalObject()`.

- Note that passing `this` would be equivalent to giving the client direct access to the bean instance, while a client should always come through the proper channel: EJBObject and the container.

Thou shalt not try to make thy bean a server

You should not program the bean to do server-like activities such as listening on a TCP/IP socket, multicasting on a socket, or accepting connections on a socket. By doing such things, the bean is violating the EJB architecture. The architecture does allow a bean to use the socket as a client, though.

Thou shalt not mess with the container

By attempting to do the job of a container inside the bean, you may be making your application less portable and less robust, and you may be creating security holes as well. To keep the benefits of the EJB architecture intact, you must practice the following restrictions to avoid doing the container's job:

- From inside the bean, never try to create, access, obtain, or set the class loader.
- The bean should never try to create or set a security manager.
- The bean should never try to stop the JVM.
- The bean should never try to change the input/output (I/O) and error streams.
- The bean should never try to set the socket factory that is used by the ServerSocket or a stream handler factory that is used by the URL.
- Inside the bean, never implement thread management tasks such as the following:
  - Starting, stopping, suspending, or resuming a thread
  - Changing the priority of a thread
  - Changing the name of a thread
- From inside the bean, never try to load a native library. It could compromise security as well.
- If a package or a class is made unavailable to the enterprise beans by the Java language, do not attempt to access this package or class.
- The enterprise bean must not define a class in a package. This is the job of the container.
- The enterprise bean should never try to access security configuration objects such as Identity, Signer, Provider, Policy, and Security.

The next category of restrictions is about input/output.

Thou shalt watch thy I/O

Do not use the bean to get input from the input device such as a keyboard/mouse or to display the output to the GUI using, for example, Abstract Window Toolkit (AWT).

If you did, you would be violating the J2EE architecture. In addition, servers generally do not allow direct communication between the standard I/O devices (keyboard/ screen display) and the application programs.

Also, from inside the bean, do not try to access the files and directories directly, such as by using the `java.io` package. To store and retrieve data, use the resource manager API, such as Java Database Connectivity (JDBC). By violating this rule, your bean may become machine dependent; also, the file system APIs are not well suited for the beans.

> **NOTE** Remember during programming to avoid the following: using AWT for output; using a keyboard/screen for I/O; trying to create, set, or get the class loaders; using the `java.io` package; loading a native library; using a read/write static variable; getting security policy information about a code source; using a bean instance as a socket server; or managing threads.

Violating the restrictions described above does not necessarily mean that your application will not run. In the real world, these rules are violated occasionally, sometimes for good reasons such as performance. If you have a valid reason to violate one or more of these rules, you can certainly do it, but be aware of the price, such as compromising portability. Violate it in such a way that you could fix it easily in the future if you needed to.

2.7 THE EJB ENVIRONMENT

The enterprise bean is deployed into an environment and is executed in that environment. Regarding the environment, you need to keep in mind two important issues. First, the application assembler and the deployer should be able to customize the business logic of the bean without changing the source code. Second, the bean should be able to access external resources such as a database even though the bean provider who wrote the bean code did not know the real names of the resources. One of the external resources that a bean may need could be another bean.

2.7.1 The bean's home in the environment: JNDI

JNDI is an interface to the Java naming and directory service that can be used to register and find beans and services. The details of JNDI are beyond the scope of this book. All you need to know is how to use JNDI to find another bean or service remotely.

We have already used JNDI lookup in listing 2.4 to find the home interface of `FortuneBean`. The relevant lines from that listing are

```
Context ictx = new InitialContext();
Object objref =
        ictx.lookup("java:comp/env/ejb/FortuneSelector");

FortuneHome home =
    (FortuneHome)PortableRemoteObject.narrow(objref,
                                 FortuneHome.class);
```

You create an instance of `InitialContext` and use it as an entry point into JNDI. There is a standard context convention to store things in JNDI and look them up. The context java:comp is the root context in a J2EE application. The ejb objects and resource objects are bound to the environment context java:comp/env under subcontexts such as ejb for beans or jdbc for database connections.

You can look at it this way: each bean type, say `FortuneBean`, has its own home in the JNDI environment. All the bean instances of a given type share that home. This is because all the instances of a bean type have the same EJBHome, and it is the EJBHome object that is accessed by a client by using JNDI. This home would be referred to by the name that was used to register with JNDI. For example, the `FortuneSelector` name in the method call `lookup("java:comp/env/ejb/FortuneSelector")` is the name by which the bean is registered with JNDI, and the container will be sure to return the EJBHome reference to the client as a result of this method call.

2.7.2 Deployment descriptor elements for the environment

Recall that enterprise beans are portable software components. That means, besides many other things, that they must stay independent of the operational environment in which the application is deployed, and they must allow customization without changing the source code in order to use external resources such as databases that are specific to a given operational environment. This two-pronged goal is achieved by declaring environment elements in the deployment descriptor file. In the following sections, we discuss three kinds of deployment descriptor elements: environment entries, EJB references, and references to the resource manager connection factories. It is the bean provider's responsibility to declare these elements in the deployment descriptor, which can be modified by the deployer.

Environment entries

Think of environment entries as parameters that you, the bean provider, declare, and their values may change depending on the operational environment in which the bean will be deployed; that is, the deployer can change their values. Assume, for example, that you want to set up a parameter that represents the maximum discount in your e-commerce application that any customer can receive. You have no idea what the value of this parameter should be, and you want to let the deployer set the value and then let your bean code read it and use it. You will define this parameter inside the element `<env-entry>` in the deployment descriptor file as follows:

```
<env-entry>
  <description> Maximum percentage discount for a customer </description>
  <env-entry-name> maxCustomerDiscount </env-entry-name>
  <env-entry-type> java.lang.Double </env-entry-type>
  <env-entry-value>  50 </env-entry-value>
</env-entry>
```

The <description> element is optional. The environment entry name specified in the <env-entry-name> element is the name of the customizable parameter and is relative to the JNDI context java:comp/env. The data type for the values of the environment entries is specified by the <env-entry-type> element and can be one of the following: Boolean, Byte, Character, Double, Float, Integer, Long, Short, or String.

You will access these parameters from your bean class using JNDI lookup as shown here:

```
InitialContext ctx = new IntialContext();
Double maxDiscount = (Double) ctx.lookup("java:comp/env/maxCustomer-
    Discount");
```

NOTE The data types for specifying the values for the environment entries must be strings or wrappers.

The bean provider may set up an initial value for the maxCustomerDiscount using the element <env-entry-value>, and the deployer may change it without having to change the bean code. Remember, from your code the <env-entry> is read-only; you cannot overwrite it from your code. Also, each <env-entry> element can have only one environment entry. That means if you have x number of environment entries, you will define x number of <env-entry> elements.

There are two things you must know about the naming collision of environment entries:

- An environment entry is defined within the scope of a given bean type, say CustomerBean. Therefore, two different bean types may have environment entries with the same name and there will be no name collision.
- A given bean type cannot have two different environment entries with the same name.

Let's take a look at an example. Consider that CustomerBean has an environment entry discount with the value of 10, and the VIPDiscount bean has an environment entry discount with the value 15. All instances of CustomerBean will see 10 as the value of discount, and all instances of the VIPDiscount bean will see the value of discount as 15. Furthermore, CustomerBean (as well as VIPDiscount) cannot assign the name *discount* to any of its other environment entries.

EJB references

Recall that a bean is registered with JNDI with a logical name and that a client can access this bean by doing a JNDI lookup on the home interface of the bean. The client could be another bean. So, the question here is, how does your bean access another bean so that if the class name or the JNDI name of the target bean is changed, you don't need to change the source code of your bean? You may not even know the JNDI name of the target bean when you are writing your bean. This is where EJB references come in handy. You make up a JNDI name for the target bean, use it in your bean code, and declare it in the `<ejb-ref>` element of the deployment descriptor. The application assembler will link the EJB reference to the target bean by using the `<ejb-link>` tag.

The following is an example where we want to access a bean from our bean, so we give the target bean a fake JNDI name, FortuneSelector, and declare it in the deployment descriptor as shown here:

```
<ejb-jar>
<enterprise-beans>
...
 <session>
 <ejb-ref>
    <ejb-ref-name>ejb/FortuneSelector</ejb-ref-name>
    <ejb-ref-type>Session</ejb-ref-type>
    <home>FortuneHome</home>
    <remote>Fortune</remote>
  </ejb-ref>
  ...
  </session>
  ...
 </enterprise-beans>
</ejb-jar>
```

The `<ejb-ref-type>` must be session or entity. The `<home>` and `<remote>` elements specify the names of the home and component interfaces of the target bean, respectively. Now from your bean code, you can access the target bean by using this JNDI name as follows:

```
        Context ctx = new InitialContext();
        Object objref =
            ictx.lookup("java:comp/env/ejb/FortuneSelector");

        FortuneHome home =
            (FortuneHome)PortableRemoteObject.narrow(objref,
                                        FortuneHome.class);
```

Note that the name ejb/FortuneSelector that you declared in the deployment descriptor is relative to the java:comp/env context in JNDI. You include this basic context in the code but not in the deployment descriptor.

The application assembler links the ejb reference to the target bean by using the `<ejb-link>` element inside the `<ejb-ref>` element as shown here:

```
<ejb-ref>
    <ejb-ref-name>ejb/FortuneSelector</ejb-ref-name>
    <ejb-ref-type>Session</ejb-ref-type>
    <home>FortuneHome</home>
    <remote>Fortune</remote>
    <ejb-link>FortuneCookieBean</ejb-link>
</ejb-ref>
```

The value of the `<ejb-link>` element must be identical to that of the `<ejb-name>` element of the target bean. Also, the application assembler must ensure the following:

- The target bean is of the same flavor as declared in the `<ejb-ref-type>` element.
- The home and component interfaces of the target bean are type compatible with the corresponding home and component interfaces declared in the ejb reference.

The target bean whose `<ejb-name>` must match with `<ejb-link>` may be in any ejb-jar file but must be in the same J2EE application as the referencing bean. The target bean can also be referenced by using local interfaces. In this case, the name of the elements in the deployment descriptor will slightly change, as shown here for our example:

```
<ejb-local-ref>
  <ejb-ref-name>ejb/FortuneSelector</ejb-ref-name>
  <ejb-ref-type>Session</ejb-ref-type>
  <local-home>FortuneLocalHome</local-home>
  <local>FortuneLocal</local>
  <ejb-link>FortuneCookieBean</ejb-link>
</ejb-local-ref>
```

The `<local-home>` and `<local>` elements contain the names of the local home interface and the local component interface of the bean, respectively. The bean may also need to access other external resources, such as a database whose name we do not want to hard-code into the bean's source code. Let's see how those resources will be referenced from the bean.

References to the resource manager connection factories

The question here is, how does your bean get a connection to a database? A *resource manager* is a system such as a database server or a message queue that makes one or more resources available for an application. A *connection factory* is an instance of a class that implements an interface such as `javax.sql.DataSource` or `javax.jms.QueueConnectionFactory`. When you are writing your bean code, you get the connection to a database through a connection factory. How do you find the connection factory? Yes, you are right—through a JNDI lookup! The object that implements the interface such as `javax.sql.Datasource` registers with JNDI, and the bean that needs the connection to the database accesses the connection factory object by doing a JNDI lookup. For example, in a bean's business method you would write the code that looks like the following:

```
InitialContext ctx = new IntialContext();
DataSource dsrc = (DataSource)ctx.lookup("java:comp/env/jdbc/discountDB");
Connection con = dsrc.getConnection();
```

At the time of writing the code, you did not know the real name of the database, so you made up the name discountDB. Now, you want to tell the deployer that your bean is depending on this database, so that the deployer could match this with the real database name in a specific operational environment. You do this by declaring the made-up name in the deployment descriptor by using the `<resource-ref>` element as shown here:

```
<resource-ref>
  <description> Defines a reference to the connection factory for the
                resource manager DiscountDB.
  </description>
  <res-ref-name>jdbc/DiscountDB</res-ref-name>
  <res-type>javax.sql.DataSource</res-type>
  <res-auth>Container</res-auth>
</resource-ref>
```

Note the following:

- The `<res-ref-name>` element contains the name referred to in the bean code without mentioning the basic context java:comp/env.

- The `<res-auth>` element specifies who would check the security access credentials for the user of the database: the Container or the Bean. The value Container means that the deployer must configure the container to handle access authorization. The value Bean means that you should use the overloaded version of the `getConnection()` method to pass the login name and password, for example:

```
Connection con = dsrc.getConnection("username", "password");
```

- The `<res-type>` element specifies the resource manager connection factory type, that is, the interface that that the connection factory object implements. The types available in EJB 2.0 are shown in table 2.3.

Table 2.3 Standard types for resource manager connection factories. These are the interfaces that the connection factory classes implement. Do not use the java:/comp/env/ part of the context in the deployment descriptor.

Resource	Type (Interface)	Recommended JNDI Context to Be Used in the Bean Code
JDBC connections	Javax.sql.DataSource	java:comp/env/jdbc
JMS connections	Javax.jms.QueueConnectionFactory Javax.jms.TopicConnectionFactory	java:comp/env/jms
JavaMail connections	javax.mail.Session	java:comp/env/mail
URL connections	java.net.URL	java:comp/env/url

Here is the big picture for access to resource managers. Because resource managers such as database management systems are specific to a given operational environment, you don't want to refer to them by their real name from your bean in order to keep the bean portable. You make up a fake JNDI name for them and use that name in your code, and then you declare it in the deployment descriptor for the deployer. The deployer learns about it from the deployment descriptor and matches your fake name to the real JNDI name under which the resource is registered. The system admin will typically configure the resource manager, say, the database server, and register it with JNDI.

Next let's look at the set of APIs and the services that are provided to the bean as part of its runtime environment.

2.7.3   Required APIs and services

The EJB 2.0 spec requires the container to guarantee the availability of the following APIs for the bean instances at runtime:

- Java 2 Standard Edition (J2SE) version 1.3 APIs
- Java Database Connectivity (JDBC) 2.0 extension
- Java Naming Directory Interface (JNDI) API 1.2
- Java Transaction API (JTA) 1.0.1 extension, the `UserTransaction` interface only
- Java Message Service (JMS) 1.0.2 standard extension
- JavaMail 1.1 extension, for sending mail only
- Java API for XML (JAXP) 1.0

It is important to note that only version 1.3 of J2SE is required and not J2SE 1.4 (or 5.0 for that matter). The required version for JDBC is 2.0, and the version for all other APIs is 1.x; you don't need to memorize the values of x. Some of the APIs may sound like one the container might be offering, but it's not required to do so. So in the exam, don't fall into that trap. The following APIs, for example, are not required of the container: JINI, JMX, JTS, JXTA, JSP, servlets.

Throughout this book, you will be learning about the services that the container provides. For now, just note that the container is required to provide the following services:

- Persistence management for entity beans
- Support for transactions including distributed transactions
- Security management
- Thread safety
- Implementation tasks, that is, generating the following classes: stub classes to serve the remote client, classes to implement the home and component interfaces, and classes for resource manager connection factories

Be aware that the EJB container/server vendors may offer additional services that are not part of the EJB 2.0 requirements, such as the following:

- Fail-over servers to support fault tolerance
- Clustering to support fault tolerance, load balancing, availability, and scalability
- Data caching for performance

After you are aware of all the programming restrictions and the APIs guaranteed by the container, you write the beans. But you are not finished yet; you still need to package the beans into a JAR file. There are rules about how to do it.

2.8 PACKAGING THE BEANS INTO A JAR FILE

The beans are packed into an ejb-jar file. This file is a deliverable from the bean provider and the application assembler. In other words, the ejb-jar file is a contract between the bean provider and the application assembler, and also between the application assembler and the deployer. We have already talked about the ejb-jar file in this chapter. In this section, we will summarize some important points about this file.

The ejb-jar file includes the following:

- The bean class files
- The bean interface files
- The deployment descriptor file

The ejb-jar file may contain more than one bean but only one deployment descriptor. The name of the deployment descriptor file must be ejb-jar.xml and it must exist inside the directory META-INF. The ejb-jar files may be created using application assembly and deployment tools.

In our example in this chapter, the files that will go into the ejb-jar file are as follows:

- FortuneBean.class
- Fortune.class
- FortuneHome.class
- Ejb-jar.xml

You may give the ejb-jar file that contains the above-listed items whatever name you please. This is your deliverable for the application assembler.

2.9 LAB EXERCISE

To show you the big picture about how the beans are written, compiled, deployed, and executed, we present a demo on a very simple but complete example. In this lab exercise, you will perform the following tasks:

1 Download J2SE 1.3 and J2EE SDK 1.3 from the java.sun.com web site.
2 Install the packages that you downloaded.

3 Configure the environment.

4 Test the installation.

5 Compile, deploy, and execute a bean.

You should complete this exercise by following the detailed instructions presented in appendix A.

The three most important takeaways from this chapter are

- The software components in the EJB tier are the enterprise beans, which come in three flavors: session beans, entity beans, and message-driven beans.
- A bean lives in a container, which provides it an environment that the bean uses to interact with other beans and with the resources that it may need.
- Six players run the EJB show: the bean provider, the container provider, the server provider, the application assembler, the deployer, and the system administrator.

2.10 SUMMARY

The Enterprise JavaBeans (EJB) architecture defines the business tier of the J2EE system, which contains the enterprise beans to implement the business logic of a J2EE application. The big picture of EJB includes the enterprise beans, the environment in which the beans operate, and the players (the EJB roles) that make it all happen.

There are three flavors of enterprise beans: session beans, entity beans, and message-driven beans. Furthermore, session beans come in two forms: stateful and stateless. Session beans are used to implement a business process, while entity beans represent in memory an entity in the database. Message-driven beans are used to handle messages from a message service such as JMS. Entity beans and session beans support synchronous communication with the client, while message-driven beans support asynchronous communication. Session beans serve only one client at a time, while entity beans can serve multiple clients concurrently.

The beans and the resources they need are registered with the environment provided by the Java Naming and Directory Interface (JNDI). The bean provider uses JNDI lookup to find other beans and resources and informs the deployer about the assumptions made about the names through the deployment descriptor, and the deployer makes sure these names match the names in the JNDI. The system admin takes care of matching between the actual resources and the JNDI.

The EJB architecture consists of three main parts: the enterprise beans, the container, and the server. The beans cannot run on their own; they run inside the container, which is supported by the server. Currently there is no practical distinction between the container and the server. The container/server implements the system (infrastructure)-level services for the beans, such as transaction and security management.

The complex and distributed nature of an enterprise application based on EJB gives rise to several distinct roles and responsibilities: bean provider, application assembler, application deployer, container/server provider, and system administrator.

The bean provider packages the bean classes, the interfaces, and the deployment descriptor file into an ejb-jar file. For one ejb-jar file there is one and only one deployment descriptor file, and it must be named ejb-jar.xml.

One of the core characteristics of enterprise beans is "write once, deploy anywhere," which refers to the portability among servers from different vendors. To keep this characteristic intact, you must follow the programming restrictions listed in the EJB specifications, and the bean must not use the proprietary services offered by a specific vendor server.

Comprehend

- Basic definitions of three bean flavors: session bean, entity bean, and message-driven bean. The difference between a stateful session bean and a stateless session bean.

- What does and does not go into an ejb-jar file. The only items that go into an ejb-jar file are .class files for beans, .class files for interfaces, and a deployment descriptor file named ejb-jar.xml.

- The EJB roles.

- Environment entries, EJB references, and references to resource manager connection factories.

- The overall architecture of EJB: beans, container, server, and the relationship among them.

Look out

- EJB 2.0 requires only J2SE 1.3 and not J2SE 1.4.

- Environment entries belong to a bean type; that is, all the instances of a bean type will get the same value of an environment entry. Two different bean types may have the same name for their environment entry; there will be no name collision.

- The value of the `<ejb-ref-type>` element could be either Session or Entity, because you do not look for a message-driven bean.

- You apply only the narrow operation on the return of a JNDI lookup and only in a remote client, and you do it before casting the returned object to the home interface.

- There is no class or interface naming standard mandated by the EJB 2.0 spec; for example, the home interface does not have to include the word *Home* in its name, and the class name does not have to include the word *Bean* or EJB in its name.

- All the bean instances of a given type, say DiscountBean, share the same EJBHome object, but each instance has its own EJBObject.

Review questions

Some questions may have more than one correct answer. Choose all that apply.

1. You have a J2EE application in which the programmer did not follow the programming restrictions listed in the EJB specification. This means that the application will surely not function properly.

    a. True
    b. False.

2. Which of the following files go into the ejb-jar file delivered by the bean provider?

    a. The bean's class files
    b. The bean's interface files
    c. The EJBObject class generated by the container that would be needed to interrupt the client calls
    d. The deployment descriptor file ejb.xml

3. The name of the deployment descriptor file must be:

    a. ejb-jar.xml
    b. deployment.xml
    c. ejb.xml
    d. Any filename with the extension .xml would be fine.

4. The name of the ejb-jar file must be ejb-jar.xml.

    a. True
    b. False

5. The EJB container offers which of the following services?

    a. Security management

    b. Transaction management

    c. Load balancing

    d. Fault tolerance

6. Which of the following kinds of beans would survive a server crash?

    a. Entity beans

    b. Stateless session beans

    c. Stateful session beans

    d. Message-driven beans

7. Which of the following are true about an enterprise bean according to the EJB 2.0 spec?

    a. A bean cannot use `java.net.Socket`.

    b. A bean instance variable cannot be declared static and final.

    c. A bean cannot listen on a socket as a server.

    d. A bean cannot use the `java.io` package.

    e. A bean cannot use this in the body of a class method.

8. As a bean provider, you can take it for granted that the EJB container will provide which of the following services?

    a. Clustering

    b. Load balancing

    c. Distributed transaction management

    d. Support for JSP and servlets

    e. Generating classes that implement the home and component interfaces of a bean

9. As a bean provider, you can take for granted that the EJB container will provide which of the following APIs?

    a. JNDI

    b. JMX

    c. JXTA

    d. JAXP

    e. JINI

10. Which of the following roles are responsible for making sure that all the declared EJB references in the deployment descriptor are bound to the homes of the enterprise beans that exist in the operational environment?
    a. Application assembler
    b. Container provider
    c. Bean provider
    d. System administrator
    e. Deployer

11. Which of the following are true about the ejb-jar file?
    a. The ejb-jar file is a contract between the application assembler and the system administrator.
    b. The ejb-jar file is a contract between the application assembler and the deployer.
    c. The ejb-jar file is a contract between the bean provider and the application assembler.
    d. The ejb jar file must have the name ejb-jar.xml.
    e. The ejb-jar file must contain only one deployment descriptor.

12. Which of the following deployment descriptor elements will the bean provider use to declare a bean reference that the bean provider is using to get access to the home of an enterprise bean?
    a. `<env-entry>`
    b. `<ejb-ref>`
    c. `<resource-ref>`
    d. `<ejb-link>`

13. Which of the following are valid entries in the deployment descriptor?
    a. `<env-entry-type> java.lang.Boolean </env-entry-type>`
    b. `<env-entry-type> int </env-entry-type>`
    c. `<env-entry-type> short </env-entry-type>`
    d. `<env-entry-type> java.lang.Character </env-entry-type>`
    e. `<env-entry-type> char </env-entry-type>`

14. In your bean code you do a JNDI lookup on a JDBC connection by the following code fragment:

```
InitialContext ctx = new InitialContext();
DataSource dsrc = (DataSource)ctx.lookup("java:comp/env/jdbc/discountDB");
Connection con = dsrc.getConnection();
```

Which of the following are correct entries into the `<resource-ref-name>` element in the deployment descriptor?

- a. `java:comp/env/jdbc/discountDB`
- b. `env/jdbc/discountDB`
- c. `jdbc/discountDB`
- d. `discountDB`
- e. All of the above

PART 2

Session beans

Now it's time to explore session beans. These components come in two flavors: stateless session beans and stateful session beans. Keep in mind these facts:

- A stateless session bean is very noncommittal. It does not remember the client from the last call. It's illusive in the sense that a create call from the client does not create it and a remove call from the client does not remove it. After servicing a client call, it goes back into the pool. Its relationship with the client ends there.

- A stateful session bean is fully committed to its client. It's created by the container upon a create call from the client, used entirely by only that client, and at the end is removed upon a remove call from the client. Its relationship with the client is enduring.

The session bean instance is constructed just like a simple Java object and gets its beanhood from two interfaces: `SessionBean` and `SessionContext`. For a session bean instance, `SessionContext` is the direct line of communication with the container. Any messages from the container come through another line of communication, the `SessionBean` interface. These calls from the container are also known as container callbacks.

A stateless session bean's life is very simple. It is created by the container without any call from the client and is put into a pool. It stays in the pool, services a client call, and goes back into the pool. It keeps doing this until the container decides to delete it to save resources.

The life of a stateful session bean is more sophisticated. It is created by the container upon a create call from a client, serves only that client, and is removed by the container at the end of the session with that client upon a remove call from the client. While it is servicing client calls, it can be put to sleep by the container between two client calls in order to save resources.

So, let's visit these two interesting beans and check them out for ourselves.

C H A P T E R   3

Client view of a session bean

EXAM OBJECTIVES

2.1 Identify correct and incorrect statements or examples about the client view of a session bean's local and remote home interfaces, including the code used by a client to locate a session bean's home interface.

2.3 Identify correct and incorrect statements or examples about the client view of a session bean's local and remote component interfaces.

INTRODUCTION

The *client view* of a bean is the part of the bean exposed to a client, specifically a set of methods that the client can invoke on the bean. The purpose of the client is to have access to the bean instance, that is, to invoke methods on it, and the client view is the means to that end. Composed of a component interface and a home interface, the client view could be a remote or a local view. Accordingly, both the home and the component interfaces come in two flavors: local and remote. The client view of a remote client consists of a remote component interface and a remote home interface, while the client view of a local client consists of a local component interface and a local home interface.

Local or remote, the client of a session bean has to use both the home and component interfaces to access the bean so that it can perform a business task, such as paying online from a credit card. The methods that the client can invoke are exposed in the interfaces, which means that the client can invoke only those methods of a bean that are exposed in the interfaces. In addition to the interfaces, another element is involved in the client call to the bean method: the container.

The prize for this chapter lies in knowing the answer to the question, what does a client of a stateless and stateful session bean go through in order to access a bean instance? The three avenues to explore in search of the answer are the home interface, the component interface, and the difference between the remote client view and the local client view. Although the next chapter details the characteristics and functionalities of session beans, we briefly introduce session beans in this chapter before we delve into the specifics of the client view.

3.1 SESSION BEANS IN EJB LAND

The EJB architecture offers three kinds of beans to satisfy a wide range of business requirements to be met by enterprise applications. Session beans are one of the three kinds of beans in the EJB container, the other two being entity beans and message-driven beans. A session bean represents a process such as verifying a credit card or determining the discount for a customer, while an entity bean represents something like an employee, product, or order stored in secondary storage, say a database.

A session bean is used by a single client; that is, a session bean instance is activated by the container to serve only a single client. After the client is done, the bean instance is either sent to the pool or killed by the container. In contrast, a single entity bean instance can be used by multiple clients, and the client calls will be serialized by the container. Although a session bean supports a transaction and can access data in the database, it does not represent an entity in the database. On the other hand, an entity bean represents an entity in persistent data storage. Therefore, a session bean has a relatively shorter life than an entity bean.

Session beans come in two flavors: stateful and stateless. A *stateful* session bean maintains a conversational state with its client; that is, it maintains the knowledge of actions performed as a result of multiple method calls by the same client. In contrast, a *stateless* session bean cannot remember client-specific information from one method call to another. Because a stateless session bean by definition does not remember anything from the previous call, the container may use different bean instances to service different method calls by the same client, or it may use the same bean instance to serve method calls from different clients.

There is another way of looking at the definition of a session bean, whether stateful or stateless. A session bean, as the name suggests, holds a one-on-one session with a client. The session includes only one call from the client in the case of a stateless session bean and may include multiple calls in the case of a stateful session bean.

A client has access only to the methods exposed in the interfaces of the bean. In other words, the client does not need to know how the bean class is written. So, in this chapter we will show you only how to write session bean interfaces and how to write a client program that can access the methods in the interfaces. Writing the bean class will be covered in the next chapter. It's always sweet to start from home, so let's begin with the home interface of the session bean.

3.2   SESSION BEAN REMOTE HOME INTERFACE

Session bean remote home interface—what kind of name is that? Is it short for something? Well, a remote home interface is the home interface that can be accessed by a client either from a remote machine or from the same machine where the bean is deployed. We will refer to a client who is using the remote interface as a *remote client*. To invoke methods on a session bean instance, a remote client needs to have a reference to the component interface of the bean: the EJBObject introduced in chapter 2. A reference to an EJBObject of a bean instance can be obtained only through the home interface: EJBHome, which was introduced in chapter 2 as well.

Let's first get our terminology straight. Throughout the book when we say that the client gets a reference to the interface, or that an interface is returned by a method call, we really mean the reference to an object that implements the interface. This is the standard terminology used in the literature for brevity. So a reference to a home interface means a reference to an instance of a class that implements the home interface, and we refer to that instance as EJBHome, EJB Home, or just Home. Similarly, a reference to a component interface means a reference to an instance of a class that implements the component interface, and we refer to this instance as EJBObject or EJB Object.

So, the first step for a remote client that wants to access the bean is to get a reference to the remote home interface of the bean. Subsequently, the client will invoke a method on the home interface, by using the reference that the client obtained.

You, the bean provider, will write the home interface. Let's look at the methods you are required to put into the home interface.

3.2.1   Required methods in the remote home interface

The main purpose for which a client uses the remote home interface is to get a reference to the remote component interface, because to invoke business methods on the bean, the client needs a reference to the component interface. The client does this by invoking a create method on the home interface. So, the only method you are required to declare in the session bean home interface is one create method. The client can also use the home interface to inform the container at the end of the session that it is done with the bean by invoking a remove method on the home interface. You do not declare the remove() method in the home interface; it is inherited from the EJBHome interface that your home interface extends. Let's take a look at a very simple example of a remote home interface.

Writing a home interface

For this chapter consider a bean called DiscountBean that can determine the discount for a customer. The code fragment for the remote home interface for our bean, DiscountHome, is presented here:

```
import java.rmi.RemoteException;
import javax.ejb.*;
public interface DiscountHome extends javax.ejb.EJBHome {
 Discount create() throws RemoteException(), CreateException();
}
```

The rules for writing a remote home interface are as follows:

- Import javax.ejb.*; you will be using EJBHome and `CreateException` from this package.

- Import java.rmi.RemoteException.

- Declare a `create()` method with the component interface as the return type.

- The `create()` method must declare `CreateException` and `RemoteException` in its `throws` clause. It can also declare other application exceptions.

These rules are the requirements for writing a stateless session bean. For a stateful session bean, all these requirements apply except that instead of using the no-argument `create()` method, or in addition to it, you can use one or more other versions of the `create()` method that we will discuss later in this chapter.

Because your home interface extends the `EJBHome` interface, it inherits all the methods of the `EJBHome` interface, and hence those methods are also exposed to the client. What are those methods, and for what purpose can the client use them?

Methods in the home interface

There are five required methods in the session bean home interface: one `create()` method that you must put into the interface and four methods inherited from the `EJBHome` interface. The methods in the home interface, `DiscountHome`, for our session bean called DiscountBean are shown in figure 3.1.

All five methods are visible to the client, and hence the client is capable of invoking them, for good or for bad. One rule in EJB land that you should learn, the earlier the better, is that just because a method is exposed to a client, it does not mean the client is allowed to invoke it. In this book, when we say that the client can invoke a method, we mean that it is legal to invoke the method. On the other hand, when we say that the client cannot invoke a method, we mean that it is illegal to invoke the method even if it is exposed to the client, and hence the client is capable of invoking it. Some methods will throw an exception if the bean is of the wrong flavor or at the wrong point in its lifecycle.

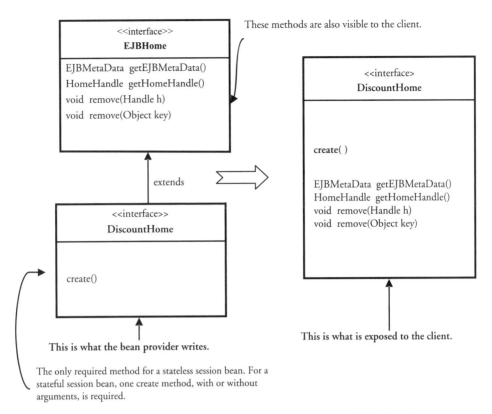

Figure 3.1 The session bean's home interface, `DiscountHome`, extends the interface `EJBHome`. A client will see all the methods declared by the bean provider in `DiscountHome` in addition to the methods of the interface `EJBHome`.

Here is a brief description of all the methods in the remote home interface:

- *create()*—The create() method is invoked by the client to get a reference to the component interface of a session bean. It does not necessarily mean that a bean instance will be created upon receiving this call. If the bean is a stateless session bean, the container may already have created some bean instances and may use one of those instances to service the method calls. Or the container may wait until the client invokes a business method before it creates a bean instance.

- *getEJBMetaData()*—This method returns the EJBMetaData interface, which can be used to get class information about the bean. The client of an enterprise application will hardly ever use this method; this is mostly used by the container provider.

- *getHomeHandle()*—This method can be used by a client to get a handle to the home interface, so that the client does not have to go through another JNDI search if it needs the home interface at a later time after losing the current reference.

- *remove(Handle h)*—A client of a session bean can call this method to inform the bean that the client does not need to use the bean anymore. It does not necessarily mean that the bean instance will be removed. If the bean is the stateful session bean, the instance will be removed; if it is a stateless session bean, its effect is a big zero—the instance has already gone back into the pool.

- *remove(Object key)*—This is the first example of how you can run into trouble for invoking a method just because it was exposed to you. The argument key here stands for the primary key, which session beans don't have. So, this method is meant only for an entity bean. If a client called this method on an entity bean, the corresponding entity in the database would be deleted. If the client called it on a session bean, the exception `javax.ejb.Remove-Exception` would be thrown. Isn't it crazy to expose a method to a client that the client cannot access? Of course it is. However, think of all the things in the real world that are exposed to you but that you cannot access. Besides, there are very good reasons here to expose this remove method to the client: simplicity and uniformity. The remote home interfaces of both the session bean and the entity bean extend the same interface, `EJBHome`, from which they inherit this method. It makes sense for the entity bean but not for the session bean. This is the price that you sometimes end up paying for standardizing for the sake of simplicity and uniformity.

ALERT If a client of a session bean invokes the method `remove(Object key)` on the bean's home interface, it receives a `javax.ejb.RemoveException`. While it can invoke the `remove(Handle h)` method, this does not necessarily mean that the session bean instance will be removed. It will be removed only if it is the instance of a stateful session bean.

Let's take a look at the responsibilities related to the home interface.

Responsibilities

You, the bean provider, write the interface, and the container implements the interface. That means EJB Object and EJB Home are references to the classes written by the container, and these classes implement the component and home interfaces, respectively.

`create()` is the first method and `remove()` is the last method that a client invokes on the home interface of a session bean. Next, we present a comprehensive description of these two methods.

3.2.2 The create and remove methods in the home interface

From the client's perspective, a `create()` method and a `remove()` method mark the beginning and end of a client session with a session bean. It is important to develop a comprehensive understanding of these two methods. There are possibly more than one `create()` method and also more than one `remove()` method.

The create() methods

A client of a session bean calls a `create()` method to get a reference to the component interface of a bean. You must understand how the `create()` method is used differently by a stateless session bean than by a stateful session bean. Table 3.1 lists these differences.

Table 3.1 Comparing the usage of the `create()` method in the home interface of a stateless session bean and a stateful session bean

Characteristic	Stateless Session Bean	Stateful Session Bean
Developer declares the method in the bean's home.	Only the no-argument `create()` method, and it is mandatory.	At least one `create()` method is mandatory.
Client's purpose.	Get an EJB object reference to a bean.	Get an EJB object reference to a bean.
Arguments/initialization.	No arguments, no client-specific initialization by the bean.	May have arguments that the bean may use to do client-specific initialization.
Bean instance creation.	Container does not create a new bean instance when `create()` is called. It pulls one out of the pool only when a business method is called afterward.	Container does make a new bean instance.

A stateless session bean must have a no-argument `create()` method, and that's the only `create()` method it can have—no choice. A stateful session bean also must have at least one `create()` method. For your stateful session bean interface, you can choose one or more `create()` methods from the following:

- A no-argument `create()` method: `create()`.

- The overloaded `create(...)` methods.

- `create<method>(...)` methods whose name must start with the prefix `create`, for example, `createDiscount(String id)`. It may or may not have an argument—it's your choice.

Each `create()` method must throw `javax.ejb.CreateException`. It should also throw `java.rmi.RemoteException`, but only if it is in a remote interface. Also for a remote interface, an argument of a `create()` method must be RMI/IIOP compatible: a primitive data type, a serializable object, a remote object, or an array or a collection of any of these. The return type of each `create()` method is always the component interface of the session bean. For example, the full signature of a `create()` method `createDiscount(String id)` would be

```
public Discount createDiscount(String id) throws CreateException,
RemoteException;
```

where `Discount` is the remote component interface for the DiscountBean. As you will see in the next chapter, for each `create<method>` in the session bean home interface, you will write one method in the bean class with a name beginning with `ejbCreate<method>`.

Recall that the session bean home interface that you write inherits two `remove()` methods from the `EJBHome` interface, and the session bean client can use one of these methods and should stay away from the other.

The remove() methods

Generally speaking, from the client's viewpoint, the purpose of the `remove()` methods is to remove the bean, which have a different meaning for each bean flavor: stateful session bean, stateless session bean, and entity bean. You will see how later in this section. The following two `remove()` methods are defined in the `javax.ejb.EJBHome` interface and inherited by the remote home interface that you write:

```
void remove(Handle h) throws RemoteException, RemoveException;
void remove(Object primaryKey) throws RemoteException, RemoveException;
```

However, because the concept of primary key exists only for entity beans, the `remove(Object primaryKey)` method can be used only for entity beans and not for session beans. The `remove(Handle h)` method can be called for both session and entity beans.

The characteristics of the `remove()` methods are summarized in table 3.2 for a stateless session bean and a stateful session bean. The main difference between the behavior of the `remove()` method in stateless and stateful session beans is that a `remove()` call on a stateful bean will kill the bean instance, while a `remove()` call on a stateless bean virtually has no effect; it will go back into the pool after every business method call it services.

Table 3.2 Comparing the usage of the `remove()` methods in the home interface of a stateless session bean and a stateful session bean

Characteristic	Stateless Session Bean	Stateful Session Bean
Client's purpose	Informs the container the client is done with the bean.	Informs the container the client is done with the bean.
Container's action in response to the method call	None. The bean has already gone to the pool.	Kills the bean instance.
Can the client use an EJB object reference after calling a successful `remove()`?	No. If used, will receive exception.	No. If used, will receive exception.
Allowed argument types	Handle	Handle

NOTE The creation and deletion of stateless session bean instances are not associated with any method call from the client. The container can create a bunch of instances of a stateless session bean and put them into the pool before any client calls a `create()` method. After serving a business method call, a stateless session bean instance goes back to the pool before any remove call from the client.

Note that the `remove()` methods must include the `RemoveException` in the `throws` clause. They also must throw the `RemoteException`, but only if the interface is remote.

You write the home interface, and the container implements the home interface in a class and creates one instance of this class. When a client accesses the bean by doing a JNDI lookup, what the client receives is a reference to this instance, and we will call it the EJBHome object, EJB Home, or simply home. There is exactly one EJB Home object for each session bean type, such as DiscountHome, which all the clients will share. The container also implements the component interface of the bean in a class and makes an instance of it called EJBObject when it creates an instance of the session bean. Therefore, each session bean instance, and hence each client, will have a reference to its own EJBObject. For example, consider 100 clients interacting with a session bean named DiscountBean at a given time. There will be only one EJB Home object, 100 instances of DiscountBean, and 100 EJBObjects corresponding to 100 instances, one each. If it were a stateless session bean the container might use less than 100 instances, but that's beside the point. The point is that multiple bean instances share the same EJBHome but not the EJBObject.

Now let's explore the component interface.

3.3 SESSION BEAN REMOTE COMPONENT INTERFACE

The remote component interface along with the remote home interface form the remote client view of a session bean. The remote client can use the home interface to receive a reference to the remote interface of a bean and then in turn use this interface to call the business methods of the bean. The remote client view of a session bean works the same way regardless of whether the client is running on a remote machine or on a local machine within or outside the same JVM in which the session bean is running. That means a client running in all these different scenarios uses the same API to communicate with the entity bean.

Once a client gets a reference to a session bean's remote component interface, it can use this reference to call the methods exposed in the interface.

3.3.1 Methods in the remote component interface

A session bean's component interface is used to expose the business methods that you wrote in the bean class. It extends `javax.ejb.EJBObject`, the same interface that the component interface of an entity bean would extend. Therefore, a client can access the methods that you implemented in the bean class and exposed in the component interface, as well as the methods in the EJBObject interface.

Figure 3.2 shows one business method written by the bean provider and the five methods that the component interface (named Discount in our example) inherits from the EJBObject interface.

The business method, getDiscount() in our example, returns a discount as a percentage such as 10%. The code fragment corresponding to figure 3.2 is shown below:

```
Import javax.ejb.*;
public interface Discount extends EJBObject {
  public int getDiscount() throws RemoteException;
}
```

The rules for writing a remote component interface are as follows:

- Import javax.ejb.*
- Import java.rmi.RemoteException, only for a remote interface.
- Extend javax.ejb.EJBObject.

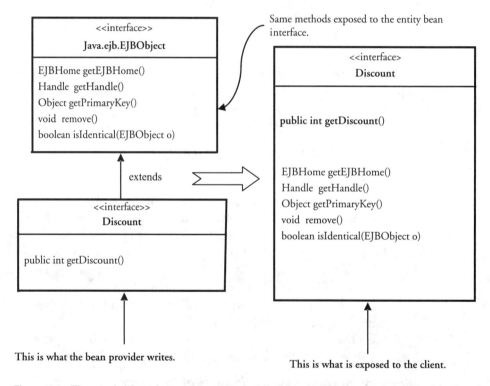

Figure 3.2 The session bean's remote component interface, Discount, extends the interface EJBObject. A client sees all the methods declared by the bean provider in the Discount interface in addition to the methods of the EJBObject interface that the Discount interface extends.

      CHAPTER 3 CLIENT VIEW OF A SESSION BEAN

You may declare one or more business methods, and they must throw a `RemoteException` only if the interface is remote. Remember the following rules about these methods:

- If the interface is remote, each method must declare a `RemoteException`, and each argument and return type must be RMI/IIOP-compliant: a primitive data type, a serializable object, a remote object, or an array or a collection of any of these.
- Because the Java language allows it, you can write overloaded methods.
- Methods may have arbitrary names, but they must not begin with the prefix `ejb`, because the prefix `ejb` is reserved for container callback methods such as `ejbCreate()` and `ejbRemove()`.
- The methods may throw application-level exceptions defined by you, but they must not be runtime exceptions. This means they would be checked at compile time.
- All methods are declared public, and no method is declared static or final.

The remote component interface extends the `EJBObject` interface. Let's take a closer look at the methods in the `EJBObject` interface.

3.3.2 Methods from the EJBObject interface

The container implements the remote component interface in a class, and we will call an instance of that class an EJBObject or an EJB Object. This object obviously contains the methods from the `EJBObject` interface that our remote component interface extends, along with the methods that you declare in the interface. In the following sections, we provide a brief description of the methods inherited from the `EJBObject` interface.

getEJBHome()

This method returns a reference to the enterprise bean's remote home interface, `EJB Home`. This is useful in a situation when you have a reference to the bean's component interface, `EJB Object`, but not to the home interface. Say you want to create more bean instances. To do that you will need a reference to the home. The long way to get a reference to the bean's home would be to go through the JNDI lookup, and the shorter and more efficient way in this situation would be to invoke `getEJBHome()` on the EJBObject reference that you already have.

getHandle()

This method returns a handle for the EJB Object. A handle in EJB lets you store a reference to a home or component interface and retrieve it at a later time. The reference is stored in a persistent fashion. Of course, the retrieved reference from a handle will work only if the bean instance to which the reference refers is still alive.

getPrimaryKey()

This method returns the primary key associated with the EJB Object. Since session beans don't have primary keys, this method can be invoked only on an entity bean. Calling it on a session bean will cause a `RemoteException` if the calling client is remote and an `EJBException` if the client is local.

isIdentical()

This method tests whether two EJB Objects are identical—that is, they refer to the same bean instance. If they are identical, the method returns true; otherwise it returns false. For a stateless session bean, this method will always return true if the references that the client is comparing were handed out by the same Home. In other words, any two instances of a stateless session bean of the same type, say DiscountBean, are identical. In contrast, in the case of a stateful session bean the two bean instances are never identical. So, the `isIdentical()` method invoked on a stateful session bean's interface will return true only if the two EJB Objects being compared refer to the same bean instance.

> **ALERT** EJB Objects are compared by using the `isIdentical()` method and not the `equals(...)` method. Even for a local client, there is no guarantee that the `equals(...)` method would do the right thing.

You have already seen two `remove()` methods in the home interface, and one of them was forbidden. The component interface includes a `remove()` method as well.

remove()

This method when invoked on a stateful session bean removes the bean instance. If invoked on a stateless session bean, it informs the container that the client has finished with the bean. You will see later in this book that in the case of an entity bean, the result of this method call will be to remove an entity in the database. Recall that the home interface includes two `remove()` methods as well. So, you have a choice of removing the bean from the home or from the component interface, whichever way is convenient. Note that the `remove()` method in the `EJBObject` interface does not have an argument. You don't need an argument here because each bean instance has its own EJBObject, and you simply invoke this method on the EJBObject whose bean instance you want to remove. However, when you want to call `remove()` on a home, the home will not know which bean instance you want to remove, because there is only one home for all bean instances of a given type. Therefore, while invoking `remove()` on the EJB Home of a bean type, you need to specify which instance you want to remove; you do so by using the argument in the `remove(...)` method. That's why the `remove(...)` methods in the `EJBHome` interface have arguments. Once a session bean instance has been removed, any call to its remote component interface will result in `java.rmi.NoSuchObjectException`.

To invoke a business method, the client must receive a reference to the component interface. Let's explore how a client gets a reference to a component interface and what the client can do with it.

3.3.3 Getting and using the remote component interface

A client can invoke business methods only on the remote component interface of the bean and not directly on the bean. The client can receive a reference to the remote component interface of a session bean by any of the following methods:

- Receive the reference by calling a `create()` method of the home interface.
- Receive the reference by using the session bean's handle. Note that handles exist only in a remote interface. More about this in the next section.
- Receive the reference as a parameter in a method call. This could be an input parameter in an incoming method call or a return of a method execution.

Once the client obtains the reference, it may use the reference to accomplish any of the following tasks:

- Call the business methods exposed in the component interface, a common use.
- Pass the reference as a parameter in a method call or a return value of a method call.
- Obtain the session bean's handle by calling `getHandle()`.
- Invoke the `remove()` method on the session bean.
- Obtain a reference to the home interface of this bean type by calling `get-EJBHome()`.
- Test whether your reference and another reference point to the same session bean instance, by calling the `isIdentical(...)` method.

NOTE The return types and the arguments of methods exposed to a remote client must be RMI/IIOP compatible: Java primitives, serializable objects, remote objects, arrays, or collections of any of these.

The EJB 2.0 spec introduces the local home and local component interfaces.

3.4 LOCAL INTERFACES

A local interface is an interface of a bean that can be used only by a client running on the same machine and in the same JVM where the bean is running. Local interfaces, introduced in EJB 2.0, improve performance and accommodate container-managed relationships (CMR) between entity beans, which are also introduced in EJB 2.0. (You will learn more about CMR in chapter 9; for now it's enough to know that CMR fields are used to establish relationships between two entity beans.) Both for session beans and entity beans, the local home and local component interfaces extend `EJBLocal-Home` and `EJBLocalObject` as opposed to remote home and component interfaces, which extend `EJBHome` and `EJBObject`, respectively.

NOTE Unlike the remote client view, the local client view is not location independent. A client using the local client view to access the bean must run in the same JVM where the bean is running.

Let's see how local interfaces are different from remote interfaces in terms of the methods that they offer.

3.4.1 Local interfaces and their methods

The local home interface and the local component interface extend the `EJB-LocalHome` interface and the `EJBLocalObject` interface, respectively, as opposed to `EJBHome` and `EJBObject` in the case of the remote interface. The methods in `EJBLocalHome` and `EJBLocalObject` are shown in figure 3.3. Note that they form a subset of the methods in the `EJBHome` and `EJBObject` interfaces. The crossed-out methods in figure 3.3 exist in `EJBHome` and `EJBObject` but not in `EJBLocalHome` and `EJBLocalObject`.

Local clients may use reflections instead of EJBMetaData to get the same information, so they don't need the `getEJBMetaData()` method. Handles are used to create a serializable object that could later be used to establish communication with a remote object. Therefore, handles are irrelevant for a local client, and hence all the methods related to handles are missing from the local interfaces, `EJBLocalObject` and `EJBLocalHome`.

Obviously, the difference between the remote interfaces and the local interfaces is the remoteness—which is just common sense. In other words, the main differences

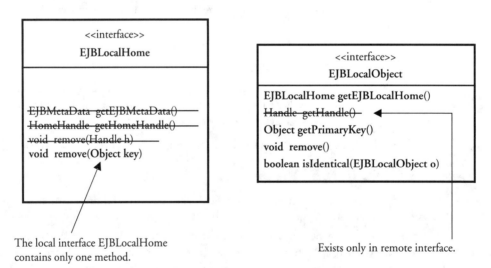

The local interface EJBLocalHome contains only one method.

Exists only in remote interface.

Figure 3.3 Methods in the `EJBLocalObject` and `EJBLocalHome` interfaces. The crossed-out methods do not belong to the local interfaces but do belong to their remote counterparts.

between the local and remote interfaces emerge from the fact that `EJBLocalHome` and `EJBLocalObject` do not extend `java.rmi.Remote`, contrary to `EJBHome` and `EJBObject`, which do. These differences, which apply to both session and entity beans, are summarized here:

- As opposed to remote interfaces, you must not declare a `RemoteException` for any method in the local interfaces.
- You are allowed to have both local and remote interfaces for a bean type, say DiscountBean. However, the remote home interface can provide a reference only to a remote component interface (i.e., EJB Object), and a local home interface can provide a reference only to a local component interface (i.e., EJB Local Object).
- A client using a local interface still needs to go through JNDI lookup in order to locate the home interface, but narrowing is not needed, since narrowing is required only on an object obtained remotely.
- Each `create()` method in the local interface must return a reference to the local component interface and not to the remote component interface.

Note from figure 3.3 that the local client has no `remove()` method left in the home interface for it to use. Recall that the session bean client cannot use the `remove (Object key)` method. So, the local client has to use the `remove()` method from the component interface when it wants to say it has finished with the client.

A reference to a session bean's local interface (that is, an EJBLocalObject) must not be passed out of the JVM in which it was created. A client can pass a local home object reference to another application through its local interface. However, a local home object reference cannot be passed as an argument of a method or as a return of the method that was invoked on an enterprise bean's remote home or remote component interface.

ALERT A remote session bean client can use the home interface to remove a bean, while a local client cannot use the home interface to remove a bean but can use the component interface to do so.

You may be wondering what options the bean provider has in writing bean interfaces; for example, can you write just a local home interface and not a local component interface, or can you write a local home interface and a remote home interface and no component interface? According to the spec, the bean provider must provide one of the following combinations of interfaces:

- Local home interface and local component interface
- Remote home interface and remote component interface
- Local home interface, local component interface, remote home interface, and remote component interface

No other combination is valid. That means home and component interfaces come in pairs. For example, if you provide a local or remote home interface, you must provide the corresponding component interface as well, and vice versa. This makes sense because to invoke business methods you need the component interface, and to get to the component interface you need the home interface. Also, without the component interface the home interface will not be very useful; it will have no access to business methods.

Let's see how local interfaces are implemented.

3.4.2 Writing local interfaces

Here are the code fragments for the local home interface, `DiscountLocal-Home`, and the local component interface, `DiscountLocal`, for the session bean DiscountBean:

```
//Local home interface: DiscountLocalHome
import javax.ejb.*;
public interface DiscountLocalHome extends javax.ejb.EJBLocalHome {
 DiscountLocal create() throws CreateException();
}
```

```
//Local component interface DiscountLocal
import javax.ejb.*;
public interface DiscountLocal extends EJBLocalObject {
  public int getDiscount();
}
```

Note that the local home interface extends `EJBLocalHome` instead of `EJBHome`, and the local component interface extends `EJBLocalObject` instead of `EJBObject`. Also, the `RemoteException` is missing from the declarations of both interfaces.

Speaking of exceptions, let's take a look at some important exceptions in local interfaces as compared to remote interfaces.

Exceptions in local interfaces

Let's see what kind of exceptions a local client has to deal with compared to a remote client:

- If a local client invokes the `getPrimaryKey()` method on a session bean, it will result in `Javax.ejb.EJBException`.
- Once a session bean instance has been removed, any call to its local component interface will result in `javax.ejb.NoSuchObjectLocalException`.

Table 3.3 shows the exceptions that you must declare in the interface methods.

Table 3.3 Exceptions that you must include in the `throws` clauses of the methods in local and remote interfaces

Methods	Remote Interface Must Declare	Local Interface Must Declare
All	`java.rmi.RemoteException`	None
Create	`Javax.ejb.CreateException` `Java.rmi.RemoteException`	`Javax.ejb.CreateException`
Remove	`Javax.ejb.RemoveException` `Java.rmi.RemoteException`	`Javax.ejb.RemoveException`

All the exceptions shown in table 3.3 are compiler-checked exceptions, and hence the client must be prepared to receive these exceptions. In addition, the local client may receive an `EJBException`, but because it is a runtime system exception, the local interfaces do not need to declare it. The `RemoteException` is also a system exception, but it is a checked exception, so it must be declared in the interfaces and the client must handle it. You will learn more about EJB exceptions in chapter 13.

By now you know the interfaces that make up the client view. Next we will see how a client accesses the session bean by using the client view of the bean.

3.5 USING THE CLIENT VIEW

The client of a session bean uses the client view, that is, the interfaces, to access the bean. The client may be another enterprise bean or just a plain Java program. A client program accesses a session bean in three steps: it locates the home interface (an instance of a class that implements the home interface), which is the same for all the bean instances of a given bean type; from the home, it gets the reference to the component interface for a particular bean instance; and then it invokes business methods on the component interface.

3.5.1 Locating the home interface

To access a session bean, a client must locate the home interface of that bean type. It does so using a JNDI lookup. An example of a remote client that locates the home interface is presented in listing 3.1.

Listing 3.1   Example of a client code for locating the home interface of a session bean remotely

```
import javax.naming.Context;
import javax.naming.InitialContext;
import javax.rmi.PortableRemoteObject;

public class DiscountClient {

    public static void main(String[] args) {
        try {
            Context ictx = new InitialContext();        Starting point for
                                                         JNDI lookup
```

```
        Object objref =                    JNDI name given to DiscountBean at deployment
            (Context)ictx.lookup("java:comp/env/ejb/Discounter");  <─┘
        DiscountHome home =
            (DiscountHome)PortableRemoteObject.narrow(objref,
                                    DiscountHome.class);  <─┐
                                        Home stub narrowed to
        Discount discounter = home.create();     make it castable to
        System.out.println(discounter.getDiscount());   DiscountHome
        System.exit(0);

    } catch (Exception ex) {
        System.err.println("Caught an exception!");
        ex.printStackTrace();
    }
  }
}
```

This simple program demonstrates the three steps each client has to go through to locate the home interface of a session bean (or an entity bean for that matter):

1. Get a reference to the InitialContext of JNDI. This is the starting point for looking up the bean name registered with the JNDI naming service at deployment time.

2. Use the reference to InitialContext to look up the bean's home interface.

3. Cast the results of the lookup to the bean home interface type.

After locating the home interface, the client may use it to invoke a home method or to get a reference to the component interface to invoke business methods. This is the general picture. A remote client gets a stub to the Home Object and a stub to the EJB Object because the Home Object and the EJB Object are remote. Instead of invoking a method call on the EJB Object directly, the client invokes the method on the local stub of the EJB Object, and the stub sends the method call to the remote EJB Object. The client communicates with the Home Object through a local Home stub as well. So, the detailed steps involved in accessing an instance of a session bean Discount-Bean for a remote client are as follows:

1. The client does a JNDI lookup for Discounter, the name for the DiscountBean that was registered with JNDI at deployment time.

2. The JNDI service returns a stub for the Home Object to the client.

3. The client calls the `create()` method on the stub.

4. The stub sends the method call to the Home Object.

5. The container may create the bean instance and the EJB Object for that instance.

6. The stub for the EJBObject is returned to the client.

7. The client uses the EJB Object stub to invoke methods on the bean instance.

8. The EJB Object stub sends the method calls to the EJB Object.

We have explained how a remote client can access a session bean. How about if more than one client tries to access a given session bean type, say DiscountBean, at the same time?

3.5.2 Accessing a session bean concurrently

Multiple clients can access a session bean type concurrently, but not the same session bean instance. Assume Client A and Client B are attempting to access the same session bean, DiscountBean. Each client gets a copy of the stub for the same EJB Home. However, the two clients will get the stubs for different EJB Objects associated with two different instances of the session bean, DiscountBean. The container activates two bean instances corresponding to each of these EJB Objects. In other words, the container activates a separate bean instance to serve each client of this bean type concurrently. This is shown in figure 3.4.

NOTE   No two clients can share the same session bean instance. While multiple clients can call a session bean type, say DiscountBean, concurrently, each client will be served by a separate bean instance.

Remember that a session bean instance does not offer concurrent access to clients.

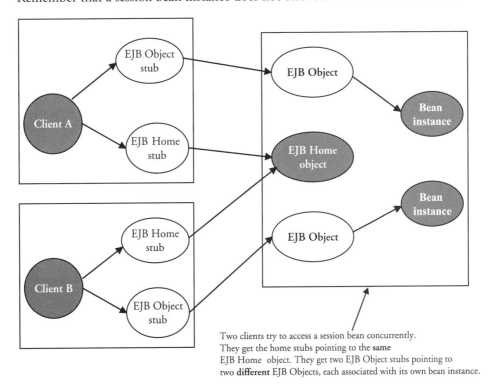

Two clients try to access a session bean concurrently.
They get the home stubs pointing to the **same**
EJB Home object. They get two EJB Object stubs pointing to
two **different** EJB Objects, each associated with its own bean instance.

Figure 3.4   Example of multiple clients accessing the same session bean type concurrently. Two clients, A and B, who are trying to access the same bean type, say DiscountBean, get stubs for the same EJB Home Object but for different EJB Objects.

The three most important takeaways from this chapter are

- The client uses the home interface to get to the component interface.
- The client uses the component interface to invoke methods on the bean.
- A local interface is equal to the corresponding remote interface minus remoteness.

3.6 SUMMARY

The client view of a session bean is a set of interfaces that the client uses to access the bean. The ultimate goal of a bean client is to have access to the bean's methods. But there is no direct access for the client to the bean's methods, and the client has to go through a number of steps to finally have access. It does a JNDI lookup on the bean's home interface and obtains a reference to EJBHome object: it will be just a stub for the EJBHome object if the client is a remote client. Once the client has access to EJB-Home, it gets a reference to EJBObject by invoking a create method on EJBHome: again the remote client will get a stub to the EJBObject. After getting access to EJB-Object, it can invoke a business method call on the bean by invoking the method on the EJBObject. The business method call propagates from the client to the EJB Object stub (only for a remote client), to the EJB Object, to the container, and finally to the bean instance. In a remote client view, the arguments and return types for the methods must be RMI/IIOP compatible and they must throw the `RemoteException`. The methods in the local client view must not throw the `RemoteException`.

The creation and deletion of stateless session bean instances are not associated with any method calls from the client. The container can create several stateless session bean instances and put them into the pool, or it can kill a few of them to save resources. So, the stateless session bean instances are totally at the mercy of the container. In contrast, a stateful session bean instance is created by the container when a client invokes a create method on the home interface and is deleted by the container with the remove call from the client.

The main function of the home interface (`EJBHome`) is to give out references to the bean's component interface, `EJBObject`. There is only one `EJBHome` for all instances of a given bean type, say DiscountBean, while every bean instance gets its own `EJBObject`. A remote client can use the Home to remove a bean instance, while a local client cannot.

In this chapter you explored the client view, which a client uses to invoke methods on a session bean instance. The next question to ask is, what does a container have to do with a deployed session bean to make it ready for servicing client calls? This defines the topic of the next chapter.

Comprehend

- Some methods exist only in remote interfaces and not in local interfaces. The reason is the absence of remoteness and handles in local interfaces.
- In the case of a remote client, the object returned from JNDI lookup must be narrowed and then cast to the home interface before you can use it.
- Rules exist for writing interfaces and methods in the interfaces; know these rules for the exam.
- The client does not have direct access to the bean; it goes through the interfaces and the container.
- The method return types and the method arguments in a remote interface must be IIOP compatible.

Look out

- A client cannot call the `remove(Object key)` method on the session bean because session beans have no keys.
- A remote client of a session bean can remove the bean by invoking the `remove()` method on the Home, but a local client cannot because there is no `remove()` method in the local home interface that can be called on a session bean.
- A stateless session bean must have one and only one `create()` method in its home interface and it must be without arguments.
- `RemoteException` must be declared in the remote interfaces and not in the local interfaces.
- You cannot call the `getPrimaryKey()` method on the session bean's EJB-Object because there is no primary key attached to a session bean instance.
- EJB objects are compared by using the `isIdentical(...)` method and not the `equals(...)` method.

Memorize

- The definitions and functionalities of methods in the `EJBHome` interface.
- The definitions and functionalities of methods in the `EJBObject` interface.
- The definitions and functionalities of the methods in the `EJBLocal-Home` and `EJBLocalObject` interfaces.

Some questions may have more than one correct answer. Choose all that apply.

1. Suppose Lottery is a reference to the component interface of a stateless session bean named LotteryBean. Which of the following are valid methods that a bean provider may put in the home interface of LotteryBean?
   a. `create()`
   b. `create(String id)`
   c. `createSuperLotto(int number)`
   d. `CreateMiniLotto()`
   e. `NewLotto(float amount)`

2. Suppose Lottery is a reference to the component interface of a stateful session bean named LotteryBean. Which of the following are valid methods that a bean provider may put in the home interface of LotteryBean?
   a. `create()`
   b. `create(String id)`
   c. `createSuperLotto(int number)`
   d. `CreateMiniLotto()`
   e. `NewLotto(float amount)`

3. Which of the following statements are true about locating or using the home interface of a session bean?
   a. Once acquired, the home interface can be used only once.
   b. Each instance of a session bean has its own EJBHome object.
   c. The InitialContext must be narrowed before it can be used to get the home interface.
   d. Only remote clients need to get the home interface; local clients can get to the component interface directly.
   e. The local client can use the home interface to remove the bean instance.
   f. None of the above.

4. Which of the following statements are true about the remote component interface of a session bean?
   a. All methods in the remote home interface and the remote component interface declare to throw `javax.ejb.RemoteException`.

b. All methods in the remote home interface and the remote component interface declare to throw `java.rmi.RemoteException`.

c. A client locates the remote component interface from JNDI and then narrows it before invoking methods on it.

d. A remote client can use the method `remove(Object key)` from the home interface to remove a stateful session bean instance.

e. A handle for an EJBObject reference may be obtained from the remote home interface.

5. Which of the following statements are true about a remote client that wants to remove a session bean?

    a. The client can remove the session bean by invoking a no-argument `remove()` method on the remote home interface.

    b. The client can remove the session bean by invoking a no-argument `remove()` method on the remote component interface.

    c. The client can remove the session bean by invoking the `remove()` method with the object handle as an argument on the remote home interface.

    d. The client can remove the session bean by invoking the `remove()` method with the object handle as an argument on the remote component interface.

6. Which of the following statements are true about a session bean client?

    a. A local client can remove the bean by invoking a method on the home interface.

    b. Only a remote client can use the `remove()` method in the component interface.

    c. A stateful session bean is created by the container when the client invokes a `create()` method on the home interface.

    d. A create call from a client on a stateless session bean may not result in creating any instance of the bean. The container can create stateless session bean instances before any call from the client.

    e. A remove call from a client on a stateless session bean instance results in removing the instance.

7. Which of the following are true about using the `isIdentical()` method of the session bean component interface?

    a. Comparing two EJB Objects given out by the same home of a stateless session bean will always return true.

    b. Comparing two EJB Objects given out by the same home of a stateful session bean will always return true.

c. You can use the `equals(...)` method instead of `isIdentical()` if you wish.

d. Comparing two EJB Objects given out by two different homes of stateless session beans will always return false.

8. Assuming L and R are the local and remote clients for session bean B, which of the following are true statements?

   a. L can pass its reference for B as a return value of a method call from R.

   b. R can pass its reference for B as a parameter in a method call to L.

   c. L cannot call methods on R.

   d. L cannot call methods on B.

9. Which of the following statements are true about session beans?

   a. You must declare a no-argument `create()` method both in the home interface and the component interface of a stateless session bean.

   b. You must write a no-argument `remove()` method in both the remote home interface and the remote component interface of a session bean.

   c. A stateless session bean does not need a `create()` method because the container creates the stateless session bean instances without any call from the client.

   d. None of the above.

10. Which of the following are the bean provider's responsibility in the case of a session bean?

    a. To declare the no-argument `create()` method in the home interface of a stateless session bean

    b. To declare the no-argument `remove()` method in the home interface

    c. To write the component interface for the session bean

    d. To implement the methods of the EJBObject interface

    e. To make sure the business methods declared in the component interface are neither final nor static

Birth of a session bean

EXAM OBJECTIVES

3.1 Identify correct and incorrect statements or examples about session beans, including conversational state, the SessionBean interface, and create methods.

3.3 Identify the interface and method for each of the following: Retrieve the session bean's remote home interface, Retrieve the session bean's local component interface, Determine if the session bean's caller has a particular role, Allow the instance to mark the current transaction as a rollback, Retrieve the UserTransaction interface, Prepare the instance for re-use following passivation, Release resources prior to removal, Identify the invoker of the bean instance's component interface, Be notified that a new transaction has begun, Be notified that the current transaction has completed.

3.4 Match correct descriptions about purpose and function with which session bean type they apply to: stateless, stateful, or both.

3.5 Given a list of responsibilities related to session beans, identify those which are the responsibility of the session bean provider, and those which are the responsibility of the EJB container provider.

3.6 Given a list of requirements, identify those which are the requirements for a session bean class, remote component interface, remote home interface, create methods, business methods, local component interface, local home interface.

4.2 Given a list of methods of a stateful or stateless session bean class, define which of the following operations can be performed from each of those methods: `SessionContext` interface methods, `UserTransaction` methods, JNDI access to java:comp/env environment naming context, resource manager access and other enterprise bean access.

INTRODUCTION

Processes are essential parts of business, for example, credit card verification, stock quotes lookup, and order fulfillment. Session beans are designed to implement the business processes in an enterprise application. You know from the previous chapter that a client interacts with a session bean by using the client view, which is composed of a component interface and a home interface. Think of an active session bean in the container servicing the client calls. How did the bean get to this stage, and who did the work? This chapter answers those questions. Obviously, first there has to be code for the bean (that is, code for the bean class, interfaces, and the classes that implement the interfaces), and two players are involved in writing/generating this code: the bean developer and the EJB container. You need to know the division of responsibilities between the two.

The container instantiates the bean class and assigns a session context to this instance, and the instance later will use this context to interact with the container, for example, "give me the info about the client who made the call." On this issue, you can roughly divide the world of bean methods into two: the first half includes the methods that you write, and the second half includes the methods of the `Session-Context` that the container implements. How your half talks to the other half is one of the core issues in this chapter, and it makes its way to the next chapter as well.

The focus of this chapter lies in the answer to these questions: how is the bean created, how does it slowly grow to acquire its full beanhood, and what does that mean? In search of the answer, you will explore the following three avenues: the bean instance, the `SessionContext` interface, and the `SessionBean` interface. And pay attention to who's in charge here; it's basically between you and the container.

4.1   INTRODUCING SESSION BEANS

A session bean represents a process such as determining the discount for a customer. Session beans come in two flavors: stateful session beans and stateless session beans. A stateful session bean maintains the conversational state with a client over a set of multiple calls called a *session*, starting with a `create()` call and ending with a `remove()` call. A client begins with a `create()` call to the home interface of a bean type such as CustomerBean, and an instance of that bean type is created by the container. The client can invoke a number of calls on this bean instance and eventually end the session by invoking the `remove()` method. The client's call to `remove()` kills that instance.

During its lifetime the bean instance of a stateful session bean serves only the client that caused its creation by invoking the `create()` method.

A stateful session bean, by definition, is well suited to implement a business process that requires you to maintain the ongoing conversation between the client and the bean in order to complete a business task. For example, a shopping cart for an e-commerce application can be implemented in a stateful session bean. The information to be maintained during the session in this case will be the customer id, a list of items the customer selects to buy, and so forth. The list is built up over multiple calls from the client, and the information needs to be maintained from one call to the next.

A stateless session bean, in contrast to a stateful session bean, does not maintain any conversational state with the client, and hence the bean treats every method call as if it were from a new client. Therefore, multiple calls from the same client to the same bean type may be serviced by different bean instances. Does that mean every method call will create a new bean instance? The answer is a resounding no. A `create()` call from the client of a stateless session bean does not necessarily create a bean instance. The container may create a number of bean instances and put them into a pool before any client makes any call on the bean. Or the container may wait and create a bean instance only when a call for a business method arrives from a client. So, the creation of a stateless session bean is not bound to the `create()` call from a client. Neither does a `remove()` call from the client kill the stateless session bean instance, because the instance goes back to the pool after servicing a call.

A stateless session bean is suitable for implementing a business task that will take just one client call. For example, the client can send the necessary information to make an online payment from a credit card in one HTML form. Therefore, the online payment from a credit card may be a suitable business process to be implemented in a stateless session bean.

Whether a session bean is stateless or stateful is determined at deployment time, based on a setting in the deployment descriptor. Both a stateless and a stateful session bean extend the same interface, `SessionBean`, and their interfaces extend the same super interfaces: `EJBHome`, `EJBLocalHome`, `EJBObject`, and `EJBLocalObject`.

The basic differences between a stateful session bean and a stateless session bean at the definition level are listed in table 4.1. You will see more differences surface as you go through this chapter.

Table 4.1 Basic differences between a stateful session bean and a stateless session bean

Characteristic	Stateful Session Bean	Stateless Session Bean
State	Maintains the bean state across multiple method calls	Does not maintain the bean state across multiple method calls
Creation of bean instance	Created by the container upon a `create()` call from the client	Created by the container before any client call or only to service a business method call

continued on next page

Table 4.1 Basic differences between a stateful session bean and a stateless session bean (continued)

Characteristic	Stateful Session Bean	Stateless Session Bean
Deletion of bean instance	Deleted upon a `remove()` call from the client	Can be deleted by the container to save resources, without any call from the client
Concurrency	Created for only one client, and deleted when the client is done	Serves a request from only one client at a time

Now that you understand the basic definition of a session bean and the difference between its two flavors, let's see what's involved in implementing a session bean.

4.2   IMPLEMENTING A SESSION BEAN

The two major players in implementing a session bean (or any other bean for that matter) are the bean provider and the container. The bean provider's responsibility is to write the home interface, the component interface, and the class for the bean. We have already covered these interfaces in the previous chapter, so in this section you will learn how the bean class is implemented. This class will include some methods from the home and component interfaces that we discussed in chapter 3. Furthermore, you also need to write some methods in this class from the `SessionBean` interface, which the bean class implements. In the following sections, we discuss all the methods you need to implement in the session bean class.

4.2.1   Implementing the methods from the client view

The methods in this category that you need to put in the bean class come from the following two interfaces: the home interface and the component interface.

Methods from the home interface

In the home interface of a stateless session bean, you must declare one and only one create method with no arguments: `create()`. In a stateful session bean's home interface, there must be at least one create method. It could be a no-argument `create()` method, a `create(...)` method with arguments, or a create method with a name of type `create<method>` (such as `createVIP()`). So, for a stateful session bean, you can declare one or more create methods in the home interface, and a no-argument `create()` method does not have to be there as long as at least one create method exists. As an example, we show in figure 4.1 a few create methods in the home interface `DiscountHome` of a stateful session bean named DiscountBean.

It is also your responsibility to write a method in the bean class corresponding to each of these create methods declared in the home interface. For each `create<method>` in the home interface, you will provide an `ejbCreate<method>` with a mandatory prefix `ejb` followed by the identical name and arguments as declared in the interface, with the first letter of `create` uppercased. For example, for the

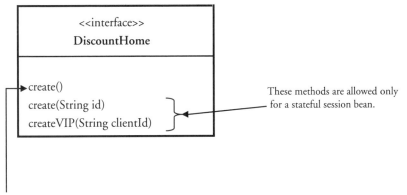

Figure 4.1   Methods declared by the bean provider in the home interface of the DiscountBean. Only one create method is required. For a stateless session bean, only one `create()` method is required and allowed.

`createVIP(String id)` method declared in the home interface, you will need to write the corresponding method `ejbCreateVIP(String id)` in the class. The implementation of the `ejbCreate<method>` methods is further discussed later in this chapter.

> **NOTE**   For every `create<method>` method in the home interface of a session bean, you need to provide an `ejbCreate<method>` method in the bean class with a mandatory prefix `ejb` followed by the identical name (with the first letter of `create` uppercased) and arguments as declared in the interface.

In the bean class, you also need to implement the methods that you declared in the component interface.

Methods from the component interface

In your bean class, you must implement each method that you declare in the component interface. In our example, the methods for the `Discount` component interface are shown in figure 4.2. A client can invoke these methods only after getting a reference to the component interface (i.e., the EJBObject) of an instance of `Discount-Bean`. The business logic related to the application can go into these methods. For example, if you want to calculate the discount for a customer, you will declare that method in the component interface and implement it in the bean class.

Following are the rules for implementing the business methods declared in the component interface:

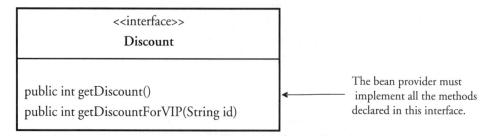

| <<interface>> |
| Discount |
| public int getDiscount() |
| public int getDiscountForVIP(String id) |

The bean provider must implement all the methods declared in this interface.

Figure 4.2 Methods in the component interface of the Discount bean. These methods must be implemented by the bean provider in the bean class. These are also called the business methods.

- A business method's name, modifiers, arguments, and return types must be identical to the version declared in the component interface.

- The method corresponding to a remote component interface (or any interface for that matter) must not declare `RemoteException` in the class. Read my lips: no `RemoteException` in the bean class.

- In the bean class implementation of a method, you don't have to declare all of the exceptions declared in the component interface. You need only declare those exceptions that your method actually throws.

- You can declare arbitrary application exceptions but only if they are also declared in the interface version of the method.

ALERT Do not include the `RemoteException` in any method definition in the bean class. If in the class you declare an application exception in a business method, make sure it is also declared in the interface version of the method. However, if an application exception is declared in the interface method, you don't have to declare it in the matching class method unless you are going to throw it from the class method.

So, now you know how to implement the methods from the home interface and the component interface inside the bean class. But you are not finished with implementing the bean class just yet. Recall that the session bean class implements the `SessionBean` interface. Therefore, you are required to implement the methods of the `SessionBean` interface inside the bean class, too.

4.2.2 Implementing methods from the SessionBean interface

A session bean class implements the `SessionBean` interface. Therefore, the bean provider must implement the methods of this interface in the bean class. The container uses these methods to notify the bean instance of events related to the lifecycle of the bean instance. You implement them, and the container calls them; that's why they are called *container callbacks*. These methods are shown in figure 4.3.

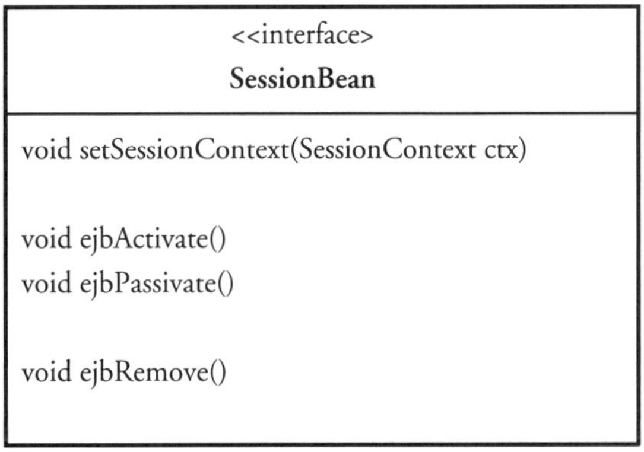

<<interface>> SessionBean
void setSessionContext(SessionContext ctx)
void ejbActivate() void ejbPassivate()
void ejbRemove()

Figure 4.3
Methods in the `SessionBean` interface. These methods must be implemented by the bean provider in the bean class. These are also called *callback* methods because the container calls them back on the bean instance.

Note that the `SessionBean` interface has three methods, `ejbActivate()`, `ejbPassivate()`, and `ejbRemove()`, that the `EntityBean` interface has as well. However, you will learn in chapter 8 that the behavior of these methods is drastically different in entity beans. The equivalent of `setSessionContext()` in the `EntityBean` interface is `setEntityContext()` and the behavior is the same: to set the context using the bean instance that can interact with the container.

NOTE   The three methods `unsetEntityContext`, `ejbLoad()`, and `ejbStore()` in the `EntityBean` interface have no equivalent in the `SessionBean` interface. You must know why their absence in the `SessionBean` makes sense: because a session bean does not represent an entity in the database.

Here is a brief justification for the existence of these methods:

- *setSessionContext()*—This method is used by the container to pass a reference to the bean's session context. Using this reference, the bean would interact with the container throughout the lifecycle of the bean.

- *ejbActivate()*—This method is called by the container just after the container brings a passivated (stored) bean instance back into memory. It applies only to a stateful session bean.

- *ejbPassivate()*—The container calls this method just before saving the bean to storage. It applies only to a stateful session bean.

- *ejbRemove()*—The container calls this method before destroying a bean instance. It will call it in response to the client's invocation of a `remove()` method on a stateful session bean. It may also call it on a stateless session bean, but without any `remove()` call from the client. The `remove()` call from the client tells the container the client is done with the bean. If the bean is stateless, it will go back to the pool, and if the bean is stateful, the container will invoke `ejbRemove()` on the instance and put it out for a garbage collector.

The setSessionContext() method is further discussed later in this chapter, and the next chapter examines the other methods in detail. By now, you have seen all the pieces of a session bean class. Let's see what the full picture looks like when we put these pieces together.

4.2.3 Putting it all together in code

Listing 4.1 shows the code for the DiscountBean class, which includes all the methods discussed in the previous sections. The main purpose for the code is not to give you a working program but to show the method declarations. You also need to know the functionalities of different methods.

Listing 4.1   Code for the DiscountBean class. This is not the complete code, just a skeleton.

```
1 import javax.ejb.*;
2 import java.util.*;
3
4 public class DiscountBean implements SessionBean {
5 initialContext ic  = new InitialContext();
6 private int discount;
7 private SessionContext context;
8 private String cId;
9 DataSource ds = (DataSource) ic.lookup("java:comp/env/jdbc/CustomerDB");
10    public void setSessionContext(SessionContext ctx){
11         context = ctx;                          ◁⎯  This method will be called only
12    }                                                 once; grab the context
13  public void ejbCreate(String clientId) {
14                  cId=clientId;      ◁⎯  The bean instance
15   }                                     is being created;
16                                         time to initialize
17 public void ejbActivate(){
18      ds.getConnection();
19   }
20
21   public void ejbPassivate(){
22      this.cleanup();  //release the resources
23   }
24
25   public void ejbRemove(){
26      this.cleanup();// release the resources    ◁⎯  The bean instance
27   }                                                 is being removed;
28                                                     time to clean up
29   public String getDiscount() {
30      int discount = (int) (Math.random() * 100);
31      return "Discount %:" + discount;
32   }
33}
```

The session bean class must not be declared final or abstract because it will disable the container from handling the class properly, such as extending it to create support classes, possibly during the deployment phase. Also, the bean class must not have any `finalize()` method because by doing this you would be stepping on the container's toes, since it is the responsibility of the container to manage the lifecycle, threads, garbage collection, and so forth.

Note that the bean class implements the `SessionBean` interface, which it must. This is the interface that makes the session bean a session bean. Optionally, it can also implement the `SessionSynchronization` interface, which contains the transaction-related methods. We will examine this interface in chapter 12 when we discuss transactions.

Also note no constructor is declared; an empty no-argument constructor will be supplied by the compiler and that's all you need. Of course, you can write your own no-argument constructor, but make sure you do not try to access any context method or anything else from it; just an empty no-argument constructor will do.

For a stateful session bean, an `ejbCreate<method>` (lines 13 to 15) is called by the container when a client invokes the corresponding `create<method>` method on the home interface. In a stateless session bean, the invocation of the `ejbCreate()` method by the container is not associated with the client call. The container may call it before any client call is made to create a number of bean instances and put them into the pool. The same is true with the `ejbRemove()` method.

The methods `ejbActivate()`, `ejbPassivate()`, `ejbCreate<method>()`, `ejbRemove()`, and `setSessionContext()`, which you implement, are called by the container while managing the lifecycle of a session bean instance, and hence they are called *container callbacks*. The container can call `ejbActivate()` and `ejb-Passivate()` repeatedly, while `setSessionContext()` and `ejbRemove()` will be called only once. We will go into the details of these methods in the next chapter when we explore the lifecycle of a session bean.

> **ALERT** A business <method> exposed in the component interface have the same name <method> in the bean class, while a create<method> declared in the home interface has the name `ejbCreate<method>` in the bean class with the first letter of <method> uppercased.

So, where does the beanhood lie in the bean class, that is, what is in the class that makes a bean instance a bean? The answer is two interfaces: `SessionBean` and `SessionContext`. You implement the `SessionBean` interface and the container calls its methods to manage the bean's lifecycle. The container implements the `SessionContext` interface and you (from inside the bean class methods) call the methods on it. In other words, a bean instance uses the methods from the `SessionContext` interface to communicate with the container.

But before a bean instance can acquire its beanhood, it needs to be created. In the process of creating a bean instance, the container calls `Class.newInstance()` to create a plain-old Java instance of the bean class. Following this, the container calls the two methods from the `SessionBean` interface, the container callbacks, namely the `setSessionContext()` method and an ejbCreate method.

4.3 CONSTRUCTING AND CREATING A SESSION BEAN

According to the spec, the life story of a session bean (or any bean for that matter) starts from the state in which a session bean does not exist. You may think of this state from this perspective: a session bean of a given type, say DiscountBean, has been deployed; the code is there, thereby the potential of an active session bean is there in form of the code, but the action has not started yet. The action starts when the server is started. The first step out of the "does not exist" state is the construction of an instance by the container using the `newInstance()` method. This is where the life of a session bean starts: just a plain-old instance of a Java class.

4.3.1 Creating a session bean instance

Creating a bean instance involves constructing the bean instance and giving it a dose of beanhood by assigning a session context to it. Creating a session bean instance is the container's responsibility, which it performs by using the following procedure:

1 Make a new SessionContext that extends EJBContext.

2 Make a new instance of the session bean using the `Class.newInstance()` method.

3 Call the `setSessionContext()` method on the bean instance and pass in the session context. This assigns the context to the bean instance, which is a reference to the `SessionContext` interface that the bean will use to interact with the container.

4 Call an ejbCreate method on the instance. The bean instance is now ready to service method calls from the client.

5 Put the bean instance (which has a context, that is, a reference to the Session-Context object) in the pool if it is a stateless session bean.

In the case of a stateful session bean, the container starts the procedure listed here with a create call from the client. The bean instance is created and the client receives the EJB Object reference to that instance. Then the client can use the EJB Object reference to invoke method calls on the bean instance. At the end of the session, the client can call a remove method, and the container will delete the bean instance.

In case of a stateless bean, the container can start the creation process without a call from the client. In this case, the container can create a bunch of bean instances and put them into a pool. Think of the pool as a chunk of memory where these instances are sitting ready to run, so the pool is using the resource: memory. When a client invokes a create method, the container does nothing related to creating the bean instance, but the client receives the EJB Object reference. When the client uses the EJB Object reference to invoke a business method on the bean instance, the container pulls an instance from the pool to service the method call. After serving the method call, the bean instance goes back to the pool. In other words, unlike the stateful bean instance, the remove call by the client does not kill the stateless bean instance. If the client does call the remove method, it will have zero effect (no instance removed, no exception thrown) because the stateless session bean instance has already gone into the pool.

Now that you know the basic steps that the container takes in creating a session bean instance, let's walk through the complete process of creating a stateful session bean instance for a client.

4.3.2 The stateful session bean creation process

The birth, life, and death of a stateful session bean instance are associated with one and only one client. When the client invokes a create method on the home interface of a stateful session bean, a bean instance is created by the container. The steps of the creation process are as follows:

1 The client calls a create method on the EJB Home stub.

2 The create method invocation is passed to the EJB Home object.

3 Upon receiving the call, the container creates the following:

   a An EJBObject

   b An instance of `SessionContext`

   c An instance of the session bean by calling `Class.newInstance()`

4 The container invokes the `setSessionContext(...)` method on the bean instance and passes the session context as an argument. The container also invokes the ejbCreate method on the bean instance corresponding to the create method invoked by the client. These two calls link the context and the EJB-Object to the bean instance.

5 The client receives the EJBObject stub, a remote reference, as the return value of the `create()` call.

The bean instance is now ready to service method calls from the client, and the client can use the EJBObject stub to invoke business methods exposed in the component interface of the bean. The steps listed above are shown in figure 4.4.

The creation process involves two kinds of create methods. The method names for the first kind begin with the word `create`, and the clients invoke these methods on the home interface to start the creation process. The method names for the second kind begin with `ejbCreate`, and the container uses them to actually create a session bean instance. Let's take a closer look at this kind of method, which you implement in the bean class.

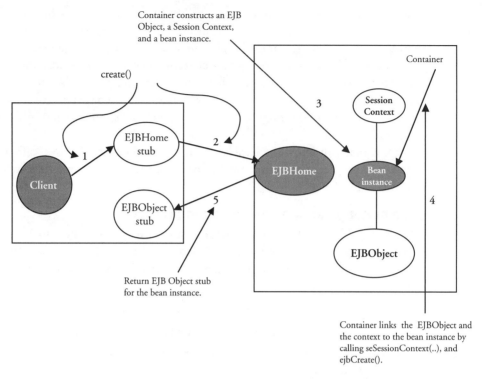

Container constructs an EJB
Object, a Session Context,
and a bean instance.

create()

Container

Return EJB Object stub
for the bean instance.

Container links the EJBObject and
the context to the bean instance by
calling seSessionContext(..), and
ejbCreate().

**Figure 4.4   The steps involved in the process of creating an instance of a stateful session bean.
The process is triggered when a client invokes a create method on the bean home interface.**

4.3.3 The ejbCreate methods

Recall that a stateless session bean in its home interface must have one and only one
create method with no arguments. A stateful session bean must have one or more create methods. It may have one or more methods from the following list: a `create()`
method with no argument, a `create(...)` method with arguments, and overloaded
`create(...)` methods. Furthermore, a stateful session bean's home interface may also
have one or more create methods with the name `create<method>` where you can
replace <method> with a word of your choice, for example, `createDiscount(...)`
or `createCart(...)`.

You must implement an `ejbCreate<method>` method in the class of the bean
corresponding to each `create<method>` method in the bean's home interface.
When a client invokes a `create<method>` method on the home interface, the container invokes the corresponding `ejbCreate<method>` method on the bean
instance. If the create method had arguments, the container would pass them into the
ejbCreate method. The rules for writing an `ejbCreate<method>` are as follows:

- To make the name of the ejbCreate<method>, the name of the create<method> is preceded with the prefix ejb and the lowercase c in create is replaced with the uppercase C.

- The signatures of an ejbCreate<method> are mostly the same as those of the corresponding create<method>. That means

  - The method must be declared public and must not be static or final.

  - The method arguments must be identical with the create<method>.

  - The method return type must be void.

  - The method arguments must be of legal RMI/IIOP type if there is a create<method> in the remote home interface corresponding to this ejbCreate<method> in the class.

  - The throws clause may include javax.ejb.CreateException and arbitrary application exceptions defined by you, but the EJB 2.0–compliant bean must not include RemoteException in the throws clause of an ejbCreate<method>, because only the container can throw the RemoteException.

- Note that you do not declare a RemoteException in your ejbCreate method because this method is called by the container and not directly by the remote client. Furthermore, just because you declared the CreateException in the create method in the interface, it does not mean you have to declare it in the ejbCreate method as well. Do not declare it if you are not going to throw it.

> **ALERT** A stateless session bean can and must have one and only one no-argument ejbCreate() method because the home interface of the stateless session bean must have one and only one create() method with no argument. A stateful session bean will have multiple ejbCreate methods, one corresponding to each create method in the corresponding home interface.

Recall that the line of communication from the bean instance to the container is through the SessionContext interface. The bean instance gets the session context during a call from the container to the bean: setSessionContext(...). The instance can use the context to receive information about the caller and to invoke other container services. In the following section, we describe the services (or operations) that can be invoked on the SessionContext interface.

4.4 USING THE SESSIONCONTEXT INTERFACE

The SessionContext interface is the line of communication from the bean instance to the container. The SessionContext interface (like EntityContext for an entity bean) extends the EJBContext interface. It has two methods of its own and inherits eight methods from the EJBContext interface. Therefore, once the container associates the SessionContext instance (that is, the instance of a class that implements the `SessionContext` interface), all 10 methods are exposed to you inside the methods of the bean instance. The session context methods are shown in figure 4.5.

The terms *CMT bean* and *BMT bean* appearing in figure 4.5 are related to transactions and need explanation. When you write a bean, you can choose to do the higher-level transaction management inside the bean code, such as marking where the transaction starts and where it ends. This is called bean-managed transaction (BMT) demarcation, and we will call such a bean a BMT bean. The other choice is to let the container mark the start and end of the transaction, and this is called container-managed transaction (CMT) demarcation; we will call such a bean a CMT bean. We will explore this further in chapter 12.

The context of a session bean instance is created and maintained by the container. The container instantiates the `SessionContext` interface (actually the class that implements the interface) and assigns it to the session bean instance by invoking the `setSessionContext(...)` method on the bean instance. The instance can use this context to invoke services offered by the container. In other words, you can use the context from inside the bean class methods to call the methods of the `Session-Context` interface. These methods along with the tasks they accomplish are listed in table 4.2.

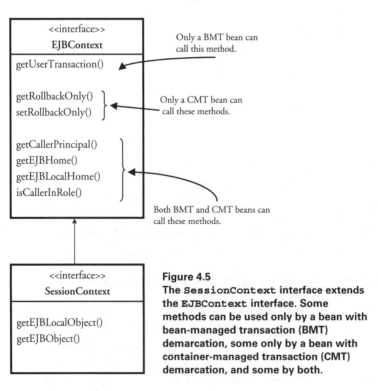

Figure 4.5
The `SessionContext` interface extends the `EJBContext` interface. Some methods can be used only by a bean with bean-managed transaction (BMT) demarcation, some only by a bean with container-managed transaction (CMT) demarcation, and some by both.

Table 4.2 Methods available in the `SessionContext` interface. Permission to use these methods reflects the lifecycle stage of the bean.

Method	Task
`getEJBHome()`	Get a reference to the bean's home interface
`getEJBLocalHome()`	Get a reference to the bean's local home interface
`getEJBObject()`	Get a reference to the bean's EJBObject; that is, a reference to the component interface
`getEJBLocalObject()`	Get a reference to the bean's EJBLocalObject, the session bean's local interface
`getCallerPrincipal()`	Return the `java.security.Principal` that identifies the caller of the method
`IsCallerInRole(…)`	Test whether the caller has a particular security role assigned to it
`setRollbackOnly()`	Mark the current transaction to roll back
`getRollbackOnly()`	Determine whether the transaction has already been marked for rollback
`getUserTransaction()`	Get a reference to the transaction; cannot by used by entity beans

NOTE The `SessionContext` interface does not have the `getPrimaryKey()` method but the `EntityContext` interface does. All other methods in the `EntityContext` and `SessionContext` are the same.

As you will see in chapter 7, an instance of an entity bean is associated with the `EntityContext` interface. Note that both interfaces `SessionContext` and `EntityContext` extend `EJBContext`. The `SessionContext` interface has all the methods that the `EntityContext` interface has except the method `getPrimaryKey()`, which `EntityContext` has but `SessionContext` does not. The `getPrimaryKey()` method will not make any sense in the case of session beans anyway, because the primary key is related to the entity that an entity bean represents. However, remember that both the `EJBObject` and `EJBLocalObject` interfaces also have the method `getPrimaryKey()`, and the component interfaces of both the session and entity beans extend the same `EJBObject` and `EJBLocalObject`. Therefore, the `getPrimaryKey()` method is exposed to the client in the remote and local component interfaces of both the session bean and the entity bean. This means it is possible that the session bean client can erroneously make a call to the `getPrimaryKey()` method by using the component interface. In this case, the client would receive an exception because session beans do not have primary keys.

ALERT Do not confuse the `SessionContext` with the JNDI context. `SessionContext` is given to the bean instance so that the bean could interact with the container, for example, invoke some container services.

Although when you have access to the context of a bean instance all 10 methods in the context are exposed to you, you are not allowed to say, "I can call any of these methods from whichever bean method I please." Permission to use these methods of the `SessionContext` interface by the bean provider from inside the bean class depends on the bean instance's lifecycle stage. In the next section, we discuss which of these methods you can use at the bean's creation stage.

4.5   OPERATIONS PERMITTED DURING BEAN CREATION

You have already learned which methods you need to implement in the bean class. From inside these methods, you can invoke method calls on the `SessionContext` interface, which is obtained when the container calls the `setSessionContext()` method. In addition to these method calls, you may also want to have the following:

- Access to the bean's JNDI environment
- Access to a resource manager such as a database
- Access to the methods of other beans

It is very important to understand that you cannot have access to all of these from any method you please in the bean class. What call you can make and what access you can have from within a method of the bean class depends on the state of the bean's life cycle at the time of the method execution.

4.5.1   Operations allowed during bean construction

Let's see what you can do from inside the class methods that belong to the construction stage, that is, the constructor method and the `setSessionContext(...)` method. The constructor is a no-argument method. As you know from plain-old Java, you don't even have to write a constructor; the compiler will provide you with a default no-argument constructor. If you define the constructor yourself, make sure it is public and has no arguments.

You cannot have access to anything (context methods, EJB Object methods, etc.) from inside the constructor because the bean instance is just being created and it has not yet acquired beanhood. The second method that belongs to the construction stage is the `setSessionContext()` method, which the container calls after constructing the bean instance. The container calls this method to pass the context to the bean instance, so this is your only opportunity to capture the context:

```
public void setSessionContext(SessionContext cxt) {
    context = cxt;
}
```

At this stage, the bean instance and its context both have been instantiated. All 10 methods of the `SessionContext` interface are exposed to you, although this does not mean that you can call them. Because a bean instance has been constructed, its home in JNDI must be available. So, it does makes sense that you can get a reference to the bean's home interface and have access to its JNDI environment from within the `setSessionContext()` method. Thus, although the bean instance is beginning to breath, you cannot do much with it yet.

Once you understand the whole lifecycle of the bean (which is the topic of the next chapter), it will become obvious why you cannot make the prohibited operations. By "making" the operations, we mean calling the methods that would make those operations. For now, let's make another observation. An EJBObject has not yet been associated with the bean instance, so it does not make any sense to try to obtain a reference to the bean's component interface. In table 4.3, we list the permitted and prohibited operations at the construction stage. We will be including a similar table for different stages of the bean's lifecycle discussed in this and the next chapter.

Table 4.3 Operations permitted and prohibited in the constructor and `setSessionContext()` methods for stateful and stateless session bean instances

Operation	Constructor	`setSessionContext()`
Get a reference to the bean's home interface	No	Yes
Get a reference to the bean's EJBObject, that is, a reference to the component interface	No	No
Get security information	No	No
Mark the current transaction to roll back	No	No
Determine whether the transaction has already been marked for rollback	No	No
Get a reference to the transaction; not used by entity beans	No	No
Get the primary key for the bean	No	No
JNDI access	No	Yes
Resource manager access	No	No
Access to other beans	No	No

If you call a prohibited method from the `SessionContext` interface, it is container's responsibility to throw a `java.lang.IllegalStateException`. However, if you attempt (at this stage) to access a resource manager or call another bean's method, the result is undefined by the EJB architecture.

ALERT If from inside any class method you call a prohibited session context method, the container will throw a `java.lang.IllegalState-Exception`. If you attempt to access a resource manager or another bean's method when you are not supposed to, the result is unspecified by the EJB architecture.

So, from inside the `setSessionContext()` method you can access the bean's home interface and the bean's JNDI context but nothing else. The `setSessionContext()` method call is followed by the ejbCreate call. You might be wondering what you can access from inside the `ejbCreate()` method.

4.5.2 Operations permitted during bean creation

By the time the `ejbCreate()` method is called, the `setSessionContext()` method has already been executed, and hence the session context has already been assigned to the bean and the EJBObject for this instance has been created. So the bean is slowly acquiring its beanhood.

Table 4.4 shows the permitted and prohibited operations in an ejbCreate method for a stateful session bean and a stateless session bean. Make sure you understand why one operation is permitted and another is prohibited in a given method. The discussion of the ejbCreate methods in the previous section should help you here. For example, you can get a reference to the EJBObject because the container creates the EJBObject before invoking an ejbCreate method. In the case of a stateful session bean, an ejbCreate method is called by the container after receiving a `create()` call from a client. Therefore, from inside the ejbCreate method of a stateful session bean, you can get the security information about the client by calling the `getCallerPrincipal(...)` method, since the container has that information. In contrast, a stateless session bean is created by the container without any call from the client; therefore, you cannot call the `getCallerPrincipal(...)` method from inside the ejbCreate method of a stateless session bean. Go through table 4.4 and make sure you understand the reasoning behind each Yes and No entry.

Table 4.4 Permitted and prohibited operations in an ejbCreate method for a stateful session bean and a stateless session bean

Operation	Stateful Session Bean	Stateless Session Bean
Get a reference to the bean's home interface	Yes	Yes
Get a reference to the bean's EJB Object, that is, a reference to the component interface	Yes	Yes
Get security information	Yes	No
Mark the current transaction to roll back; CMT beans	No	No
Determine whether the transaction has already been marked for rollback; CMT beans	No	No
Get a reference to the transaction; BMT beans	Yes	No
JNDI access	Yes	Yes
Resource manager access	Yes	No
Access to other beans	Yes	No

CHAPTER 4 BIRTH OF A SESSION BEAN

Keep in mind that simply instantiating the bean class does not make a bean instance a real functional bean instance; it needs its session context and an EJBObject to become a full bean.

Throughout this chapter, we have been pointing out what you are responsible for and what the container is responsible for. Basically, it is your responsibility to implement all the required methods in the bean class. In the next section, we reiterate in one place all the container's responsibilities in bringing the session bean to life.

4.6 RESPONSIBILITIES OF THE CONTAINER

The following list outlines the responsibilities of the container to bring you a unified picture:

- The container generates the following classes:
  - The session `EJBHome` class that implements the remote home interface for the bean
  - The session `EJBObject` class that implements the remote component interface for the bean
  - The session `EJBLocalHome` class that implements the local home interface for the bean
  - The session `EJBLocalObject` class that implements the local component interface for the bean
- The container generates and maintains the class that implements the `SessionContext` interface.
- A session bean instance can support only one client at a time. Therefore, the container must make sure that only one thread is executing the instance at any time.
- The container invokes the callback methods to maintain the bean's lifecycle.

The three most important takeaways from this chapter are

- The container makes the bean instance from the bean class.
- The container uses the `SessionBean` interface to communicate with the bean instance.
- The bean instance uses the `SessionContext` interface to communicate with the container.

4.7 SUMMARY

In this chapter, we saw a session bean instance rising from the code and getting into a state in which it is ready for method calls from the client. The creation process is triggered either by a create call from the client if it is a stateful session bean or by the container without any call from the client if it is a stateless session bean. The creation process involves the following method calls from the container: `Class.newInstance()`, `setSessionContext()`, and `ejbCreate<method>`.

It is your responsibility to write the methods of the bean class, which fall into these categories:

- An ejbCreate method corresponding to each create method in the home interface
- The four methods from the `SessionBean` interface: `ejbActivate()`, `ejbPassivate()`, `setSessionContext()`, and `ejbRemove()`
- The business methods exposed in the component interface

The container uses the methods in the `SessionBean` interface to communicate with the bean instance, while the bean instance uses the methods in the `SessionContext` interface to communicate with the container. The container, after instantiating the bean class, assigns a session context to the bean instance; do not confuse this context with the JNDI context. The container implements and maintains the session context. The bean instance interacts with the container by invoking methods on the session context. Depending on the state of the bean's lifecycle, some of the context methods may be prohibited; that is, calling them will generate the `java.lang.IllegalStateException`. The rule of thumb here is to use common sense. Do not ask the container for something it does not have at the time; for example, you cannot call the `getCallerPrincipal()` method from inside the ejbCreate method of a stateless session bean because there is no caller yet—the container is creating the bean instance without any call from the client.

In this chapter, you learned how a session bean instance develops. In the next chapter, we will explore everything that can happen to the bean during its lifecycle.

Comprehend

- You must know what methods you are required to write in the bean class and the rules to write them, for example, an ejbCreate method corresponding to each create method in the home interface, all the methods in the component interface, and the methods of the `SessionBean` interface.

- Multiple clients cannot access a session bean instance concurrently.

- A stateful session bean instance serves one and only one client during its lifecycle, while a stateless session bean can serve more than one client but only one at a time.

- Looking at the client code, you must be able to tell whether the client is remote or local, or whether the client is for a stateful session bean or for a stateless session bean. Pay attention to the methods being called; for example, only a remote client can call a remove method with a handle as an argument, and only a client for a stateful session bean can call a create method with arguments.

Look out

- The definition of the session bean class does not have to implement the component interface, but you have to provide code for the methods declared in the component interface.

- There is no remove method in the component interface, but you have to implement the `ejbRemove()` method in the bean class, because it is in the `SessionBean` interface that your class implements.

- There is no `RemoteException` in the method definitions inside the bean class.

- If you declare an application exception in the method definition inside the class, you must declare that exception in the interface version of the method definition as well.

- A create method is in the home interface and an ejbCreate method is in the bean class. The container callbacks are in the bean class and not in the bean's home interface.

Memorize

- Definitions and functionalities of the methods in the `SessionBean` interface.
- Definitions and functionalities of the methods in the `Session-Context` interface.
- The methods that can be called during the lifecycle of a session bean at different states and during the transition from one state to another.

Review questions

Some questions may have more than one correct answer. Choose all that apply.

1. Which of the following interfaces are implemented by the bean provider?
   a. `javax.ejb.SessionBean`
   b. `javax.ejb.SessionContext`
   c. `javax.ejb.EJBContext`
   d. `javax.ejb.EnterpriseBean`
   e. `javax.ejb.EJBObject`
   f. `javax.ejb.EJBHome`

2. Which of the following are correct statements about a session bean class?
   a. It extends the interface `SessionBean`.
   b. It is written by the bean provider.
   c. Its business method must not throw `RemoteException`.
   d. It can have a `finalize()` method.
   e. It implements `SessionContext`.

3. Which of the following show the correct sequence in which the methods would be invoked in the process of creating a session bean instance?
   a. `newInstance(), ejbCreate(), setSessionContext()`
   b. `newInstance(), getSessionContext(), ejbCreate()`
   c. `newInstance(), setSessionContext(), ejbCreate()`
   d. `setSessionContext(), newInstance(), ejbCreate()`
   e. `ejbCreate(), newInstance(), setSessionContext()`
   f. `ejbCreate(), setSessionContext(), newInstance()`

4. Which of the following statements are true about a stateful session bean?

    a. An `ejbRemove()` call from the container removes the bean instance and puts it out for the garbage collector.

    b. An `ejbCreate()` call is made by the container only when a client invokes a create method.

    c. You can get the security information about a client from inside the `ejbCreate()` method.

    d. The container will call the `setSessionContext()` method only once.

    e. All of the above.

5. Which of the following statements are true about a stateless session bean?

    a. An `ejbRemove()` call from the container removes the bean instance and puts it out for the garbage collector.

    b. An ejbCreate call is made by the container only when a client invokes a create method.

    c. You can get the security information about a client from inside the `ejbCreate()` method.

    d. The container will call the `setSessionContext()` method only once.

    e. All of the above.

6. Which of the following statements are correct about a session bean whose class contains the following method? `public void ejbCreate(String id){}`

    a. It is a stateless session bean.

    b. The home interface of the bean has the method `create (String id)` declared in it.

    c. It is a stateful session bean.

    d. The component interface of the bean has the method `ejb-Create(String id)` declared in it.

    e. None of the above.

7. For a session bean, which of the following are the container's responsibilities?

    a. Call `ejbCreate()`.

    b. Implement `javax.ejb.SessionBean`.

    c. Implement `javax.ejb.EJBContext`.

    d. Implement `ejbRemove()`.

    e. Implement `setSessionContext()`.

8. Which of the following statements are true about a business method implemented in the session bean class and declared in the component interface?

    a. The method must declare `RemoteException` in the bean class if the method is exposed in a remote interface.

    b. If the method definition declares an application exception in the interface, it must do so in the class as well.

    c. The method must not be declared final or static.

    d. The method must not begin with `ejb`.

    e. You cannot have overloaded methods.

9. From which of the following methods can you call the `isCallerInRole()` method of the SessionContext?

    a. `setSessionContext()`

    b. `ejbCreate()` method of a stateless session bean

    c. `ejbCreate()` method of a stateful session bean

    d. None of the above

10. Which of the following exceptions are thrown if a bean instance makes a prohibited method call to its session context?

    a. `java.lang.IllegalStateException`

    b. `java.rmi.RemoteException`

    c. `javax.ejb.IllegalMethodCall`

    d. `javax.ejb.NoSuchMethodException`

    e. `javax.ejb.NoSuchObjectException`

CHAPTER 5

Lifecycle of a session bean

EXAM OBJECTIVES

3.2 Identify the use of, and the behavior of, the ejbPassivate method in a session bean, including the responsibilities of both the container and the bean provider.

4.1 Identify correct and incorrect statements or examples about the lifecycle of a stateful or stateless session bean instance.

4.2 Given a list of methods of a stateful or stateless session bean class, define which of the following operations can be performed from each of those methods: SessionContext interface methods, UserTransaction methods, JNDI access to java:comp/env environment naming context, resource manager access and other enterprise bean access.

4.3 Given a list of scenarios, identify which will result in an ejbRemove method not being called on a bean instance.

INTRODUCTION

In the beginning, a session bean type, say DiscountBean, is a class along with the interfaces, and the bean instance does not exist. At runtime, the container makes an instance of the bean, and from this point on the bean instance goes through different stages until it is destroyed and made available for the garbage collector. It is important to understand this whole cycle—known as the *session bean lifecycle*—because the bean instance can do different things in different states of its lifecycle.

As you know from the previous chapter, session beans come in two flavors: stateless and stateful. The stateless session bean has a simple lifecycle since it exists in only two states: the *method ready* state, in which it is able to service the business method calls from the client, and the *does not exist* state, in which, well, it does not exist. The stateful session bean has an additional state called the *passive* state: the container can pull the bean from the method ready state and put it to bed, that is, save it into secondary storage from where it can be brought back into action at a later time.

The focus of this chapter is the answer to the question, How do the behavior and capabilities of a bean instance change as it progresses through different states of its lifecycle? In other words, what can (or can't) a bean instance do at different states and in between the two given states? In our search for the answer, we will be exploring the following three avenues: various states of the lifecycle, the transition from one state to another, and the bean's changing access to its session context. We'll also pay attention to the roles played by the container and the bean provider in running the show.

5.1 THE STATEFUL SESSION BEAN LIFECYCLE: AN OVERVIEW

To understand the lifecycle of a stateful session bean, keep in mind that a bean instance is created by the container for a client when the client invokes a create method on the bean interface. Furthermore, the bean instance maintains its conversational state with the client through all the client calls during a session. The instance serves only the client that caused its creation until the instance is killed by the container upon the client's request, for example, to save memory.

The lifecycle of a stateful session bean consists of the following three states:

- The does not exist state
- The method ready state
- The passive state

Figure 5.1 shows the three states as well as the methods that are invoked during the transition of the bean from one state to another. These methods are called *container callbacks*.

These three states are explained in the following sections.

5.1.1 The does not exist state

Yes, according to the EJB spec, the *does not exist* state does exist. We don't need to read Jean-Paul Sartre or study existentialism to make sense of the existence of this nonexistent state. All we have to do is follow the instance. The does not exist state of the session bean refers to the bean state when the bean instance does not exist. However,

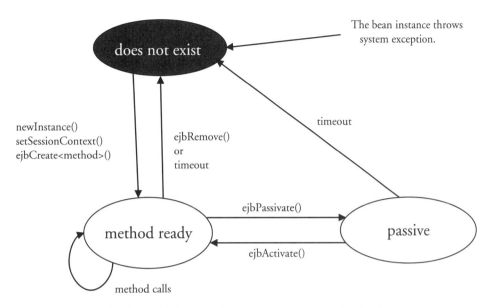

Figure 5.1 Lifecycle of a stateful session bean. The bean has two kinds of methods: the methods that can be called in the method ready state and the methods that are called in the process of transitioning the bean from one state to another.

we know that the bean does exist even when the instance does not. After all, you wrote it, and the deployer deployed it. So, before an instance is created, the bean is in the does not exist state.

The bean steps out of the does not exist state when a client invokes a create method, and as a result the container does the following:

1 Makes a new `SessionContext` instance, that is, the instance of the class that implements the `SessionContext` interface. This step does not have to be repeated for each instance of the session bean. The point is that the container maintains the `SessionContext`.

2 Makes a new instance of the session bean by invoking the `Class.newInstance()` method on the bean class, which in turn calls the class constructor.

3 Calls the `setSessionContext()` method on the bean instance and passes in the session context. This assigns a context to the bean instance and thereby provides the bean instance a reference to the `SessionContext` interface.

4 Calls the ejbCreate method corresponding to the create method invoked by the client.

So, the life of a session bean instance starts when the container constructs it out of the session bean class by calling the `newInstance()` method, which in turn calls the no-argument constructor of the bean class. We discussed the three methods mentioned in the list above and the `SessionContext` interface in detail in the previous chapter.

The execution of these three methods puts the bean into the *method ready* state, which we explore next.

5.1.2 The method ready state

A bean instance in the method ready state is ready to serve; that is, the container can use it to service the method calls invoked by the client. A stateful session bean in the method ready state is tied to a client, as it was created as a result of a create call from the client. Therefore, in this state the bean is either executing a client call or waiting for the next call from the same client. There are only two exits for the bean instance out of this state, and they are described below.

Go back to nonexistence

When the client is done with the bean, it invokes a `remove()` method, which triggers an `ejbRemove()` call on the bean instance. The container can also invoke the `ejbRemove()` method without the `remove()` call from the client if the bean times out. The timeout is determined by the deployer to specify the maximum wait time between two consecutive client calls. The life of a session bean instance ends with an `ejbRemove()` call, and the container puts it out for garbage collection. In other words, the bean goes back to the does not exist state.

Go passive

When a stateful session bean in the method ready state is waiting for the next call from the client, the container can execute `ejbPassivate()` on it to save resources, for example, memory. After this call the container puts the instance into the passive state. That means the container puts the state of the bean (the instance variables, etc.) into secondary storage by using a method such as Java serialization.

The three transaction-related container callbacks for the session bean instance in the method ready state are discussed in chapter 12.

So, in the method ready state, the bean services the client's call to business methods of the bean, and maintains the conversational state with the client. One of the exits from the method ready state takes the bean instance to the passive state, which we explore next.

5.1.3 The passive state

Why would the container passivate a session bean instance that's in the method ready state and serving its client? Well, there is a maximum limit on how many bean instances the container can keep in memory. Also, recall that one bean instance can serve only one client. Consider a case where the maximum number of bean instances have already been created, and each instance is serving its own client. Now assume that one more client calls, but we already have the maximum number of bean instances created and tied to their clients, and no room is available to create a new instance to serve the new client. So, we are in trouble, and the container comes to our rescue. By using some algorithm, it singles out an instance that is waiting for the next call from its client and says, "You are just sitting around here idle; why don't you go take a nap?" Then the container puts this instance temporarily out of memory and saves its state (values of the instance variables, etc.) in secondary storage. Now the container can create a new instance to serve the new client. This process is called *passivation*.

You may be wondering how the container says to an instance, "Go take a nap." Well, the container calls the `ejbPassivate()` method on the instance just before passivating it. However, note that the container can passivate a bean instance only if the instance is not in a transaction.

ALERT   A session bean instance in a transaction cannot be passivated.

There are only two exits for a bean instance out of the passive state: one leads back to the method ready state, and the other leads to the does not exist state, where it came from originally. If the client invokes a method on the passivated bean instance, the container activates the bean by reassigning the stored values to the bean instance. After restoring the bean state, the container calls `ejbActivate()` on the instance. It is the container's way of telling the instance to reinitialize itself. On the other hand, if the bean times out while in the passive state, the container will put it back into the does not exist state. The bean does not even get an `ejbRemove()` call in this case, because before the container could invoke `ejbRemove()`, it would have to bring the instance back into the memory, that is, activate it. The instance is going to be removed anyway, so why waste resources by activating it just for the purpose of removing it?

ALERT   If a session bean instance in a passive state times out, the container will remove it without calling `ejbRemove()` on it.

The lifecycle of a stateless session bean is much simpler, as you'll see in the next section.

5.2   THE STATELESS SESSION BEAN LIFECYCLE: TO BE OR NOT TO BE

To be or not to be, that is the stateless session bean lifecycle. It contains only two states: the method ready state and the does not exist state. To understand the lifecycle of a stateless session bean, keep in mind that the stateless session bean does not maintain any client-specific information between method calls. This property decouples the stateless session bean instances from a specific client. The container creates several instances of a specific bean type, for example, DiscountBean, and puts them into a pool. All of these instances are equally able to serve any client's call.

When a client invokes a method on the bean, the container fetches any instance from the pool to service the call. The instance services the call and goes back into the pool. For another call from the same client, all instances are equally qualified because none of them is maintaining a conversational state with the client. So, when the time comes to save some memory, the container can select several instances and send them to the does not exist state. There is no need for passivation because the bean does not have any client state information that has to be stored. As a result, the stateless bean's lifecycle contains only two states: the does not exist state and the method ready state. The lifecycle of a stateless session bean is shown in figure 5.2.

The transition between the does not exist and the method ready states involves the same set of methods as in the case of the stateful session bean, but differences exist in how the transition is carried out:

- The container creates bean instances and puts them into a method ready pool without waiting for a call from a client. Remember, in the case of a stateful session bean, the container creates a session bean instance as a result of a create call from a client.

- After serving a client, the stateless bean instance goes back into the pool instead of being removed. Client calls to remove() are ignored.

- The concept of a stateless session bean instance timing out in the method ready state does not exist because the bean is not committed to servicing two consecutive calls from a specific client. It services a call and goes back into the pool. When the next call comes from the same client, this bean instance does not remember anything from the previous call.

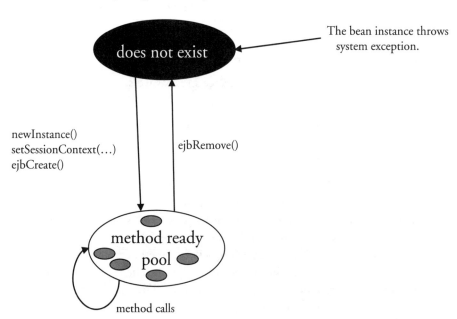

Figure 5.2   Lifecycle of a stateless session bean. The bean has two kinds of methods: the methods that can be called in the method ready state and the methods that are called in the process of transitioning the bean from one state to another.

Because a stateless session bean instance is not committed to just one client, and because it has a simple lifecycle, it makes stateless session beans highly scalable and more efficient in performance.

As you know by now, the passive state exists only for the stateful session bean and not for the stateless session bean. Let's explore the details of the passive state; for example, how does a bean go into a passive state and how does it come out of it?

5.3 INTO AND OUT OF A NAP: PASSIVATION AND ACTIVATION

You have already learned that passivation and activation make sense only for a stateful session bean and not for a stateless session bean, because passivation is all about saving the state of a bean in secondary storage, and the stateless session bean does not maintain the conversational state with the client. In this section, we explore the details of passivation and activation: the implementation of the `ejbPassivate()` and `ejbActivate()` methods and the access that the bean instance has to its session context during passivation and activation.

5.3.1 Implementing ejbPassivate() and ejbActivate()

Just before passivation, the container calls the bean method `ejbPassivate()`, and just after activating the passivated bean, the container calls the method `ejbActivate()`. It is the responsibility of the bean provider to implement these two methods in the bean class.

The ejbPassivate() method

The signatures of the `ejbPassivate()` method look like the following:

```
public void ejbPassivate() {

}
```

The container calls the `ejbPassivate()` method just before saving the bean state in secondary storage. The process of storing and retrieving objects is called *object serialization*. Inside the `ejbPassivate()` method, you have to prepare the bean state for passivation. By the completion of the `ejbPassivate()` method, all the non-transient fields (which will be saved) of the bean state must be one of the following:

- A serializable object, that is, its class implements the `Serializable` interface.
- Null.
- A reference to an enterprise bean's remote component interface or remote home interface.
- A reference to an enterprise bean's local component interface or local home interface.
- A reference to a `SessionContext` object.

- A reference to the bean's JNDI context (for example, java:comp/env) or any of its subcontexts.
- A reference to a user transaction interface: `javax.transaction.User-Transaction`. You will meet this interface again in chapter 12 in all of its glory.
- A reference to a resource manager connection factory, for example, javax.sql. DataSource.

Making the bean instance serializable means that any reference held by the bean instance that does not belong to one of the above must be replaced with one of the above or set to null. For example, you must close all the database connections in the `ejbPassivate()` method and set the references to these connections to null.

When a client call arrives for a passivated bean instance, the container brings the instance back into memory and invokes the `ejbActivate()` method on it.

The ejbActivate() method

The signatures of the `ejbActivate()` method look like the following:

```
public void ejbActivate() {

    }
```

When the client of a passivated bean instance makes a method call for the instance, the container brings the bean instance back into memory (for example, by deserializing it) and invokes the `ejbActivate()` method on it. In this method, you can reassign the resources that you released in the `ejbPassivate()` method.

Note that the EJB 2.0 spec does not mandate a particular mechanism for saving the bean state to secondary storage, although Java serialization is the popularly used mechanism.

You may wonder what kind of access—for example, to its session context—a bean instance has while it is going into the passive state or coming out of it.

5.3.2 Permitted operations and access

Recall that during the creation of a bean instance, the container creates a `SessionContext` and assigns it to the instance by calling the method `setSessionContext()` that you implement. The question is, which methods of the `SessionContext` can you invoke from inside the `ejbActivate()` and `ejbPassivate()` methods of the bean class? In other words, what operations are allowed from inside these two methods? Table 5.1 presents the answer to this question. The only "No" entry is that a bean going into the passive state or coming out of it cannot possibly be in a transaction.

Table 5.1 Permitted and prohibited operations from inside the ejbPassivate() and ejbActivate() methods of a session bean class

Operation	ejbPassivate()	ejbActivate()
Get a reference to the bean's home interface	Yes	Yes
Get a reference to the bean's EJBObject, that is, a reference to the component interface	Yes	Yes
Get security information about the client	Yes	Yes
Mark the current transaction to roll back	No	No
Determine whether the transaction has already been marked for rollback	No	No
Get a reference to the transaction; BMT beans only	Yes	Yes
JNDI access	Yes	Yes
Resource manager access	Yes	Yes
Access to other beans	Yes	Yes

While the ejbActivate() method is being executed no meaningful transaction context exists because the bean has just been brought into memory from the passivated state. Therefore, it does not make sense to mark a transaction for rollback or to find out whether it is marked for rollback. However, if it is a bean-managed transaction (BMT) bean, you can get a reference to the UserTransaction interface. Also, because the bean is being activated upon a call from a client, you can have access to the security information about the client. All these permissions and accesses are also valid in the ejbPassivate() method, because the actual passivation is done after the method is executed.

ALERT   If you attempt to invoke a method of the SessionContext interface from a method of a session bean instance and the access is not allowed, the container must throw a java.lang.IllegalStateException. If you attempt to access a resource manager (say, a database) or a method of another bean and the access is not allowed, the behavior is undefined by the EJB architecture.

Remember that the only thing you cannot do with the session context in the ejbActivate() and ejbPassivate() methods is mark the instance for transaction rollback or to ask whether the instance is marked for rollback. This is because the container will not passivate a bean instance while it is in a transaction, so no transaction context exists when you are in the ejbPassivate() method. And obviously you do not expect to see a transaction context in the ejbActivate() method: the bean has just come out of the passive state.

The ultimate destination of a bean instance is, well, where it came from: the does not exist state. It goes back to this state when the container removes it. The instance is removed for different reasons in different ways, as we'll see in the next section.

5.4 REMOVING A SESSION BEAN INSTANCE

Removing a session bean instance means putting it back into the does not exist state, in other words, making it available for the garbage collector. A stateful session bean instance is removed by the container in two situations: (1) the bean, while in the method ready state or in the passive state, times out, or (2) the client invokes a remove() method on the bean interface. In the case of a stateless session bean, however, the container can remove the bean as it pleases without waiting for a remove call from the client. The container also removes a bean instance if the instance throws a system exception.

Implementing the ejbRemove() method

The ejbRemove() method is called by the container to inform the instance that it is being removed. It's your responsibility to implement the ejbRemove() method with the following signatures:

```
public void ejbRemove() {

    }
```

You usually release the same resources in the ejbRemove() method that you would in the ejbPassivate() method.

Operations permitted during ejbRemove()

The container may call the ejbRemove() method before removing the bean. Now that the bean is on its way to the does not exist state, what can it do with the session context; in other words, what operations is it allowed to make? Table 5.2 answers this question.

Table 5.2 Permitted and prohibited operations in the ejbRemove() method for a stateful session bean and a stateless session bean. The list, in the case of a stateful session bean, is identical to those for the ejbCreate(), ejbActivate(), and ejbPassivate() methods.

Operation	Stateful Session Bean	Stateless Session Bean
Get a reference to the bean's home interface	Yes	Yes
Get a reference to the bean's EJB Object, that is, a reference to the component interface	Yes	Yes
Get security information	Yes	No
Mark the current transaction to roll back; CMT beans	No	No
Determine whether the transaction has already been marked for rollback; CMT beans	No	No
Get a reference to the transaction; BMT beans	Yes	Yes

continued on next page

CHAPTER 5   LIFECYCLE OF A SESSION BEAN

Table 5.2 Permitted and prohibited operations in the `ejbRemove()` method for a stateful session bean and a stateless session bean. The list, in the case of a stateful session bean, is identical to those for the `ejbCreate()`, `ejbActivate()`, and `ejbPassivate()` methods. *(continued)*

Operation	Stateful Session Bean	Stateless Session Bean
JNDI access	Yes	Yes
Resource manager access	Yes	No
Access to other beans	Yes	No

The situation is the same as in the `ejbActivate()` or `ejbPassivate()` method: the bean instance has no transaction context. Before calling `ejbRemove()`, the container makes sure the instance is not in a transaction, so you cannot mark a transaction to roll back, and you cannot ask whether a transaction is marked for a rollback. In other words, you cannot tell a bean on its way to the does not exist state, "I am going to mark your transaction for a rollback." Common sense is in play again. All other standard operations and accesses are permitted for a stateful session bean. For a stateless session bean, more accesses are prohibited because it is removed without a request from the client.

Exceptions caused by the bean removal

If the client of a stateful session bean instance invokes a method on the bean's interface after the instance has been removed, this results in `java.rmi.NoSuchObjectException` if the client is a remote client and `javax.ejb.NoSuchObjectLocalException` if the client is a local client. When a client attempts to remove a bean instance, and the bean has already been removed, the container, instead of invoking `ejbRemove()`, throws `javax.ejb.RemoveException` to the client.

The missed ejbRemove() calls

A session bean instance can return to the does not exist state and thus complete its lifecycle in one of two ways: removal by the container or deletion as a result of a server crash. The container will invoke an `ejbRemove()` method before removing the bean instance except under the following situations:

- The bean instance times out while in the passive state. The deployer sets the timeout value.
- The bean instance throws a system exception on the container.
- The server crashes.

> **ALERT** A bean timing out in the method ready state will receive an `ejbRemove()` call before deletion, while a bean timing out in the passive state will not receive an `ejbRemove()` call.

Because the bean instance can go to the does not exist state directly from the passive state, you should do the same cleanup in the `ejbPassivate()` method that you do in the `ejbRemove()` method—in other words, prepare the bean instance for removal before passivating it.

Now, we will take an in-depth look at the method ready state of a session bean.

5.5 WHERE THE BEAN ROCKS: THE BUSINESS METHODS

In the method ready state, a bean instance is at the prime of its lifecycle. It can do what it was created for: execute its business methods. In other words, it can service the business method calls from the client, and that is the very reason the client accessed the bean in the first place. It's your responsibility to implement the business methods in the bean class and expose them in the component interface of the bean.

5.5.1 Implementation of business methods

You can define zero or more business methods in a session bean class, and the signatures of these methods must obey the following rules:

- A business method name can be arbitrary, but it must not start with `ejb`. This rule exists to avoid conflicts with the container callback methods such as `ejbCreate()` or `ejbPassivate()`.

- A business method must be declared public.

- A business method must not be declared final or static.

- The arguments and return types for a business method must be in compliance with the RMI/IIOP (Internet Inter-ORB Protocol) legal types (that is, primitives, serializable objects, an array or collection of primitives or serializable objects, or a remote object) if the method is exposed in the session bean's remote interface.

- The name, return types, and arguments of a business method in the bean class must be identical to the corresponding method declared in the component interface.

- The business methods in the class must not declare `RemoteException`: no `RemoteException` in the class whatsoever. You don't have to declare other exceptions declared in the interface in the class method unless you might actually throw them from the method.

- You must not declare any exception in the method that was not declared in the interface. You can declare arbitrary application exceptions, but you have to declare them in the interface for the corresponding method as well.

  ALERT A business method must not throw an application exception that is not declared in the component interface for the matching method.

What kind of access does the bean have while executing its business methods?

5.5.2   Operations from the business methods

You have seen that in the bean methods discussed so far, such as `ejbCreate()` and `ejbActivate()`, the bean's access to the session context methods and other resources is very limited. However, in the business methods, the bean can have access to all the session context methods, its JNDI context, resource managers, and other beans, as table 5.3 shows.

Table 5.3   Operations permitted and prohibited from inside the business methods of a session bean class. These apply to both stateful and stateless session beans.

Operation	Any Business Method
Get a reference to the bean's home interface	Yes
Get a reference to the bean's EJBObject, that is, a reference to the component interface	Yes
Get security information about the client	Yes
Mark the current transaction to roll back	Yes
Determine whether the transaction has already been marked for rollback	Yes
Get a reference to the transaction; only for BMT beans	Yes
JNDI access	Yes
Resource manager access	Yes
Access to other beans	Yes

To remember what accesses a session bean instance has within different bean methods, bear in mind the following two facts:

- A stateful session bean has no transaction context in the following methods: `ejbCreate()`, `ejbRemove()`, `ejbActivate()`, and `ejbPassivate()`. Therefore, the instance in these methods has access to everything except the two transaction-related methods of the session context.

- The stateless session bean also has no transaction context in the `ejbCreate()`, `ejbRemove()`, `ejbActivate()`, and `ejbPassivate()` methods, so there's no access to two transaction-related methods. In addition to this, the stateless session bean instance when being created or removed is not tied to any client, so you cannot ask for client information in the `ejbCreate()` and `ejbRemove()` methods of a stateless session bean.

The three most important takeaways from this chapter are

- Business methods can be executed only in the method ready state.
- Container callbacks are executed during the transition from one state to another.
- The passive state exists only for stateful session beans and not for stateless session beans.

5.6　SUMMARY

The lifecycle of a stateful session bean involves three states: the does not exist state, which exists before an instance of the bean is constructed; the method ready state, in which the bean can service the business method calls; and the passive state, which is the stored state of the bean instance. The lifecycle of a stateless session bean has only two states: the does not exist state and the method ready state. The bean instance has limited access to the methods of the `SessionContext` interface from its methods except from the business methods, where it can call any session context method. So, three kinds of methods define the lifecycle of a session bean: the business methods exposed in the component interface, the `SessionBean` methods (container callbacks) called by the container during the transition from one state to another, and the methods of the `SessionContext` interface called from within the bean class methods. Activation and passivation are meaningful only for a stateful session bean.

The major difference between the lifecycles of a stateful session bean and a stateless session bean stems from the fact that a stateful session bean has a lifetime commitment to its client, while a stateless session bean has a single obligation. In other words, a stateful session bean is created upon a `create()` call from the client; it serves only that client and maintains its state with that client during its lifecycle; and it is killed upon a `remove()` call from the client. So, if the container needs to delete a stateful session bean that's still in session, it puts the bean into the passive state. Stateless session beans are created and removed as needed by the container to service multiple client calls. They do not need a passive state because they do not keep client-specific information that has to be saved. This also explains why a stateless session bean instance does not need a passive state: there is no state with the client that needs to be saved. No concurrent access by multiple clients is allowed to a stateless or a stateful session bean. Furthermore, none of the stateful and stateless session bean instances can survive a container crash.

Compared with the stateless session bean, you might think the stateful session bean is extremely sophisticated. Wait until you meet the entity bean in the next chapter!

Comprehend

- Know the lifecycles of a stateless session bean and a stateful session bean.

- A stateless session bean has no passive state because it does not maintain any state with the client that would need to be saved.

- Be able to describe the information you can get from the session context and what other accesses you can have from inside a given bean class method.

- Container callbacks include an ejbCreate method corresponding to each create method in the home interface and all the methods from the `SessionBean` interface. The bean provider must implement these callback methods in the class.

Look out

- You cannot passivate a bean that is in a transaction.

- A remove call from a client removes only a stateful session bean instance and not a stateless session bean instance because the creation and deletion of a stateless session bean do not depend on client calls.

- By the end of the `ejbPassivate()` method all the nontransient instance variables must be in a form ready to be serialized by the container: null, serializable object, remote component interface, remote home interface, etc.

- Know the situations under which the container will not call `ejb-Remove()` before killing the bean instance: the bean instance throws a system exception, the bean times out in passive state, or the container/server crashes.

Memorize

- The acceptable type for passivation.

- The methods that can be called during the lifecycle of a session bean at different states and during the transition from one state to another.

Some questions may have more than one correct answer. Choose all that apply.

1. Which of the following methods can be called from the code of a stateless session bean's client?
   a. ejbCreate()
   b. remove()
   c. create()
   d. ejbRemove()
   e. createDiscount()

2. Which of the following methods can be invoked by the container on the stateless session bean?
   a. ejbCreate()
   b. remove()
   c. create()
   d. ejbRemove()
   e. createDiscount()

3. Which of the following methods belong to the SessionBean interface?
   a. ejbCreate()
   b. ejbActivate()
   c. create()
   d. setSessionContext()
   e. getRollbackOnly()

4. Which of the following methods belong to the SessionContext interface, directly or by inheritance?
   a. ejbCreate()
   b. ejbActivate()
   c. create()
   d. setSessionContext()
   e. getRollbackOnly()
   f. getEJBHome()

5. Which of the following lists presents the correct sequence in which the listed methods would be executed in the lifecycle of a stateful session bean?
   a. ejbCreate(), setSessionContext(), ejbActivate(), ejbPassivate()

b. `ejbCreate()`, `ejbActivate()`, `ejbPassivate`, `set-SessionContext()`

c. `setSessionContext()`,`ejbCreate()`,`ejbPassivate()`, `ejbActivate()`

d. `setSessionContext()`, `ejbCreate()`, `ejbActivate()`, `ejbPassivate()`

e. `ejbActivate()`,`ejbCreate()`, `setSessionContext()`, `ejbPassivate()`

6. In which of the following cases will the container remove a session bean instance without invoking the `ejbRemove()` method ?

   a. The bean instance throws a system exception.

   b. The bean instance in a passive state times out.

   c. The bean instance in the method ready state times out.

   d. The bean instance calls a prohibited method of its session context.

   e. The client invokes the method `remove()`.

7. Which of the following statements show what happens when a client invokes a session bean instance that does not exist?

   a. `javax.ejb.NoSuchObjectLocalException` for the local client

   b. `javax.ejb.NoSuchObjectException` for the remote client.

   c. `javax.ejb.RemoveException`

   d. `javax.ejb.ObjectNotFoundException`

   e. `java.rmi.NoSuchObjectException` for the remote client

8. Which of the following statements are true about the lifecycle of a session bean?

   a. Only a stateful session bean, and not a stateless session bean, in a transaction can be passivated.

   b. The client cannot invoke a `create()` or `remove()` call on a stateless session bean.

   c. Only a stateful session bean can be activated or passivated.

   d. The container will invoke an `ejbRemove()` call on a stateful session bean only in response to a `remove()` call from the client.

   e. Two clients may end up using the same stateless session bean instance, one after the other.

9. Which of the following are valid declarations for the business methods in the class of a session bean?

   a. `public void ejbSetDiscount(float number);`

   b. `public void setDiscount(float number) throws RemoteException;`

```
c. public static void setDiscount(float number);
d. public void setDiscount();
```

10. From which of the following methods can't a stateful session bean access the methods of another bean?

    a. `ejbRemove()`

    b. `ejbPassivate()`

    c. `setSessionContext()`

    d. `ejbCreate()`

    e. None of the above

PART 3

Entity beans

The entity bean is the most sophisticated component of EJB and it has the most interesting lifecycle. The single defining property of an entity bean is its ability to represent an entity in the database. The most important characteristics of an entity bean are the following:

- To allow a client to operate on an entity in the database, it offers the client view with business methods exposed in both the home interface and the component interface.
- It can get involved in a relationship with another entity bean.
- It has a whole new language called the Enterprise JavaBeans query language (EJB QL) attached to it, which you must learn in order to tell the container how to manage the persistence of entity beans.

You will learn three important things about an entity bean. From a client's perspective, as long as the entity is alive, the entity bean will survive even a server crash. A remove call from the client for an entity bean will not remove an entity bean instance. The third fact is from the container's perspective: All instances in the pool are constructed equal, and they remain equal as long as they are in the pool.

Let's explore this sophisticated bean.

C H A P T E R   6

Client view of
an entity bean

EXAM OBJECTIVES

5.1 Identify correct and incorrect statements or examples about the client of an entity bean's local and remote home interface, including the code used to locate an entity bean's home interface, and the home interface methods provided to the client.

5.2 Identify correct and incorrect statements or examples about the client view of an entity bean's local component interface (`EJBLocalObject`).

5.3 Identify correct and incorrect statements or examples about the client view of an entity bean's remote component interface (`EJBObject`).

5.4 Identify the use, syntax, and behavior of, the following entity bean home method types, for CMP: finder methods, create methods, remove methods, and home methods.

125

INTRODUCTION

The main purpose of entity beans is to let the client operate on the entities in the database, for example, to change the email address of a customer. When they are deployed in the EJB container, entity beans bring with them the business methods that implement the business logic of the application; this often involves interaction with the database. The client in general may make database operations that fall into three categories: create a new entry in a database table, conduct operations on an existing specific entry whose identity is known to the client, or conduct operations on multiple entries that meet certain criteria but whose identity is not known to the client before the operation. The client can make these operations using the client view of an entity bean.

The client view is composed of the home interface and the component interface. Just like with session beans, the client starts by locating the home interface of an entity bean. The client may just need to conduct operations on multiple entities in the database whose identification is not known, for example, to list all the customers who have made more than 10 orders. In this case, the client may invoke the methods exposed in the home interface, called home business methods (not available in session beans). If the client is interested in performing operations on a specific entity, it can use the home reference to get a reference to the component interface and invoke the business methods exposed in the component interface.

So, this chapter focuses on determining how a client uses the client view to perform operations on a specific entity in the database or on multiple entities in the database whose identification is not known to the client. To find the answer, we will explore the following three avenues: the home interface of an entity bean, the component interface of an entity bean, and the differences between the client views of a session bean and an entity bean. Although we will explore the characteristics and functionalities of an entity bean in the next chapter, we'll take a brief look in this chapter at this interesting bean from the client's perspective before we get into the details of the client view.

6.1   INTRODUCING ENTITY BEANS

Entity beans are the most sophisticated of three kinds of beans in the EJB container, the others being session beans and message-driven beans. In this section, you will learn what an entity bean is and how to distinguish the different concepts related to it. An entity bean represents a thing such as an employee, product, or order, while a session bean represents a process such as credit card verification. Any kind of enterprise bean or simple Java program can act as a client to use an entity bean when it needs to deal with data, for example, to store, retrieve, or change the data.

You may still be dragging your feet and saying, "I can access the database with session beans, so why do I have to write entity beans?" The fact of the matter is you don't have to write entity beans. You don't have to write session beans either, and you don't even have to use EJB, and you can still accomplish all the things that you accomplish with an EJB application, but it would be more difficult, cumbersome, messy, and prone to errors. The whole idea of a bean (or a component) is that its design specializes in certain functionality, and the specialty of an entity bean is database access. For example, its design deals with database access issues, and the solutions to most of those issues are automated and offered by the container as services. You will see this as you continue exploring this book.

Having justified the existence of an entity bean, let's see what entity beans live on and live for.

6.1.1 The core functionality of an entity bean

An entity bean offers access to data about an entity stored in persistent storage such as a database, file, or any other form. From the client view, an entity bean is an object that is an in-memory representation of the entity. An instance (object) of an entity bean encapsulates the persistent data about an entity and the methods to manipulate the data. Business logic is implemented in the methods.

In this chapter, we will work with a simple example of an entity bean as a tool to illustrate the basic concepts. We will call our entity bean the Customer bean, which is composed of a class named `CustomerBean`, a remote home interface named `CustomerHome`, and a remote component interface named `Customer`.

The skeletons of the class and the interfaces are shown here. First, let's look at the `CustomerBean` class:

```
public class CustomerBean implements EntityBean {
  private String id;
  private String name;
  private String email;
// methods go here.
}
```

Next, we have the `CustomerHome` interface:

```
public interface CustomerHome extends EJBHome {
 // We will fill in some code here later in this chapter.
}
```

Finally, the `Customer` interface looks like this:

```
public interface Customer extends EJBObject {
 // We will fill in some code here later in this chapter.
}
```

Note that the `CustomerBean` class implements the interface `EntityBean`, which makes it an entity bean. The home interface `CustomerHome` extends `EJBHome`, the same `EJBHome` that a session bean's home interface extends. Similarly, the remote component interface `Customer` extends `EJBObject`, the same `EJBObject` that a session bean's remote component interface extends.

A specific instance of an entity bean may represent an entity from the database. In our simple example, an entity occupies one row in the database table shown in figure 6.1. It is possible that an entity may contain more than one row from multiple tables. As shown in figure 6.1, each entity may be represented by a specific entity bean.

An entity bean represents a persistent entity, and persistence management will handle the interaction with the database. Persistence management may be coded inside the bean, which is called bean-managed persistence (BMP), or it may be offered by the container, which is called container-managed persistence (CMP). You'll learn more about persistence management in the next chapter.

A specific instance of an entity bean may represent an entity from the database. The reason we say "may" is that it's possible to have an instance of an entity bean class that is not representing any entity at this time. Also, it is possible to have an entity in the database that is not being represented by an entity bean instance at this time. For example, consider a pool of 90 instances of an entity bean and a database table with 500 customers. A pool is a collection of instances of a bean type (say Customer); each instance has a context attached to it, and an instance in the pool does not represent a specific entity. Therefore, in the beginning, none of the entity bean instances represents any entity. Now assume that 50 client requests come in for 50 different entities. The container pulls 50 instances out of the pool and assigns a specific entity to each one. At this point, there are 50 entity bean instances representing 50 entities in the database, there are 450 entities in the database not being represented at all, and there are 40 bean instances in the pool that are not attached to any entity.

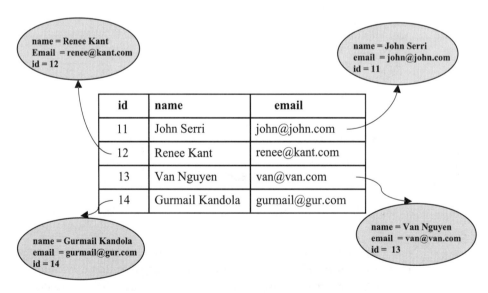

Figure 6.1 Customer information table in the database and the entity beans representing the entities. In the simplest scenario, an entity is a row in the table.

So, it should be clear by now that entity and entity bean can exist independently of each other. We know that an entity can certainly exist independently of the entity bean in a database outside the EJB container, but what about the entity bean? That depends on the definition of *entity bean*, which can mean more than one thing. So the question is, what are we referring to when we say *entity bean*? Let's explore.

6.1.2 Entity, entity bean, and entity bean instance

An entity can exist independently of any entity bean but may be represented by the entity bean. By using this representation, the client can use the entity bean to operate on the entity. Three players are related to the concept of entity bean: an entity bean class, an entity bean instance, and an entity bean instance representing an entity. To mistake one for the other is a common source of confusion for folks who are just starting to work with EJB. Let's clarify these three concepts and their relationships with the entity.

Entity and entity bean

Decoupling these two concepts is easy. An entity is a thing that exists in the database outside of the EJB container, and an entity bean is the bean in the EJB container that can represent this entity. For example, a customer with *name* equal to John Serri, *id* equal to 11, and *email* equal to john@john.com in a database table (figure 6.1) is an entity. When needed, the container would ask an entity bean instance to represent this entity. We will discuss the details of when and how this happens later in this chapter and the next. The entities shown in figure 6.1 contain one row each. Remember that an entity bean may contain more than one row across multiple tables in a relational database.

An entity bean represents an entity, not vice versa. However, there could be an entity without the existence of any entity bean. The story begins with the entity; the entity bean is there just to represent the entity. You shouldn't consider entities as some sort of backup of entity beans. As you saw in an example presented earlier in this chapter, there could be entities in the database that are not being represented by entity beans at a given time. When the EJB server goes down, the entities, regardless of whether they were being represented by entity beans, still live and may be represented by entity beans when the server comes back. The point is that the entities live in the database independently of the EJB container and independently of the entity beans. The reverse is not true. For example, if there is no entity called John Serri in the database, there can be no Customer entity bean representing John Serri for the client.

A beginner may get confused by statements like "There can be no entity bean without an entity." You can argue against this statement, because after all the developer wrote the entity bean (a class and interfaces), the deployer deployed it to the container, and all that was done without mention of a specific entity in the database. The problem here is that when we talk about an entity bean, we might be referring to any of the following: the entity bean class, an entity bean instance not assigned to any entity (that is, the instance in the pool), or an active entity bean instance representing a specific entity. Being a Java developer, you already know the difference between a class and an instance. By an active entity bean instance, we mean the bean instance that represents an entity. If by an entity bean we mean only an entity bean instance that represents an entity, then of course there could be no entity bean without an entity.

NOTE   When we say there can be no entity bean without an entity, we mean there can be no specific entity bean instance representing a specific entity that does not exist in persistent storage.

Let's explore further the relationship between an entity bean and an entity bean instance.

Entity bean and entity bean instance

When describing the relationship between an entity and an entity bean, we used the term *active entity bean* because *entity bean* by itself is a concept with a broad scope. From the perspective of a bean provider and bean deployer, an entity bean is a component composed of a class, interfaces, and a deployment descriptor. When the application is running, another player comes on the scene: the entity bean instance. So, during runtime what do we mean when we say *entity bean*? Do we always mean the entity bean instance, then? The answer is no.

For example, consider a customer named Renee Kant (figure 6.1) being represented by an entity bean instance in memory. Assume the server crashes. Of course, the bean instance in memory would die. However, the entity bean representing customer Renee Kant is not dead from the client's viewpoint because when the server is restarted, the client can access this customer again. The container will make another entity bean instance to represent the customer (entity) Renee Kant. Therefore, from the client's viewpoint, the entity bean (not a particular bean instance) representing Renee Kant did not die during the server crash. However, if the customer were removed from the database, then the entity bean would die because the client could not access it anymore. So, as long as the entity exists, the possibility of representing it in memory exists, and the entity bean exists. This is the client's perspective.

NOTE   When you read something like "an entity bean survives the server crash," it means that even though entity bean instances die with a server crash, when the server is restarted, the container can always create an instance to represent the entity as long as the entity is alive in persistent storage. So, from the client's perspective, the entity bean *survived* the server crash.

Thus, an entity always exists in persistent storage, and an entity bean can represent it in memory. By *entity bean* we may mean one of the following three things: the entity bean class written by the bean developer, entity bean instances in the pool representing no specific entity, or entity bean instances representing a specific entity. And what we mean by entity bean (a class, an instance in the pool, or an instance representing an entity) depends on the context.

Having examined the different faces of an entity bean, let's now explore its main characteristics.

6.1.3   Characteristics of an entity bean

The following are some characteristics of entity beans relevant to the client view:

- Multiple entity bean types can be deployed in a container. For example, a container may have a Customer bean and an Account bean.
- Each bean type has its own home interface and a component interface, and the two combined make the client view for that bean type.
- All instances of a particular bean type share the same home interface reference, but each bean instance gets its own component interface reference.
- During its entire lifecycle, an entity bean instance lives inside the container.
- The container provides management services for the bean, including security, transaction, and concurrency. The container also manages persistence for the CMP beans.
- Unlike for a session bean, multiple clients can access an entity bean concurrently. The container manages the concurrency.
- Entity beans survive a server crash. This means that if a client can access an entity using an entity bean before the crash, it can access the same entity using an entity bean after the crash as well when the server is restarted.

In order to manipulate entities in the database, the client can use the home interface and the component interface. Depending on the nature of the operation, it may not need a component interface, but it will always need the home interface.

6.2   ENTITY BEAN REMOTE HOME INTERFACE

The bean provider writes the remote home interface, which extends `javax.ejb.EJBHome`, the same `EJBHome` that the remote home interface of session bean extends. Just like in session beans, all the bean instances of a bean type will have the same home interface reference, while each instance will have its own component interface reference.

When a client needs to access a bean, the story starts with the home interface. The process is described in section 6.5. The client does the JNDI lookup on the home interface, uses the home interface reference to get a reference to a bean's component interface, and then uses the component interface to call business methods of the bean. This is true for both session and entity beans. As you will see, a client can make some operations without having to get a reference to the bean's component interface. This obviously implies that the home interface of an entity bean may have business methods.

First, we will look at the methods required to be included in the home interface.

6.2.1 Required methods in the remote home interface

The purpose of the home methods is to allow the client to make certain kinds of operations on the entity, such as finding a specific entity (say a particular customer), removing a specific entity, and performing some operations on the database that are not targeted at a specific entity, such as listing all the customers who have made more than 10 orders. The method that finds a specific entity, called `findByPrimaryKey(...)`, is declared by the bean provider in the home interface, and the methods that remove the entity are inherited from the `EJBHome` interface.

There are five required methods in the entity bean home interface: four methods inherited from `EJBHome` and one method called `findByPrimaryKey(...)` that you must put into the interface. The home interface for our example of the Customer bean is presented in figure 6.2.

Like a session bean home interface, an entity bean home interface must extend the `javax.ejb.EJBHome` interface, inheriting four methods from the `EJBHome` interface. The `EJBHome` methods have already been discussed in detail in Part 2, "Session beans." Here is the summary:

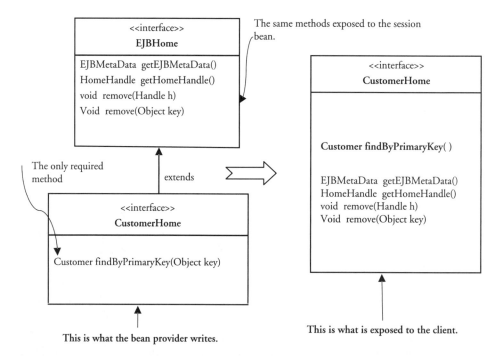

Figure 6.2 The entity bean's home interface, `CustomerHome`, extends the interface `EJBHome`. A client would see all the methods declared by the bean provider in the `CustomerHome` interface in addition to the methods of the interface `EJBHome`.

- *getEJBMetaData()*—This method returns the EJBMetaData interface, which can be used to get the class information about the bean. This method is typically called only by the container, not by bean clients.
- *getHomeHandle()*—This method can be used by the client to get a handle to the home interface, so that the client would not have to go through another JNDI search if it needed the home interface at a later time after losing the current reference.
- *remove(Handle h)*—This method can be used by the client to remove an entity.
- *remove(Object key)*—This is another method a client can use to remove an entity.

You should develop a clear understanding of the differences between the session bean home interface and the entity bean home interface. For example, a session bean can use only the remove() method with Handle as an argument, while an entity bean can use both remove() methods in the home interface.

NOTE There is only one method, findByPrimaryKey(), that the bean developer is required to put into the entity bean home interface. The create() method is not required.

Furthermore, the create() method in the entity bean home interface is optional, while it is required in the session bean home interface. In the entity bean home interface, you (the bean developer) are required only to define the findByPrimary-Key() method. The other find methods are optional. In the case of entity beans, the create() method is used to insert entries into the database. Making this method optional gives you the option of preventing the client from inserting data into the database.

To summarize, the following five methods at minimum are exposed to the client in a remote home interface:

- findByPrimaryKey(Object key), which you define with the remote component interface as the return type
- getEJBMetaData() from EJBHome with EJBMetaData as the return type
- getHomeHandle() from EJBHome with HomeHandle as the return type
- remove(Handle h) from EJBHome with void as the return type, that is, returns nothing
- remove(Handle key) from EJBHome with void as the return type

The home interface for our example is

```
public interface CustomerHome extends EJBHome {
  public Customer findByPrimaryKey(String primaryKey) throws
     FinderException, RemoteException;
}
```

The method `findByPrimaryKey(...)` must throw `FinderException`, and of course also `RemoteException`, like any other method in the remote interface.

A client uses the `findByPrimaryKey(...)` method to get a reference to the component interface of an entity bean that would represent a specific entity in the database. But the client might need to conduct other kinds of operations, such as creating a new entity in the database, deleting an existing entity, searching for a set of entities that meet a certain criterion, and updating a set of entities that meet a certain criterion. To allow the client to perform these operations, you may define additional methods in the home interface. Let's see how to do that.

6.2.2 Additional methods in the home interface

In addition to the required methods, you may define other methods in the entity bean home interface. The methods that you are allowed to define fall into the following categories.

The finder methods

We will be referring to these methods as the *find* methods and the *finder* methods alternatively. The purpose of a finder method is to get a reference to the component interface of an entity bean instance that represents an existing entity, that is, a reference to an EJBObject. The client will use this reference to interact with the entity by invoking methods on the bean instance. As you already know, you are required to define one finder method, `getByPrimaryKey(...)`, in the home interface of any entity bean you write. This method allows the client to find an entity bean with a specific primary key, that is, an entity bean representing a specific entity in the database. Even if we say that the client accesses (or finds) an entity, we always mean an entity bean instance representing that entity. The method takes one argument that must be of type primary key for that bean. If the entity with the specified primary key does not exist, the client receives a `javax.ejb.ObjectNotFoundException`, a subclass of `FinderException`.

Optionally, you may define more finder methods. Each finder method must start with the prefix `find`, as in `findByPrimaryKey()`. The return type of a finder method is either the remote component interface of the entity bean or a Collection of it. In the latter case, the client will get references to multiple EJBObjects: one for each bean instance that was found. If the return type is a Collection and no entity was found, an empty Collection is returned and no exception is thrown.

> **ALERT** If an entity is not found, the client gets an `ObjectNotFoundException` in the case of a single-entity finder and an empty Collection (and no exception) in the case of a multiple-entity finder.

For a CMP bean, you will not need to write any finder methods in the bean class. The container will implement them for you. However, for a BMP bean, you will need to write a matching method named `ejbFind<method>` in the bean class for each find<method> in the home interface. You will learn the details about this in the next chapter.

The finder methods are used only to find the entities that already exist in the database, that is, to get a reference to the remote component interfaces of the entity bean instances that represent those entities. You can allow the clients to create an entity that currently does not exist in the database by defining the create methods in the home interface.

The create methods

With a create method, a client creates a new entity in the database and receives a reference to the component interface for the bean instance representing that entity. Using the reference to the component interface, the client can make other operations on that specific entity.

You must know how a create method is used differently in session beans and entity beans. Table 6.1 lists these differences.

Table 6.1   Comparing the usage of a create method in the home interface of a stateless session bean, a stateful session bean, and an entity bean

Characteristic	Stateless Session Bean	Stateful Session Bean	Entity Bean
Developer declares the method in the bean's home.	Mandatory to declare one and only one create method: create().	Mandatory to declare at least one create method.	Not mandatory.
Client's purpose.	Get an EJB object reference to a bean.	Get an EJB object reference to a bean.	Create a new entity in the database and get an EJB object reference to a bean representing that entity.
Arguments/ initialization.	No arguments, no client-specific initialization by the bean.	May have arguments that the bean can use to do client-specific initialization.	Arguments not mandatory, but a meaningful call will always have arguments.
Bean creation.	Container does not create a new bean instance. When create() is called, it pulls one out of the pool only when a business method is called afterward.	Container does make a new bean instance.	Container does not create a new bean instance. Pulls one out of the pool and loads it to represent the entity.

You may define more than one create method for an entity bean type corresponding to different ways of creating an entity. In addition to overloading the create() method, you may define create<method> methods whose names must start with the prefix create. Each create method must throw javax.ejb.CreateException and also `java.rmi.RemoteException` if it is in a remote interface. The return type of each create method is always the component interface of the entity bean.

ALERT A create method call on an entity bean will create an actual entity in the database, while a create method call on a session bean does not trigger interaction with the database.

For each create method in the entity home interface, you will write two methods in the bean class with names beginning with `ejbCreate` and `ejbPostCreate`. You will learn more about this in the next chapter. Recall that in the case of a session bean, you need to write only one method, `ejbCreate()`, in the bean class corresponding to each `create()` method in the home interface.

The entity bean home interface inherits the `remove()` methods from the `EJBHome` interface, and the client can use these methods to remove entities from the database.

The remove methods

Generally speaking, from the client's viewpoint, the purpose of the remove methods is to remove the bean, which have a different meaning for the different bean flavors (stateful session, stateless session, and entity), which you will see later. The following two remove methods are defined in the `javax.ejb.EJBHome` interface used by both session and entity beans:

```
void remove(Handle h) throws RemoteException, RemoveException;
void remove(Object primaryKey) throws RemoteException, RemoveException;
```

Therefore, the home interfaces of an entity bean and a session bean will both inherit these methods from the `EJBHome` interface. However, because the concept of primary key exists only for entity beans, the `remove(Object primaryKey)` method can be invoked only on entity beans and not on session beans. The `remove(Handle h)` method could be invoked on either session or entity beans.

The usage of the remove methods by a client and its effects are summarized in table 6.2 for the various bean flavors.

Table 6.2 Comparing the usage of the remove methods in the home interface of a stateless session bean, a stateful session bean, and an entity bean

Characteristic	Stateless Session Bean	Stateful Session Bean	Entity Bean
Client's purpose.	Inform the container that the client has finished with the bean.	Inform the container that the client has finished with the bean.	Delete an entity from the database.
Container's action in response to the method call.	None. The bean has already gone into the pool.	Kill the bean instance.	The entity in the database is removed. The bean instance goes back into the pool.

continued on next page

CHAPTER 6 CLIENT VIEW OF AN ENTITY BEAN

Table 6.2 Comparing the usage of the remove methods in the home interface of a stateless session bean, a stateful session bean, and an entity bean *(continued)*

Characteristic	Stateless Session Bean	Stateful Session Bean	Entity Bean
Can client use EJB object reference after calling a successful `remove()`?	No. If used, it will receive an exception.	No. If used, it will receive an exception.	No. If used, it will receive an exception.
Allowed argument types.	Handle.	Handle.	Both Handle and Object for the primary key.

Note that the remove methods throw `RemoveException` and also `Remote-Exception`, but only if the interface is remote.

> **ALERT** A remove method call on an entity bean will delete an actual entity in the database, while a remove method call on a session bean does not trigger interaction with the database.

The remove methods are implemented by the container. One main difference between the session bean home interface and the entity bean home interface is that you can define business methods in the entity bean home interface. These methods can handle operations that do not need a specific entity identified by the client.

The home business methods

Unlike in the session bean home interface, you can define business methods in the entity bean home interface. However, in these methods, you can implement only the business logic that is not related to a specific entity bean representing a specific entity in the database. This is because a home business method is not required to return a reference to an EJBObject that the client would need to interact with a specific entity. You can implement home business methods that allow clients to perform operations on a set of entities that meet a certain criterion but whose identification is not known to the client. For example, a client can apply discounts to all customers who qualify.

Here are the rules for defining home business methods:

- You can give your home business methods arbitrary names but they must not begin with `create`, `find`, or `remove` to avoid conflict with the create, find, and remove methods.

- In the home business methods, you may declare application-level exceptions.

- These methods may return the EJBObject type or some other type.

- Business methods in the remote home interface must declare `java.rmi.RemoteException` in their `throws` clause, and their arguments and return types must be compliant with the RMI-IIOP: primitives, serializable objects, an array of primitives, an array of serializable objects, or a remote object.

ALERT   The home business methods of entity beans may have arbitrary names, but they must not begin with `find`, `remove`, or `create`.

For each home business `<method>`, you are required to write a method in the bean class with the name `ejbHome<method>`. You will learn more about this in the next chapter.

The home business methods do not deal with a specific entity. If a client has to perform operations on a specific entity, the client needs a reference to the component interface of the entity bean (EJBObject) representing that specific entity.

6.3 ENTITY BEAN REMOTE COMPONENT INTERFACE

The remote component interface along with the remote home interface constitute the remote client view of an entity bean. The remote client can use the home interface to receive a reference to the remote interface of a bean and then in turn use this interface to call the business methods of the bean. The remote client view of an entity bean works the same way regardless of whether the remote client is running on a remote machine or on a local machine within or outside the same JVM in which the entity bean is running.

Once a client gets a reference to an entity bean's remote component interface, it can use this reference to call the methods exposed in the component interface. Let's see what those methods are.

6.3.1 Methods in the remote component interface

An entity bean's component interface is used to expose the business methods written in the bean class. Just as in a session bean, it extends `javax.ejb.EJBObject`. Therefore, a client can access the methods that you implemented in the bean class and exposed in the component interface, as well as the methods in the `EJBObject` interface. The `EJBObject` interface methods have already been discussed in detail in Part 2, "Session beans."

Figure 6.3 shows some business methods and the five methods that the component interface (named `Customer` in our example) inherits from the `EJBObject` interface. You write the business methods in the component interface to allow the client to access an entity bean that would represent a specific entity such as (name: John Serri, email:john@john.com, id:11).

The code fragment corresponding to figure 6.3 is shown here:

```
public interface Customer extends EJBObject {
  public String getName() throws RemoteException;
  public void setName(String name) throws RemoteException;

  public String getEmail() throws RemoteException;
  public void setEmail(String email) throws RemoteException;
}
```

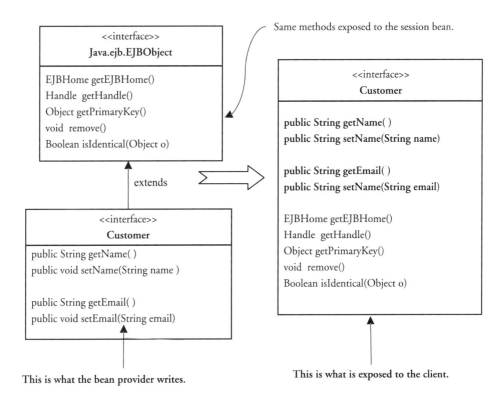

Same methods exposed to the session bean.

<<interface>>
Java.ejb.EJBObject

EJBHome getEJBHome()
Handle getHandle()
Object getPrimaryKey()
void remove()
Boolean isIdentical(Object o)

extends

<<interface>>
Customer

public String getName( )
public void setName(String name)

public String getEmail( )
public void setEmail(String email)

This is what the bean provider writes.

<<interface>>
Customer

public String getName( )
public String setName(String name)

public String getEmail( )
public String setName(String email)

EJBHome getEJBHome()
Handle getHandle()
Object getPrimaryKey()
void remove()
Boolean isIdentical(Object o)

This is what is exposed to the client.

Figure 6.3   The entity bean's remote component interface, `Customer`, extends the `EJBObject` interface. A client sees all the methods declared by the bean provider in the `Customer` interface in addition to the methods of the `EJBObject` interface that the `Customer` interface extends.

Just as for session beans, the container implements the home interface in a class, and the instance of that class is called the EJBHome object. The container also implements the component interface in a class, and an instance of that class is called the EJBObject object. All the bean instances of the same type (for example, CustomerBean) have the same home (`EJBHome`), but each bean instance has its own EJBObject. We will illustrate this with an example. A client who wants to perform operations on a specific entity (say John Serri with primary key #11), can get a reference to the component interface of the bean representing that entity by calling `findByPrimary-Key("11")` on the home. This call will return the component interface of the bean representing John Serri. Now the client can use this reference to perform operations on the entity John Serri (for example, change the email address). The client performing operations on John Serri can get a reference to the home by calling `getEJBHome` on the component interface, and then from the home can get a reference to the component interface of a bean representing another entity, say Renee Kant. This is because Home is common to all the bean instances of the same bean type.

The rules for writing the remote component interface are as follows:

- Import `javax.ejb.*`.
- Import `java.rmi.RemoteException`.
- Extend `javax.ejb.EJBObject`.

You may declare one or more business methods, which must throw `Remote-Exception` only if the interface is remote. Remember the following rules about these methods:

- A method must declare `RemoteException`, and its arguments and return types must be RMI-IIOP–compliant: primitives, serializable objects, an array of primitives, an array of serializable objects, or a remote object.
- Because the Java language allows it, you can write overloaded methods.
- Methods may have arbitrary names, but they must not begin with the prefix `ejb`. You will learn in the next chapter that the prefix `ejb` is reserved for another kind of method; you also know it from Part 2, "Session beans."
- The methods may throw application-level exceptions defined by you, but they must not be runtime exceptions. This means you must declare them in the `throws` clause, and the client must handle them.

To operate on a specific entity, the client must receive a reference to the remote component interface.

6.3.2 Getting and using the remote component interface

A client may receive a reference to the remote component interface, that is, the `EJBObject`, of an entity bean instance by any of the following methods:

- By calling a find method in the home interface.
- By using the entity bean's handle. Recall that handles exist only in a remote interface.
- As a parameter in a method call.

Once obtained, the reference may be used to accomplish any of the following tasks:

- Call the business methods exposed in the component interface, a common use.
- Pass the reference as a parameter in a method call or a return value of a method call.
- Obtain the primary key of an entity by calling the method `getPrimaryKey()`.
- Obtain the entity beans handle by calling `getHandle()`.
- Delete the entity bean (actually the entity in the database) by calling the remove method.
- Obtain a reference to the home interface of the bean type by calling `getEJB-Home()`.

Note that if you use the reference to call a method on the entity bean that has already been removed, you will get the `java.rmi.NoSuchObject` exception.

Just as for session beans, the EJB 2.0 spec also introduces the local home and local component interfaces for entity beans.

6.4   *LOCAL INTERFACES*

Local interfaces were introduced in EJB 2.0 to improve performance and accommodate the container-managed relationships (CMR) between entity beans, which were also introduced in EJB 2.0. (You will learn more about CMR in chapter 9; for now it's enough to know that CMR fields are used to establish relationships between two entity beans.) Both for session beans and entity beans, the local home and local component interfaces extend `EJBLocalHome` and `EJBLocalObject` as opposed to the remote home and component interfaces, which extend `EJBHome` and `EJBObject`, respectively. The methods in `EJBLocalHome` and `EJBLocalObject` are shown in figure 6.4. They form a subset of the methods in the `EJBHome` and `EJBObject` interfaces. The crossed-out methods in figure 6.4 exist in `EJBHome` and `EJBObject` but not in `EJBLocalHome` and `EJBLocalObject`.

Local clients may use reflection instead of `EJBMetaData` to get the same information, so they don't need the `getEJBMetaData()` method. In the remote interfaces, the handles are used to create a serializable object that could later be used to establish communication with a remote object. Therefore, handles are irrelevant for a local client, and hence all the methods related to the handles are missing from the local interfaces: `EJBLocalObject` and `EJBLocalHome`.

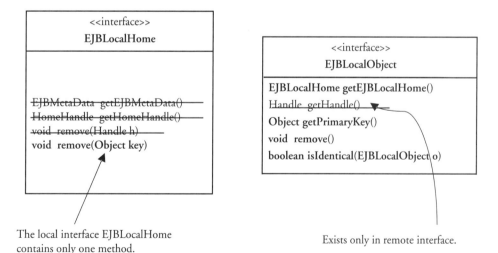

The local interface EJBLocalHome contains only one method.

Exists only in remote interface.

Figure 6.4   Methods in the `EJBLocalObject` and `EJBLocalHome` interfaces. The crossed-out methods do not belong to the local interfaces but do belong to their remote counterparts. They are shown so that you can compare the two kinds of interfaces.

The main differences between local and remote interfaces emerge from the fact that EJBLocalHome and EJBLocalObject do not extend java.rmi.Remote, contrary to EJBHome and EJBObject, which do. These differences, which have been discussed in detail in chapter 3, apply to both session and entity beans and are summarized here:

- As opposed to remote interfaces, you must not declare a RemoteException for any method in local interfaces.
- You may have both local and remote interfaces for a bean type, say Customer-Bean. However, the remote home interface can provide only a reference to a remote component interface, EJBObject, and a local home interface can provide a reference only to a local component interface, EJBLocalObject.
- A client using a local interface still needs to go through JNDI in order to locate the home interface; however, the narrowing is not needed.
- Unlike the remote interface, each create method in the local interface must return a reference to the local component interface and not the remote component interface.

You may be wondering what options the bean provider has in writing bean interfaces. For example, can you write just a local home interface and not the local component interface, or can you write a local home interface and a remote home interface and no component interface? According to the spec, the bean provider must provide one of the following combinations of interfaces:

1 Local home interface and local component interface
2 Remote home interface and remote component interface
3 Local home interface, local component interface, remote home interface, and remote component interface

No other combination is valid.

A client accesses an entity bean by using the client view of the bean, which we look at next.

6.5   USING THE CLIENT VIEW

The client of an entity bean uses the client view, that is, the interfaces, to access the bean. The client may be another enterprise bean or just a plain Java program. A client program accesses an entity bean in the same way it accesses a session bean: it locates the home interface, which is the same for all the bean instances of a bean type, and from the home gets the reference to the component interface for a particular entity bean instance. Then the client can invoke methods on both the home interface and the component interface. But how does a client locate the home interface of a bean?

6.5.1 Locating the home interface

To access an entity bean, a client must locate the home interface of that bean type. The process of locating the home interface is the same as for a session bean. An example of client code that locates the home interface is presented in listing 6.1.

> **Listing 6.1 Example of a client code for locating the home interface of an entity bean**

```
import java.util.*;
import javax.naming.Context;
import javax.naming.InitialContext;
import javax.rmi.PortableRemoteObject;

public class CustomerClient {

    public static void main(String[] args) {

        try {                                      Starting point
                                                   for JNDI lookup
            Context ctx = new InitialContext();
            Object objref = ctx.lookup("java:comp/env/ejb/AnyCustomer");
                                                   JNDI name for CustomerBean

        CustomerHome home =  (CustomerHome)        Home stub narrowed to
        PortableRemoteObject.narrow(objref,        cast to CustomerHome
        CustomerHome.class);
        Customer renee =  home.findByPrimaryKey("12");

         } catch (Exception ex) {
            System.err.println("Exception: " );
            ex.printStackTrace();
        }
     }
  }
```

This simple program demonstrates the three steps each client has to go through to locate the home interface of an entity bean:

1. Get a reference to InitialContext of JNDI. This is the starting point for looking up the bean name registered with the JNDI naming service.

2. Use the reference to InitialContext to look up the bean's home interface.

3. Cast the results of the lookup to the bean's home interface type. Narrow the JNDI lookup results before casting if the home interface is a remote one.

After locating the home interface, the client may use it to invoke a home method or get a reference to the component interface of an entity bean to perform operations on a specific entity. It is important to understand how the EJB architecture responds to a method invocation by a client; for example, the client invokes the findBy-PrimaryKey() method.

6.5.2   Accessing an entity bean

To access an entity bean, a client first accesses the home interface of that bean type, as shown in the previous section. After that, it may either invoke methods exposed in the home interface or get a reference to the component interface of a specific entity and invoke methods on that interface to perform operations on the entity. Figure 6.5 shows what happens when a client calls the method `findByPrimaryKey()`.

After the client receives the `EJBHome` stub as discussed in the previous section, the following things happen:

1 The client calls the method `findByPrimaryKey("11")` on the `EJBHome` stub.
2 The method invocation is passed to the EJBHome object.
3 The container selects a bean instance in the pool and uses it to find out if entity #11 exists in the database.
4 The bean interacts with the database to verify whether entity # 11 exists.
5 The bean informs the EJBHome object that entity #11 exists.
6 The container creates an EJBObject and assigns it the entity id #11.
7 The container returns the `EJBHome` stub to the client.

Unlike for a session bean, multiple clients may access the same entity bean concurrently. This means that more than one client may perform operations on a specific entity concurrently.

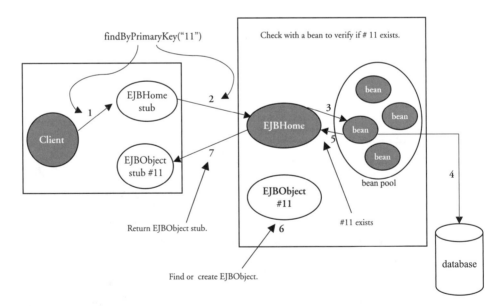

Figure 6.5   How the EJB architecture works in the process of a client getting a reference to the component interface of an entity bean. The process happens in sequential steps, shown by numbers on the arrowed lines.

CHAPTER 6   CLIENT VIEW OF AN ENTITY BEAN

6.5.3   Accessing an entity bean concurrently

Multiple clients can access a client bean concurrently, as shown in figure 6.6. Client A and client B are trying to access the same entity, the customer with id #11. Each client gets a copy of the stub for the same EJBObject #11. The container would take care of concurrency by providing synchronization. It may activate one bean instance or two instances to serve these two concurrent requests. The bean provider does not have to know which of these methods the container would use to handle synchronization.

Remember that a session bean does not offer concurrent access to multiple clients. The three most important takeaways from this chapter are:

- A client of an entity bean performs operations on an entity in the database by invoking methods on an instance of the bean.

- A create method call and a remove method call on an entity bean create and delete an entity in the database, respectively.

- The client of an entity bean can use the home interface to perform operations on the entities in the database without knowing their identifications, while the client has to use the component interface to perform operations on a specific entity in the database whose identity is known to the client.

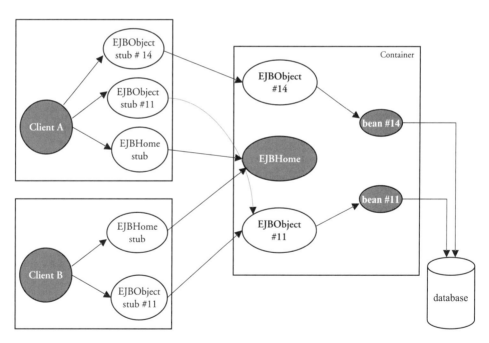

Figure 6.6   Concurrent access to an entity bean by multiple clients. Two clients, A and B, who are trying to access the same entity, #11, get stubs for the same `EJBObject` that holds the entity id #11.

6.6 SUMMARY

The purpose of the client view of an entity bean is to allow the client to perform the following kinds of operations on database: insert an entity into or remove it from the database, operate on a specific existing entity, and operate on a set of entities whose identification is not already known to the client. The client view of an entity bean is composed of a component interface and a home interface. All the beans in a bean type, such as CustomerBean, have the same home interface object, EJBHome, while each bean instance in the bean type would have its own component interface object, EJBObject. Therefore, operations on a specific entity may be performed by using the component interface, while operations on a set of entities whose identification is not known to the client may be conducted using the home interface.

Although both remote interfaces (home and component) of an entity bean, like those of a session bean, extend EJBHome and EJBObject, respectively, they have different rules. For example, the `create()` method in the entity bean home interface is optional, unlike in the session bean home interface. Also unlike in the session bean home interface, you can have business methods in the entity bean home interface. You are required to define a `findByPrimaryKey()` method, the only required method, in the entity bean home interface. However, you may define more finder methods of the following kinds: single-entity finder methods that return a reference to the component interface and multiple-entity finders that return a Collection of references. If no match is found in the database, the single-entity finder methods must throw `ObjectNotFoundException`, while the multiple-entity finder methods simply return an empty Collection.

When a client calls `create()`, it means to insert a row into the database table. Similarly, a client calls `remove()` to delete an entity from the database, and once that entity is deleted, no entity bean is able to represent that entity. It's gone. On the other hand, if an entity bean instance dies, for example, due to the server crash, the entity represented by this bean still persists and may be represented by another bean instance when the server is restarted.

In this chapter, you have learned what kind of calls a client can make to entity beans to perform operations on the database and what an entity bean is from the client's perspective. In the next chapter, you will learn exactly how the entity beans get to the stage where they are able to work for the clients.

Comprehend

- An entity is a thing, such as a customer, that exists in a database outside of EJB, while an entity bean is a bean inside an EJB container whose instance can represent an entity in memory.

- The component interface of an entity bean contains methods that can be used by the client to perform operations on a specific entity whose id is known to the client; for example, to change the email address of a specific customer.

- As opposed to a session bean, the home interface of an entity bean may contain home business methods that can be used by a client to perform operations on multiple entities that satisfy a given criterion, for example, to get the email addresses of all the customers who have status equal to VIP.

- Unlike for a session bean, a create method call on an entity bean creates an entity in persistent storage, and a remove method call deletes an entity in persistent storage.

Look out

- Contrary to a session bean, you are not required to have a create method in the home interface of an entity bean, but you are required to have a finder method instead: `findByPrimaryKey(...)`.

- The return type of a single-entity finder method must be the component interface type of the bean, while the return type of a multiple-entity finder method must be a Collection of the component interface type.

- Although the return type for home methods is generally the component interface, the return type for home business methods of the entity bean home interface does not have to be the component interface; it could be any legal type.

- If no entity is found in the database, a call to a single-entity finder method will result in `ObjectNotFoundException`, while a call to a multiple-entity finder will simply return an empty Collection, and there will be no exception.

Review questions

Some questions may have more than one correct answer. Choose all that apply.

1. Which of the following statements are true about the entity bean's remote home interface?
   a. Both the `create()` and `remove()` methods are declared in the interface by the bean developer.
   b. Both the `create()` and `remove()` methods are inherited from `javax.ejb.EJBHome`.
   c. The `create()` method is declared by the bean developer, and the `remove()` methods are inherited from `javax.ejb.EJBHome`.
   d. The `remove()` methods are declared by the developer, and the `create()` method is inherited from `javax.ejb.EJBHome`.
   e. The bean provider must provide the `create()` method.

2. The developer is required to put which of the following methods in the entity bean home interface?
   a. `create()` and `findByPrimaryKey()` methods
   b. One or more `create()` methods
   c. One or more business methods
   d. Only one method, `findByPrimaryKey()`

3. Which of the following are illegal names for the business methods defined in an entity bean home interface?
   a. `findAllCustomers(...)`
   b. `removeTheCustomer(...)`
   c. `createCustomer(...)`

d. `create()`

e. `retrieveCustData(…)`

4. How many create methods can you declare in the entity bean home interface?

    a. One or more

    b. Zero or more

    c. Exactly one

    d. Zero

5. How many find methods can you declare in the entity bean home interface?

    a. One or more

    b. Zero or more

    c. Exactly one

    d. Zero

6. Consider an entity bean with `Customer` as its remote component interface and `CustomerHome` as its remote home interface. Which of the following are legal method declarations in the home interface?

    a. `public      CustomerHome      findCustomerBy-`
       `Email(String email);`

    b. `public   Customer   findCustomerByEmail(String`
       `email);`

    c. `public   Customer   findCustomerByEmail(String`
       `email) throws FinderException, RemoteException;`

    d. `public   Customer   findCustomerByEmail(String`
       `email) throws FinderException;`

    e. `public    String    findCustomerByEmail(String`
       `email) throws FinderException, RemoteException;`

7. Consider an entity bean with `Customer` as its local component interface and `CustomerHome` as its local home interface. Which of the following are legal method declarations in the home interface?

    a. `public CustomerHome findCustomerByEmail(String`
       `email);`

    b. `public   Customer   findCustomerByEmail(String`
       `email);`

    c. `public   Customer   findCustomerByEmail(String`
       `email) throws FinderException, RemoteException;`

    d. `public   Customer   findCustomerByEmail(String`
       `email) throws FinderException;`

    e. `public String findCustomerByEmail(String email)`
       `throws FinderException, RemoteException;`

8. Which of the following are the valid ways a client can get a reference to the remote component interface of an entity bean representing a specific entity?

    a. Call a create method.
    b. Call a find method.
    c. Obtain a reference from the handle.
    d. Call `getBeanReference()`.
    e. Obtain the reference as a parameter in a method call.

9. A client calls a finder method whose return type is a Collection of references to the remote interface of an entity bean. Assume no match for that entity is found. Which of the following will be the result of this call?

    a. `ObjectNotFoundException`.
    b. An empty Collection will be returned.
    c. An entity would be created and a reference to that entity would be returned.
    d. `EntityNotFoundException`.

10. Which of the following are true statements about what happens when a `remove()` method is called using the component interface of an entity bean representing a specific entity in the database?

    a. The entity bean instance is deleted.
    b. The entity in the database is deleted.
    c. Both the entity and the entity bean instance survive, but that entity bean instance does not represent that entity anymore.
    d. Nothing happens; the container simply ignores the call.

Birth of an entity bean

EXAM OBJECTIVES

6.1 Identify correct and incorrect statements or examples about the entity bean provider's view and programming contract for CMP, including the requirements for a
CMP entity bean.

6.6 Identify the interface(s) and methods a CMP entity bean must and must not
implement.

8.1 From a list of behaviors, match them with the appropriate `EntityContext`
method responsible for that behavior.

8.2 Identify correct and incorrect statements or examples about an entity bean's primary key and object identity.

INTRODUCTION

As you learned in the last chapter, a client interacts with an entity bean by using the
client view, which is composed of a component interface and a home interface. Think
of an active entity bean in the container as representing a specific entity and serving
the clients. The question arises: What procedure and work were involved in getting
this bean to this stage and who did the work? This chapter is the answer to this question. Obviously, first there has to be a bean class and other related code. Two players

are involved in writing/generating the code: the bean developer and the EJB container. You need to know the division of responsibilities between the two. The container instantiates the bean class and assigns an entity context to this instance, and the instance uses this context to interact with the container. The bean class must implement the `EntityBean` interface, which contains the methods that the container uses to communicate with a bean instance through its lifecycle. So the `EntityBean` interface is the line of communication from the container to the bean instance, while the `EntityContext` interface is the line of communication from the bean instance to the container.

The container may construct a number of such bean instances, which is called a pool of entity beans. At this stage the bean is in the pool and does not represent any specific entity in the database. However, even at this stage, it can serve a client's request if it does not involve operations on a specific entity. When a method call from a client arrives related to a specific (existing or to be created) entity, the container pulls a bean instance from the pool and enables it to represent that specific entity. At this stage the bean instance is ready to conduct operations requested by the client on the entity the instance represents. This is the big picture, and the rest is detail. The focus of this chapter lies in determining how an entity bean instance comes into being and slowly grows to acquire its full beanhood. The three avenues we will explore are the `EntityBean` interface, the `EntityContext` interface, and the differences between the session bean and the entity bean going through the creation process. Also pay attention to who's in charge; it's between the bean provider and the container.

7.1   HERE COMES ENTITY BEAN PERSISTENCE

You were introduced to entity beans in the previous chapter. In this section, let's explore a salient feature of entity beans called *persistence*, which stems from the fact that an entity bean represents an entity in persistent storage. So, consider an entity bean instance as representing an entity from the database. As long as the entity is present in the database, the entity bean persists through a server shutdown, crash, or similar incident. This means that even if a particular bean instance dies, the server will find another instance for representing the entity as long as the entity is there. However, if an entity is removed from the database, then the corresponding entity bean dies, even if the instance does not; the instance might simply go back to the pool.

The data fields in the bean class corresponding to the data fields of the entity in the database are called persistent fields, and they compose the state of the bean. A client that interacts with the bean changes the entity in the database by changing the state of the bean, that is, by changing the values of one or more persistent fields in the bean. However, it is a two-step process: the client causes the change of the entity bean state, and the container propagates the change to the database. That means we have an issue of keeping the bean state and the entity in the database synchronized with each other.

7.1.1 Synchronizing entity and entity bean

The synchronization issue arises because we have an entity in the database and the corresponding persistent fields in the bean instance that represent the entity. For true representation, they need to stay synchronized with each other. Consider a bean as representing an entity in the database. Now assume that someone manually changes, or another application changes, the values of one or more fields of that entity in the database. As a result, the state of the entity bean goes stale and no longer truly represents the entity until those changes in the database are propagated to the bean. The reverse is true as well; that is, if a client changes the state of the entity bean, any application that accesses that entity in the database before the change is propagated to the database is dealing with a stale entity.

To the outside world, the entity bean and the entity should always appear synchronized. The container implements synchronization by ensuring the following:

- Before a bean starts executing a business method that could potentially interact with the bean state, it must be loaded with the fresh entity from the database.

- During the time the client is interacting with the bean to potentially change its state, nobody should be allowed to access the entity in the database.

- Once the client has finished interacting with the bean state, the entity in the database must be updated with the current values of the persistent fields in the bean before it is made available to the rest of the world.

This is how the container implements synchronization by using a transaction. If you are not familiar with the term *transaction*, think for now that transaction means an atomic action; that is, either all the changes to the entity required by a set of business methods would be made in the database or none of them would be made. It's all or none. You will learn more about this topic in chapter 12, a whole chapter devoted to transactions in EJB.

When a client call to a business method arrives, the container starts a transaction by requesting the database to lock the entity. The container then loads the bean with the current values of the entity fields. The bean will run one or more business methods in the same transaction. After the business methods have been executed, the container updates the entity in the database with the new bean state. Finally, the container ends the transaction and requests the database to unlock the entity.

The whole idea of synchronization by transaction is part of bean persistence management. It's obvious by now that persistence management involves interacting with the database, which requires writing the database access code. When it comes to writing/generating the code, only two players are involved: you (the bean provider) and the container.

7.1.2 CMP and BMP entity beans

The question is, who writes the database access code, such as code that gets the database connection and the JDBC statements that interact with the database? In bean-managed persistence, the bean developer does this job and the bean is called a BMP entity bean; in container-managed persistence, the container does this job and the bean is called a CMP entity bean.

BMP bean

In a BMP bean, it is your responsibility to write the database access code, such as JDBC statements. You write it in the appropriate callback methods of your bean class that the container calls. So it is still the container that decides when it's time to interact with the database. At that time the container calls a method in your bean class that you wrote and the method will do its JDBC work.

CMP bean

In a CMP bean, the container is responsible for all the database access code. For this reason, the CMP bean class that you write for a CMP bean must be an abstract class. However, you will still need to give any necessary information to the container—for example, identifying the bean fields that correspond to the entity fields in the database. These fields compose the persistent state of the bean. You will also need to give enough information to the container to build appropriate select queries. You pass all this information through the deployment descriptor and by defining appropriate abstract get and set methods in the bean class. You will learn exactly how you do it in the next two chapters.

> **ALERT** A CMP bean class is always declared abstract because it contains persistence-related methods, which are declared abstract and will be implemented by the container.

Note that in both CMP and BMP beans, it's still the container that is running the entity part of the show, that is, deciding when to make which database call. In the case of CMP, it makes the database calls by itself, while in the case of BMP, it invokes a method on the bean when it needs to interact with the database, and the bean makes the database call. The main differences between a BMP entity bean and a CMP entity bean are listed in table 7.1

Table 7.1 Differences between a CMP entity bean and a BMP entity bean

Characteristic	CMP Bean	BMP Bean
Class	Abstract	Not abstract
Database access code	Generated by container/tools	Written by the bean provider

continued on next page

Table 7.1   Differences between a CMP entity bean and a BMP entity bean *(continued)*

Characteristic	CMP Bean	BMP Bean
Persistent state	Composed of virtual persistent fields represented by abstract getter and setter methods	Composed of persistent fields coded as instance variables
Finder methods	Implemented by the container	Written by the bean provider
Return value of `ejbCreate()`	Should be null	Must be the primary key

As of EJB 2.0, developers are encouraged to use CMP beans, and the exam does not emphasize BMP beans. Nevertheless, we recommend that you know the basic differences between BMP and CMP beans covered in this chapter. From this point on, by entity beans we mean CMP entity beans unless stated otherwise. You should know what roles the bean provider and the container play in implementing a CMP entity bean.

7.2   IMPLEMENTING A *CMP* ENTITY BEAN

Who implements an entity bean class? The answer is both the bean provider and the container. The bean provider's responsibility is to provide an abstract class for a CMP entity bean. The class is abstract because you will declare some abstract methods in it that the container will complete to implement persistence. The concrete class will be generated at deployment time by the container (or the container provider's tools). This class will include some methods from the home and component interfaces, which we discussed in chapter 6. Furthermore, you also need to write some methods in this class that the container will call back at various stages. For this reason, they are called container callback methods, similar to those in the session bean class. In the following sections, we discuss all kinds of methods you need to implement or declare in the bean class.

7.2.1   Implementing methods from the interfaces

The methods in this category that you need to put in the bean class come from the following three interfaces: the home interface, the component interface, and the `EntityBean` interface.

Methods from the home interface

In the home interface, you can declare one or more finder methods, zero or more create methods, and zero or more home business methods. It is your responsibility to put a method in the class corresponding to each of these methods except the finder methods in the case of CMP beans (the container implements the finder methods). Read my lips: no finder methods in the bean class for a CMP bean. The methods in the `CustomerHome` interface of our example from chapter 6 are shown in figure 7.1. As you know from that chapter, the only required method is `findByPrimaryKey(...)`, but we have added other (optional) methods to illustrate some concepts.

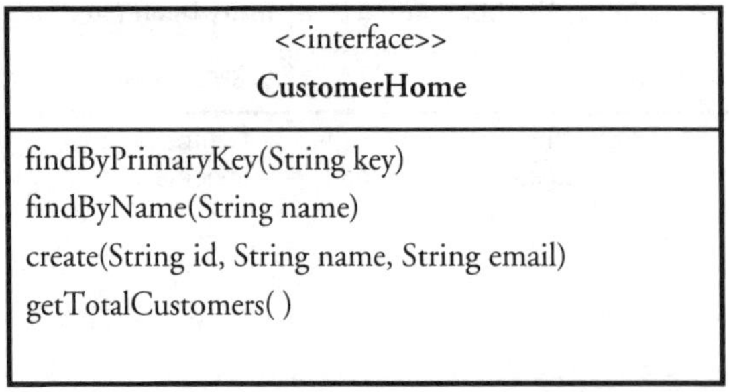

| findByPrimaryKey(String key) |
| findByName(String name) |
| create(String id, String name, String email) |
| getTotalCustomers( ) |

Figure 7.1
Methods declared by the
bean provider in the home
interface of the Customer
bean. Only the
findByPrimaryKey()
method is required; the
others are optional.

ALERT   For CMP beans, you will not write or declare any finder method in the bean class corresponding to the finder methods in the home interface. The container will implement these methods.

For each `create<method>` method in the home interface, you will provide an `ejbCreate<method>` method and an `ejbPostCreate<method>` method in the bean class. For each business method, say `<method>`, in the home interface, you will provide an `ejbHome<method>` method in the bean class with the first letter of `<method>` uppercased, for example, the `ejbHomeGetTotalCustomers` method in the class for the `getTotalCustomers` method in the home interface. For a CMP bean, you will not write any method corresponding to a finder method in the home interface. In a BMP bean, you will write an `ejbFind<method>` method corresponding to each `find<method>` in the home interface.

ALERT   For each create method in the home interface of an entity bean, you will write two methods in the bean class: an ejbCreate method and an ejbPost method. Note the difference from the session bean class where you would write only the ejbCreate method.

Let's take a look at the contributions of the component interface to the bean class.

Methods from the component interface

In your bean class, you must implement each method declared in the component interface. In our example, the methods for the `Customer` component interface are shown in figure 7.2. A client can invoke these methods only after getting a reference to the component interface (the `EJBObject`) of an entity bean instance representing a specific entity. Therefore, the business logic related to the specific entities can go into these methods. For example, if you want to let a client change the email address of a specific customer, you will declare a method in the component interface to facilitate this and implement this method in the bean class. For example, once a client has the `EJBObject` (the reference to it) for the bean instance representing the customer with id #11, the client can invoke the method `getCustEmail()` on it in order to get the email address of this particular customer.

```
          <<interface>>
            Customer

setCustName(String name)
getCustName()


setCustEmail(String email)
getCustEmail()


setCustId(String id)
getCustId()
```

Figure 7.2
Methods in the component interface of the Customer bean. These methods must be implemented by the bean provider in the bean class. These are commonly called the business methods.

Although your bean class must include all the methods declared in the component interface, you do not implement the component interface in the definition of the bean class, just like for a session bean class. Your class must also include the methods in the EntityBean interface.

Methods from the EntityBean interface

An entity bean class implements the EntityBean interface in its definition. Therefore, the bean provider must implement the methods of this interface in the bean class. The container uses these methods to notify the bean instance of events related to the lifecycle of the bean instance. So, you always implement the seven methods (also called container callbacks) from the EntityBean interface in the bean class. These methods are shown in figure 7.3.

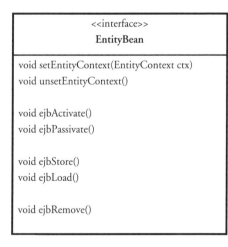

```
            <<interface>>
             EntityBean

void setEntityContext(EntityContext ctx)
void unsetEntityContext()


void ejbActivate()
void ejbPassivate()


void ejbStore()
void ejbLoad()


void ejbRemove()
```

Figure 7.3
Methods in the EntityBean interface. These methods must be implemented by the bean provider in the bean class. These are commonly called container callback methods.

Recall that the `SessionBean` interface also has the three methods `ejbActivate()`, `ejbPassivate()`, and `ejbRemove()` that the `EntityBean` interface has. However, you will learn in the next chapter that the behavior of these methods in entity beans is dramatically different from that in session beans. The equivalent of `setEntityContext()` in `SessionBean` is `setSessionContext()` and the behavior is the same: it sets the context which is used by the bean to interact with the container. The other three methods in the `EntityBean` interface, namely `unsetEntityContext()`, `ejbLoad()`, and `ejbStore()`, have no equivalent in the `SessionBean` interface. Why do they exist in the `EntityBean` interface, then? This is because, unlike a session bean, an entity bean represents an entity in the database. You will see the connection of these methods with the entity more clearly in the next chapter.

> **NOTE** The three methods `unsetEntityContext()`, `ejbLoad()`, and `ejbStore()` in the `EntityBean` interface have no equivalent in the `SessionBean` interface. You must know why their absence in the `SessionBean` interface makes sense. This is because a session bean does not represent an entity.

All these methods are invoked by the container on a bean instance. The following is a brief summary of what these methods are used for:

- *setEntityContext()*—Used by the container to pass a reference to the entity context of this bean instance. Using this reference the bean would interact with the container.
- *unsetEntityContext()*—Called by the container to send an entity bean instance from the pool to the does not exist state.
- *ejbActivate()*—Called when the bean is pulled out of the pool to execute a client's call to a business method.
- *ejbPassivate()*—Called just before sending an entity bean instance back to the pool.
- *ejbStore()*—Called by the container just before updating the entity in the database with the current bean state.
- *ejbLoad()*—Called by the container after refreshing the bean state with the current entity fields in the database.
- *ejbRemove*—Called by the container in response to the client's invocation of the `remove()` method. This method call means the client wants to remove the entity from the database.

The method `setEntityContext()` is further discussed later in this chapter. The other methods will be discussed in detail in the next chapter. In a nutshell, the `EntityBean` interface is the line of communication that the container uses to communicate with the bean instance at different stages of the bean's lifecycle.

Never lose sight of the fact that an entity bean instance represents a persistent entity, and this representation is done through the entity bean's state. The bean state is composed of the persistent fields in the bean that map back to the entity fields in the database. The bean handles these fields through methods.

7.2.2 Methods for virtual persistent fields

The fields in an entity bean that also exist in the database are called persistent fields. The values of these fields constitute the state of the bean. For our example, figure 7.4 shows these fields for the entity bean instance representing John Serri (id #11) in the database table. In a CMP bean, these fields are managed by the container, so they must not be defined as instance variables in the entity bean class. From the perspective of the bean provider, these fields are virtual (hence the name virtual persistent fields) and are accessed through getter and setter accessor methods, which must be declared in the bean class by the bean provider.

For each persistent field, you will declare an abstract get method and an abstract set method in the bean class. We have also included an abstract select method in our bean class, which relates to database queries. We will talk more about the select methods in chapters 9 and 10. The container will implement all these abstract methods. You will need to help the container implement these methods by making some entries in the deployment descriptor file. We will visit those entries in chapters 9 and 10 also. For now, bear in mind that these abstract methods are not directly exposed to the client; for example, you should not expose them as business methods in the component interface. You can, but you should avoid doing so for the sake of a good programming practice and encapsulation, if nothing else.

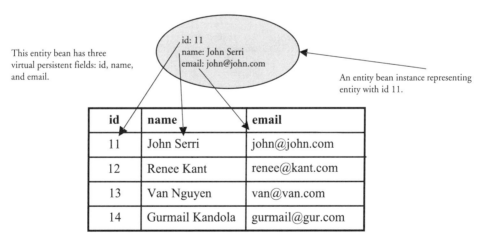

This entity bean has three virtual persistent fields: id, name, and email.

id: 11
name: John Serri
email: john@john.com

An entity bean instance representing entity with id 11.

id	name	email
11	John Serri	john@john.com
12	Renee Kant	renee@kant.com
13	Van Nguyen	van@van.com
14	Gurmail Kandola	gurmail@gur.com

Figure 7.4 Mapping of the virtual persistent fields of an entity to the entity fields in the database. Mapping is shown for one entity bean instance representing a specific customer with id #11.

So in a CMP bean class, the bean provider implements the container callbacks and declares the abstract methods corresponding to the persistent fields that compose the bean state. Because of these abstract methods, the class is declared abstract. The container will implement the abstract methods and generate the concrete class at deployment time. In the following section, we show the class that would be written by the bean provider for our simple example.

7.2.3 Putting it all together in code

Listing 7.1 shows the code for the CustomerBean class that includes all the methods discussed in the previous sections. The class has to be declared abstract because it contains abstract methods. Each pair of abstract getter and setter methods (lines 75–80) represents a persistent field of an entity in the database (the columns of a database table). It may sound obvious, but make sure the return type of a getter method matches the argument type of the corresponding setter method: you get what you set. The class must be declared public and it must implement the EntityBean interface.

> **NOTE** The return type of an abstract getter method representing a persistent field must match the argument type of the corresponding setter method.

This is a moment when you can close your eyes and say, "Now I understand how an entity bean represents an entity in the database." This is where the connection is: virtual persistent fields in the entity bean map to the entity fields in the database— columns of a database table in the simplest case. However, because this is a CMP bean, the container will actually implement these methods, but you have to declare them in the bean class. The getter and setter business methods (lines 25–48) that we exposed in the component interface for the client to interact with the entity data call the abstract getter and setter methods.

Listing 7.1 Code for the CustomerBean class. This is a CMP bean.

```
1. import javax.ejb.*;
2. import java.util.*;

3. public abstract class CustomerBean implements EntityBean
4. {
5. // Bean instance variables
6. private EntityContext context;
7.
8. // Methods from home interface
9. public String ejbCreate(String id, String name,
    ➡ String email) throws  CreateException
10. {
11.     setId(id);
12.     setName(name);
13.     setEmail(email);
14.     return null;
15. }
```

```
16. public void ejbPostCreate(String id, String name,
       String email) throws CreateException
17. {
18. }

19. // home business method
20. public int ejbHomeGetTotalCustomers() throws FinderException
21. {
22.   return ejbSelectGetAllCustomers().size();
23. }

24. // Methods from the component interface
25.  public String getCustId()
26.  {
27.      return getId();
28.  }

29. public void setCustId(String id)
30. {
31.      setId(id);
32. }

33. public String getCustName()
34. {
35.   return getName();
36. }

37. public void setCustName(String name)
38. {
39.   setName(name);
40. }

41. public String getCustEmail()
42. {
43.   return getEmail();
44. }

45. public void setCustEmail(String email)
46. {
47.   setEmail(email);
48. }

49. // Methods from EntityBean interface
50. //give the context to the bean
51. public void setEntityContext(EntityContext ctx)
52. {
53.   context = ctx;
54. }

55. public void unsetEntityContext()
56. {
57.   context = null;
```

```
58. }

59. public void ejbActivate()
60. {
61. }

62. public void ejbPassivate()
63. {
64. }

65. public void ejbStore()
66. {
67. }

68. public void ejbLoad()
69. {
70. }

71. public void ejbRemove()
72. {
73. }

74. // Access methods for virtual persistent field
75. public abstract String getId();

76. public abstract void setId(String id);

77. public abstract String getName();                    Pair of abstract
                                                          methods for the virtual
78. public abstract void setName(String name);           persistent field, name

79. public abstract String getEmail();

80. public abstract void setEmail(String email);

81. // Select methods
82. public abstract Collection ejbSelectGetAllCustomers()
        throws FinderException;        Abstract select method
    }                                  that would be implemented
}                                      by the container
```

Note that no variables are declared in the bean class corresponding to the virtual persistent fields. These fields exist only in the form of abstract methods.

ALERT The bean provider declares a pair of getter and setter methods corresponding to each entity field, and no variable, in the bean class.

The `ejbCreate(...)` method (lines 9–15) that the container would call as a result of the client call to `create()` method in the home also deals with the data by making calls to the abstract getters and setters. In other words, the abstract getter and setter methods act as a gateway to the entity data for the data-related client calls. Another method that needs an explanation is `ejbHomeGetTotalCustomers()` (line 20) corresponding to the home business method `getTotalCustomers()` exposed in the home interface. This method calls an abstract method, `ejbSelectGetAll-Customers()`, on line 82. Abstract select methods like this one are also implemented by the container. The bean provider makes the connection in the deployment descriptor file by using a query language called EJB-QL. You will learn more about it in chapter 10.

The EntityBean methods (lines 50–73), for example, `ejbActivate()`, `ejb-Passivate()`, `ejbStore()`, and `ejbLoad()`, are called by the container while managing the lifecycle of the entity bean. We will talk in detail about these methods in the next chapter.

> **ALERT** A business <method> exposed in the component interface has the same name <method> in the bean class, while a business <method> declared in the home interface has the name `ejbHome<method>` in the bean class, with the first letter of <method> uppercased.

For entity beans, construction and creation are two different things. Constructing the bean means constructing an instance of the bean, and creating means inserting an entity into the database and assigning a bean instance to represent this entity. In the next chapter, you will see how construction and creation fit into the big picture of the entity bean lifecycle.

7.3 CONSTRUCTING AN ENTITY BEAN

According to the spec, the life story of an entity bean starts from the state in which an entity bean does not exist. You might think of this state like this: the entity bean has been deployed, the code is there, therefore the potential of an active entity bean is there in the form of the code, but the action has not started yet. The action starts when the server is started. The first step out of the does not exist state occurs when the container constructs an instance of the bean using the `newInstance()` method. This is where the life of an entity bean starts.

7.3.1 Constructing a bean instance

Constructing a bean instance is the container's responsibility. The container follows this procedure to construct a bean instance:

1 Make a new `EntityContext`, that is, create an instance of the class that implements the `EntityContext` interface. `EntityContext`, like `Session-Context`, extends `EJBContext`.

2 Make a new instance of the entity bean using the `Class.newInstance()` method.

3 Call the `setEntityContext()` method on the bean instance and pass in the entity context. This assigns the context to the bean instance and provides the bean instance with a reference to the `EntityContext` interface that the bean would use to interact with the container.

4 Put the bean instance (which now has a context) into the pool.

At this stage, the bean instance is in the pool and is not attached to any specific entity in the database. Each bean type (CustomerBean, AccountBean, OrderBean, etc.) will have its own pool. All beans of the same type are constructed equal: when needed, the container can pull out any bean instance from the pool to make it represent an entity so that a client could operate on the entity through that instance.

In step 2, when the container constructs a bean instance by using the no-argument constructor for the bean, the instance is just like a plain-old Java instance. After the execution of the `setEntityContext()` method, the bean instance has access to the `EntityContext` interface: its line of communication with the container. At this stage the bean instance has acquired some beanhood because it is now connected to the container. In the following section, we describe the services that the bean instance can invoke by using the `EntityContext` interface.

7.3.2 Using the EntityContext interface

You learned in chapter 4 that a session bean communicates with the container using the `SessionContext` interface. Similarly, an entity bean communicates with the container using the `EntityContext` interface shown in figure 7.5.

> **NOTE** `SessionContext` does not have the `getPrimaryKey()` method while `EntityContext` does. All other methods in the `EntityContext` and `SessionContext` interfaces are the same.

The terms *CMT bean* and *BMT bean* appearing in figure 7.5 are related to transactions and need some explanation. When you write a bean, you can choose to do the higher-level transaction management inside the bean code, such as marking where the transaction starts and where it ends. This is called bean-managed transaction (BMT) demarcation, and we will call such a bean a BMT bean. The other choice is to let the container mark the start and end of a transaction, and this is called container-managed transaction (CMT) demarcation. We will call such a bean a CMT bean. We will explore these topics in chapter 12. However, note that entity beans use only CMT demarcation, so they can never use the method `getUserTransaction()`.

> **ALERT** Entity beans can use only container-managed transaction (CMT) demarcation, so they can never use the `getUserTransaction()` method.

The context of an entity bean instance, the EntityContext, is created and maintained by the container. The container instantiates the `EntityContext` interface (the class that implements the interface) and assigns it to an entity bean instance. The instance can use this context to invoke services offered by the container, such as marking a

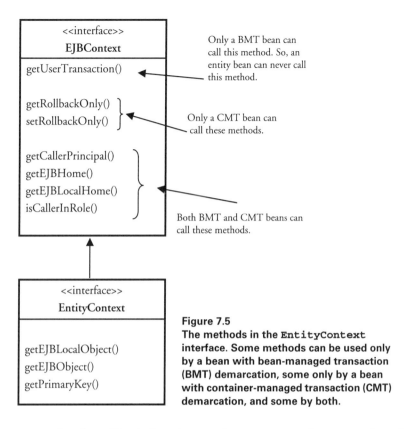

Figure 7.5
**The methods in the `EntityContext`
interface. Some methods can be used only
by a bean with bean-managed transaction
(BMT) demarcation, some only by a bean
with container-managed transaction (CMT)
demarcation, and some by both.**

transaction for rollback. In other words, you can use the context from inside the bean class methods to call the methods of the `EntityContext` interface. These methods along with the tasks they accomplish are listed in table 7.2.

Table 7.2 Methods available in the `EntityContext` interface. Permission to use these methods depends on which stage of its lifecycle the bean is in.

Methods	Task
getEJBHome() getEJBLocalHome()	Get a reference to the bean's home interface.
getEJBObject() getEJBLocalObject()	Get a reference to the bean's `EJBObject`, that is, a reference to the component interface.
getCallerPrinciple() IsCallerInRole()	Get security information.
setRollbackOnly()	Mark the current transaction to roll back.
getRollbackOnly()	Determine whether the transaction has already been marked for rollback.
getUserTransaction()	Get a reference to the transaction. Cannot by used by entity beans.
getPrimaryKey()	Get the primary key for the bean.

ALERT Do not confuse the EntityContext with the JNDI context. EntityContext is given to the bean instance so that the bean can interact with the container, for example, invoke some container services. The JNDI context contains the bean's environment.

Note that the only difference between the `EntityContext` interface and the `SessionContext` interface described in chapter 4 is the addition of the `get-PrimaryKey()` method. The primary key identifies the entity that the entity bean represents, so it doesn't make any sense for a session bean to have this method. However, remember that both the `EJBObject` and `EJBLocalObject` interfaces also have the method `getPrimaryKey()`, and the component interfaces of both the session and entity beans extend the same `EJBObject` and `EJBLocalObject`. Therefore, the `getPrimaryKey()` method is exposed to the client in the remote and local component interfaces of both the session bean and the entity bean. This means it is possible that session bean client can erroneously make a call to `getPrimaryKey()` by using the component interface. In this case, the client would receive an exception, since session beans do not have primary keys.

Permission to use the methods of the `EntityContext` interface by the bean provider from inside the bean class methods depends on at what stage of its lifecycle the bean instance is. In the next section, we discuss which of these context methods you can use at the bean's construction stage.

7.3.3 Operations allowed during bean construction

You have already learned which methods you need to implement in the bean class. From inside these methods, you can invoke method calls on the `EntityContext` interface, which is obtained when the container calls `setEntityContext()` method. In addition to these method calls, you might like to have the following:

- Access to the bean's JNDI environment
- Access to a resource manager such as database
- Access to other beans methods

It's very important to understand that you cannot have access to all of these from any method you want in the bean class. What call you can make and what access you can have from within a method of the bean class depend on which state of its lifecycle the bean is in when your method is being executed.

Let's see what you can do from inside your methods that belong to the construction stage. You cannot put anything inside the bean constructor. It is a no-argument bean constructor. As you know from plain Java, you don't even have to write a constructor; the compiler will provide you with a default no-argument constructor. If you define the constructor yourself, make sure it is public and has no arguments.

The second method that belongs to the construction stage is the `setEntity-Context()` method that the container calls after constructing the bean instance.

The container calls this method to pass the context to the bean instance. So this is your only opportunity to capture that context:

```
public void setEntityContext(EntityContext cxt) {
      context = cxt;
}
```

At this stage, the bean instance has been constructed and a context has been assigned to it. So it is able to communicate with the container, that is, it can call methods on the `EntityContext` interface from inside the `setEntityContext(...)` method. In table 7.3, we list the permitted and prohibited operations at the construction stage. We will be showing this table for different stages of the bean's lifecycle discussed in this and the next chapter.

Table 7.3   Operations permitted and prohibited in the constructor and `setEntityContext` methods

Operation	Constructor	setEntityContext
Get a reference to the bean's home interface	No	Yes
Get a reference to the bean's `EJBObject`, that is, a reference to the component interface	No	No
Get security information	No	No
Mark the current transaction to roll back	No	No
Determine whether the transaction has already been marked for rollback	No	No
Get a reference to the transaction; not used by entity beans	No	No
Get the primary key for the bean	No	No
JNDI access	No	Yes
Resource manager access	No	No
Access to other beans	No	No

Once you understand the whole lifecycle of the bean (which is the topic of the next chapter), it will become obvious why you cannot perform the prohibited operations, and there are lots of them at this stage. For now, just understand that in the constructor the bean instance is simply being instantiated, just like a plain-old Java instance; it has no beanhood at all at this stage. So, inside the bean constructor the bean cannot perform any bean-like activity. By the time the setEntityContext method is called, the bean instance has just been constructed and it does not represent any entity. Therefore, it does not make any sense to try to obtain a reference to its specific component interface (that is, `EJBObject`), because it does not exist yet. And it does not make sense to get information about a client, because there is no client yet. The only thing it has going for it so far is its JNDI home. Therefore, the only two things it can ask from the container are access to JNDI and a reference to its home interface. In other words, the bean instance has been constructed and its communication line with the container (`EntityContext`) has been set up, but the bean is still pretty grumpy: it's like waking up on Monday morning.

If you call a prohibited method in the `EntityContext` interface, it is container's responsibility to throw a `java.lang.IllegalStateException`. However, if you try to attempt (at this stage) to access a resource manager or call another bean's method, the result is undefined by the EJB architecture.

All constructed bean instances of a given type, say CustomerBean, in the pool are equal, and none of those represents any entity. After the container constructs a bean instance, assigns it a context, and puts it into the pool for that bean type, the bean is ready for creation when needed, that is, to acquire its full beanhood.

7.4 CREATING AN ENTITY BEAN

Before a bean instance can go through the creation process, it must go through the construction process that we discussed in the previous section. After construction, creating an entity bean means the following two things:

- Inserting an entity into the database
- Having a bean instance to represent that entity

The process of creating an entity through EJB is triggered by a client.

7.4.1 CMP entity bean creation process

When a client invokes a create method in the home interface, the bean is created by the container. The process for a remote client is as follows:

1. The client calls a create method on the EJBHome stub.
2. The create method invocation is passed to the EJBHome.
3. Upon receiving the call, the container pulls a bean instance out of the pool and sends it the entity data, received in the arguments of the create method, by calling the corresponding ejbCreate method on it. The bean instance now can build its persistent state.
4. The container stores the entity in the database. Now, the bean state and the entity in the database are consistent with each other.
5. The container creates an EJBObject, an instance of the class that implements the component interface of the bean.
6. The container provides the EJBObject and the EntityContext of the bean with the primary key and assigns the entity bean instance pulled out of the pool to the EntityObject.
7. The container calls the `ejbPostCreate()` method so that the bean can finish initializing itself, and EJBHome sends the EJBObject stub to the calling client.

These steps are shown in figure 7.6.

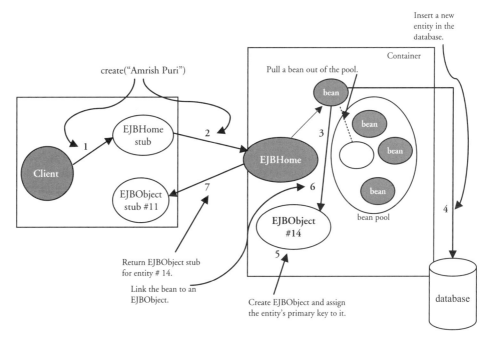

Figure 7.6 **The steps involved in the process of inserting an entity in the database by a remote client. The process is triggered by invoking a `create()` method by the client.**

After the entity has been created, the remote client can use the EJBObject stub to call the business methods exposed in the component interface.

Note the differences from how a create method works in a session bean. Unlike the creation of a session bean, the creation of an entity bean includes the creation of an entity in the database. Furthermore, the entity bean has the ejbPostCreate(...) method, which the session bean does not. So, in entity beans we do not have an EJBObject during the execution of ejbCreate(). However, we do have an EJBObject by the time ejbPostCreate(...) is executed. This means that the bean developer cannot get a reference to the EJBObject in the ejbCreate() method. However, there are a few things that you can do in this method.

The ejbCreate methods

You must implement an ejbCreate method in the bean class corresponding to each create method in the bean's home interface. When a client invokes a create method, the container invokes the corresponding ejbCreate method. Here are the rules for writing the ejbCreate methods:

- To make the name of the ejbCreate method, the name of the create method is preceded with the prefix ejb and the lowercase c in create is replaced with an uppercase C.

- The signatures of an ejbCreate method are the same as those of the corresponding create method. That means:
  - The method must be declared public and must not be static or void.
  - The method arguments must be identical with the corresponding create method.
  - The method return type must be the primary key class, and the return value should be null.
- Before the end of the ejbCreate method you must assign valid values to all the persistent fields that make up the primary key. Otherwise, the container will not be able to build the primary key for this entity and hence the entity will not be inserted into the database.
- The method may declare `CreateException` or any other application exception if it was declared in the home interface. It must not declare a `java.rmi.RemoteException`, as only the container can throw that.

ALERT   Inside the ejbCreate method, the bean provider must assign valid values to all the persistent fields that make up the primary key. Otherwise, the container will not be able to build the primary key and hence will not do the insert in the database.

How will the container know which of the persistent fields make up the primary key? The bean provider gives this information to the container in the deployment descriptor. The null value returned from the ejbCreate method whose return type is the primary key is not required but recommended. The reason for this is that the container will figure out the primary key given that you have assigned valid values to all the persistent fields in the bean that compose the key. Therefore, there is no need for introducing any overhead in the method to instantiate the key class in order to return it.

For every ejbCreate method, there must be an ejbPostCreate method. After executing an ejbCreate method, the container performs a few actions, such as building a primary key, inserting the entity into the database, creating an `EJBObject`, and assigning the entity's primary key to the `EJBObject` and to the EntityContext of that bean instance. This enables the bean instance to represent the entity. Then, the container calls the corresponding ejbPostCreate method so that the bean instance can finish initializing itself.

ejbPostCreate<method>

You must implement an ejbPostCreate method in the class of a bean corresponding to each create method in the bean's home interface. When a client invokes a create method, the container invokes the corresponding ejbPostCreate method, after invoking the ejbCreate method. Here are the rules for writing an ejbPostCreate method:

- To make the name of the ejbPostCreate method, the name of the corresponding create method is preceded with the prefix `ejbPost` and the lowercase `c` in `create` is replaced with an uppercase C.

- The method must be declared public and must not be declared static or final.

- The return type must be void, as opposed to the ejbCreate method where the return type must be the primary key class.

- The method may declare `CreateException` and any other application exception if it was declared in the home interface, but it must not throw `java.rmi.RemoteException` even if the method corresponds to a remote interface.

You need an ejbPostCreate method in an entity bean because an ejbCreate method is too early for certain things that need to be done to finish the initialization of the bean. For example, you can get a reference to the `EJBObject` in the ejbPostCreate method but not in the ejbCreate method. The `EJBObject` does not exist during the execution of the ejbCreate method.

It is important to know what you can and cannot put into an ejbCreate method and an ejbPostCreate method, such as which EntityContext methods can be called and what kind of access the bean can have.

7.4.2 Operations allowed during bean creation

During the execution of the bean construction, a context (instance of EntityContext) is assigned to the bean instance. The bean provider can use this context to invoke methods on EJBContext from the methods that the bean provider writes inside the bean, such as the ejbCreate and ejbPostCreate methods. The method calls on EntityContext and the method calls used to get access to its JNDI environment are also known as *operations*.

Table 7.4 shows the permitted and prohibited operations in an ejbCreate method and the corresponding ejbPostCreate method. Make sure you understand why an operation is permitted and another operation is prohibited in a given method, taking into account what you have learned about the ejbCreate and ejbPostCreate methods in the previous section. For example, you cannot get a primary key in an ejbCreate method from the EntityContext because the container assigns the primary key to the context only after the execution of this method is complete. You can get a reference to the `EJBObject` in the ejbPostCreate method and not in the ejbCreate method because the container creates the `EJBObject` after executing the ejbCreate method and before invoking the ejbPostCreate method. Because both the ejbCreate and ejbPostCreate methods are running in a transactional context, you can do the transaction-related things in these methods, such as marking the transaction for rollback. Go through table 7.4 and make sure you understand each Yes and No entry.

Table 7.4 Permitted and prohibited operations in the ejbCreate and ejbPostCreate methods

Operation	ejbCreate	ejbPostCreate
Get a reference to the bean's home interface	Yes	Yes
Get a reference to the bean's EJBObject, that is, a reference to the component interface	No	Yes
Get security information	Yes	Yes
Mark the current transaction to roll back	Yes	Yes
Determine whether the transaction has already been marked for rollback	Yes	Yes
Get a reference to the transaction; not used by entity beans	No	No
Get the primary key for the bean	No	Yes
JNDI access	Yes	Yes
Resource manager access	Yes	Yes
Access to other beans	Yes	Yes

Thus, during the ejbCreate and ejbPostCreate methods, the bean instance gets its remaining beanhood. By the end of the execution of these methods the bean instance has an EJBObject with a primary key assigned to it, and it also get its Entity-Context stamped with the primary key. So, one important point you must learn from the construction and creation of the bean is that the container enables an entity bean instance to represent an entity in the database by doing the following two things:

- Assigning the primary key of the entity to the EntityContext of the bean
- Assigning the primary key of the entity to the EJBObject of the bean

Now, we'll discuss the issue of identifying the entity bean instances by using the primary keys.

7.5   IDENTIFYING ENTITY BEANS

Each entity bean instance of a given type (say CustomerBean) representing an entity has a unique primary key that serves as its identity. This should not come as a surprise because the entities in the database tables are uniquely defined by their primary keys, and the bean instances representing those entities to the clients must be uniquely identifiable, too. Even in cases where the data that the beans are representing is not in a relational database table, it must be in uniquely identifiable pieces, that is, the client should be able to tell one customer (say John Serri) from another (say Gurmail Kandola).

A client may use the primary key to call the method findByPrimaryKey(...) in order to get a reference to the component interface of an entity bean. Subsequently, the client can use this reference to call the business methods of the bean exposed in the component interface. Although the container would build the primary key, insert it, and assign it, it's still your responsibility to give enough information to the container to build the key. In other words, you need to provide a primary key class, specify it in the deployment descriptor, and assign valid values to the fields that compose the key.

7.5.1   Constructing the primary key

You must choose or create a class to contain the primary key and specify it in the deployment descriptor. If you decide that one or more persistent fields in the bean class will compose the key, then you have to tell this to the container in the deployment descriptor. Make sure you assign valid values to these fields in the ejbCreate method. You can take the values passed in by the customer or generate the values of the key fields, or both. For example, you may decide to simply use the customer id, a persistent field, as the primary key. In this case, you must make sure you assign a valid value to the customer id in the ejbCreate method.

A key could be composed of a single field or multiple fields.

Single-field key

Consider a simple scenario in which the data is in a database table, and a single field in each row represents the primary key; that is, it uniquely defines each row. In this case you can use the corresponding persistent field in the bean class to define the primary key for any bean representing a row in this table. Suppose the name of the entity bean persistent field that you are using for the primary key is ID (represented by the abstract `getID()` and `setID()` methods) and it is of type int. You specify it in the deployment descriptor of the CMP bean by using the elements `<prim-key-class>` and `<primkey-field>` as shown below:

```
<ejb-jar>
  <enterprise-beans>
    ...
  <entity>
    ...
      <prim-key-class>java.lang.Integer</prim-key-class>
      <primkey-field>ID</primkey-field>
    ...
  </entity>
  </enterprise-beans>
</ejb-jar>
```

This single-field primary key is a simple case where we just use the wrapper class `Integer` to make the one-field key where the field type is int. However, if your entity beans represent data from a table whose primary key is composed of multiple fields, you need to provide a primary key class.

Multiple-field key

You define a multiple-field primary key when it takes more than one field to uniquely identify an entity in the database. You specify it in the deployment descriptor by using the element <prim-key-class> and you do not include the element <primkey-field>. But you have to write a primary key class. You must follow these rules for the primary key class:

- A primary key class must be serializable.
- A primary key class must be declared public.
- The key should be composed of the fields that are defined as persistent in the bean class.
- The persistent fields in the bean class composing the key must be accessible by methods declared public.

By the end of the execution of ejbCreate method, all the fields composing the primary key must have obtained valid values. In other words, you must have specified the values of the fields that compose the primary key for your bean before the ejbCreate method is complete.

Once all the entity bean instances representing entities have been assigned primary keys, the keys can be used to uniquely identify them within their entity bean type.

7.5.2   Identifying entity beans with primary keys

A client communicates with an entity bean that represents a specific entity through a reference to the component interface of that bean. In other words, the primary key is an object identity of the entity because it is associated with both a reference to the component interface of the bean, EJBObject, and the context of the bean instance, EntityContext. This object identity does not change over the lifetime of the reference. Therefore, entity beans that are accessible to clients can always be identified by using primary keys.

A client can retrieve the primary key from the component interface of an entity bean by calling the getPrimaryKey() method. Invoking this method on a remote or local interface would return the same value. If a client receives two entity references from the same Home, it can determine whether they refer to the same or different beans by comparing their primary keys with the equals() method. The client can also find out whether the two references refer to the same bean by comparing them with each other using the isIdentical() method, as shown in this code fragment:

```
Customer customerOne = ...;
Customer customerTwo = ...;
if (customerOne.isIdentical(customerTwo)) {
 System.out.println("customerOne and customerTwo refer
 ➥ to the same entity bean");
} else {
 System.out.println("customerOne and customerTwo refer
 ➥ to different entity beans");
}
```

You should never use the `==` operator or the `equals()` method to compare two object references, because their results are unspecified in EJB. Always use the `isIdentical()` method for this purpose. As already stated, the `equals()` method is used to compare the primary keys to determine whether two references belong to the same bean instance.

> **NOTE** If a client receives two entity references from the same Home, it can determine whether they refer to the same or different beans by comparing their primary keys using the `equals()` method. The client can also find out whether the two references refer to the same bean by comparing the references with each other by using the `isIdentical()` method.

So, an entity bean instance becomes able to represent an entity in the database when the container gives it a unique identity by assigning the primary key of the entity to the context of the bean instance, EntityContext, and also to the EJBObject of the bean instance. From this point on, the bean is ready to serve client calls for that specific entity.

The three most important takeaways for this chapter are

- The container makes a bean instance from the bean class.
- The container uses the `EntityBean` interface to communicate with the bean instance.
- The bean instance uses the `EntityContext` interface to communicate with the container.

7.6 SUMMARY

In this chapter we saw an entity bean rising from the code and getting into a state in which it has a unique identity and represents a specific entity in the database. The container and the bean developer are responsible for generating the code for the bean class. The container creates instances of the bean class, assigns an EntityContext to them, and keeps them in the pool. Do not confuse this context with the JNDI context; this is the instance of the class that implements the `EntityContext` interface. At this stage, an entity bean, although not representing a specific entity, is ready to do some work for clients that do not involve a specific entity (such as finder methods and home business methods). When a method call arrives from a client that involves a specific entity, the container pulls a bean out of the pool and enables it to represent that specific entity. This involves assigning the primary key of the entity to the context of the bean instance and to the `EJBObject` of the bean instance, and of course loading the entity data into the bean instance. Now, because there are two things carrying the same data—the entity and the bean instance—they need to stay in synch with each other. In the case of CMP entity beans, the container is responsible for this synchronization. The bean class for a CMP bean must be declared abstract, because some of the methods will be implemented by the container.

The bean class must be declared public and it must implement the `EntityBean` interface. While the `EntityContext` interface is the communication line from the bean instance to the container, the `EntityBean` interface is the communication line from the container to the entity bean instance. Which EntityContext methods can be called from within a bean method depends on at which stage of its lifecycle the entity bean is. The methods that are common to the entity and session beans behave very differently in the two bean kinds.

In this chapter, you learned how an entity bean is born, looking like a plain Java object, and then acquires its beanhood through the construction and creation process. In the next chapter, we will explore everything that can happen to the bean during its entire life.

Comprehend

- What methods go into the bean class and their relationship with the interfaces.
- The difference between creating an entity bean and a session bean. A `create()` call on an entity bean inserts an entity into the database.
- Comparing two bean references with each other and their primary keys with each other: the primary keys can be compared using the `equals(...)` method while the references must be compared by using the `isIdentical(...)` method.
- Permitted and prohibited operations from inside the following class methods during the bean construction and creation stage: constructor, setEntityContext, ejbCreate, and ejbPostCreate.

Look out

- An entity bean can never call the getUserTransaction method, because only a BMT bean can call this method and an entity bean is always a CMT bean.
- EntityContext has only one method that SessionContext does not have and that is `getPrimaryKey()`. Remember, there is also a `getPrimaryKey()` method in the `EJBObject` and `EJBLocalObject` interfaces that the remote component and the local component interfaces of both session beans and entity beans extend.
- The class for a CMP bean must be declared abstract because it contains abstract methods that will be implemented by the container.
- You do not implement a find method in the class of a CMP bean; the container will do that.

Memorize

- Names and functionalities of the methods in the `EntityBean` interface as compared to the `SessionBean` interface.
- Names and functionalities of the methods in the `EntityContext` interface as compared to the `SessionContext` interface.

Some questions may have more than one correct answer. Choose all that apply.

1. Consider two references, customerOne and customerTwo, to the component interface `Customer` of an entity bean. What is the correct way to find out if the two references refer to the same bean instance?

    a. `customerOne == customerTwo`
    b. `customerOne.equals(customerTwo)`
    c. `customerOne.isIdentical(customerTwo)`
    d. All of the above

2. Consider an entity bean whose primary key is defined by two fields, courseID and teacherID, in a class named `CoursePK`. The key class is specified in the deployment descriptor with the following code fragment:

```
<prim-key-class> CoursePK </prim-key-class>
<primkey-field> courseID </primkey-field>
<primkey-field> teacherID </primkey-field>
```

Which of the following are valid statements about this code fragment?

    a. This is valid only for a BMP bean.
    b. This is valid only for a CMP bean.
    c. This is valid for both CMP and BMP beans.
    d. This is an invalid specification of the primary key in the deployment descriptor.

3. Which of the following methods are allowed to be invoked from within the method `setEntityContext()`?

    a. `getEJBHome()`
    b. `getEJBLocalHome()`
    c. `getEJBObject()`
    d. `getPrimaryKey()`

4. Which of the following statements are true about a CMP entity bean?

    a. You cannot write JDBC code in the bean class to make a connection and send queries to any database.
    b. You cannot write JDBC code in the bean class to change the values of virtual persistent fields of your bean.
    c. You can write JDBC code and get connected to any database you want.
    d. You can write JDBC code to read the virtual persistent fields, but you cannot change their values.

5. Which of the following are not legal method declarations in a CMP entity bean class to set the value of a persistent field?

    a. `public abstract String setEmail(String email);`
    b. `public void setEmail(String email);`
    c. `public abstract void setEmail(String email);`
    d. `public abstract void SetEmail(String email);`

6. Which two of the following are a legal pair of getter and setter accessor methods declared in a CMP entity bean class to set and get the values of a persistent field?

    a. `public abstract void setID(int id);`
    b. `public abstract String getID();`
    c. `public abstract Object getID();`
    d. `public abstract int getID();`

7. How many `ejbPostCreate()` methods can a CMP bean class have?

    a. Zero or more
    b. One or more
    c. One only
    d. Zero only
    e. Zero or one only

8. Which methods of the `EntityContext` interface can be called from within an `ejbCreate<method>` of an entity bean class?

    a. `getEJBObject()`
    b. `getPrimaryKey()`
    c. `getEJBHome()`
    d. `getRollbackOnly()`
    e. `getUserTransaction()`

9. Which methods of the `EntityContext` interface can be called from within an `ejbPostCreate<method>` of an entity bean class?

    a. `getEJBObject()`
    b. `getPrimaryKey()`
    c. `getEJBHome()`
    d. `getRollbackOnly()`
    e. `getUserTransaction()`

10. Which of the following statements about the entity bean are true?

    a. All entity bean instances of the same type (say CustomerBean) have the same Home, that is an instance of an object that implements the home interface of this bean.

    b. A specific entity bean instance can be accessed by only one client at a time.

    c. If two clients wanted to access the same entity in the database concurrently, the container would make two entity bean instances to represent that entity.

    d. If two clients wanted to access the same entity in the database concurrently, the container would make one entity bean to represent that entity, and the two clients would get their own references to the same EJBObject corresponding to that one entity bean instance.

Lifecycle of an entity bean

EXAM OBJECTIVES

7.1 Identify correct and incorrect statements or examples about the lifecycle of a CMP entity bean.

7.2 From a list, identify the responsibility of the container for a CMP entity bean, including but not limited to: setEntityContext, unsetEntityContext, ejbCreate, ejbPostCreate, ejbActivate, ejbPassivate, ejbRemove, ejbLoad, ejbStore, ejbFind, ejbHome, and ejbSelect.

7.3 From a list, identify the purpose, behavior, and responsibilities of the bean provider for a CMP entity bean, including but not limited to: setEntityContext, unsetEntityContext, ejbCreate, ejbPostCreate, ejbActivate, ejbPassivate, ejbRemove, ejbLoad, ejbStore, ejbFind, ejbHome, and ejbSelect.

INTRODUCTION

The entity bean is the most sophisticated of all the three bean flavors, and so is its lifecycle. In the beginning, an entity bean type, say CustomerBean, is a class along with the interfaces, and the bean instance does not exist. The container makes an instance of a bean, and from this point on the bean instance goes through different stages (or states) until it is destroyed for the garbage collector to collect. This whole cycle is called the entity bean lifecycle. It is important to understand the lifecycle because at its different stages the bean instance can do different things.

The lifecycle of an entity bean involves three states: life before birth, life after birth without an entity, and life after birth with an entity. In the previous chapter, you learned that a bean is born when the container constructs an instance, gives it an entity context, and puts it into the pool. This is life without an entity. You also learned how in response to a `create()` call by a client, the container promotes the bean to represent a specific entity. This is the life devoted to an entity. The lifecycle is largely about method invocations of two kinds: the methods invoked on the bean instance and the methods invoked on the entity context of the bean instance from inside the methods of the bean class.

This chapter focuses on how the behavior and capabilities of a bean instance change as it progresses through different states of its lifecycle—in other words, what a bean instance can and cannot do at different states and in between the two given states. We will explore three avenues marked with three questions. Two questions are related to the methods invoked on the entity bean instance: Which methods of an entity bean class can be invoked on the entity bean instance at each of these three states, and which methods are invoked on the entity bean instance in the process of transitioning between any two states? The third question is related to the bean context: Which methods can be invoked on the context of the bean instance from inside the methods of the bean class? In this chapter, we will probe the lifecycle of an entity bean with these three questions in mind.

Oh, another thing: pay attention to who is running the show in this lifecycle. It is largely between you (the bean provider) and the container. We begin with a high-level view of the lifecycle, followed by further probing.

8.1   ENTITY BEAN LIFECYCLE OVERVIEW

From its construction to its destruction, all the states that a bean instance goes through are collectively called the bean's lifecycle. In chapter 5, we explored the lifecycle of a session bean. The lifecycle of an entity bean consists of three states:

- The does not exist state
- The pooled state
- The ready state

Figure 8.1 shows the three states and also the methods that can be invoked on the bean in each of these three states. The figure also shows the methods that are called in the process of transitioning the bean from one state to another.

8.1.1   The does not exist state

The does not exist state of the entity bean refers to the bean state when the bean instance does not exist. However, the bean does exist before its instance is constructed.

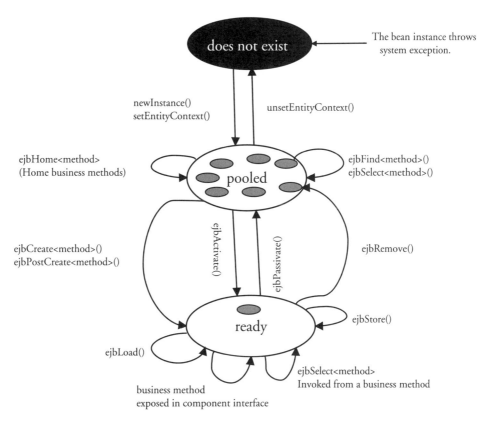

Figure 8.1 Lifecycle of an entity bean. The bean has two kinds of methods: the methods that could be called inside each of the three states and the methods that are called in the process of transitioning the bean from one state to another.

After all, you wrote it, and the deployer deployed it. So before an instance is created, the bean is in the does not exist state.

The bean comes out of the does not exist state when the container does the following:

- Makes an EntityContext. The EJB spec does not require a new context for each bean instance.

- Makes a new instance of the entity bean by calling the `Class.newInstance()` method on the bean class that in turn would call the class constructor.

- Calls the `setEntityContext(...)` method on the bean instance and passes in the context. This assigns a context to the bean instance, and provides the bean instance with a reference to the `EntityContext` interface.

- Puts the bean instance (which now has an entity context) in the pool.

The `EntityContext` interface and the `setEntityContext(...)` method were discussed in detail in the previous chapter. When the container needs to reduce the size of the pool, it puts an instance back into the does not exist state by calling the method `unsetEntityContext()`.

> **NOTE** A session bean has the `setSessionContext(...)` method, while an entity bean has the `setEntityContext(...)` method to accomplish the same goal. There is no `unsetSessionContext(...)` method for the session bean corresponding to the `unsetEntityContext()` method for entity beans; that is, there is no `unsetSessionContext` method in the `SessionBean` interface.

So, the life of an entity bean instance starts when the container constructs it out of the entity bean class by calling the `newInstance()` method (which in turn calls the no-argument constructor of the bean class) and assigns it a context by calling the `setEntityContext(...)` method. The container can put a number of instances of a bean of the same type (say CustomerBean) in a pool. At this point all these instances are in the pooled state.

8.1.2 The pooled state: No strings attached

Each bean type (CustomerBean, OrderBean, etc.) has its own pool. A bean instance in a pooled state is ready to serve, that is, the container can use it to serve client calls, which would invoke ejbHome and ejbFind/ejbSelect methods. However, in this state an instance, although connected to the container through the context, is not connected to any entity in the database. In other words, it's not representing any specific entity in the database. Because none of the instances in the pool are attached to any specific entity in the database, the instances have no unique identities, and hence all of them are free and equal. Therefore, any of them are equally capable of serving a suitable request from the client at this state. The requests that they serve do not involve operations on any specific entity in the database. Examples of such requests that an entity bean instance in the pool can serve are those that come through the calls to the find and home business methods. The container can use the instance in the pooled state to execute the following methods:

- An ejbFind method as a result of client invocation of a find method
- An ejbHome method as a result of a client invocation of a home business method
- An ejbSelect method called from within an ejbHome method

Note that although the find methods are targeted at a specific entity, the bean does not leave the pool during the execution of these methods. The container would choose a bean instance in the pool to find the requested entity, and it will send the bean to the next state only if the client calls a business method on that entity. The process of how a find method works was explained in chapter 6. The other methods (in addition to ejbFind, ejbHome, and ejbSelect) that can be invoked by the container on a bean instance in the pool are those that would transition its state either back to the does not exist state or to the next state, called the ready state. There is only one method that the container calls to put the instance back to the does not exist state: unsetEntityContext().

When a client invokes a create method on the bean's interface, the container inserts an entity (sent by the client) into the database, pulls a bean out of the pool, and enables it to represent that entity. In the process of doing so, the container invokes the ejbCreate and ejbPostCreate methods on the bean corresponding to the create method invoked by the client. This would put the bean instance into the ready state, where it is ready to serve requests from the clients for that specific entity. We covered this situation in chapter 7. In order to save resources, beans in the ready state can be kicked back into the pool by using the ejbPassivate method. Remember, in the pool, no instance represents any specific entity and all instances are equal; in other words, the instance that has been passivated can be called by the container to represent any entity in the future.

So, in the ready state each bean represents a specific entity in the database. In other words, each bean instance of a specific bean type (say CustomerBean) has a unique identity.

8.1.3 The ready state: I'm yours until I go back to the pool

The ready state is the state in which a bean instance represents a specific entity, even though it can serve multiple clients. There are only two ways for a bean to enter the ready state: through creation, which involves two methods—the ejbCreate method and the corresponding ejbPostCreate method—or through activation, which involves one method—ejbActivate. The creation path is taken in response to a create call by a client, and the activation path is taken when the entity that needs to be represented already exists. You will learn more about activation and passivation on the following pages.

While a bean instance is in the ready state, these methods may be invoked on it:

1 The container may invoke the synchronization related methods ejbStore() and ejbLoad().

2 A client may invoke business methods exposed in the component interface.

3 An ejbSelect method may be invoked from a business method, ejbStore() or ejbLoad().

An entity bean instance in the ready state has the following characteristics:

- It has a state, that is, the values of its persistent fields representing the fields in the entity.

- It has a context that holds the primary key of the entity.

- An EJBObject corresponds to this bean that holds the same primary key as the bean context.

NOTE In the pooled state, an entity bean instance does not represent any specific entity in the database, while in the ready state it does represent a specific entity in the database.

The bean instance in the ready state is attached to a specific entity until it receives an ejbRemove call or an ejbPassivate call from the container and goes back to the pool. So, an entity bean can have three possible states in its lifecycle: the does not exist state, the pooled state, and the ready state. The container will transition the bean from one state to another either due to a client call such as `create()`, or on its own as a part of its management process such as `ejbPassivate()`. As figure 8.1 shows, a number of methods can be invoked on a bean instance depending on its state. Inside each of these methods you can invoke methods on the context of the bean—the methods of the `EntityContext` interface. In the previous chapter, you learned what those methods are. Which of those context methods can you invoke from inside a method of the bean instance? This is a common issue running through all the following sections of this chapter.

8.2 FINDING A BEAN AND DOING A SELECT

Corresponding to every find method in the home interface of an entity bean is an ejbFind method implemented by the container, and corresponding to each business method in the home interface of an entity bean is an ejbHome method in the bean class implemented by the bean provider. While an entity bean instance is in the pool, the container may invoke any ejbFind or ejbHome method on the bean. An ejbHome method may in turn call an ejbSelect method. None of these method calls transition the bean to another state.

8.2.1 The ejbFind methods

The find methods are exposed in the home interface for the client to find entities in the database—think of SELECT queries. The bean provider never writes an ejb-Find<method> and doesn't even declare it in the bean class. These methods are implemented by the container corresponding to the find methods in the home interface. A client may invoke a find method such as `findByPrimaryKey()` to search for a specific entity or a find method that would search for entities that fulfill a condition such as "find all the customers who have made more than 10 orders in the last month." In the former case, at most one entity would be found, while in the latter case more than one entity may be found. Whether or not an entity was found in the database as a result of the find calls, the bean instance still stays in the pool after the execution of these methods is complete. When one or more entities are found as a result of a find method call, and if the client invokes a business method on one of those entities, the container would transition a bean instance from the pool to the ready state via activation (by executing the `ejbActivate()` method). We will learn about activation and passivation later in this chapter. The bean instance that moved to the ready state via activation would represent the specific entity.

The bean provider neither declares nor implements the ejbFind methods in the bean class. The container takes care of implementing these methods.

Let's work through an example in order to clarify the process described above. Assume a client wants to change the email address of John Serri, which is an entity in the database with primary key 11.

1 The client invokes the method `findByPrimaryKey("11")` on the EJB-Home object.

2 The container selects a bean instance in the pool and calls its method `ejbFindByPrimaryKey("11")`.

3 The bean (through the container) searches the database for an entity with primary key 11. If the entity is not found, the client would get an `ObjectNotFoundException`.

4 If the entity is found, the container makes an EJBObject and assigns it the primary key 11 if it does not exist.

5 The reference to this EJBObject is sent to the client.

You have already seen this process discussed in detail in chapter 6. Note that no bean instance has been sent to the ready state yet in order to represent this entity. The bean instance on which the `ejbFindByPrimaryKey("11")` method was invoked is still in the pool. The client, after receiving the reference to the EJBObject, invokes a business method on it, say `setEmail()`. After the invocation of this method, the container will pull a bean instance out of the pool and transition it to the ready state through activation (discussed later in this chapter) in order to represent the entity with primary key 11. Then, it will invoke the business method on it that was called to change the email address. After the method execution is complete, the container may keep the bean in the ready state or it may send it back to the pool through passivation.

8.2.2 The ejbSelect methods

The ejbSelect methods, introduced in EJB 2.0, are used to make select queries on the database. They are not exposed to the client. These methods are declared abstract in the bean class by the bean provider just like the accessor methods for the virtual persistent fields. That means the container implements them according to the information provided in the deployment descriptor files. We will learn more about how this works in the next two chapters.

The ejbSelect methods may be invoked by the home business methods on the bean instances in the pool. They may also be invoked by the business methods on the bean instances in the ready state. Also in the ready state, they may be invoked from within an `ejbLoad()` or `ejbStore()` method.

NOTE The ejbSelect methods are not exposed to the client, and they are declared abstract in the bean class. The ejbFind methods are exposed to the client (through the find methods declared in the home interface), but they are not put in the bean class by the bean provider.

Both the ejbFind and ejbSelect methods are implemented by the container according to the information provided in the deployment descriptor by using EJB-QL; you will learn more about this query language in chapter 10. While you should never write or declare an ejbFind method in a CMP bean class, you may need to declare the ejbSelect methods in the bean class. Therefore you must know the following rules for writing these methods:

- The method name must begin with `ejbSelect`, such as `ejbSelectList-Customers()`.
- The method must be declared public.
- The method must be declared abstract as it would be implemented by the container.
- The `throws` clause in the method definition must include `javax.ejb.FinderException`. It may include arbitrary application-specific exceptions as well.

While the ejbFind methods are exposed to the client in the interface via the find methods, the ejbSelect methods are not exposed to the client and are generally invoked by the business methods. Two kinds of business methods are invoked on an entity bean: the business methods exposed in the component interface, which can be invoked on the bean in the ready state, and the business methods exposed in the home interface, which can be invoked on the bean in the pooled state. The latter are also called home business methods, which we explore next.

8.3 DOING BUSINESS FROM HOME

Unlike a session bean, an entity bean can have business methods exposed in its home interface. The reason for this is there are some operations that a client may perform on a set of entities without having to have a reference to the component interface of a specific entity. Such operations are not targeted at a specific entity. For example, a client wants to know the names of all the customers who have made more than 10 orders in the last month. The client can look up the home interface of a bean type (say CustomerBean) through JNDI. Then the client will invoke an appropriate method (say `listAllCustomersByOrders()`) on the home interface, which will be forwarded to the EJBHome object. The container will select a bean in the pool and invoke the method `ejbHomeListAllCustomersByOrders()`, which in turn may call a select method to access the database. The bean will return the data that the container passes back to the client. In the whole process, the bean will stay in the pool: no corresponding EJBObject will be created, no primary key will be assigned, and no `ejbActivate()` method will be executed. There are some rules you should follow in writing the home business methods.

8.3.1 Writing home business methods

The home business methods are the business methods declared in the home interface of an entity bean. These methods trigger operations that do not target a specific entity. In the bean class, you need to implement the home business methods that you exposed in the home interface. The names of these methods in the class are not identical but match those in the home interface. You must adhere to these rules in writing these methods:

- The name of the home business method in a bean class corresponding to a business <method> in the home interface must be ejbHome<method> with the first character of <method> uppercased. For example, the method in the bean class corresponding to the method listCustomers() in the home interface would be ejbHomeListCustomers().
- The method must be declared public.
- The method must not be declared static.
- If the method is exposed in the remote home interface, the arguments and return types must be RMI-IIOP compliant.
- The throws clause in the method declaration may include application-specific exceptions if they were declared in the home interface, but it must not include RemoteException.

The two key points to remember when you are writing a home business method are that no EJBObject for this bean exists yet, and no primary key either. Therefore, do not write code in these methods that assumes the existence of the primary key or the EJBObject. However, the bean does have a context (an instance of EntityContext) that you can use to get some information from the container.

8.3.2 Using EntityContext: Communicating with the container

What kind of information can you get from EntityContext from inside the home business methods—in other words, what methods of EntityContext can you invoke? Table 8.1 provides an answer to this question. To understand each Yes and No in the table, remember that the home business methods do not involve a specific entity.

Table 8.1 Operations allowed and not allowed from inside the home business methods of an entity bean class

Operation	Any Home Business Method
Get a reference to the bean's home interface	Yes
Get a reference to the bean's EJBObject, that is, a reference to the component interface	No
Get security information about the client	Yes

continued on next page

Table 8.1 Operations allowed and not allowed from inside the home business methods of an entity bean class *(continued)*

Operation	Any Home Business Method
Mark the current transaction to roll back	Yes
Determine whether the transaction has already been marked for rollback	Yes
Get a reference to the transaction; not used by entity beans	No
Get the primary key for the bean	No
JNDI access	Yes
Resource manager access	Yes
Access to other beans	Yes

The home business methods are invoked on the bean instances in the pool. There, the bean has no `EJBObject` and no primary key because it does not represent a specific entity. Therefore, from inside the home business methods, you cannot invoke the context methods on the bean to get its primary key or a reference to the `EJBObject`. Entity beans cannot get a reference to the transaction because they always use a container-managed transaction.

Remember the exception rule for accessing an EntityContext method from any of the entity bean class methods: If from a method of an entity bean instance you attempt to invoke a method of the `EntityContext` interface, and the access is not allowed, the container must throw `java.lang.IllegalStateException`. However, if you attempt to access a resource manager (say a database) or a method of another bean, and the access is not allowed, the behavior is undefined by the EJB architecture.

ALERT If from a method of an entity bean instance you attempt to invoke a method of the `EntityContext` interface, and the access is not allowed, the container must throw the `java.lang.IllegalStateException`. If you attempt to access a resource manager (say a database) or a method of another bean, and the access is not allowed, the behavior is undefined by the EJB architecture.

The home business methods are executed on a bean instance in the pool. If a client calls a business method that requires handling a specific entity, the container promotes a bean instance in the pool state to the ready state. One way of doing that is the creation process, which was discussed in chapter 7. The other method is activation, which is discussed in the next section.

8.4 IN AND OUT OF THE POOL

A pool is a collection of instances of an entity bean of a specific type (such as Customer-Bean), the instances that have an entity context associated with each of them but not a primary key. To serve a client that's invoking operations on a specific entity, the container has to send a bean instance from the pool to the ready state through either the creation path or the activation path. Once in the ready state, the container can put the bean instance back into the pool through either the passivation path (in order to save the resources) or the remove path (see figure 8.1).

8.4.1 Activating a bean instance

Activating a bean instance means transitioning the bean instance from the pooled state to the ready state. When a client call arrives for an operation on a specific existing entity and there is no entity bean instance in the ready state representing that entity, the container pulls an entity bean instance out of the pool and sends it to the ready state through activation. Taking the bean from the pool through the activation path in order for it to represent an entity in the ready state involves creating an EJBObject for the bean instance (if one already does not exist), assigning the entity's primary key to the context of the bean instance, executing the ejb-Activate() method on the bean, and then loading the bean with the entity data followed by executing ejbLoad() on the bean instance.

Recall that both the ejbActivate() method and the ejbLoad() method are inherited from the EntityBean interface that the bean class implements. Both of them are public and return nothing (void as the return type). Table 8.2 shows what context-related information you can get from inside these methods.

Table 8.2 Permitted and prohibited operations from inside the ejbActivate() and ejbLoad() methods of an entity bean class

Operation	ejbActivate()	ejbLoad()
Get a reference to the bean's home interface	Yes	Yes
Get a reference to the bean's EJBObject, that is, a reference to the component interface	Yes	Yes
Get security information about the client	No	Yes
Mark the current transaction to roll back	No	Yes
Determine whether the transaction has already been marked for rollback	No	Yes
Get a reference to the transaction; not used by entity beans	No	No
Get the primary key for the bean	Yes	Yes
JNDI access	Yes	Yes
Resource manager access	No	Yes
Access to other beans	No	Yes

While the ejbActivate() method is being executed, no meaningful transaction context exists—in other words, it runs with an unspecified context; you will learn more about the transaction context in chapter 12. Therefore, you cannot have access to a resource manager or the methods of other beans. Obviously, without a transaction context, it does not make sense to mark a transaction for rollback or to find out whether it is marked for rollback. The bean instance at this stage cannot access the security information about the client either.

Before executing a business method, the container synchronizes the state of the entity bean instance with the entity in the database by refreshing the persistent fields in the entity bean with the current values of the corresponding fields in the database. Immediately after doing this, the container calls the `ejbLoad()` method. In this method, the bean provider should reinitialize all the instance variables that depend on the persistent fields of the bean. The `ejbLoad()` method runs in the transaction context of the business method that triggered the call to `ejbLoad()`. Therefore, the transaction-related information that is not available to the `ejbActivate()` method is available to the `ejbLoad` method. This should help you understand each Yes and No entry in the `ejbLoad()` column of table 8.2.

The reverse of activation is passivation. While activation involves the `ejbActivate()` and `ejbLoad()` methods, passivation involves the `ejbStore()` and `ejbPassivate()` methods.

8.4.2   Passivating a bean instance

When the container decides to send a bean instance in the ready state back to the pool, it calls two methods, `ejbStore()` and `ejbPassivate()`, on the bean in the process of doing so. The container may decide to do so in order to release the resources allocated to the bean in the pool. The context information that you are allowed and not allowed to access from inside these two methods is shown in table 8.3.

Table 8.3   Permitted and prohibited operations from inside the `ejbPassivate()` and `ejbStore()` methods of an entity bean class

Operation	`ejbPassivate()`	`ejbStore()`
Get a reference to the bean's home interface	Yes	Yes
Get a reference to the bean's EJBObject, that is, a reference to the component interface	Yes	Yes
Get security information about the client	No	Yes
Mark the current transaction to roll back	No	Yes
Determine whether the transaction has already been marked for rollback	No	Yes
Get a reference to the transaction; not used by entity beans	No	No
Get the primary key for the bean	Yes	Yes
JNDI access	Yes	Yes
Resource manager access	No	Yes
Access to other beans	No	Yes

CHAPTER 8   *LIFECYCLE OF AN ENTITY BEAN*

The container calls the `ejbStore()` method to give the bean provider (who wrote the code) a chance to update the persistent state of the bean instance. After this call, the container synchronizes the bean's state with the entity in the database. During the `ejbStore()` execution the transaction context still exists. Before the container calls `ejbPassivate()`, it is no longer associated with a transaction; therefore it is not in a meaningful transaction context. This should help you understand each Yes and No entry in table 8.3. The `ejbPassivate()` method gives the instance a chance to release any resources that don't need to be held while in the pool. The instance still holds the primary key until the end of the `ejbPassivate()` execution.

> **NOTE** The bean provider can assume that the persistent state of the entity bean instance has been synchronized with the entity in the database just before `ejbLoad()` and after `ejbStore()`.

So, the bean instance goes from the pooled state to the ready state either through creation (the ejbCreate and ejbPostCreate methods) or through activation. The ready state is the state in which the bean is at the prime of its beanhood. It can service the business method calls from the client, and it has maximum access to the EntityContext methods and to the JNDI environment. Let's take a closer look at the ready state.

8.5 WHERE THE BEAN ROCKS: THE READY STATE

In the *ready* state, a bean instance is at the prime of its lifecycle. It can do what it was created for: execute its business methods for the client. In other words, it can service the business method calls from the client, and that is the very reason the client accessed the bean in the first place. It is your responsibility to implement the business methods in the bean class and expose them in the component interface of the bean.

8.5.1 Implementation of business methods

You can define zero or more business methods in an entity bean class, and the signatures of these methods must obey the following rules:

- A business method name can be arbitrary, but it must not start with `ejb`. This rule is there in order to avoid conflicts with the container callback methods such as `ejbCreate()` or `ejbPassivate()`.
- A business method must be declared public.
- A business method must not be declared final or static.
- The arguments and return types for a business method must be in compliance with the RMI/IIOP legal types if the method is exposed in the entity bean's remote interface.
- The name, return types, and arguments of a business method in the bean class must be identical to the corresponding method declared in the component interface.

- The business methods in the class must not declare `RemoteException`: no `RemoteException` in the class whatsoever. As for other exceptions declared in the interface, you don't have to declare them in the class method unless you might actually throw them from the method.

- You must not declare any exception in the method that was not declared in the interface. You can declare arbitrary application exceptions, but you have to declare them in the interface for the corresponding method as well.

ALERT A business method in the class must not throw an application exception that is not declared in the component interface for the matching method, and it must never throw `RemoteException` under any situation.

What kind of access does the bean have while executing its business methods?

8.5.2 Operations from business methods

You have seen that in the bean methods discussed so far such as `setEntityContext()` and `ejbActivate()`, the bean's access to the session context methods and other resources is very limited. However, in the business methods, the bean can have access to all the entity context methods, its JNDI context, resource managers, and other beans. Remember that an entity bean, being a CMT bean, can never have a reference to a transaction, that is, the `getUserTransaction()` method. As table 8.4 shows, the bean rocks.

Table 8.4 Operations permitted and prohibited from inside the business methods from a component interface implemented in an entity bean class

Operation	Any Business Method
Get a reference to the bean's home interface	Yes
Get a reference to the bean's `EJBObject`, that is, a reference to the component interface	Yes
Get security information about the client	Yes
Mark the current transaction to roll back	Yes
Determine whether the transaction has already been marked for rollback	Yes
Get a reference to the transaction; only for BMT beans	No
JNDI access	Yes
Resource manager access	Yes
Access to other beans	Yes

The most unique feature of the ready state is that a bean instance in the ready state represents a specific entity. If a client makes a call to delete that entity from the database, and the client's request is met, there is no entity for that bean instance to represent. So the bean instance is brought back into the pool. This is called the remove path, and it is triggered by a remove call from the client.

8.5.3 Removing a bean instance

As you well know by now, two things are involved in the term *entity bean*: the entity bean instance and the entity that it represents. Therefore, when you talk about removing an entity bean, you should always consider whether you are removing the entity bean instance or the entity.

Executing remove on a bean instance

When a client invokes a remove method on a bean interface, the container invokes the corresponding ejbRemove method on the bean instance that represents a specific entity. As a result of this call, it is actually the entity in the database that is removed, and the bean instance simply goes back to the pool. After the execution of this method, the container deletes the entity from the database, or so it should appear to the application. The context information that you can access from within the `ejbRemove()` method is shown in table 8.5.

Table 8.5 Permitted and prohibited operations from inside the `ejbRemove()` method of an entity bean class.

Operation	`ejbRemove()`
Get a reference to the bean's home interface	Yes
Get a reference to the bean's `EJBObject`, that is, a reference to the component interface	Yes
Get security information about the client	Yes
Mark the current transaction to roll back	Yes
Determine whether the transaction has already been marked for rollback	Yes
Get a reference to the transaction; ot used by entity beans	No
Get the primary key for the bean	Yes
JNDI access	Yes
Resource manager access	Yes
Access to other beans	Yes

The container synchronizes the persistent state of the entity bean with the entity before it invokes the `ejbRemove()` method. That may involve invoking `ejbStore()` on the bean instance before `ejbRemove()`. The bean state is synchronized with the entity before deletion, because there may be a cascade delete that would need to be done (you will learn more about the cascade deletes in the next chapter). The `ejbRemove()` method and the database delete operations run in a transaction context. Therefore, you have access to all the context information from within the `ejbRemove()` method. After the execution of the `ejbRemove()` method, the container removes the instance from all the relationships and puts it back into the pool. Now, it is only as good as any other instance in the pool. Remember, it is the entity that has been removed and not the bean instance.

Unlike in stateful session beans, a `remove()` call from the client does not kill the entity bean instance. It does delete the entity in the database that the bean instance represents.

Note that the entity has been removed as a result of a `remove()` call, but the bean instance has survived. The bean instance can be deleted in various ways, sending the entity bean back to the does not exist state and hence completing its lifecycle.

End of the story

An entity bean can complete its existence in one of two ways: removal by the container and "accidental" deletion. The lifecycle completion of an entity bean means, of course, going back to the does not exist state. An entity bean is deleted when the container wants to reduce the number of entity bean instances in the pool and removes the bean instance by executing the method `unsetEntityContext()` on it. In this method, you should release the resources you assigned to the instance in the `setEntityContext()` method, such as a reference to the Home.

Accidental deletion can take place when an entity instance throws a system exception and the container must remove the instance. A server crash or shutdown will also result in the removal of the entity instance.

The three most important takeaways from this chapter are the methods that define the lifecycle of an entity bean:

- The business methods in the home interface and the component interface
- The methods called during the transition from one state to another
- The methods of the `EntityContext` interface

8.6 SUMMARY

The lifecycle of an entity bean involves three states: the does not exist state that exists before an instance of the bean is constructed, the pooled state that exists after an instance of the bean is constructed but does not yet represent any entity, and the ready state in which the bean instance represents a specific entity. As long as the bean instance is alive, that is, it is in the pooled state or in the ready state or in a transition between the two, it has the context with it.

Three kinds of methods define the lifecycle of an entity bean: the business methods in the home interface and the component interface, the methods during the transition from one state to another, and the methods of the `EntityContext` interface called from within the bean class methods.

Because in the pooled state a bean instance does not represent any specific entity, it cannot serve requests for operations on specific entities, such as changing the email address of a customer. Therefore, the container can use the instance to execute only those methods that do not involve operations on a specific entity, such as home business methods and not the business methods exposed in the component interface, which would require an EJBObject, which the instance in the pool does not have yet. For the same reason, there are restrictions on what operations you (the developer) can invoke on the context of the bean instance from inside the methods of the bean instance that can be executed only in the pooled state. For example, the bean instance does not have an EJBObject and a primary key, so you cannot use the context to get the primary key or to get the reference to the remote component interface of the instance.

In the ready state, the bean instance is at its prime: it has its context, its EJBObject, and a primary key assigned to its context and to the EJBObject. In other words, it represents a specific entity with that primary key. Now the container can use the instance to execute the business methods related to the specific entity the instance represents. Another job for the container is to keep the instance in synch with the entity, and that involves calling `ejbStore()` and `ejbLoad()` methods on the instance. And then there are methods that the container calls in the process of transitioning the bean instance from one state to another, such as `ejbCreate()` with `ejbPostCreate()`, or `ejbActivate()` during the transition from pooled to ready state, `ejb-Passivate()` or `ejbRemove()` during the transition from ready to pooled state, constructor and `setEntityContext()` during the transition from does not exist to pooled state, and `unsetEntityContext()` during the transition from pooled to does not exist state. Either each of these methods runs in a meaningful transaction context or it does not. If it does, you can perform the transaction-related operations on the context from inside the method, such as marking the transaction for rollback.

So far in this book we have discussed entity beans as isolated individuals. However, entity beans represent specific entities in a database, and databases are most of the time relational databases. The entities in a relational database are related to each other, such as a specific order belonging to a specific customer. Therefore, the entity beans representing the entities are bound to have relationships of some sort with each other. This is the topic of the next chapter.

Comprehend

- Permitted and prohibited operations from inside the entity bean class methods
- The differences in behavior of the create, remove, passivate, and activate methods in session beans and entity beans
- The difference in the lifecycles of entity beans and session beans
  - A call to a create method in an entity bean results in the insertion of an entity into the database, while in the case of a stateful session bean it creates an instance of the bean and does nothing for a stateless session bean.
  - A call to a remove method in an entity bean results in the deletion of an entity in the database, while in the case of a stateful session bean it deletes an instance of the bean and does nothing for a stateless session bean.
  - Passivation in session beans means saving the bean in persistent storage, for example, by serializing it, while passivation in entity beans simply means sending the instance back to the pool: no serialization.

Look out

- In an entity bean lifecycle, each ejbCreate method must have a corresponding ejbPostCreate method with the same arguments.
- An instance that throws a system exception will be deleted by the container.
- For entity beans, the ejbCreate method is executed between the pooled state and the ready state, and not between the does not exist state and the pooled state.
- No `RemoteException` should appear in any bean class method.

Memorize

- The bean methods that can be executed at different states of the bean's lifecycle

Some questions may have more than one correct answer. Choose all that apply.

1. Which of the following statements are true about the method `ejbFindBy-PrimaryKey("25")`?
    a. It can be invoked only on a bean instance in the pooled state.
    b. It can be invoked only on a bean instance in the ready state.
    c. It can be invoked on a bean instance that is either in the ready state or in the pooled state.
    d. It can be invoked only on a bean instance that is representing the entity with the primary key 25.
    e. By the time the results of the method invocation are returned to the client, the entity with the primary key 25 if found is associated with a bean instance.

2. Which of the following should you, the bean provider, do in the bean class about the ejbFind methods?
    a. Declare them as public and abstract.
    b. Declare then as private and abstract.
    c. Declare them as public.
    d. Declare them as private.
    e. Do not declare them at all.

3. When an `ejbCreate<method>` method is invoked, what other methods must the container invoke?
    a. `ejbActivate()`
    b. `ejbStore()`
    c. `ejbFindByPrimaryKey()`
    d. `ejbPostCreate()`

4. Consider the method `getUserTransaction()` of the interface `Entity-Context`. From which methods of an entity bean class can this method be called?
    a. `ejbCreate<method>`
    b. Home business methods
    c. Business methods exposed in the component interface
    d. `ejbStore()`
    e. None of the above

5. Which of the following does an entity bean instance have in the ready state?
   - a. It has an EntityContext assigned to it.
   - b. It has a primary key assigned to its context.
   - c. It has an EJBObject.
   - d. Its EJBObject has a primary key assigned to it.
   - e. None of the above.

6. Which of the following methods, invoked on an entity bean, are always associated with the state change in the bean's lifecycle?
   - a. `setEntityContext(...)`
   - b. `ejbLoad()`
   - c. `ejbPassivate()`
   - d. `ejbRemove()`
   - e. `ejbSelect()`

7. Which of the following are the legal method declarations for an entity bean class?
   - a. `public static Collection ejbHomeListCustomers()`
   - b. `public Collection ejbHomeListCustomers() throws RemoteException`
   - c. `public Collection ejbHomeListCustomers()`
   - d. `public Collection ejbHomelistCustomers()`
   - e. `public Collection EJBHomeListCustomers()`

8. Which of the following methods can be invoked on the EntityContext from inside the `ejbActivate()` method of an entity bean class?
   - a. `getPrimaryKey()`
   - b. `getCallerPrincipal()`
   - c. `getRollbackOnly()`
   - d. `getEJBObject()`
   - e. `isCallerInRole()`

9. Which of the following actions can you achieve by invoking an appropriate method on the EntityContext from inside the `ejbPassivate()` method of an entity bean class?
   - a. Get the primary key
   - b. Get security information about the client
   - c. Mark a transaction for rollback
   - d. Call another bean's method
   - e. Access the JNDI environment of the bean

10. Which of the following actions can you achieve by invoking an appropriate method on the EntityContext from inside the `ejbStore()` method of an entity bean class?

    a. Get the primary key

    b. Get security information about the client

    c. Mark a transaction for rollback

    d. Call another bean's method

    e. Access the JNDI environment of the bean

CHAPTER 9

Entity bean relationships

EXAM OBJECTIVES

6.2 Identify correct and incorrect statements or examples about persistent relationships, remove protocols, and about the abstract schema type, of a CMP entity bean.

6.3 Identify correct and incorrect statements or examples about the rules and semantics for relationship assignment, and relationship updating, in a CMP bean.

6.4 Match the name with a description of purpose or functionality, for each of the following deployment descriptor elements: ejb-name, abstract-schema-name, ejb-relation, ejb-relationship-role, cmr-field, cmr-field-type, and relationship-role-source.

6.5 Identify correctly implemented deployment descriptor elements for a CMP bean (including container-managed relationships).

INTRODUCTION

Entity beans represent entities in a database, and those entities are often related to each other—for example, a customer's relationship to the orders made by the customer. Therefore, the beans that represent two related entities are naturally related to each other. The fields of an entity are represented by container-managed persistence (CMP) fields inside the entity bean representing that entity. The relationship between two beans representing two related entities is defined through fields called container-managed relationship (CMR) fields, which are similar to CMP fields. The bean provider declares these fields in the bean class in the form of abstract get and set methods, and the container implements these methods by using the information provided by the bean provider in the deployment descriptor. The referential integrity of the related entities is maintained by introducing multiplicity into the relationships, for example, one-to-one relationships and one-to-many relationships.

This chapter focuses on how the container manages the relationship between two entities in the database as represented by the relationship between two entity beans. We will explore the following three avenues: the CMR fields declared in the deployment descriptor as compared to the CMP fields, the corresponding get and set methods in the bean class, and the multiplicity of the relationships. Of course, once again you must also pay attention to who's in charge; it's between you and the container.

9.1   USING BEANS TO REPRESENT DATABASE TABLES

In chapter 6, we presented a simple mapping of the entity bean fields to the database table columns. Recall that the entity bean fields are declared by the bean provider in the form of get and set methods. In this section, we will present the mapping between the bean methods and the table columns for an entity bean and the mapping between several entity beans and the related tables in the database.

An entity bean represents an entity, and the entity lives in a database table. Let's consider the simplest case in which the entity is a row in the database table. The table contains several rows, which can be represented by several instances of the entity bean, one row per instance. A client can use the bean instance to perform operations on the row the instance represents: read it, modify it, or delete it. Note that the different instances of the bean are of the same bean type, say CustomerBean. So, when you think of a bean type, think of the database table, and when you think of a bean instance, think of a row in the table. Although in a more sophisticated situation, an entity may occupy multiple rows across tables, it does not change the fundamentals of the picture we are presenting here: the entities (and the bean instances representing them) represent rows in the tables, the beans (the bean types) represent the tables, and those tables could be related to each other.

9.1.1   Beans representing related tables

In this section, we will present a simple mapping between the persistent fields of an entity bean and the columns of the corresponding table in the database. We will show this mapping for several entity beans and related tables. Again, each persistent field in the bean is represented by a pair of get and set methods.

Consider an application that maintains the customer database containing tables such as Customer, Order, and OrderBackup, shown in tables 9.1, 9.2, and 9.3, respectively. These tables are related to one another, reflecting, for example, that an order is made by a customer.

Table 9.1 The Customer table. Four rows are shown, with each row containing a record for each customer.

CustomerID	Name	Email	Age	Member
11	John Serri	john@john.com	47	FALSE
12	Renee Kant	renee@kant.com	22	TRUE
13	Van Nguyen	van@van.com	30	TRUE
14	Gurmail Kandola	gurmail@gur.com	40	FALSE

Table 9.2 The Order table. Four rows are shown, each row representing a separate order.

OrderID	CustomerID	TotalAmount	OrderStatus	OrderDate
101	11	100.00	Pending	01-FEB-05
102	11	50.75	Shipped	25-JUL-01
201	12	200.00	Cancelled	15-DEC-03
202	12	500.75	Approved	12-MAR-04

Table 9.3 The OrderBackup table, which has the rule that OrderBackupID is identical to OrderID. The second column gives the filename in which the order is backed up.

OrderBackupID	BackupFileName
101	order_101.xml
102	order_102.xml
201	order_201.xml
202	order_202.xml

The Customer table with CustomerID as the primary key contains the basic information about each customer: name, email address, age, and member status. For this example, the TRUE value of the Member field means that the customer holds a membership card, which makes the customer eligible for certain discounts. The Order table contains the orders made by the customers. Each row in the Order table represents a unique order, with OrderID as the primary key. The CustomerID field in the Order table is the foreign key that identifies to which customer an order belongs and hence relates the two tables, Order and Customer. For example, in table 9.2, both orders identified by OrderIDs 101 and 102 are made by the same customer with CustomerID 11, whose name is John Serri and who does not have a membership. In our example, the OrderBackup table is related to the Order table with the rule that the OrderBackupID is identical to the OrderID. This means that the order with OrderID 101 is backed up in the file named order_101.xml.

The database tables in our example may be represented by the entity beans of types CustomerBean, OrderBean, and OrderBackupBean, whose component interfaces are shown in figure 9.1. The figure also shows the get methods used to retrieve the values of the column fields in the tables. We know that the tables are related. The question is what kind of relationship the entity beans representing these tables have with one another. Let's focus on the two entity beans Customer and Order. Consider that a client has a reference to an order and wants to get a reference to the corresponding customer. The client will first get the CustomerID by indirectly invoking the method `getCustomerID()` on the Order bean and then use the CustomerID to get the reference to the Customer by, for instance, invoking the method `findByPrimaryKey(…)`. This can be done without setting up any relationship between the two beans.

It's clear that the indirect relationship between the two beans shown in figure 9.1 comes directly from the relationship between the tables they represent. However, it would be convenient, efficient, and more consistent with object-oriented philosophy if we could get the reference to the CustomerBean bean directly from the OrderBean bean without going through the CustomerID. The EJB architecture provides for such relations, and this is the type of entity bean–level relations that we are going to explore in this chapter.

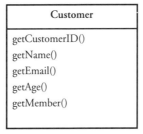

Figure 9.1 The entity beans corresponding to the database tables Customer, Order, and OrderBackup. The methods in the component interfaces of the beans are also shown.

9.1.2 Establishing a relationship between two entity beans

In the previous section, you saw how we can get a reference to Customer from Order by going through the CustomerID, that is, by using the relationship between the tables. However, it would be more convenient and efficient to have a direct relationship between the two beans at the bean level. In other words, you should be able to get a reference to a Customer directly from the Order that belongs to that Customer without going through the CustomerID. Once you have a reference to the Customer, you could invoke methods to perform all kinds of operations on the Customer as well as joint operations on the Customer and the Order made by the Customer. In terms of data, it means you should be able to conduct queries on the Order bean that involve data from the entity represented by the Customer bean, such as "give me all the orders made by the customer Renee Kant."

> **NOTE** There are exactly two entity beans participating in any entity bean relationship. The relationship between the two beans may be one-to-one, one-to-many, or many-to-many. The term *one* or *many* here refers to the bean instance(s).

Instead of asking for the CustomerID from the Order, you would ask for a reference to the Customer. This is accomplished by replacing the `getCustomerID()` method (figure 9.1) with the `getCustomer()` method (figure 9.2) in the Order bean.

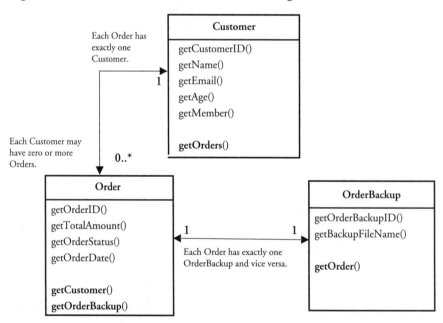

Figure 9.2 Relationships between the three beans shown by their component interfaces, Customer, Order, and OrderBackup; the relationships are represented by arrows. The number close to a bean indicates how many instances of this bean the partner bean may have; for example, a Customer may have zero or more orders.

The arrows in figure 9.2 show the relationships between the beans. The number close to a bean shows how many instances of this bean the partner bean's instance may have. This is called the *multiplicity* of the bean. For example, a Customer may have zero or more Orders, while an Order may belong only to one Customer. This means the Customer bean has a multiplicity of one and the Order bean has a multiplicity of many. Such a relationship is called one-to-many. Also the arrows between Order and OrderBackup show that an Order can have exactly one OrderBackup, and vice versa. Such a relationship is called one-to-one. In the following section, we discuss all three kinds of relationships: one-to-one, one-to-many, and many-to-many.

9.2   CONTAINER-MANAGED RELATIONSHIPS

The container manages a relationship between two beans by using the abstract get and set methods declared by the bean provider in the bean classes along with the CMR fields declared by the bean provider in the deployment descriptor. The relationship may be one-to-one, one-to-many, or many-to-many. In the following examples, we discuss these relationships for two entity beans, A and B, with instances denoted by ai or aij for A, and bi or bij for B, where i and j are integers. This means the instances of bean A would be denoted by a1, a2, a3, a12, a13, and so on. Bean A has methods `getB()` and `setB()` to manage its relationship with B, and bean B has methods `getA()` and `setA()` to manage its relationship with A. These methods would be declared by the bean provider and implemented by the container by using the information in the deployment descriptor provided by the bean provider.

9.2.1   One-to-one relationships

In a one-to-one relationship, bean A can have only one of bean B, and vice versa. By this we mean you can get a reference to the component interface of an instance of B by invoking a get method on an instance of A, and vice versa. You can also establish, or reestablish, the relationships between instances by invoking the set methods. Let's work through an example. Consider the following lines of code:

```
B b1 = a1.getB();
B b2 = a2.getB();
```

The `getB()` method returns exactly one instance of B. This shows the relationship between a1 and b1 and between a2 and b2, as shown in figure 9.3. Now, let's see what happens if a1, which already has a relationship with b1, tries to set up a relationship with b2. Assume the following line of code is executed:

```
a1.setB(a2.getB())
```

This would set the relationship between a1 and b2, which means the `getB()` method on a1 will return b2 and the `getA()` method on b2 will return a1. What happened to a1's relationship with b1? Remember? It is one-to-one; a1 can have a relationship with only one instance of B. So, b2, which was assigned to a2 before and is now

Before executing the line a1.setB(a2.getB())

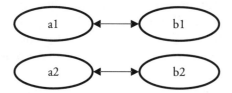

After executing the line a1.setB(a2.getB())

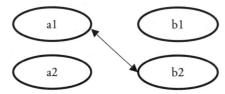

Figure 9.3
Example of reestablishing a one-to-one relationship between two beans, A and B. Note that the assignment is moved and not copied because each instance of one bean type can be related to only one instance of the other bean type.

assigned to a1, has to be moved and not copied. That means b2 will have no relationship with a2 anymore, nor will a1 have any relationship with b1 anymore. In other words, b2's relationship with a2 has been removed; therefore, `a2.getB()` will return null. Similarly, `b1.getA()` will return null as well. As a result, the following expressions will be true:

```
a2.getB() == null
b1.getA() == null
b2.isIdentical(a1.getB())
a1.isIdentical(b2.getA())
```

So, a2 no longer has any relationship with any instance of B, and b1 no longer has any relationship with any instance of A. Two relationships have been removed as a result of reestablishing one relationship. As shown in figure 9.3, the relationship between A and B has been reestablished.

When a bean can be associated with more than one instance of the other bean, the assignment is copied and not moved. This is the case in one-to-many relationships, which we explore next.

9.2.2 One-to-many relationships

In a one-to-many relationship, bean A can have more than one instance of bean B, but bean B may have only one instance of A. This means you can get a Collection of instances of B by invoking a get method on an instance of A, and you can get only one instance of A by invoking a get method on an instance of B. You can also establish or reestablish the relationships between instances by invoking set methods. For example, consider the following lines of code:

```
Collection b1 = a1.getB();
Collection b2 = a2.getB();
```

The getB() method returns b1, which is a Collection of instances of B, say b11, b12, b13, and so on. This shows the one-to-many relationship between a1 and the instances in the Collection b1, and between a2 and instances in the Collection b2, as shown in figure 9.4. Now assume the following line of code is executed:

```
a1.setB(a2.getB())
```

This would set up a relationship between a1 and b2. This means the getB() method on a1 returns b2, which is a Collection of b21, b22, b23, and so on. The getA() method on b21, b22, or b23 returns a1. Because B can have only one instance of A, the assignment of a1 has been moved (and not copied) from b1 to b2. So, b1i.getA() and a2.getB() will return null. Figure 9.4 shows how the relationship is reestablished as a result of the set method execution.

Now let's look at a many-to-one relationship, which would be from the perspective of B. Consider the following lines of code:

```
Collection b1 = a1.getB();
Collection b2 = a2.getB();
```

The getB() method returns b1, which is a Collection of instances of B, say b11, b12, b13, and so on. This shows the one-to-many relationship between a1 and the instances in the Collection b1, and between a2 and the instances in the Collection b2, as shown in figure 9.4. Now assume the following line of code is executed:

```
b11.setA(b21.getA())
```

The change of relationships as a result of the execution of this line is shown in figure 9.5. Because bean A can accept a relationship with multiple instances of bean

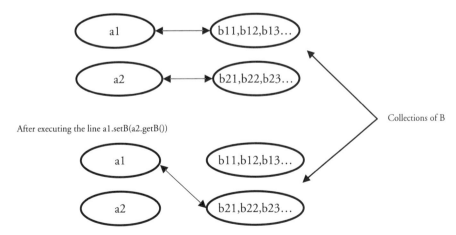

Figure 9.4 Example of reestablishing a one-to-many relationship between two beans, A and B. Note that the assignment is moved and not copied.

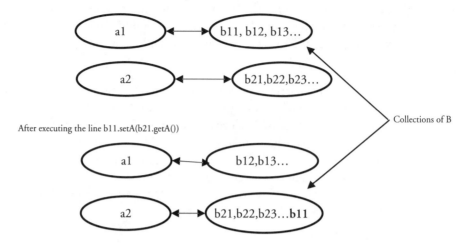

Before executing the line b11.setA(b21.getA())

After executing the line b11.setA(b21.getA())

Collections of B

Figure 9.5   Example of reestablishing a relationship between two beans, A and B, in a many-to-one relationship. Note that b11's relationship has been moved from a1 to a2, but the rest of the relationships have not been overwritten, unlike in figure 9.4.

B, the reassignment of b11 to a2 is not going to overwrite the existing relationships of a1 or a2. So again, it's only the one-to-one side of one-to-many relationships that causes the removal of the relationships when an instance that is already in a relationship establishes a new relationship.

> **NOTE**   If you reassign a bean instance to a different instance of the related bean whose multiplicity is one, the assignment is moved and not copied. For example, if an order is reassigned to another customer, the order is moved and not copied. This makes sense because due to the multiplicity, a particular order can have only one customer.

The most complex relationship is many to many, which we explore next.

9.2.3   Many-to-many relationships

In a many-to-many relationship, bean A can have more than one instance of bean B, and vice versa. You can get a Collection of instances of B by invoking a get method on an instance of A, and you can get a Collection of instances of A by invoking a get method on an instance of B. You can also establish or reestablish the relationships between instances by invoking set methods.

Many-to-many is the most complex relationship. However, in terms of reestablishing the relationships this is the simplest situation. From the previous two sections, it is easy to realize that if a relationship is reestablished in a many-to-many situation, it's not going to overwrite any existing relationship. So the instances survive. For example, if a student instance who is registered for four courses gets registered for another course, there is a new relationship between this other course and the student,

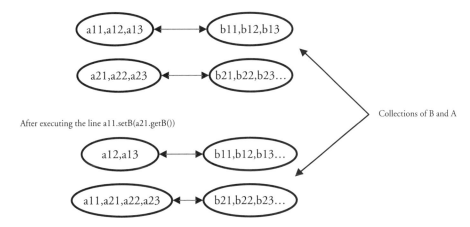

Before executing the line a11.setB(a21.getB())

After executing the line a11.setB(a21.getB())

Collections of B and A

Figure 9.6 Example of reestablishing a relationship between two beans, A and B, in a many-to-many relationship. Note that the relationship of a11 to b1i has been overwritten with the relationship of a11 to b2i, where i = 1,2,3, etc. The rest of the relationships have not been overwritten.

but it does not rewrite any existing relationship. In another scenario, the student may cancel the registration and reregister for a new set of courses. That will also not affect any relationship other than this student's relationship with the courses. Such a scenario is shown in figure 9.6.

A relationship between two beans is managed by using the set and get methods, called access methods, which are declared by the bean provider in the classes of the participating beans. The access methods are used not only for managing the relationships between the beans but also for managing the persistence of the beans.

9.3 MANAGING PERSISTENCE AND RELATIONSHIPS

Persistence management and relationship management are facilitated through fields called container-managed persistence (CMP) fields and container-managed relationship (CMR) fields, respectively. The CMP fields map to the columns of the database table, in other words, to the entity that the bean represents. A CMR field of a bean is the local interface type of the related bean or a Collection of it. To be more specific, the get method corresponding to a CMR field of a bean will return a reference to the local component interface of the related bean or a Collection of it. Therefore, a bean that does not have a local interface cannot be a target of a relationship. So, remember, beans are not interested in long-distance (remote) relationships.

The bean provider's responsibility is to declare a pair of get and set methods for each CMP field and a separate pair of set and get methods for each CMR field. The container implements the methods by using the declaration of these methods along with the information provided by the bean provider in the deployment descriptor.

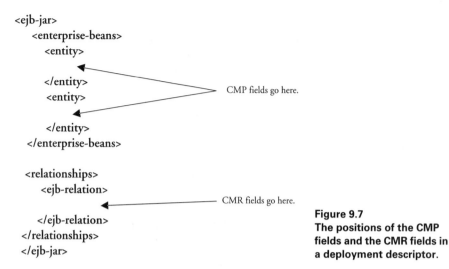

```
<ejb-jar>
    <enterprise-beans>
        <entity>

        </entity>              ◄──────────────  CMP fields go here.
        <entity>

        </entity>  ◄
    </enterprise-beans>


    <relationships>
        <ejb-relation>
                    ◄──────────────  CMR fields go here.
        </ejb-relation>
    </relationships>
</ejb-jar>
```

Figure 9.7
**The positions of the CMP
fields and the CMR fields in
a deployment descriptor.**

Figure 9.7 shows the positions of the CMP and CMR fields in the deployment descriptor of an application. Note that the CMP fields are declared in the `<entity>`, which is a subelement of the `<enterprise-beans>` element, while the CMR fields are declared in the `<ejb-relation>` element, which is a subelement of the `<relationships>` element. Both the `<enterprise-beans>` and the `<relationships>` elements are subelements of the `<ejb-jar>` element.

In the following sections, you will see the details of how a bean provider would declare the CMP and the CMR fields for our example of Customer and Order beans.

9.3.1   Container-managed persistent fields

The CMP fields of a bean map to the columns of the database table in which the entity lives. The bean provider declares a pair of abstract get and set methods in the bean class corresponding to each persistent field. These abstract methods would be implemented by the container using the information provided by the bean provider in the deployment descriptor. Listing 9.1 shows the CMP fields for the CustomerBean and the OrderBean (in our example) defined in the deployment descriptor. Only the relevant part of the deployment descriptor is shown.

Listing 9.1   The CMP fields for the OrderBean and the CustomerBean

```
1. <enterprise-beans>
2.   <entity>
3.     <display-name> OrderBean </display-name>
4.     <ejb-name>OrderBean</ejb-name>
5.     <local-home>OrderLocalHome</local-home>
6.     <local>OrderLocal</local>
7.     <ejb-class>OrderBean</ejb-class>

8.     <persistence-type>Container</persistence-type>
```

```
9.    <prim-key-class>java.lang.String</prim-key-class>
10.   <reentrant>False</reentrant>          ⟵┐ Indicates a single-threaded
11.   <cmp-version>2.x</cmp-version>           │ non-reentrant entity bean
12.   <abstract-schema-name>OrderSchema</abstract-schema-name>
13.   <cmp-field>
14.     <description>description goes here</description>
15.     <field-name>orderID</field-name>
16.   </cmp-field>
17.   <cmp-field>
18.     <description>description goes here</description>
19.     <field-name>totalAmount</field-name>
20.    </cmp-field>
21.   <cmp-field>
22.     <description>description goes here</description>
23.     <field-name>orderStatus</field-name>
24.   </cmp-field>
25.   <cmp-field>
26.     <description>description goes here</description>
27.     <field-name>orderDate</field-name>
28.   </cmp-field>

29.   <primkey-field>orderID</primkey-field>
30.   <security-identity>
31.     <description>description goes here</description>
32.     <use-caller-identity/>
33.   </security-identity>
34.   </entity>

35.   <entity>
36.     <display-name>CustomerBean</display-name>
37.     <ejb-name>CustomerBean</ejb-name>
38.     <local-home>CustomerLocalHome</local-home>
39.     <local>CustomerLocal</local>
40.     <ejb-class>CustomerBean</ejb-class>        ⟵┐ Indicates
41.     <persistence-type>Container</persistence-type>  │ Customer bean
42.     <prim-key-class>java.lang.String</prim-key-class> ⟵┘ is a CMP bean
43.     <reentrant>False</reentrant>
44.     <cmp-version>2.x</cmp-version>
45.     <abstract-schema-name>CustomerSchema</abstract-schema-name>
46.     <cmp-field>
47.       <description>description goes here</description>
48.       <field-name>customerID</field-name>
49.     </cmp-field>
50.     <cmp-field>                                 ⟵┐ Defines the
51.       <description>description goes here</description>  persistent
52.       <field-name>name</field-name>                    field, name
53.     </cmp-field>                                 ⟵┘
54.     <cmp-field>
55.       <description>description goes here</description>
56.       <field-name>age</field-name>
57.     </cmp-field>
58.     <cmp-field>
```

```
59.      <description>description goes here</description>
60.      <field-name>email</field-name>
61.    </cmp-field>
62.    <cmp-field>
63.      <description>description goes here</description>
64.      <field-name>member</field-name>
65.    </cmp-field>

66.    <primkey-field>customerID</primkey-field>
67.    <security-identity>
68.      <description>description goes here</description>
69.      <use-caller-identity/>
70.    </security-identity>
71.  </entity>
72. </enterprise-beans>
```

The description of the CMP fields and CMR fields provided by the bean provider through the deployment descriptors and the get and set methods is called the *abstract persistence schema*. The name is drawn from the fact that these fields are used to maintain persistence, and the persistence would actually be managed and implemented by the container, so at this stage it is abstract. Line 12 in listing 9.1 specifies the name for the OrderBean schema, while line 45 does the same for the CustomerBean schema. The abstract persistence schema name for a bean is defined in the element <abstract-schema-name>, which is a subelement of the <entity> element and which must be unique inside a deployment descriptor.

Lines 13 to 28 define the persistent fields for the OrderBean. Each field name is defined in the element <field-name>, which is a subelement of <cmp-field>. The field name maps to the column name in the database table, table 9.2 in this case. Note that the field type is not provided in the deployment descriptor. The container will get the type information from the get and set methods that you will see later in this chapter. As an exercise, locate the CMP fields defined for the CustomerBean in listing 9.1 and compare them with table 9.1 (hint: lines 46 to 65).

NOTE   No two schemas defined inside the same deployment descriptor may have the same name.

So, you inform the container about the persistent fields by defining them in the deployment descriptor and by declaring a pair of abstract get and set methods for each persistent field. The name of the field is given in the deployment descriptor, and the type (also the name) appears in the get and set methods. You do something very similar for the CMR fields as well.

9.3.2 Container-managed relationship fields

The relationship between two beans is defined within the element <ejb-relation>, which is a subelement of <relationships> in the deployment descriptor. The <ejb-relation> element contains exactly two <relationship-role> elements corresponding to the two beans participating in the relationship. The relationship between the OrderBean and the CustomerBean is defined in listing 9.2. Only the relevant part of the deployment descriptor is shown.

```
1. <relationships>
2.  <ejb-relation>
3.   <ejb-relationship-role>
4.     <ejb-relationship-role-name>
5.       CustomerBean
6.     </ejb-relationship-role-name>
7.     <multiplicity>One</multiplicity>
8.     <relationship-role-source>
9.       <ejb-name>CustomerBean</ejb-name>
10.     </relationship-role-source>
11.     <cmr-field>
12.      <cmr-field-name>orders</cmr-field-name>
13.      <cmr-field-type>java.util.Collection</cmr-field-type>
14.     </cmr-field>
15.   </ejb-relationship-role>

16.   <ejb-relationship-role>
17.    <ejb-relationship-role-name>
18.        OrderBean
19.      </ejb-relationship-role-name>
20.    <multiplicity>Many</multiplicity>
21.    <cascade-delete/>
22.    <relationship-role-source>
23.      <ejb-name>OrderBean</ejb-name>
24.    </relationship-role-source>
25.    <cmr-field>
26.       <cmr-field-name>customer</cmr-field-name>
27.    </cmr-field>
28.   </ejb-relationship-role>
29.  </ejb-relation>
30. </relationships>
```

The relationship role for the customer bean is defined in lines 3 to 15. The multiplicity of one means that the partner of CustomerBean (the OrderBean) may have only one instance of CustomerBean; that is, an order can belong to only one customer. The <ejb-name> element under the <relationship-role-source> element specifies which bean is playing this role. This ejb-name must match the ejb-name given to this bean in the <entity> element. The <cmr-field> and its child elements identify the abstract CMR field declared in the bean class. The <cmr-field-name> must match the name used in the get and set methods; for example, orders match with getOrders() and setOrders(). The <cmr-field-type> element specifies the type of CMR field. It is used only when the get method is going to return a Collection, that is, when the partner bean has a multiplicity of many. The value of the element <cmr-field-type> could be either java.util.Collection or java.util.Set.

The role of the OrderBean is defined in lines 16 to 28. It has a multiplicity of many; that is, an instance of the CustomerBean may have many instances of the OrderBean but not vice versa because CustomerBean has a multiplicity of one. By having an instance of a bean, we mean a reference to the local component interface of the instance, EJBLocalObject, which would be returned by the get method. Note that the <cmr-field-type> element is missing from the role of the OrderBean. This is because CustomerBean has a multiplicity of one, and we do not have to decide whether the return type of the getCustomer() method is going to be the Collection or the Set of the local component interface of the CustomerBean. It is simply going to be the local component interface type of the CustomerBean.

NOTE   A CMR field of a bean is always the local component interface type of the related bean or a Collection of it. This means the get method corresponding to the CMR field would return a reference to the local component interface of the related bean or a Collection of it. The return type of Collection CMR fields can return either java.util.Collection or java.util.Set, and the bean developer must specify it in the deployment descriptor.

The element <cascade-delete/> in line 21 is an instruction to the container that when a Customer instance is deleted, all the instances of Order related to that customer must be deleted as well. It needs to happen because an Order has only one customer, and if that customer is being deleted, the order would have nowhere to go for the customer information. Note that there is no <cascade-delete> in the role of the CustomerBean. This is because the CustomerBean is related to the OrderBean, which has a multiplicity of many. In other words, if an order is deleted, the customer does not have to be deleted because other orders may be associated with that customer.

ALERT   The CMP fields do not have <cmp-field-type> elements. The container figures out the type from the get and set methods. The CMR fields do have <cmr-field-type> elements if the multiplicity of the partner bean is many.

So, entity bean persistence and the relationships between any two entity beans are managed by the container by using the information provided by the bean provider through the deployment descriptor and the abstract get/set access methods. In this section, you learned how to provide this information in the deployment descriptor. The next section shows you how the get and set access methods fit into the class code and how they relate to the deployment descriptor.

9.4 PROGRAMMING FOR CMP AND CMR

The container implements the access methods for entity bean persistence and the entity bean relationships. These methods are declared in the bean class by the bean developer and are related to the CMP and CMR fields declared in the deployment descriptor. Listing 9.3 shows the code for the `OrderBean` class in our example.

> **Listing 9.3 The OrderBean class. Lines 14 to 24 show the abstract access methods for the CMP and CMR fields.**

```
1. import javax.ejb.*;
2. import javax.naming.*;
3. import java.util.*;
4. public abstract class OrderBean implements  EntityBean {
5. // Instance variables
6. // define status code
7.  static final int STATUS_PENDING = 1;
8.  static final int STATUS_APPROVED = 2;
9.  static final int STATUS_SHIPPED = 3;
10. static final int STATUS_CANCELLED= 4;
11. // EntityContext
12.      private EntityContext  context;
13. // getters and setters for the CMP fields
14. public abstract String getOrderID();                    ◁┐
15. public abstract void setOrderID(String id);             │
16  public abstract  double getTotalAmount();               │  Methods
17. public abstract void setTotalAmount(double amount);     │  corresponding
18. public abstract int getOrderStatus();                   │  to CMP fields
19. public abstract void setOrderStatus(int status);        │
20. public abstract Date getOrderDate();                    │
21. public abstract void setOrderDate(Date, date);          ◁┘
22. // getter and setter for a CMR field
23. public abstract CustomerLocal getCustomer();
24. public abstract void setCustomer(CustomerLocal customer);


25. // Select methods
26. public abstract Collection ejbSelectGetAllOrders()
       throws FinderException;
27. public abstract Collection ejbSelectGetOrdersByCustomer
       (String cust)throws FinderException ;
28. public abstract Collection
       ejbSelectGetOrdersByCustomerAndStatus
       (String cust, String   status) throws FinderException;

29. // Business methods
30. public String fetchOrderID() {
       return getOrderID()
    }
31. public int fetchOrderStatus() {
32.    return getOrderStatus()
```

```
33. }
34. public void changeOrderStatus(int status) {
35.     setOrderStatus(status)
36. }
37. public String fetchCustomerID() {
38.     return getCustomerID();
39. }
40. public String fetchTotalAmount() {
41.     return getTotalAmount();
42. }

43. //Home business methods
44. public String ejbHomeFetchAllOrders( ) {
45.   String orderList = null;
46.   try {
47.     Collection orderCollection = ejbSelectGetAllOrders ( );
48.     Iterator orderIt = orderCollection.iterator();
49.     while ( orderIt.hasnext()) {
50.      Order order = (Order) orderIt.next();
51.      orderList + = " " + order.fetchOrderID();
52.     }
53.   }catch(Exception ex) {
54.     // handle exception
55.   }
56.     return orderList;
57. }
58. public String ejbHomeFetchAllOrdersByCustomer
    ➥ (CustomerLocal customer ) {
59.   String orderList = null;
60.   try {
61.     String custId = customer.fetchCustomerID();
62.     Collection orderCollection =
        ➥ ejbSelectGetAllOrdersByCustomer(custId);
63.     Iterator orderIt = orderCollection.iterator();
64.     while ( orderIt.hasnext()) {
65.      Order order = (Order) orderIt.next();
66.      orderList + = " " + order.getOrderID();
67.     }
68.   }catch (Exception ex) {
69.         // handle exception
70.     }
71.       return orderList;
72. }

73. public String ejbHomeFetchAllOrdersByCustomerAndStatus
    ➥ (CustomerLocal customer, String Status ) {
74.   String orderList = null;
75.   try {
76.     String custId = customer.fetchCustomerID();
77.     Collection orderCollection =
        ➥ ejbSelectGetAllOrdersByCustomerAndStatus (cust_id, status);
78.     Iterator orderIt = orderCollection.iterator();
```

```
79.     while ( orderIt.hasnext()) {
80.       Order order = (Order) orderIt.next();
81.       orderList + = " " + order.getOrderID();
82.     }
83.   } catch (Exception ex) {
84.       // handle exception
85.   }
86.       return orderList;
87.   }

88. //Entity  callbacks
89. public String ejbCreate(String orderId, CustomerLocal customer,
    ➡ double totalAmount, int status, Date date) {
90.   setOrderID(orderId);
91.   setTotalAmount(totalAmount);
92.   setOrderStatus(status);
93.   setOrderDate(Date);
94.   return NULL;
    }

95. public void ejbPostCreate(String orderId, CustomerLocal
    ➡ customer,double totalAmount, int status, Date date) {
96.   setCustomer(customer);
97. }

98. public void setEntityContext (EntityContext etx) {
99.    context = etx; }
100.   public void ejbLoad ( ) {  }
101.   public void ejbStore ( ) {  }
102.   public void ejbActivate ( ) { }
103.   public void ejbPassivate ( ) { }
104.   public void ejbRemove ( ) { }
105.   public void unsetEntityContext () {
106.   context = null;
107. }
```

Lines 14 to 21 show the declarations for the get and set methods related to the CMP fields. Note that each CMP field has it own pair of get and set methods. For example, consider the CMP field OrderID, which is a column in the Order database table (table 9.2). This field is entered into the deployment descriptor (listing 9.1, lines 13 to 16) as a value of the element <field-name> inside the element <cmp-field>. Note how the <field-name> orderID is used in the method name getOrderID() and setOrderID() in lines 14 and 15 of listing 9.3. This syntax is mandatory. The CMP access methods must be declared public and abstract, and the argument type of the set method must match the return type of the get method. The container learns from the return type of the get method (or the argument type of the set method) about the type of the CMP field that it would use to implement this method. Note that there is no type defined for the CMP field in the deployment descriptor.

In the case of CMR, instead of methods returning or setting the CMP fields that map to a database table, you define methods that return or set a reference to the local component interface of the related bean or a Collection of it. Lines 23 and 24 in listing 9.3 declare the abstract get and set methods for the CMR field customer defined in the deployment descriptor (line 24, listing 9.2). Again, notice that the syntax is the same as in the case of CMP fields. The get and set methods corresponding to the <cmr-field-name> customer are getCustomer() and setCustomer().

The following are the important points to remember about CMP and CMR fields and their corresponding access methods:

- The names of the CMP and CMR fields defined in the deployment descriptor must be valid Java identifiers beginning with a lowercase letter, such as "orders" and "customer."

- The bean provider must declare the class containing the CMP and CMR fields as abstract. The container provides the implementation for this class.

- A CMP or a CMR field is not declared in the class as a variable; it exists only in the form of a pair of accessor methods. The bean provider must declare an abstract get and set method for each CMP field and CMR field.

- The accessor methods must contain the name of the corresponding field (CMP or CMR) with the first letter of the field name uppercased and prefixed by get or set, for example, getCustomer() and setCustomer() for the CMR field customer.

- The get accessor method for a CMR field with a multiplicity of one should return a reference to the local component interface of the related bean. Get methods for fields with a multiplicity of many should return a Collection (java.util.Collection or java.util.Set) of references to the local component interface.

- The return type of CMP get methods must match the argument type of the corresponding set method.

- The accessor methods for the CMR fields must not be exposed in the remote interface of an entity bean.

ALERT   The CMP and CMR fields must not be declared as variables in the bean class. They are accessed only through the corresponding get and set methods.

When two beans are in a relationship, removing one may hurt the other. In the next section, we discuss how to handle this.

Lines 26 to 28 in listing 9.3 declare abstract ejbSelect methods, which were discussed, in general, in the previous chapter. These methods, used to make the database queries, are also implemented by the container. The bean developer tells the container how to implement them by giving the required information in the deployment descriptor. That information is given using the language called EJB-QL, which is covered in the next chapter.

The relationships create dependencies, and that complicates the removal of an entity. Let's explore this issue next.

9.5 RELATIONSHIPS AND REMOVE PROTOCOLS

The remove protocols refer to the ways entities may be removed. In chapter 8, we discussed the use of remove methods for removing an entity. However, when two beans are related to each other, removal of an entity may create complications. In order to handle various situations, EJB offers the following two ways to remove entities:

- Invoke the `remove()` method either on the home interface or on the component interface of the entity bean instance that represents the entity. You have seen this in the previous three chapters.
- Write the cascade-delete specification in the deployment descriptor. We mentioned this approach earlier in this chapter. Note, however, that cascade-delete is an option for maintaining referential integrity and not a way for a client to remove an entity.

In both cases, the container invokes the `ejbRemove()` method of the appropriate bean instance. The cascade-delete may cause the container to invoke an `ejbRemove()` on several bean instances. For example, consider that a `remove()` is called on the interface of a CustomerBean. This would cause the container to invoke the `ejbRemove()` method on the corresponding instance of the CustomerBean. Assume that five orders are related to this customer bean, and the OrderBean has cascade-delete specified in its ejb-relationship-role in the deployment descriptor. This would cause the container to invoke `ejbRemove()` on all the OrderBean instances related to the customer bean instance on which the `ejbRemove()` method was invoked.

The three most important takeaways from this chapter are

- The relationship between two entity beans reflects the relationship between the entities the two beans represent. The container manages the relationship by using the CMR fields that you declared in the deployment descriptor and as abstract methods in the bean class.
- The container uses multiplicity in a relationship to maintain the referential integrity of the data. For example, a one-to-many relationship may mean that when an instance of one entity gets an ejbRemove call from the container, multiple instances of the related bean will also get the ejbRemove call from the container.
- A CMR field declared in the deployment descriptor determines the names of the corresponding get and set methods declared in the bean class: they must match.

9.6 SUMMARY

A container-managed relationship exists between exactly two entity beans. The container manages the relationship through the container-managed relationship (CMR) fields declared by the bean provider in the deployment descriptor. The bean provider also declares a pair of abstract get and set methods, called accessor methods, corresponding to each CMR field in the bean class. The CMR fields are never declared as variables in the bean class; they exist only in the accessor methods, from the viewpoint of a bean provider. The relationship between two entity beans is set up in terms of the local component interfaces. This means that the return type of a get method and the argument type of the set method for a CMR field of a bean are references to the local component interface of the related bean or a Collection of it, depending on whether the multiplicity of the related bean is one or many. If the return type is a Collection, then it must be either java.util.Collection or java.util.Set, and it must be specified in the deployment descriptor. An entity bean that does not have a local component interface cannot become the target of a relationship.

The accessor methods must be declared public and abstract, and they must contain the name of the corresponding CMR field with the first letter uppercased and prefixed by get or set. The CMP and CMR fields are declared in different areas of the deployment descriptor: the CMP fields in the subelements of the <enterprise-beans> element and the CMR fields in the subelements of the <relationships> element. Depending on how many instances of an entity bean are related to another bean (the multiplicity), the relationship between two entity beans may be one-to-one, one-to-many, or many-to-many.

In a nutshell, the container manages the persistence and the relationships through the CMP and CMR fields defined by the bean provider in the deployment descriptor along with the accessor methods for these fields declared in the bean class. The container implements the accessor methods in the bean class.

Comprehend

- The relationship between the get/set accessor methods and the CMP fields in the deployment descriptor
- The relationship between the get/set accessor methods and the CMR fields in the deployment descriptor
- The difference between the get/set accessor methods for the CMP and the CMR fields.
- How the multiplicity maintains the referential integrity of the entities

Look out

- The get/set accessor methods corresponding to CMR and CMP fields must be declared public and abstract.
- The return type of a CMP field's get method must match the argument type of its set method. The same is true for a CMR field.
- The return type of a get method and the argument of a set method corresponding to a CMR field must be the local component interface type of the related bean or a Collection of it, depending on the multiplicity of the relationship.
- The CMP and CMR fields must not be defined as variables in the bean class. From the bean provider's perspective they are virtual fields represented only by pairs of get/set methods.

Memorize

- The names and locations of the elements involved in defining a CMP field in the deployment descriptor
- The names and locations of the elements involved in defining a CMR field in the deployment descriptor
- The difference in the structure of the `<cmp-field>` and `<cmr-field>` in the deployment descriptor

Some questions may have more than one correct answer. Choose all that apply.

1. Which of the following are the responsibilities of a bean provider for an entity bean using container-managed persistence and container-managed relationships?

   a. The bean provider must define the CMR fields in the deployment descriptor.
   b. The bean provider must declare the get and set methods in the bean class.
   c. The bean provider must implement the get and set methods in the bean class.
   d. The bean provider must declare the CMR fields as variables in the bean class.
   e. None of the above.

2. Which of the following statements are true about an entity bean that has a bidirectional container-managed relationship with another bean?

   a. The bean must have a local component interface.
   b. The bean must have a remote component interface.
   c. The return type of the get method for its CMR field must be RMI-IIOP compatible.
   d. The get method return type may be java.util.List.
   e. The bean should have only a local component interface and no remote interface.

3. Which of the following are possibly valid tags in defining the type of a CMR field in a deployment descriptor?

   a. `<cmr-field-type> java.util.List </cmr-field-type>`
   b. `<cmr-field-type> java.util.Map </cmr-field-type>`
   c. `<cmr-field-type> java.util.Collection </cmr-field-type>`
   d. `<cmr-field-type> java.util.Set </cmr-field-type>`
   e. `<cmr-field> java.util.Collection</cmr-field>`

4. Which of the following are valid declarations for the get method corresponding to the CMR field orders where the CMR field points to the Order bean that has the remote component interface Order and the local component interface OrderLocal ?

a. `public abstract Order getOrders();`

b. `public abstract OrderLocal getOrders();`

c. `private abstract Order getOrders();`

d. `private abstract OrderLocal getOrders();`

e. `public abstract OrderLocal getOrder();`

5. Which of the following statements are true about an entity bean that uses container-managed persistence and relationships?

    a. It can have a relationship with only one other bean.

    b. It can have a relationship with many other beans.

    c. It can have a relationship with only a session bean.

    d. Its class must be declared abstract by the bean provider.

6. Which of the following deployment descriptor elements are used to declare the name of a CMR field?

    a. `<cmr-field> teacher </cmr-field>`

    b. `< cmr-field-name> teacher </cmr-field-name>`

    c. `<field-name> teacher </field-name>`

    d. `<field-name> Teacher </field-name>`

    e. `<cmr-name> teacher </cmr-name>`

7. Which of the following statements are true for an entity bean that uses a container to manage its persistence and relationships?

    a. The type of a CMP field is determined from the corresponding get and set methods.

    b. The type of a CMR field is determined from the corresponding get and set methods.

    c. The type of a CMP field is declared in the deployment descriptor.

    d. The type of a CMR field must be declared in the deployment descriptor if it is a Collection.

    e. The type of a CMP or CMR field is declared inside the bean class in the form of a variable declaration.

8. Which of the following statements are true about the relationships between entity beans that use container-managed persistence?

    a. The relationship can be only bidirectional.

    b. The relationship can be only unidirectional.

    c. The relationship may be one-to-one, one-to-many, or many-to-many.

    d. Only two bean instances at maximum may be involved in a relationship.

9. Consider the following lines in the deployment descriptor:

```
1. <ejb-relationship-role>
2.    <ejb-relationship-role-name>
3.        OrderBean
4.      </ejb-relationship-role-name>
5.    <multiplicity>Many</multiplicity>
6.    <cascade-delete />
7.    <relationship-role-source>
8.    <ejb-name>OrderBean</ejb-name>
9.    </relationship-role-source>
10.   <cmr-field>
11.       <cmr-field-name>
12.           customer
13.         </cmr-field-name>
14.   </cmr-field>
15. </ejb-relationship-role>
```

Line 6 in the above listing means which of the following?

   a. If a customer is deleted, all the orders related to that customer will be deleted.
   b. If a customer is deleted, all the orders related to all the customers will be deleted.
   c. If an order is deleted, the customer related to the orders will also be deleted.
   d. If all the orders related to a customer are deleted, the customer will be deleted too.

10. Consider the following relationship between two beans, Order and BackupOrder:

o1 ↔ b1
o2 ↔ b2

where o1 and o2 represent the instances of the Order bean and b1 and b2 represent the instances of the BackupOrder bean, and the relationship shown is one to one. Now, the following code is executed:

```
b1.setOrder(b2.getOrder())
```

After the execution of this code, which of the following will be true?

   a. o1.getBackupOrder() == null
   b. o2. getBackupOrder == null
   c. b1.getOrder() == null
   d. b2.getOrder() == null
   e. None of the above

C H A P T E R   1 0

EJB query language

EXAM OBJECTIVES

9.1 Identify correct and incorrect syntax for an EJB QL query including the SELECT, FROM, and WHERE clauses.

9.2 Identify correct and incorrect statements or examples about the purpose and use of EJB QL.

9.3 Identify correct and incorrect conditional expressions, between expressions, in expressions, like expressions, and comparison expressions.

INTRODUCTION

The Enterprise JavaBeans query language (EJB QL) allows a bean provider to write SQL-like statements in the deployment descriptor. Entity beans represent entities in a database, and clients use some methods exposed in the client view to perform operations on the entity through the entity bean. In container-managed persistence, the container generates the database access code. That means the database-query-related methods, such as find methods declared by the bean provider in the home interface and select methods declared in the bean class, are implemented by the container. The bean provider tells the container how to implement these methods by declaring the CMP fields, the CMR fields, and the EJB QL queries in the deployment descriptor.

In this chapter, we will explore the basics of EJB QL. You will see that EJB QL queries consist of clauses that use a navigation path, operators, and expressions. We will also explore the find and select methods that the container will implement. We will then examine the missing pieces between the find and select methods on one end and database queries on the other end. To accomplish this, we will investigate three avenues: the connection of find and select methods with EJB QL queries; the structure of EJB QL queries; and what the EJB QL queries return and how it is affected by the navigation path, operators, and expressions.

10.1   THE ROLE OF EJB QL IN PERSISTENCE

EJB QL allows a bean provider to write SQL-like statements without making assumptions about the underlying database system. This means EJB QL lets you write portable queries. EJB QL is only one piece of the persistence puzzle. When we talk about entity bean persistence, we are referring to database-related methods (find and select methods) declared by the bean provider, implemented by the container, and used by the client to interact with the entity represented by the entity bean. What happens between these declarations of methods and the database tables? How does the container know how to implement these methods? In this section, you will get the answers to these questions.

10.1.1   Pieces of the persistence puzzle

You have seen find and select methods in previous chapters (6 to 9), which you declare in the home interface and the bean class, respectively. You also know that the container will actually implement these methods. The puzzle is how the container knows how to implement these methods. The three pieces used in solving this puzzle are find and select methods, CMP/CMR fields, and EJB QL. The bean provider writes EJB QL queries in order to facilitate the implementation of the find and select methods by the container. Recall that the find methods are defined by the bean provider in the home interface of an entity bean and are not mentioned in the bean class. In contrast, the bean provider declares the select methods in the bean class, but they are not exposed in the bean interfaces.

The bean provider specifies how to implement these methods by providing the following information in the deployment descriptor:

- CMP fields
- CMR fields
- EJB QL queries

We discussed CMP and CMR fields in chapter 9. The CMP fields of an entity bean map to the columns of the database table in which the entity lives, and a CMR field relates an entity bean to another entity bean. EJB QL queries are based on selection and navigation by using the CMP and CMR fields. The following list shows how all the pieces fit together:

- The bean provider declares the find methods in the home interface of an entity bean.
- The bean provider also declares the ejbSelect methods in the bean class.
- The bean provider defines the bean's CMP and CMR fields in the deployment descriptor.
- The bean provider defines the EJB QL queries in the deployment descriptor, using the names of the CMP and CMR fields.
- The bean provider also declares abstract getter and setter methods in the bean class for each CMP and CMR field.
- The container generates the database access code corresponding to the EJB QL queries and implements the getter, setter, find, and select methods.
- When a client calls a find method, or a business method that uses an ejbSelect method, the container executes the database access code it generated.

A CMP field of an entity bean declared in the deployment descriptor will match a pair of abstract get and set methods declared in the bean class, and it will also map to the columns of a database table. The CMP and CMR fields are part of the abstract schema of the bean that makes the connection of the bean class with the database table.

10.1.2 From abstract schema to database table

You can think of *abstract persistence schema* as a fancy name for the CMP and CMR fields defined in the deployment descriptor. EJB QL allows the bean provider to write queries based on the CMP and CMR field names. The CMP fields correspond to columns in a database table, as shown in figure 10.1 for the OrderBean. Note that the OrderBean doesn't have a CMP field for CustomerID. We don't need it because we have access to the CustomerBean through the CMR field customer.

Figure 10.1 shows the mapping of CMP fields to the database table. What is missing is the query. To help the container fill this gap, the bean provider provides an EJB QL query corresponding to each select or find method in the deployment descriptor. As an example, consider the following method that the bean provider declares in the OrderBean class:

```
public abstract Collection ejbSelectGetAllOrders()
    throws FinderException;
```

To support this method, the bean provider writes the following code in the deployment descriptor:

```
<query>
   <query-method>
```

```
        <method-name>ejbSelectGetAllOrders</method-name>
        <method-params />
    </query-method>
    <ejb-ql>
            SELECT   OBJECT  (o)  FROM  OrderSchema  o
    </ejb-ql>
</query>
```

This `<query>` element goes inside the `<entity>` element along with the `<cmp-field>` elements. The deployment tool will convert this EJB QL query into a SQL query at the time of deployment. A word of caution is in order here. The sample mapping and translation of EJB QL to SQL are described here to clarify the semantics of EJB QL. There are multiple ways to define a mapping to a set of tables in a relational database, and this area is beyond the scope of the EJB spec. The database does not even have to be a relational database. The result of a query must be a CMP field type or the abstract schema type.

You have already seen in chapter 9 how to declare an abstract schema (for example, OrderSchema) and CMP field in the deployment descriptor.

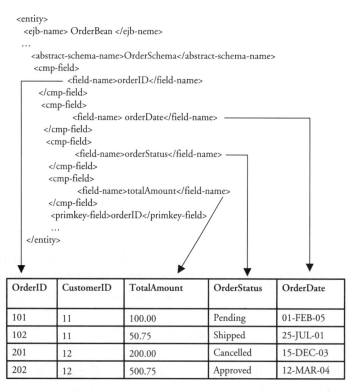

Figure 10.1 Mapping the CMP fields in the deployment descriptor to columns in a database table

10.2 ABSTRACT SCHEMA AND QUERY SYNTAX

The abstract schema for an entity bean is declared in the deployment descriptor in terms of the abstract schema name and the CMP fields. An EJB QL query returns either the CMP fields or the abstract schema type. Returning the entity bean's abstract schema means returning the entity itself.

EJB QL is a very simple language with SQL-like syntax, which we explore next.

10.2.1 EJB QL syntax and definitions

Like any other language, EJB QL has syntax—a set of rules that must be followed in order to use the language correctly. To put the syntax in perspective, recall that the bean provider uses EJB QL to define portable queries for entity beans with container-managed persistence. To be more precise, EJB QL queries are written for the following two kinds of methods:

- The find methods declared in the home interface of an entity bean by the bean provider
- The select methods declared in the entity bean class by the bean provider

The container uses an EJB QL query to generate database access code in order to implement the method to which the query is tied.

> **NOTE** EJB QL queries are written for the find and select methods. The find methods are declared by the bean provider in the home interface of the bean, while the select methods are declared by the bean provider in the bean class and are not exposed to the client.

An EJB QL query is composed of two mandatory clauses, SELECT and FROM, and one optional clause, WHERE. The SELECT clause determines the type of the objects or values to be returned by the query, while the WHERE clause is used to limit the results that would be returned. The FROM clause specifies the schema name to which the expressions in the SELECT and WHERE clauses apply. The structure of the EJB QL query is shown in figure 10.2.

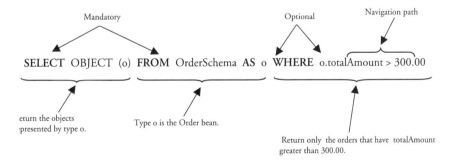

Figure 10.2   Different pieces of an EJB QL query. It is composed of three clauses: SELECT, FROM, and WHERE. The WHERE clause is optional, and the keyword AS is optional too.

The purpose of this query is to find and return all the instances of OrderBean that have a `totalAmount` value greater than 300.00. The variable o declared in the FROM clause is called an *identification variable* (a valid identifier declared in the FROM clause), and it is used to represent the bean in the rest of the query. You must declare an identification variable, but the AS keyword itself is optional. The expression o.`totalAmount` in the WHERE clause is called a *navigation path*, and it means "the totalAmount field of the OrderBean."

10.2.2 Handling the query return types

The query return type of an EJB QL query is specified by the SELECT clause in the query. It must be either the schema type itself or a CMP field from the schema. When the return type is a CMP field type, then the SELECT part of the query looks like this:

```
SELECT  o.orderStatus  FROM OrderSchema o
```

where `orderStatus` is a CMP field declared in the deployment descriptor as

```
<cmp-field>
         <field-name> orderStatus </field-name>
</cmp-field>
```

Note that no keyword OBJECT is used in the above query. However, when the return type is an abstract schema type, then you do use the keyword OBJECT in the SELECT clause of the query:

```
SELECT  OBJECT (o)  FROM OrderSchema o
```

where `OrderSchema` is the abstract schema for an OrderBean declared in the deployment descriptor as

```
<abstract-schema-name> OrderSchema </abstract-schema-name>
```

Remember that the abstract schema type refers to the bean itself, which is an object, while the CMP field is only a field inside the object and not the bean object. The rule of thumb is that if you are using a dot to navigate a path in the SELECT clause of your query, you should not use the keyword OBJECT. In the previous queries, the identification variable o is called a *range variable* because it ranges over the entire entity bean, while o.`orderStatus` is called a *single-valued path expression*.

If a query returns a CMP field, the type would be determined from the corresponding get (or set) method. However, if it returns an abstract schema, then what is this type, really? Recall that an abstract schema refers to the entity bean in which it is defined in the deployment descriptor. So, the abstract schema type is the type of component interface of the bean. Is it the local component interface (`EJBLocalObject`) or the remote component interface (`EJBObject`)? The container will figure this out by determining from which interface the query was invoked: local or remote. The return type of an EJB QL in this case is a component interface or a Collection of it.

NOTE   The return type of an EJB QL query is either a CMP field type or the abstract schema type of an entity bean. If it is the abstract schema type, this implies that it is the component interface type of the bean or a collection of it.

The results to be returned from a query are selected from the query domain, and the selection may involve navigation. So, let's explore query domains and navigation next.

10.3   QUERY DOMAINS AND NAVIGATION

In SQL, one may ask what tables can be included in a query. Similarly, in an EJB QL, it's a valid question to ask what beans can be included in a query. This is just another way of asking what the domain of the query is. So, the domain of an EJB QL query is the scope within which you can build the query. The domain includes the abstract schema types of all the CMP entity beans defined in the same deployment descriptor, that is, all the CMP entity beans in a single ejb-jar file.

You can write queries within the schema of one bean, or you can write queries involving more than one bean, for example, by navigating from one entity bean to another by using the CMR fields in the EJB QL query.

10.3.1   Navigating the path

In an EJB QL query, you can return either the CMP field type or the abstract schema type. When you are writing the `SELECT` clause to return a CMP field type, you are navigating a path within the bean. You can also navigate a path to the related bean, and while doing so you must follow some rules in order for the queries to be valid.

Navigating within the bean

Objects or values related to an entity bean are accessed by a navigation path expression in an EJB QL query. A path expression is composed of an identification variable and a CMP or CMR field separated by a dot. When the field in the path expression is a CMR field, that is, the related bean object, it may be extended. A single-valued path expression, when it resolves to a CMP field, cannot be extended.

You saw examples of both cases (involving CMP and CMR) in the previous section. However, note that although both the CMP field and the abstract schema of a bean are allowed as return types, the multivalued (Collection) CMR field is not. As an example, assume the OrderBean has a one-to-many relationship with the LineItem bean. Consider, for instance, the following query:

```
SELECT  o.orderStatus  FROM OrderSchema o
```

It is valid because `orderStatus` is a CMP field of OrderBean. Now consider a slightly different query:

```
SELECT  o.lineitems  FROM OrderSchema o
```

where the CMR field `lineitems` is a collection of instances of the abstract schema type LineItem. It is not a valid query because `lineitems` is a multivalued CMR field of the OrderBean, and hence you cannot return it from the query. Although you cannot return a multivalued CMR field, you can use a CMR field for navigation, as you will see next.

Navigating to the related bean

You cannot navigate to a multivalued CMR field in the SELECT clause, but you can navigate through the CMR field in the WHERE clause to limit the query results. Consider the following example:

```
SELECT OBJECT (o) FROM OrderSchema o WHERE o.customer.age > 30
```

This means return all the orders made by customers older than 30. In other words, return references to the component interfaces of the OrderBean instances that are related to the instances of CustomerBean that represent customers with the value of the age field greater than 30. However, you should always make sure no Collection is involved in the navigation path. For example, the following query is invalid:

```
SELECT  OBJECT (c)  FROM  CustomerSchema  c
WHERE  c.orders.totalAmount > 300.00
```

This query is invalid because `c.orders` refers to a Collection of orders, while `totalAmount` is a field corresponding to one order. You also need to make sure that you are not comparing apples with oranges. For example, look at this query:

```
SELECT OBJECT (o) FROM OrderSchema o WHERE o.customer >30
```

This is invalid because `customer` refers to a bean, and the number 30 may become a value for a field of the bean but not the bean itself. However, sometimes you may need to use Collections during navigation in order to make a query. There is a way to handle that. Let's explore it next.

10.3.2   Dealing with Collections in path navigation

You cannot compose a path expression from another path expression that evaluates to a Collection. For example, `c.orders.totalAmount` is invalid because `c.orders` evaluates to a Collection. It makes sense to ask for the total amount of an order, but it does not make sense to ask for the total amount of a Collection of orders. For example, this query is invalid:

```
SELECT  OBJECT (c)  FROM  CustomerSchema  c
WHERE  c.orders.totalAmount > 300.00
```

But what if we do want to get all the customers who have orders over 300.00? This is where the IN operator comes to the rescue. The following is a valid query to accomplish this:

```
SELECT   OBJECT (c)
FROM  CustomerSchema  c, IN (c.orders) o
WHERE  o.totalAmount > 300.00
```

This query examines all the orders from each customer and returns all the customers who have made one or more orders with the amount greater than 300.00. Because of the `IN` operator, `o` represents an individual order and not a Collection; it loops through all the orders and checks the `totalAmount` field on each order.

So, navigation within the query domain lets you have control over the query return in two ways: controlling the return type by navigating in the `SELECT` clause and putting constraints on the returns by navigating in the `WHERE` clause.

Two players determine the return of a query: identifiers and input parameters, which we explore next.

10.4   IDENTIFIERS AND INPUT PARAMETERS

You use an identifier, for example, to determine the return type of a query and input parameters to let the client put constraints on the return.

10.4.1   Identifiers

An identifier is an identification variable declared in the `FROM` clause and used in the `SELECT` clause of an EJB QL query. In addition to the standard Java programming language rules for naming, you must exercise the following constraints in naming identifiers:

- Do not use any of the EJB QL reserved words: `SELECT`, `FROM`, `WHERE`, `DISTINCT`, `OBJECT`, `NULL`, `TRUE`, `FALSE`, `NOT`, `AND`, `OR`, `BETWEEN`, `LIKE`, `IN`, `AS`, `UNKNOWN`, `EMPTY`, `MEMBER`, `OF`, and `IS`.

- Do not use other SQL reserved words either, because they could possibly be used as EJB QL reserved words in future versions.

- Do not use the value of an `<ejb-name>` or `<abstract-schema-name>` element for naming an identifier because `<ejb-name>` and `<abstract-schema-name>` must be unique in the deployment descriptor.

When you avoid the EJB QL reserved words in naming an identifier, keep in mind that EJB QL is not case sensitive (but the fields are). For example, the following is an invalid query:

```
SELECT   OBJECT (products)  FROM   Products  products
```

In this query, `Products` is the abstract schema name and `products` is the identifier. Considering that EJB QL is not case sensitive, we have a name conflict between the schema name and the identifier name. A correct form of the query could be

```
SELECT   OBJECT (p) FROM   Products p
```

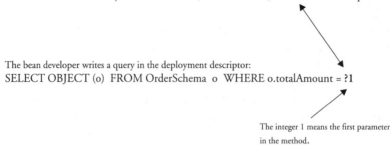

The bean developer declares a method in the bean class:
public abstract Collection ejbSelectGetOrders(double **amount**) throws FinderException

The bean developer writes a query in the deployment descriptor:
SELECT OBJECT (o) FROM OrderSchema o WHERE o.totalAmount = ?1

The integer 1 means the first parameter
in the method.

Figure 10.3 A query refers to an input parameter in a method by an integer number that specifies the position of the parameter in the method, such as first parameter, second parameter, and so on.

While identifiers are used to determine the query return, input parameters are used to let clients put constraints on the return by passing the parameters in the method corresponding to the query.

10.4.2 Input parameters

To make queries flexible, you want to let the clients decide the constraints on the return. This is accomplished through the input parameters passed in by the clients through the method calls directly in the find method and indirectly in the select methods (because select methods are not exposed in the interface, they are called from within the business methods).

The WHERE clause is used to put constraints on the returned values. In this example, we want to return only those orders that have totalAmount less than 30.00:

```
SELECT   OBJECT (o)  FROM  OrderSchema  o
WHERE  o.totalAmount  < 30.00
```

However, since the number 30.00 is hard-coded by the bean developer, the query can't be used for a different amount. To allow the client to decide this number, we must add input parameters to the find and ejbSelect methods. The methods would be declared with one or more arguments, the client would pass in the values as method arguments, and the values of parameters would be used in the WHERE clause instead of a hard-coded value. This is demonstrated in figure 10.3, in which the query returns all the orders with totalAmount greater than the first input parameter value passed through the method.

The number of distinct references in the query to the input parameters must not exceed the total number of parameters in the method—which is just common sense. For example, using ?2 in the above example would be invalid because there is no second parameter in the method. The parameters can be used only in the WHERE clause, and you are not required to use all the available parameters from the method in the clause.

So, an identifier is used in determining the return type, and the input parameters are used to allow the clients to decide the constraints on the return. The constraint technology includes two important tools: operators and expressions. Let's take a closer look at them.

10.5 OPERATORS AND EXPRESSIONS

A number of operators and expressions can be used in the WHERE clause of EJB QL queries.

10.5.1 Operators

Operators are used to further specify the query in order to determine the return type and the constraints on the return. Here is a list of operators that can be used in EJB QL queries:

- Navigation operator dot (.) used to navigate the path
- Arithmetic operators:
  - Unary: +, −
  - Multiplication and division: *, /
  - Addition and subtraction: +, −
- Comparison operators:
  - Equal to: =
  - Greater than and smaller than: >, <
  - Greater than or equal to: >=
  - Smaller than or equal to: <=
  - Not equal: <>
  - Logical operators: NOT, AND, OR

The comparison operators, >, <, =, >=, <=, can be used only with numeric values, and String and Boolean comparison can be done only with the = and <> operators. Note that the not equal operator is <> and not ! =.

ALERT Note that the comparison operator not equal is <> and not ! =. Also, the equal operator is = and not ==.

You have already seen some examples of how to use these operators in an EJB QL query, and you will see more examples in the following sections. In addition to operators, another important tool used in determining constraints on query returns is the *expression*, which we explore next.

10.5.2 Expressions

A number of expressions are available in EJB QL that can be used to build the logic for the constraint on the query return. In the sections that follow, you will see what those expressions are and how you can use them.

The BETWEEN and NOT BETWEEN expressions

These expressions are used to specify a range of values. Consider the following query:

```
SELECT   OBJECT (c)  FROM  CustomerSchema  c
    WHERE  c.age  BETWEEN 30 AND 40
```

This query will return all the customers whose age is between 30 and 40, including those customers whose age is 30 or 40. The following query will return the customers whose age is either greater than 40 or less than 30:

```
SELECT   OBJECT (c)  FROM  CustomerSchema  c
    WHERE  c.age  NOT BETWEEN 30 and 40
```

Make sure you understand that BETWEEN is an inclusive expression; in other words, BETWEEN 7 AND 10 means that 7 and 10 are included in the selected range, and NOT BETWEEN 7 AND 10 means that 7 and 10 are not included in the selection.

The IS EMPTY and IS NOT EMPTY expressions

These expressions are used to test whether the Collection resulting from a Collection-valued path expression in a query is empty. Consider the following query:

```
SELECT   OBJECT (c)  FROM  CustomerSchema  c
    WHERE c.orders IS EMPTY
```

This query will return all the customers who have no order attached to them. To select the customers who have at least one order, you would write the following query:

```
SELECT   OBJECT (c)  FROM  CustomerSchema  c
    WHERE c.orders IS NOT EMPTY
```

The LIKE and NOT LIKE expressions

The LIKE and NOT LIKE expressions are used to match the result of a single-valued path expression with a pattern that is a string literal. The pattern may include two wildcard characters: the underscore (_), which matches any single character, and the percent character (%), which matches a sequence of zero or more characters. For example, the following query will return all the customers whose name starts with Ralph and ends with Kant:

```
SELECT   OBJECT (c)  FROM  CustomerSchema  c
    WHERE c.name  LIKE   'Ralph%Kant'
```

The full name could be of any length; for example, "Ralph Kant," "RalphKant," and "Ralph A. Kant" will all match.

The following query will match "Ralph Kant" or "RalphAKant" but not "Ralph A. Kant," because there are four characters between the h and the K, and the wildcard matches only one:

```
SELECT   OBJECT (c)  FROM  CustomerSchema   c
    WHERE c.name  LIKE   'Ralph_Kant'
```

The IN and NOT IN expressions

The IN and NOT IN expressions may be used in the WHERE clause to impose a condition on the query results based on whether an item exists in a list. For example, the following query will return the customers who are from either of two cities: Sunnyvale or Phagwara:

```
SELECT   OBJECT (c)  FROM  CustomerSchema   c
    WHERE c.city  IN   ('Sunnyvale', 'Phagwara')
```

Now, consider this query:

```
SELECT   OBJECT (o)  FROM  OrderSchema   o
    WHERE o.orderStatus  NOT IN   ('approved', 'cancelled')
```

This will return the orders whose status is neither approved nor cancelled.

Note that we have used the string literals with single quotes such as IN ('Sunnyvale', 'Phagwara'). You must not use double quotes for the string literals.

> **ALERT**   You must use single quotes for the string literals in an EJB QL query and not double quotes.

The three most important takeaways from this chapter are

- EJB QL queries are written by the bean developer in the deployment descriptor to support the find and ejbSelect methods.
- An EJB QL query can return either a CMP field type or a bean's abstract schema type.
- The SELECT clause specifies what is to be returned from the query, the FROM clause specifies the domain of search, and the WHERE clause puts limits on the results. These clauses can use the navigation path, and the WHERE clause can also use operators and expressions.

10.6   SUMMARY

The Enterprise JavaBeans query language (EJB QL) provides a way to write portable SQL-like queries. The purpose of these queries, when combined with the abstract schema type and the CMR fields of an entity bean, is to help the container implement database-related methods of the bean, such as the find and select methods. EJB QL queries are written by the bean provider in the deployment descriptor of an ejb-jar file, and the container uses these queries to generate the database access code. An EJB QL query is based on the abstract schema type of an entity bean, including CMP fields and possibly CMR fields in order to navigate to related beans. An EJB QL query relates either to a find method or to a select method that is implemented by the container.

Each EJB QL query contains up to three clauses: SELECT and FROM are mandatory, while WHERE is optional. You cannot have a Collection (multiple values) type in the middle of a navigation path such as customer.orders.totalAmount where orders is a CMR field in a customer bean and is of type Collection. You can resolve this situation by using the IN operator in the FROM clause. Expressions such as BETWEEN, LIKE, and IS EMPTY can be used in the WHERE clause to impose constraints on the selection of the objects or values to be returned by a query.

Comprehend

- How the find and ejbSelect methods relate to EJB QL queries
- The structure and syntax of EJB QL queries

Look out

- In an EJB QL query, the SELECT clause and the FROM clause are mandatory, while the WHERE clause is optional.
- In EJB QL, you use <> and not ! = as the comparison operator not equal to.
- String literals use single quotes, not double quotes.
- You cannot have a Collection (multiple values) type in the middle of a navigation path such as customer.orders.totalAmount where orders is a CMR field in the customer bean and is of type Collection. You can resolve this situation by using the IN operator.

Memorize

- Understand how an EJB QL query is written in the deployment descriptor.
- In order to handle the BETWEEN expression on the exam correctly, make sure you understand that this is an inclusive expression; for example, BETWEEN 7 AND 10 means that 7 and 10 are included in the selected range, and NOT BETWEEN 7 AND 10 means that 7 and 10 are not included in the selection.

Some questions may have more than one correct answer. Choose all that apply.

In the following questions, assume that OrderSchema and CustomerSchema are the abstract schemas for the beans OrderBean and CustomerBean, respectively.

1. Which of the following are valid EJB QL queries?

   a. `SELECT OBJECT (o)`
      `FROM OrderSchema o`
   b. `SELECT OBJECT (o.totalAmount)`
      `FROM OrderSchema o`
   c. `SELECT o FROM OrderSchema o`
   d. `SELECT o.totalAmount`
      `FROM OrderSchema o`

2. Which of the following are valid EJB QL queries?

   a. `SELECT OBJECT (o) FROM OrderSchema o`
      `WHERE o.customer > 30`
   b. `SELECT OBJECT o.customer`
      `FROM OrderSchema o`
   c. `SELECT OBJECT (o) FROM OrderSchema o`
      `WHERE o.customer.member = TRUE`
   d. `SELECT OBJECT (c)`
      `FROM CustomerSchema c`
      `WHERE c.orders.orderStatus = 'pending'`

3. Which of the following are a valid use of a WHERE clause in EJB QL?

   a. `WHERE o.totalAmount > 100`
   b. `WHERE o.totalAmount == 100`
   c. `WHERE o.totalAmount != 100`
   d. `WHERE o.totalAmount <> 100`
   e. `WHERE o.totalAmount = 100`

4. Consider the following expression:

   `o.totalAmount  BETWEEN 100.00  AND 500.00`

   This expression may be replaced by which of the following expressions in order to produce the same result?

   a. `o.totalAmount < 500.00`
      `AND o.totalAmount > 100.00`

b. `o.totalAmount <= 500.00`
   `AND o.totalAmount >= 100.00`
c. `o.totalAmount <= 500.00`
   `AND o.totalAmount > 100.00`
d. `o.totalAmount < 500.00`
   `AND o.totalAmount >= 100.00`

5. Consider the following expression:

   `o.totalAmount NOT BETWEEN 100.00  AND 500.00`

   This expression may be replaced by which of the following expressions in order to produce the same result?

   a. `o.totalAmount > 500.00`
      `OR o.totalAmount < 100.00`
   b. `o.totalAmount >= 500.00`
      `OR o.totalAmount <= 100.00`
   c. `o.totalAmount >= 500.00`
      `OR o.totalAmount < 100.00`
   d. `o.totalAmount > 500.00`
      `OR o.totalAmount <= 100.00`

6. In EJB 2.0, EJB QL queries are written for which of the following methods?

   a. The get and set methods corresponding to the CMP fields
   b. The find methods
   c. The ejbSelect methods
   d. The create methods
   e. The remove methods

PART 4

Message-driven beans

In this part we are going to explore message-driven beans (MDB). The distinctive feature of these components is that they have no clients: no interfaces and no client view. This feature largely shapes their behavior and distinguishes them from the other bean flavors. Here are the three most common statements you will hear about message-driven beans in EJB:

- An MDB has a very simple lifecycle, similar to that of a stateless session bean.

- An MDB has only one business method: `onMessage(...)`. If you start a transaction in this method, you must end it before the method ends. And you cannot declare any application (checked) exceptions in an MDB; if an MDB started throwing checked exceptions, there would be no client to catch them.

- The container provides a line of communication, the MessageDrivenContext, which the MDB can use with lots of restrictions. For example, it cannot ask for EJBObject, EJBHome, or security information about the caller, because it has no client.

So, let's visit these interesting components.

<space>C H A P T E R   1 1</space>

Message-driven beans

<space>11.1 Using message-driven beans for asynchronous communication 248</space>
<space>11.2 Implementing a message-driven bean 251</space>
<space>11.3 The lifecycle of a message-driven bean 254</space>
<space>11.4 The message destination types 258</space>
<space>11.5 Summary 259</space>

EXAM OBJECTIVES

10.1 Identify correct and incorrect statements or examples about the client view of a message-driven bean, and the lifecycle of a message-driven bean.

10.2 Identify the interface(s) and methods a JMS Messaged-Driven bean must implement.

10.3 Identify the use and behavior of the `MessageDrivenContext` interface methods.

10.4 From a list, identify the responsibility of the bean provider, and the responsibility of the container provider for a message-driven bean.

INTRODUCTION

Each application has a communication aspect to it. Communication involves the exchange of data between two applications or between two components of the same application, and it can be one of two types: synchronous or asynchronous. In synchronous communication, both communicating parties have to be present at the same time. A telephone conversation is an example of synchronous communication. EJB offers entity and session beans to support synchronous communication. This means the following:

247

- When a client invokes a call on a bean instance, the bean instance on which the call is invoked has to be present at the time of the call.

- When the client makes the call, it waits for the call to return, and the call will return only after the called method completes.

You can imagine applications where the simultaneous presence of the two parties and the client's waiting for the method to return are neither desired nor needed. For example, a client in an application wants to submit a newsletter to the server that the server will send to selected customers at an appropriate time. Such applications are better served by asynchronous communication, in which the communicating parties don't have to be present at the same time. An email message is another example of asynchronous communication. EJB 2.0 has introduced message-driven beans (MDB) to support asynchronous communication in enterprise applications. This asynchronous communication is made possible by using the Java Messaging Service (JMS), which guarantees reliable message delivery.

You will see that an MDB has a simple lifetime just like a stateless session bean. When the container creates an MDB instance, it gives the instance a context, Message-DrivenContext, which the instance uses as a line of communication with the container. The container's line of communication with the instance is composed of two interfaces: `MessageDrivenBean` and `MessageListener`. The focus of this chapter lies in knowing this very simple component of EJB: the message-driven bean. To help you understand this bean we will explore three avenues: the absence of the client view, the lifecycle of an MDB, and the lines of communication between the container and an MDB instance. And as usual pay attention to who's in charge; it's largely between you and the container.

11.1 USING MESSAGE-DRIVEN BEANS FOR ASYNCHRONOUS COMMUNICATION

A message-driven bean is an asynchronous consumer of a JMS message. JMS is a vendor-independent Java API that can be used on the J2EE platform for messaging in enterprise applications. An application (or a component of an application) that sends a message is called a *JMS client*. A JMS client that generates messages is called a *JMS producer*, and the application (or component) that receives the messages is called a *JMS consumer*. In between the producer and the consumer is the JMS server. It receives message requests from the JMS clients and stores them in a JMS "destination." Sooner or later, the JMS consumer connects to the destination and retrieves the message. So, the destination decouples the message producers from the consumers, and thus it allows the communication between them to be asynchronous. Although full JMS support is a requirement in J2EE 1.3, JMS itself is not a part of EJB. An MDB gets into the JMS picture as an asynchronous message consumer with the help of the container.

11.1.1 Message-driven bean: A JMS message consumer

The method calls that come from a client of a session bean or an entity bean are synchronous. The EJB architecture offers an asynchronous environment for the client to communicate with an MDB by using JMS. The architecture and the process shown in figure 11.1 demonstrate how this asynchronous communication happens.

Here are the steps in the process:

1 A client, that is, the producer, sends a message to a queue on a JMS server. The client then goes on with its business.

2 The messaging service delivers the message to the EJB container.

3 The container notifies the messaging service (not the producer of the message) that the message has been received. The messaging service may remove the message from the queue. Removing it from the queue does not remove it from the server, however.

4 The container selects an MDB instance from the pool, invokes its `onMessage(msg)` method, and passes the message as the argument in the call. The `onMessage(...)` method is the only business method of MDB.

Subsequently, the bean instance processes (consumes) the message. If the processing fails (which means that the transaction rolls back in a CMT bean or the BMT bean throws a runtime exception), the container tells the messaging service to put the mes-

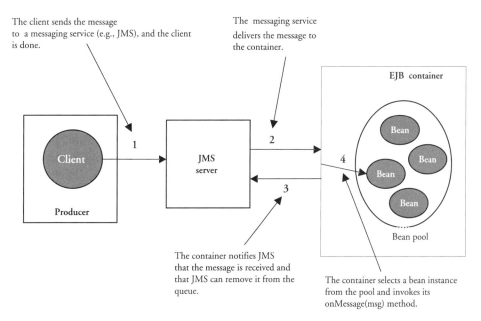

Figure 11.1 The architecture and the process for asynchronous communication with MDBs using queues. While the EJB 2.0 specification requires support only for JMS, a future goal is to provide support for other kinds of messaging services as well.

sage back into the queue, and the container will make the bean instance available to process other messages in case the bean has not thrown a system exception.

If the message is processed successfully (which means the transaction commits in a CMT bean or the onMessage() method completes successfully in a BMT bean), the container makes the bean instance available to process other messages, and a message acknowledgment is sent. Remember that the container automatically handles the message acknowledgment. In a CMT bean, the acknowledgment is a part of the transaction commit; that is, no commit means no acknowledgment. There will be situations where you want to decouple the acknowledgment from the transaction status. To handle such situations, you should use the BMT bean, where you can tell the container how to send the acknowledgment by using the <acknowledge-mode> element of the deployment descriptor, which has two possible values: AUTO-ACKNOWLEDGE and DUPS-OK-ACKNOWLEDGE. These values just tell the container how quickly to send the acknowledgment (if the container decides to send one) in order to avoid duplicate messages from the container.

As you can see, the MDB is hidden from the client, the message producer. In other words, the client has no view of the MDB instance with which the client could communicate. The client here communicates with the JMS server and not with the client view of MDB. So where is the client view of MDB, or is there any? Let's find out.

11.1.2 Client view of an MDB

You may run into statements in EJB literature such as "message-driven beans have no clients." This is just another way of saying that a message-driven bean has no client view, that is, no component interface and no home interface. This means the bean exposes no methods to the client. In other words, a message-driven bean has no identity that is visible to the client. If a bean wants to claim that it has a client, it must present a client view. It is in this sense that we say that an MDB has no client, because it has no client view. So the casualty of asynchronous communication is the client view: JMS server in, client view out.

The client of JMS (the producer) sends a message to a JMS destination, and the MDB is simply a message listener to the destination. An MDB is associated with a JMS destination by the deployer at bean deployment time. The client sends the message to the destination and then goes on to do other things.

JMS destinations can be one of two types: Queue or Topic. You will learn more about these later in this chapter. A client locates the destination attached with an MDB by using a JNDI lookup. For example, these lines of code locate the Queue for the message-driven CustomerNotificationBean:

```
Context initialContext = new InitialContext();
Queue customerNotificationQueue =
    (javax.jms.Queue)initialContext.lookup
    ("java:comp/env/jms/CustomerNotificationQueue");
```

So, the MDB is hidden behind the JMS destination and exposes no methods to the client. The absence of a client view has significant consequences for an MDB, among them:

- Because an MDB has no client, its `onMessage()` method cannot throw any checked exception. There is no client to handle the exceptions! More on exceptions in chapter 13.

- The `onMessage()` method is never run in a preexisting transaction context. If you start a transaction inside `onMessage()` (in the case of BMT), you must complete it (commit it or roll it back) before the method is completed. More on transactions in the next chapter.

- Due to the absence of the client view, many methods in the context of the bean cannot be invoked. You will learn more about this later in this chapter.

ALERT   Message-driven beans have no clients because they have no home or remote interfaces that the clients could use.

So, a message producer sends the message to a destination at a JMS server, and the container gets the message from the destination and passes it to an MDB instance. Where does this bean instance come from? The container creates it from a message-driven bean class. Next, we explain how to write an MDB class.

11.2 IMPLEMENTING A MESSAGE-DRIVEN BEAN

An instance of a message-driven bean is constructed by the container from a bean class of a certain type, such as `CustomerNotificationBean`. The MDB class has two kinds of methods:

- A business method, which is invoked to service a message
- Container callback methods, which are used by the container to maintain the lifecycle of the bean

In this section we will walk you through a simple example of an MDB class, and we will list the requirements that a bean provider must meet in writing the class.

11.2.1 Writing an MDB class

It is the bean provider's responsibility to provide a message-driven bean class. As an example, the code for a simple MDB class called `CustomerNotificationBean` is shown in listing 11.1.

> **Listing 11.1   Code for the MDB class `CustomerNotificationBean`**

```
1. import javax.ejb.*;
2. import javax.jms.*;

3. public class CustomerNotificationBean
      implements MessageDrivenBean, MessageListener {
```

```
4. private MessageDrivenContext context = null;

5. public void setMessageDrivenContext
     ( MessageDrivenContext  ctx) {
6.     context = ctx;          ←── Captures context
7. }                                 sent by container

8. public void ejbCreate( ){ }   ←── Writes initialization
                                      code here
9. public void ejbRemove( ) { }  ←── Releases resources
                                      in this method
10. public void onMessage(Message msg) {  ←── Writes only required
                                              business method
11. try {
12.  if ( msg instanceof TextMessage ) {
13.   TextMessage txtMsg = (TextMessage) msg;
14.   System.out.println("The text message is:"
        + txtMsg.getText());
15.  } else {
16.     System.out.println("Not a text message!");
17.  }
18. } catch (JMSException ex) {
19.    ex.printStackTrace();
20. }
21.  }
22. }
```

As shown in line 3 of the listing, the class must be public and must implement two interfaces: MessageDrivenBean and MessageListener. Therefore, you have to implement the three methods in these two interfaces shown in figure 11.2: setMessageDrivenContext(), ejbRemove(), and onMessage().

NOTE   You must declare an MDB class public, and it must implement two interfaces: MessageDrivenBean and MessageListener. The only required business method in the MDB class comes from the Message-Listener interface.

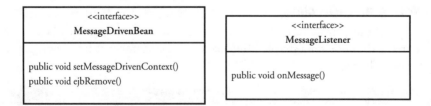

Figure 11.2 An MDB class must implement two interfaces: `javax.ejb.MessageDrivenBean` and `javax.jms.MessageListener`. The methods of these interfaces are shown. The methods `onMessage()` and `setMessageDrivenContext()` expect parameters.

The container invokes the method `setMessageDrivenContext()`, shown in lines 5 to 7, on a bean instance in order to associate it with its context, which is an instance of the interface `MessageDrivenContext`. The container maintains the context. The container calls the `ejbRemove()` method, shown in line 9, to inform you that the instance is being removed. The bean developer can put the code in the `ejbRemove()` method in order to release the resources that the instance may be holding. The `onMessage()` method, shown in lines 10 to 21, is called by the container when a JMS message arrives that needs to be serviced. The container passes the message as an argument in the method call. In the `onMessage()` method, you write the business logic to process the message.

During the process of creating an instance of an MDB, the container calls the `ejbCreate()` method shown in line 8. Recall that in an entity bean and in a session bean, the `ejbCreate()` method corresponds to the `create()` method in the home interface of the bean. Because an MDB does not have any home (or component) interface, the `ejbCreate()` method does not come from any interface, but you are required to implement it. You can include the initialization code and assign resources (for example, resolve resource factories) to the bean instance in this method.

> **NOTE**　　The `ejbCreate()` method in an MDB class does not come from any interface, but you are required to implement it.

In addition to these required messages, you are allowed to implement other methods such as helper methods in the bean class.

Because each bean class must implement the interfaces `MessageDrivenBean` and `MessageListener`, it must also implement the methods of these interfaces. This is a plain-Java language requirement. In the next section, we discuss the requirements for writing an MDB class in a more comprehensive fashion.

11.2.2　Requirements for an MDB class

It is the bean provider's responsibility to provide the class for a message-driven bean. The requirements for an MDB class, which must be met in order to ensure portability among different EJB containers, are described in the following sections.

Class definition requirements

Here are the requirements for defining an MDB class:

- The class must implement the interface `javax.ejb.MessageDrivenBean`.
- The class must implement the interface `javax.jms.MessageListener`.
- The class must be public, must not be abstract, and must not be final.

These three requirements mean that the class definition should look like this:

```
public class  CustomerNotificationBean implements
     MessageDrivenBean, MessageListener {  }
```

Requirements for writing methods

These are the requirements for writing methods in an MDB class:

- You must implement the ejbRemove() and setMessageDriven-Context() methods from the MessageDrivenBean interface. You should define them exactly the way they are defined in the interface: they must be public, not static, and not final; the return type must be void; and they must not have any arguments.

- You must implement the onMessage() method from the javax.jms. MessageListener interface, and it must be public, not static, and not final. The return type of the onMessage(...) method must be void, and it should take a single argument of type javax.jms.JMSMessage.

- Although it is not part of any interface, you must implement the ejb-Create() method in the class, and it must be public, not static, and not final. The return type of the ejbCreate() method must be void, and it must have no arguments.

- If you write a constructor for the class, it must be public and it should take no arguments. If you don't write any constructor, the compiler will supply a no-argument constructor for you. The container uses this constructor to create an instance of the bean.

- The methods in the class must not throw application exceptions, since there is no client to catch these exceptions.

> **ALERT** Do not declare checked exceptions in the methods of a message-driven bean because there is no client to catch them.

Note that an MDB class is required to implement two interfaces, while a session bean or entity bean class is required to implement only one interface. Furthermore, no MDB method can throw application exceptions, since there is no client to catch them.

11.3 *The lifecycle of a message-driven bean*

The lifecycle of an MDB is very simple, like the lifecycle of a stateless session bean. There are only two states: the does not exist state and the pooled state. During this lifecycle, the container calls the methods that you implemented in the bean class. From inside these methods you can invoke methods on the context of the bean instance. First, let's take a look at the states of the lifecycle.

11.3.1 States of the lifecycle

The states of the lifecycle of an entity bean are shown in figure 11.3.

An MDB instance comes to life when the container instantiates it by invoking the method newInstance() on the class. After constructing an instance, the container invokes two methods on the instance: setMessageDrivenContext(ctx)

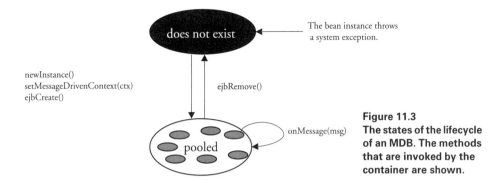

newInstance()
setMessageDrivenContext(ctx)
ejbCreate()

ejbRemove()

The bean instance throws
a system exception.

onMessage(msg)

Figure 11.3
The states of the lifecycle
of an MDB. The methods
that are invoked by the
container are shown.

followed by `ejbCreate()`. These three methods transition the bean from the does not exist state to the pooled state. The container can create a number of bean instances and put them into the pool. Each bean type, for example, `Customer-NotificationBean`, has its own pool.

A bean instance in the pool is able to process a message, that is, execute the `onMessage(msg)` method. All instances in the pool are equal; when a message arrives at the destination, the container can ask any instance to process the message by invoking its `onMessage()` method. It is the responsibility of the container to ensure that only one thread can execute a particular instance at any given time. The container ensures that the bean instances are non-reentrant by serializing the calls to each MDB instance. However, multiple bean instances from a pool can be used to service a stream of messages; in other words, bean instances can be executed concurrently.

NOTE Multiple instances of an MDB can be executed concurrently. However, a given instance is executed by only one thread at any given time—bean instances are non-reentrant.

When the container wants to remove an instance, for example, to save resources, it will invoke the method `ejbRemove()` on it, which will take the instance back to the does not exist state. The instance at this state is ready to be garbage collected. You should use the `ejbRemove()` method to release any resources acquired in `ejbCreate()`. However, remember that the container will not call `ejbRemove()` methods in the following two cases:

- The instance is being removed by the container because the instance has thrown a system exception.
- The container crashes.

To handle these situations, the application should have some mechanism to release the resources.

The bean provider should not assume that the container will always call `ejbRemove()` before removing an instance of a message-driven bean. The `ejbRemove()` call will be missed if the bean is being removed because it has thrown a system exception or because the container crashed.

The lifecycle of an MDB is very similar to the lifecycle of a stateless session bean. An MDB is also stateless; that is, it does not hold the conversational state with a client—there is no client.

After instantiating the bean, the container assigns a context to it by invoking the method `setMessageDrivenContext()`. This context is an instance of the `MessageDrivenContext` interface (the instance of a class that implements the `MessageDrivenContext` interface). Let's see how an MDB uses this context.

11.3.2 Using the MessageDrivenContext interface

As discussed in the previous section, the container constructs an instance of an MDB and assigns a context (an instance of a class that implements the `MessageDriven-Context` interface) to it. The container manages this context. The bean instance can call methods on this context. This is the communication line from the instance to the container. The `MessageDrivenContext` interface has no methods of its own. It inherits the methods from the `EJBContext` interface. Table 11.1 shows these methods and the tasks that can be accomplished by invoking these methods. The table also lists from which methods of the bean the context methods can be called.

Table 11.1 Methods available in the `MessageDrivenContext` interface. The permissions to use these methods from inside the methods of MDB are shown.

Method Task	Constructor	setMessage- DrivenContext()	ejbCreate(), ejbRemove()	onMessage()
getEJB-Home() getEJB-LocalHome()				
Get a reference to the bean's home interface	No	No	No	No
getCaller-Principle() IsCaller-InRole()				
Get security information	No	No	No	No
setRoll-backOnly() (for CMT)				
Mark the current transaction to roll back	No	No	No	Yes
getRoll-backOnly() (for CMT)				
Determine whether the transaction has already been marked for rollback	No	No	No	Yes

continued on next page

Table 11.1 Methods available in the `MessageDrivenContext` interface. The permissions to use these methods from inside the methods of MDB are shown. *(continued)*

Method Task	Constructor	setMessage- DrivenContext()	ejbCreate(), ejbRemove()	onMessage()
`getUser-Transaction()` `(for BMT)`				
Get a reference to the transaction; cannot by used by entity beans	No	No	Yes	Yes
JNDI Access	No	Yes	Yes	Yes
Resource manager access; access to other beans	No	No	No	Yes

Recall that an MDB has no client view—no home or component interface. This implies that the getEJBHome() and getEJBLocalHome() methods cannot be called from inside any method of an MDB instance. Because there is no client view, there is no issue of client security information. Hence the getCallerPrinciple() and isCallerInRole() methods cannot be called either. If a bean instance attempts to invoke a method of MessageDrivenContext when it is not allowed, the container must throw java.lang.IllegalStateException.

> **ALERT** Because an MDB does not have a home interface, you should never call the getEJBHome() or getEJBLocalHome method on the bean's context. If you do, the container will throw java.lang.IllegalState-Exception.

Therefore, only the transaction-related methods, such as getRollbackOnly(), setRollbackOnly(), and getUserTransaction(), can be called by appropriate methods of the bean. The business method of MDB, onMessage(), can call getUserTransaction() if the bean is BMT and the other two methods if the bean is CMT. The getRollbackOnly() and setRollbackOnly() methods can be called only from the methods of an MDB that execute in a transaction context.

All the MDB bean methods except the constructor can have access to the JNDI context. In addition, the onMessage() method can access the resource manager (such as a database) and the methods of other enterprise beans.

Before a bean instance can receive a message, its bean type needs to be associated with a JMS destination. Let's explore the JMS destinations next.

11.4 THE MESSAGE DESTINATION TYPES

A client sends a message to a JMS destination, an address on a JMS server. A message-driven bean is associated with a destination, and the destination can be one of two types: Topic or Queue. By using the `<message-driven-destination>` element in the deployment descriptor, the bean provider informs the deployer what destination type the bean should use, as shown here:

```
<enterprise-beans>
   <message-driven>
     <ejb-name> CustomerNotificationBean  </ejb-name>
     <ejb-class> CustomerNotificationBean </ejb-class>
     <message-driven-destination>
         <destination-type> javax.jms.Queue </destination-type>
     </message-driven-destination>
</message-driven>
</enterprise-beans>
```

The destination type in this deployment descriptor tells the deployer that this bean will expect messages from a Queue. Should your bean expect messages from a Topic destination, you would replace `javax.jms.Queue` in the code (shown in bold) with `javax.jms.Topic`. Let's see what the difference is between these two destination types.

11.4.1 The Queue destination

The `javax.jms.Queue` interface supports the point-to-point messaging model in which only one consumer (MDB instance) can receive a message sent by a producer (client). Once the message has been processed by a bean instance, the message is removed from the queue, and no other bean instance can process it. A Queue ensures that the consumer does not miss the message even if the EJB server was down at the time the message arrived.

You can associate only one bean type to a queue. For example, if `Customer-NotificationBean` is associated with `CustomerNotificationQueue`, no other bean type such as `CustomerHelpBean` can be associated with `Customer-NotificationQueue`. Furthermore, only one bean instance in the `Customer-NotificationBean` pool can receive a message that arrived at the queue.

11.4.2 The Topic destination

The `javax.jms.Topic` interface supports the publish/subscribe messaging model in which multiple beans can receive the same message. All consumers who subscribed to the Topic can receive the message sent by a producer (client). Multiple consumers (called subscribers in this case) who are interested in a Topic can subscribe to it. When a message arrives on that Topic destination, all subscribers of this topic can receive the message. Subscriptions are of two kinds: durable and nondurable. In a nondurable subscription, the subscriber can consume the message only if it was up and running when the message arrived; otherwise it would miss it. In a durable subscription, the subscriber will receive the message when it comes up even if it was down when the message arrived.

The durability is specified in the deployment descriptor with the `<subscription-durability>` element:

```
<message-driven-destination>
    <destination-type> javax.jms.Topic </destination-type>
        <subscription-durability> Durable <subscription-durability>
</message-driven-destination>
```

For a nondurable topic subscription, replace `Durable` with `NonDurable` as the value of the element `<subscription-durability>`. If the destination type is Topic and you do not specify the subscription durability element, a nondurable subscription is assumed by default.

The subscription is at a bean-type level, and more than one bean type can subscribe to a topic and hence receive a message when it arrives at the topic. For example, say that two bean types, MarketingBean and BusinessBean, subscribe to the topic CustomerInfoTopic. When a message at the CustomerInfoTopic arrives, one (and only one) instance of MarketingBean and one instance of BusinessBean will receive the message.

> **NOTE** From a Queue destination, only one instance receives the message, while from a Topic destination, only one instance from each subscribing bean type will receive a copy of the message.

So regardless of whether it is Topic or a Queue, only one instance from a pool will receive a given message. The difference between a Topic and a Queue is that more than one bean type can be associated with one Topic, while only one bean type can be associated with a Queue. Applications that require reliable delivery of messages should use Queue or durable subscriptions, because message delivery is not guaranteed in a nondurable Topic subscription.

11.5 SUMMARY

The EJB architecture offers message-driven beans (MDB) to support asynchronous communication in enterprise applications. An MDB does not have a client view, that is, no home interface and no component interface. This prevents an MDB from doing many things, such as throwing checked exceptions and invoking many of the methods in its MDB context.

An MDB class implements two interfaces: `javax.ejb.MessageDrivenBean` and `javax.jms.MessageListener`. The two container callback methods `ejb-Remove()` and `setMessageDrivenContext()` come from the `Message-DrivenBean` interface, and the `onMessage()` method comes from the `MessageListener` interface. The bean provider must provide another method that does not come from any interface: the `ejbCreate()` method. The container calls the `ejbCreate()` method in the process of creating a bean instance and putting it into the pool, the `ejbRemove()` method in the process of deleting the bean instance, and `onMessage()` in order to service a message from a destination. Multiple bean instances of the same type (from the same pool) can execute concurrently in order to handle a stream of messages. However, one instance can handle only one message at a time; in other words, bean instances are non-reentrant.

A message-driven bean can be associated with a Topic or Queue destination. A message from a Queue destination can be sent to only one bean instance, while a message from a Topic destination may be sent to several instances, where each instance belongs to a different bean type. That means only one instance from each bean type that has subscribed to the Topic can receive the message, but more than one bean type can subscribe to the same Topic.

One of many consequences of the absence of the MDB client view is that there cannot be a preexisting transaction context for the `onMessage()` method of an MDB instance. Also, if you start a transaction in the `onMessage()` method, you must complete it before the method ends. We will explore EJB transactions in the next chapter.

Comprehend

- The lifecycle of a message-driven bean
- The absence of the client view and its implications: no checked exceptions by the bean instance, can't call most of the methods in the `MessageDrivenContext` interface, and so on

Look out

- You must implement the `ejbCreate()` method in the MDB class, even though it does not correspond to any method in any interface.
- An MDB bean instance will miss the `ejbRemove()` call before its removal in two cases: the instance throws a system exception or the server crashes.
- Because there is no client, you cannot declare a checked exception in an MDB class.
- If you begin a transaction in the `onMessage(...)` method (which would be a BMT bean), you must end it before the end of the method.
- Only one bean instance receives the message from a Queue destination, while one instance of each subscribing bean type receives a copy of the message from the Topic destination.

Memorize

- The names and functionalities of the methods in the `MessageDriven-Context` interface
- The names and functionalities of the methods in the `MessageDriven-Bean` interface and the `MessageListener` interface

Some questions may have more than one correct answer. Choose all that apply.

1. Which of the following methods will the compiler expect you to implement in an MDB class?
   a. `ejbRemove()`
   b. `onMessage()`
   c. `setMessageDrivenContext()`
   d. `ejbCreate()`

2. If an MDB bean instance invokes the method `getEJBLocalHome()` on the context of the bean instance, what will be the result?
   a. You will not be able to compile the code.
   b. A reference to the local home interface of the bean will be returned.
   c. A handle to the local home interface of the bean instance will be returned.
   d. The container will throw the exception `java.lang.Illegal-StateException`.

3. Which of the following are valid statements about a message-driven bean?
   a. A message-driven bean can have only a local home interface.
   b. The identity of a message-driven bean is hidden from the client.
   c. You can invoke the `getEJBLocalHome()` method on the bean's context from inside the `onMessage()` method.
   d. The container invokes the `ejbActivate()` method on the bean instance before invoking the `onMessage()` method.

4. Which of the following interfaces must be implemented, directly or indirectly, in a message-driven bean class?
   a. `javax.ejb.MesageDrivenContext`
   b. `javax.ejb.MessageDrivenBean`
   c. `javax.jms.MessageListener`
   d. `javax.jms.MessageProducer`
   e. `javax.jms.MessageConsumer`

5. Consider two message-driven beans: MarketingService and BusinessService. Both beans have subscribed to a Topic destination, CustomerInfo. A message arrives at the Topic destination. Which of the following can happen?

    a. Only one instance of MarketingService and one instance of BusinessService will receive the message.

    b. Multiple instances of MarketingService and BusinessService will receive the message.

    c. Only one instance either from MarketingService or from BusinessService will receive the message.

    d. All the instances of MarketingService and BusinessService will receive the message.

6. Consider that method `A()` in an application sends a message; in response the method `onMessage()` of an MDB is called. The `onMessage()` method invokes another method, `B()`. Method `B()` throws an application (checked) exception. Which of the following are the correct ways to deal with this exception in the `onMessage()` method?

    a. Throw the exception back to method `A()`.

    b. Handle the exception inside the method `onMessage()`.

    c. Throw the exception back to the container.

    d. Throw RemoteException.

7. Which of the following show the correct sequence of methods invoked on an MDB during its lifecycle?

    a. `newInstance()`, `ejbCreate()`, `setMessageDriven-Context()`, `onMessage()`, `ejbRemove()`

    b. `onMessage()`, `ejbCreate()`, `ejbRemove()`

    c. `newInstance()`, `setMessageDrivenContext()`, `ejbCreate()`, `onMessage()`, `ejbRemove()`

    d. `setMessageDrivenContext()`, `ejbCreate()`, `onMessage()`

8. Which of the following are true statements about an MDB associated with a Queue?

    a. Only one instance from the pool of an MDB type can process a message at a given time.

    b. Multiple instances from the pool of an MDB type can process messages at the same time.

    c. One instance can handle only one message at a time.

    d. A message will go to only one bean instance.

9. From which of the following methods can a message-driven bean with a BMT demarcation get a reference to the transaction?

    a. `ejbCreate()`

    b. `ejbRemove()`

    c. `onMessage()`

    d. `setEJBMessageDrivenContext()`

10. From which of the following methods can a message-driven bean with a CMT demarcation invoke methods on another bean?

    a. `ejbCreate()`

    b. `ejbRemove()`

    c. `onMessage()`

    d. `setEJBMessageDrivenContext()`

EJB services

One of the great promises of EJB is to offer services so that you can concentrate on the business logic of an application. You've already learned about some of these services, such as persistence management, in previous parts of this book. In this part, you'll explore two more services, transaction management and security management, and a facility called EJB exceptions. You'll encounter all three bean flavors again, and see transactions passing through methods and beans. You'll see exceptions, the messengers of bad news, originating from a method in the bean and reaching all the way to the client, changing their colors along the way. Here are some of the things you'll learn about EJB services:

- Entity beans can never call a method from the `UserTransaction` interface.
- The container kills the bean instance and rolls back its transaction whenever a bean instance hits the container with a system exception.
- A user of an application changes into a Principal and then into a security role, such as manager.

Let's visit the most interesting aspect of EJB: EJB services.

EJB transactions

EXAM OBJECTIVES

11.1 Identify correct and incorrect statements or examples about EJB transactions, including bean-managed transaction demarcation, and container-managed transaction demarcation.

11.2 Identify correct and incorrect statements about the Application Assembler's responsibilities, including the use of deployment descriptor elements related to transactions, and the identification of the methods of a particular bean type for which a transaction attribute must be specified.

11.3 Given a list of transaction behaviors, match them with the appropriate transaction attribute.

11.4 Given a list of responsibilities, identify which of these are the container's with respect to transactions, including the handling of getRollbackOnly, setRollbackOnly, getUserTransaction, SessionSynchronization callbacks, for both container and bean-managed transactions.

INTRODUCTION

The support for transactions is a significant benefit offered by the EJB architecture. A transaction is a very common business concept in the real world that represents an exchange between two business participants. You participate in transactions in your everyday life, such as buying a book online, withdrawing cash from an ATM, and purchasing something from a store. Therefore, an enterprise application developed to address real-world problems must deal with transactions.

A transaction consists of a precisely defined set of actions and therefore has a beginning and an end. The process of marking these boundaries is called *transaction demarcation*. Who will do the demarcation, you or the container? During a transaction, multiple users may be accessing shared data concurrently. Furthermore, a transaction may involve more than one database and EJB server. Who will coordinate the access and changes to possibly multiple resources, you or the container? The good news is that the container will handle much of the complex work. You have the choice of taking some responsibility at the demarcation level. If you choose to do the demarcation yourself, it is called *bean-managed transaction (BMT) demarcation*. If you choose to let the container to do the demarcation, it is called *container-managed transaction (CMT) demarcation*. And this choice has implications for coding the bean.

If you decide your bean will be a CMT bean, you help the container by defining *transaction attributes* in the deployment descriptor. You assign these attributes to the bean methods, and they determine whether a method will run with or without a transaction when it is called by another method. Two interfaces offer transaction-related methods: `UserTransaction` and `EJBContext`. You can use these methods for demarcation (in a BMT bean) and for other transaction-related tasks.

Your goal for this chapter is to understand how the transaction attributes are used to facilitate CMT demarcation. To accomplish that, we will explore three avenues: the two interfaces offering the transaction-related methods, the specific methods from all bean flavors for which you are required to specify transaction attributes, and the difference between the transactional behavior of a BMT bean and a CMT bean. Pay attention to how the responsibility for these transactions is split among the bean provider, the application assembler, and the container. Let's start by exploring the basic concept of a transaction.

12.1   UNDERSTANDING TRANSACTIONS

The real world is full of transactions. For example, you go to an ATM and transfer some money out of your account and into your wallet. Or you go into a grocery store, fill up your shopping cart with items, pay the cashier, and put the items into your car. A transaction is involved in this process, too. So it is natural that software applications that solve real-world problems have to deal with transactions. In this section we explore the definitions of transactions and distributed transactions.

12.1.1   Defining transactions

A *transaction* is an operation that contains a set of tasks in which either all the tasks succeed as a unit or the effect of each task in the unit must be undone as if nothing happened; that is, everything must be rolled back to the point immediately before the transaction started. In other words, either the whole unit succeeds (commits) or the whole unit reverses by leaving things where they were before any task was executed on them—the transaction rolls back.

In computer science, a transaction is a very well-defined term. It is an operation that meets the following four requirements, collectively called an ACID (atomicity, consistency, isolation, and durability) test.

Atomicity

This requirement refers to the tasks that make up a transaction. A transaction is based on the all-or-none philosophy. It must be atomic. This means the tasks inside the transaction must be considered as a single atomic unit: either all of them succeed or all of them are undone. Think of buying something from the store. If you make the payment, you will either get the product that you pay for or you will get your money back. Paying for a product and receiving the product are a single atomic unit; either both happen or neither happens.

Consistency

This requirement refers to the aftermath of a transaction. Whether the transaction fails (rolls back) or it succeeds (commits), it must leave the data involved in the transaction in a consistent state. Think of a bank transaction where you deposit some money into your account. The process of taking x amount of money from you and incrementing the balance in your account by x keeps the data consistent. This is because the money that comes out of your wallet must be equal to the money added to the balance in your bank account.

Isolation

This requirement deals with concurrency—two transactions executing at the same time. Isolation means that if multiple transactions are executing concurrently and interacting with the same data, the effect must be as if they were executed sequentially. The failure to meet this condition may result in violating the consistency condition.

Durability

This requirement deals with the persistent nature of a transaction. A transaction must be durable. If the transaction succeeds, the changes made must be permanently stored; thus the results of a committed transaction must persist even if the server fails. For example, if you are changing an entity in the database, just changing its representation in computer memory will not be good enough. The transaction is not complete until the changes make it to the database.

So, a transaction by definition must be atomic, consistent, isolated, and durable. A transaction may involve more than one database and more than one server interacting with those databases. Such a transaction is called a *distributed* transaction, which we explore next.

12.1.2 Distributed transactions

Support for distributed transactions is a significant feature of the EJB architecture. It allows a transaction to span multiple databases distributed over multiple sites, possibly using EJB servers from different vendors. You can relate to a distributed transaction if you have experienced synchronizing the sale of an old house with the purchase of a new house: money obtained from selling the old house goes into buying the new house at about the same time.

Distributed transactions in EJB are implemented in the server by using a *two-phase commit* protocol. The players in this protocol are the transaction managers, such as EJB servers, and the transaction participants, such as beans and databases. A local transaction manager manages the transactions on each EJB server by interacting with the local transaction participants. A distributed transaction manager coordinates the commit with the local transaction managers on all the EJB servers involved in a distributed transaction. In phase one, the distributed transaction manager sends the `prepare to commit` command to all local transaction managers that are participating in the distributed transaction. Each local manager is responsible for coordinating the local part of the transaction by interacting with the local transaction participants. The local transaction managers respond to the distributed transaction manager with `ready to commit` or with `error`, and the distributed manager enters phase two. In phase two, the distributed manager sends the `commit` command to the local managers, if all the local managers in phase one responded with `ready to commit`. If one or more local managers did not report to the distributed manager with `ready to commit` (in phase one), the distributed manager will tell all the local managers (in phase two) to roll back.

Now that you are comfortable with the basic concept of a transaction, it's time to explore how transactions are implemented in the EJB framework.

12.2 IMPLEMENTING EJB TRANSACTIONS

Support for transaction management is an important feature of EJB. Transaction management in EJB consists of two levels. The higher level of management is concerned with marking the boundaries of a transaction, such as where the transaction starts and where it ends, and is called *transaction demarcation*. The bean provider has two choices here: declare the transaction boundaries in the deployment descriptor (container-managed transactions, or CMT) or code the demarcation in the bean methods (bean-managed transactions, or BMT). In the latter case, you delegate the responsibility for starting and ending transactions to the container. BMT and CMT demarcations are also called *programmatic* and *declarative* demarcations, respectively. Regardless of whether a bean uses CMT or BMT demarcation, the responsibility for low-level transaction management, such as implementing a two-phase commit and the enlistment of resources, always falls on the container.

In order to support transactions, EJB offers two interfaces that contain the methods that can be used by BMT and CMT beans. This is the topic that we explore in this section.

12.2.1 Interfaces for transactions

If you use BMT demarcation, you are responsible for calling the methods to start and end (commit or roll back) a transaction. These methods are in the `User-Transaction` interface. If you are using CMT, the container is responsible for calling the methods to start and end a transaction. But you can still call some other transaction-related methods, such as marking a transaction for rollback. All these transaction-related methods exist in two interfaces: `EJBContext` and `User-Transaction`, shown in figure 12.1.

All the methods in the `UserTransaction` interface can be used only by a BMT bean. The `EJBContext` interface contains three transaction-related methods: one for BMT beans only and the other two for CMT beans only. The `getUserTransaction()` method can be used only by a BMT bean to get the transaction context. The other two methods, `setRollbackOnly()` and `getRollbackOnly()`, can be invoked on the `EJBContext` only by a CMT bean in order to mark a transaction for rollback and to find out whether a transaction is already marked for a rollback, respectively. If in a CMT bean you realize that a transaction cannot succeed, you mark

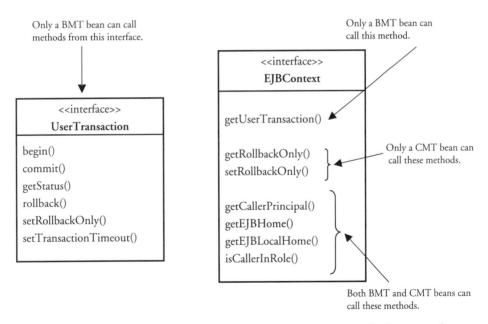

Figure 12.1 The interfaces `UserTransaction` and `EJBContext` contain the transaction-related methods used by CMT and BMT beans; no parameters are shown. Only a BMT bean can use the methods in the `UserTransaction` interface, while the `EJBContext` interface has methods for both BMT and CMT beans.

it for rollback by calling `setRollbackOnly()`. Afterwards, any other CMT bean that is called within this transaction can find out whether it is marked for rollback by calling the method `getRollbackOnly()` on its context. This way a bean can keep from wasting its time working on a transaction that is already marked for rollback. Recall that the contexts of all beans (SessionContext, EntityContext, and Message-DrivenContext) extend `EJBContext`, so the transaction-related methods are available to all three kinds of bean. Once the transaction of a CMT bean is marked for rollback, the container must not commit.

> **NOTE**   Once a transaction of a CMT bean is marked for rollback, the container must not commit.

The `setRollbackOnly()` method is also available in the `UserTransaction` interface for BMT beans. However, no `getRollbackOnly()` method is available for BMT beans. A BMT bean can find out if a transaction is marked for rollback by calling the `getStatus()` method instead. The `getStatus()` method returns more information about the status of a transaction, including whether the transaction is marked for rollback.

> **ALERT**   The `getRollbackOnly()` method is not available for a BMT bean. Instead, a BMT bean calls the `getStatus()` method to find out if a transaction is marked for rollback. Also, a BMT bean can use the `setRollbackOnly()` method only from the `UserTransaction` interface (not the `EJBContext`), and a CMT bean cannot use any method from the `UserTransaction` interface.

The `setTransactionTimeout()` method is also available only for BMT beans, and you can use it to override the default timeout value of the transaction set by the server. You can do this only before beginning the transaction.

As you have seen, the `EJBContext` and `UserTransaction` interfaces have methods for both BMT and CMT demarcations. Let's explore further how these two demarcations work.

12.2.2 Using bean-managed transactions demarcation

If you want to use bean-managed transaction demarcation, you declare it in the deployment descriptor by specifying the `<transaction-type>` element at the same hierarchy level where you specify the `<ejb-name>` element for your bean:

```
<ejb-name> FortuneCookieBean </ejb-name>
<transaction-type> Bean </transaction-type>
```

Having declared the bean's `<transaction-type>` as `Bean`, you can begin and end the transaction in the bean's methods. Before you can begin the transaction, you must get the transaction context by invoking the `getUserTransaction()` method on the `EJBContext` interface. The following example shows the skeleton of a method with transaction-related method calls:

```
public void aTransactionalMethod(){

  UserTransaction utx = context.getUserTransaction();
//start a transaction
  utx.begin();
// do other stuff in the transaction

  ...

//complete the transaction
  utx.commit();
}
```

In this code, `context` is a reference to the bean's EJBContext (SessionContext, EntityContext, or MessageDrivenContext, depending on the bean kind). You get the transaction context, `utx`, by invoking the method `getUserTransaction()` on the bean context. Any method call between `utx.begin()` and `utx.commit()` (or `utx.rollback()`) is made with the transaction context. Any method call made after `utx.commit()` is made without a transaction context.

When you are implementing a BMT transaction, you must obey the following rules:

- EJB does not allow nested transactions. This means when you begin a transaction in your code, you must end it (with a call to commit or roll back) before beginning another transaction.

- For a message-driven bean or a stateless session bean, you must end the transaction before ending the method in which you began the transaction.

- A transaction can propagate out of a BMT bean, but it can never flow into a BMT bean. In other words, a BMT bean method will never run in another bean's transaction. If a method from another bean makes a call to a BMT bean method with a transaction context, the calling bean's transaction will be suspended.

NOTE   If you started a transaction in a method of a stateless session bean or a message-driven bean, you must complete it before the method ends. Furthermore, there can be no nested transactions in a BMT bean.

When a method with a transaction context calls another method, the called method may suspend the caller method's transaction under certain circumstances that will become clear later in this chapter. You may be wondering what it means to *suspend* a transaction. This means that when a method call returns, the transaction will continue from the point where it was suspended, and whatever happened in the called method is not a part of the calling method's transaction. For example, if the transaction of the calling method is rolled back, whatever happened in the called method will not be rolled back.

Only session beans and message-driven beans can be BMT beans. Entity beans always use CMT demarcations. Therefore, they cannot use the `UserTransaction` interface.

Let's now look at container-managed transaction demarcation.

12.2.3 Using container-managed transaction demarcation

Contrary to a BMT bean, in a CMT bean, transactions are started and ended by the container. You make a bean a CMT bean by specifying the `<transaction-type>` in the deployment descriptor, as shown here:

```
<transaction-type>Container</transaction-type>
```

How does the container know which method of your bean will run in a transaction? You tell it by assigning the transaction attributes to the methods in the deployment descriptor. Here is an example:

```
<method>
  <ejb-name>FortuneCookieBean</ejb-name>
  <method-name>aTransactionalMethod</method-name>
</method>
<trans-attribute>RequiresNew</trans-attribute>
```

This code assigns the RequiresNew transaction attribute to the method `aTransactionalMethod()` in the bean FortuneCookieBean. This tells the container that if `aTransactionalMethod()` is called by another method, it should run `aTransactionalMethod()` in its own transaction. You will learn more about transaction attributes in the next section.

You can use BMT for one bean and CMT for another bean in the same deployment descriptor, but you cannot use both BMT and CMT for the same bean. In other words, you cannot assign a `<trans-attribute>` to one method in a bean and code a transaction (for example, make calls to `begin()`, `commit()`, and so on) for another method in the same bean.

NOTE   You can use BMT for one bean and CMT for another bean in the same deployment descriptor, but you cannot use both BMT and CMT for the same bean.

So, in a CMT bean, you tell the container about the transactional behavior of a bean method by assigning it a transaction attribute in the deployment descriptor. Transaction attributes are discussed in the next section.

12.3 TRANSACTION ATTRIBUTES

A transaction may propagate across multiple methods. For example, consider a method in which you start and end a transaction. Between the start and end of the transaction, you may be making calls to other methods. The question is, will those other methods run inside this transaction or not? The answer is not a simple yes or

no. There are many possible answers: yes; no; maybe; no thanks, I have my own transaction; if you come in with a transaction, you will die; if you don't come in with a
transaction, you will die. You get the idea. Of course, you write these answers in the
civilized language of transaction attributes.

Which specific answer will a called method give and how will it give that answer?
You determine the answer by specifying a transaction attribute for that method in the
deployment descriptor. Let's explore the definitions and uses of the transaction
attributes available in EJB.

12.3.1 Defining transaction attributes

Transaction attributes assigned to a method determine the behavior of the method
toward the incoming transaction in a method call. EJB offers the following six transaction attributes:

- Mandatory
- Never
- NotSupported
- Required
- RequiresNew
- Supports

These six attributes can be grouped into two categories: attributes that require a transaction and those that do not require a transaction.

Attributes that require a transaction

If a method is marked with any attribute from this category, then the method when
invoked will either run in a transaction or it will not run. This category includes three
attributes. In the following list we discuss how a called method will behave if it is
marked with one of these attributes:

- *Mandatory*—If a method marked with the Mandatory attribute is called with an
  existing transaction context, then the called method runs in that transaction. If
  the called method is called without an existing transaction context, then the
  container will throw an exception. That means the called method will always
  run in a transaction, if it does run, regardless of whether the calling method
  called it with or without a transaction. So, a method with the attribute Mandatory says to the outside world: "Whoever wants to come in, you better come in
  with a transaction context, or I'm going to throw an exception on you."

- *Required*—If a method marked with the Required attribute is called with an
  existing transaction context, then the called method runs in that transaction. If
  the called method is called without an existing transaction context, then the
  container will start a new transaction. That means the called method will always

run in a transaction regardless of whether the calling method called it with or without an existing transaction. The message to the outside world is: "If you come in with a transaction, thank you, I will run in it; otherwise, no problem, I will start my own."

- *RequiresNew*—If a method marked with the RequiresNew attribute is called with an existing transaction context, then that transaction is suspended, and the called method runs in a new transaction. If the called method is called without an existing transaction context, then the container will start a new transaction. That means the called method will always run in a new transaction regardless of whether the calling method called it with or without an existing transaction. The message to the outside world is: "I am always going to run in a transaction, and in my own transaction. If you come in with a transaction, I'm going to gently suspend it, and after I'm done, you can restart your transaction from the point where I suspended it. So the bottom line is no, thanks, I will start my own."

Attributes that do not require a transaction

These attributes are used to accommodate the "maybe" answer in EJB. If a method is marked with any attribute from this category, then the method when invoked may or may not run in a transaction. This category includes the following three attributes; we describe how a called method will behave if it is marked with one of these attributes:

- *Never*—If a method marked with the Never attribute is called with an existing transaction context, then the container will throw an exception. If the called method is called without an existing transaction context, then the called method runs with an unspecified transaction context. The message to the outside world is: "Don't even think about it; never come to me with a transaction."

- *NotSupported*—If a method marked with the NotSupported attribute is called with an existing transaction context, then that transaction is suspended, and the called method runs with an unspecified transaction context. If the called method is called without an existing transaction context, then the called method runs with an unspecified transaction context, too. The message to the outside world is: "No thanks, I like to run in an unspecified transaction context."

- *Supports*—If a method marked with the Supports attribute is called with an existing transaction context, then the called method runs in that transaction. If the called method is called without an existing transaction context, then the called method runs with an unspecified transaction context. The message to the outside world is: "If you come in with a transaction, I will run in it; otherwise I will run in an unspecified transaction context."

The transactional behavior of methods determined by these transaction attributes is summarized in table 12.1. This table shows the transactional behavior of method B under each attribute when it is called by method A under two different conditions:

with a transaction and without a transaction. The transactional contexts for methods A and B are denoted by TA and TB, when they are running in a transaction.

Table 12.1 Transactional behavior of bean methods determined by the transaction attributes. TA and TB refer to the transaction contexts of methods A and B, respectively.

Transaction Attribute of Called Method B	Method A Calls Method B from within Transaction TA	Method A Calls Method B without a Transaction Context
Mandatory	Method B runs in TA.	Container throws an exception.
Required	Method B runs in TA.	Method B runs in TB.
RequiresNew	Method B runs in TB.	Method B runs in TB.
Never	Container throws an exception.	Method B runs in unspecified transaction context.
NotSupported	Method B runs in unspecified transaction context.	Method B runs in unspecified transaction context.
Supports	Method B runs in TA.	Method B runs in unspecified transaction context.

By now you may be wondering what an unspecified transaction context is. First, only a method with the transaction attributes Supports, NotSupported, or Never can run in an unspecified transaction context. This means you just don't know the transaction behavior of the method when it is running. The EJB specification basically leaves the implementation of unspecified context to the server vendor. For example, depending on the vendor's implementation, a method in an unspecified transaction may treat each access to a resource manager as a transaction, treat multiple accesses to a resource manager as a single transaction, or use no transaction at all. Because of this uncertainty, you should always use the transaction attributes Never, Supports, and NotSupported with great caution.

The methods `ejbCreate()`, `ejbRemove()`, `ejbPassivate()`, and `ejbActivate()` of a CMT session bean always run in an unspecified transaction context. The methods `ejbCreate()` and `ejbRemove()` of a CMT message-driven bean also run in an unspecified transaction context. For a message-driven bean, only the NotSupported and Required attributes can be used.

In table 12.1 you see two cases in which the container throws exceptions: when a method call with a transaction context tries to get into a method with the Never attribute and when a method call without a transaction context attempts to get into a method with the Mandatory attribute. The container also must throw the `java.lang.IllegalStateException` if you invoke the `EJBContext.setRollbackOnly()` method from inside a CMT bean marked with any of these attributes: Supports, NotSupported, or Never.

In an application, there could be a sequence of method calls: method A calls method B, method B in turn calls method C, and so on. In the next section, we present an example involving sequences of method calls in order to help you develop a better understanding of transaction attributes.

12.3.2 Transaction attributes in action

To develop a concrete understanding about the transaction attributes, let's consider the two sequences of method calls shown in figure 12.2.

In the first sequence, `Method_A()` is in transaction Tx1 when it calls `Method_B()`, which starts executing in the same transaction (Tx1). While `Method_B()` is executing in transaction Tx1, it calls `Method_C()`, which starts executing in a new transaction, Tx2, and before completing calls `Method_D()`, which executes in an unspecified transaction. In the second sequence, `Method_A()`, while executing in transaction Tx1, calls `Method_E()`, which starts executing in a new transaction, Tx3, and before completing calls `Method_F()`, which executes in the same transaction, and so on. The question is, what is the possible combination of transaction attributes that we can assign to these methods that will make these two sequences of method calls possible? Some possible and impossible scenarios are presented in table 12.2.

Table 12.2 Several combinations of transaction attributes for the methods shown in figure 12.2. Only one combination makes the two sequences of method calls shown in figure 12.2 possible.

`Method_A()`	Requires	Supports	Mandatory	RequiresNew
`Method_B()`	Supports	Requires	RequiresNew	Mandatory
`Method_C()`	RequiresNew	RequiresNew	Required	RequiresNew
`Method_D()`	NotSupported	NotSupported	Supports	Required
`Method_E()`	RequiresNew	RequiresNew	NotSupported	RequiresNew
`Method_F()`	Mandatory	Supports	Never	Required
`Method_G()`	Required	NotSupported	Requires	Supports
Possible?	No	Yes	No	No

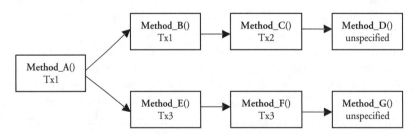

Figure 12.2 Two sequences of method calls. There may be several scenarios about what attributes we assign to these methods in order to make these sequences possible or not possible.

The scenario shown in the first column of table 12.2 is not possible. Let's see where it breaks down. Consider both figure 12.2 and table 12.2. `Method_A()` while in transaction Tx1 calls `Method_B()`, which runs in the same transaction (Tx1). This is possible because `Method_B()` has the attribute Supports. Now, `Method_B()` calls `Method_C()`, which executes in a different transaction, Tx2, which is possible because `Method_C()` has the attribute RequiresNew. If `Method_C()`, for instance, had the attribute Required, the sequence would have broken down right here. When `Method_C()` calls `Method_D()`, `Method_D()` runs in an unspecified context, which is okay because the attribute for `Method_D()` is NotSupported. Similarly, you can go through the second sequence and see that everything is all right until you get to the step where `Method_F()` calls `Method_G()`. Because `Method_G()` has the attribute Supports, and `Method_F()` is calling it within transaction Tx3, `Method_G()` would run in transaction Tx3. But figure 12.2 shows that `Method_G()` runs in an unspecified transaction. Hence, the scenario is not possible. It would be possible, for instance, if the transaction attribute for `Method_G()` was NotSupported. You can go through the rest of the columns in table 12.2 and convince yourself that only the combination presented in column 3 starting with the transaction attribute Supports is a possible combination.

Transaction attributes also limit the code that you can write in bean methods. In a CMT bean, your call to a transaction-related method in the `EJBContext` interface from a business method must be consistent with the transaction attribute assigned to the business method. For example, if you assign the attribute Supports, NotSupported, or Never, the business method will execute in an unspecified transaction context. So, any method call to `EJBContext.getRollbackOnly()` or `EJBContext.set-RollbackOnly()` from such a business method will cause the container to throw `java.lang.IllegalStateException`. The container will also throw this exception if you try to invoke `EJBContext.getUserTransaction()` in a CMT bean, because only BMT beans can invoke this method. Note that there are other situations in which the bean is in an unspecified transaction context, such as execution of the `ejbCreate<Method>()` method of a CMT session bean.

> **ALERT**   In a CMT bean, a call to `getRollbackOnly()` or `setRollback-Only()` from a method with the attribute Never, Supports, or NotSupported will cause a `java.lang.IllegalStateException`.

So, in a CMT bean, you tell the container about the transaction behavior of certain methods. Which methods need transaction attributes? The next section answers this question.

12.3.3   Using transaction attributes

In the case of a container-managed transaction, it is your responsibility to specify transaction attributes for certain methods in session beans, entity beans, and message-driven beans. The container uses these attributes to manage transactions for the bean instances.

Methods of session beans

The only methods in a session bean for which the transaction attributes must be defined are the methods in the component interface and the methods in its super-interfaces that it inherits directly or indirectly, with the exception of methods in the EJBObject and EJBLocalObject interfaces. Recall that the remote component interface of a session bean or an entity bean extends EJBObject, and the local interface extends EJBLocalObject. However, no methods in these interfaces should be marked. The methods of all other interfaces that the component interface extends must be marked. The methods of the session bean's home interface must not be marked with transaction attributes.

Bottom line: only the business methods in the component interface of a session bean should be marked.

Methods of entity beans

The following methods in an entity bean must be marked with a transaction attribute:

- All the methods in the component interface and the remove() method in the EJBObject interface that the component interface extends

- All the methods in the home interface and both remove() methods in the EJBHome interface that the home interface extends

- All the methods in the superinterfaces that the component interface inherits directly or indirectly, with the exception of the getEJBHome(), getEJB-LocalHome(), getHandle(), getPrimaryKey(), and isIdentical() methods

- All the methods in the superinterfaces that the home interface inherits directly or indirectly, with the exception of the getEJBMetaData() and get-HomeHandle() methods

Note that for a session bean, you do not mark any method from EJBObject and EJBHome with a transaction attribute, while for an entity bean you do mark the remove() methods from EJBObject and EJBHome. This is because the remove() methods behave differently in an entity bean. They are part of a delete in the database. Once you develop enough understanding about these methods, it will become obvious why you are required to specify transaction attributes for some methods and not for others.

Methods of message-driven beans

A message-driven bean (MDB) does not have any client interface, so the only method that must be marked with a transaction attribute is the onMessage() method. Furthermore, because an MDB does not have a component interface, the interface-related attributes do not make sense. Therefore, the onMessage() method can be marked only with either Required or NotSupported.

12.3.4 Transaction attributes used by beans

Not all transaction attributes make sense for all kinds of beans. Table 12.3 shows a list of transaction attributes that can be used for a session bean, an entity bean, and a message-driven bean.

Table 12.3 Transaction attributes that can be used for a session bean, an entity bean, and a message-driven bean

Bean	Transaction Attributes
Session bean	Mandatory, Never, NotSupported, Required, RequiresNew, Supports
Entity bean (CMP)	Mandatory, Required, RequiresNew
Message–driven bean	NotSupported, Required

Transactions do not necessarily have to involve databases, but they generally do. Because entity beans are designed to represent the entities in databases, they are more transactional. You should assign only the Mandatory, Required, or RequiresNew attribute to an entity bean method. In other words, a CMP entity bean method that requires an attribute assignment always runs in a transaction when called by another method. The container that you are using may optionally allow you to assign other attributes to entity bean methods, but then your entity bean will not be portable.

ALERT   A message-driven bean can use only two transaction attributes: Not-Supported and Required.

Although session beans can use databases too, by their design they are less transactional than entity beans. So, you can assign any of the six attributes to a session bean method that requires an attribute. However, if a bean implements the `javax.ejb.SessionSynchronization` interface, the application assembler can use only Mandatory, Required, or RequiresNew for a bean method, because in this case a session bean becomes as transactional as an entity bean. In other words, this ensures that the method runs only in a transaction that is necessary for the synchronization to work.

Because an MDB does not have any client interface, and because it has only one business method, `onMessage()`, that is called by the container, the issue of an incoming method call with or without a transaction does not exist. If the method `onMessage()` has a transaction, it must have been started for this method (by the container) and must complete (commit or roll back) before the method execution is complete. Therefore, `onMessage()` either runs in a transaction or it does not, and this can be handled with two transaction attributes: Required and Not-Supported. In the case of Required, the container starts the transaction before invoking `onMessage()`.

Now that you know for which bean methods you are required to specify transaction attributes, you may be wondering how exactly to do that. In the next section, we address this issue.

12.4 SPECIFYING TRANSACTIONS IN A DEPLOYMENT DESCRIPTOR

In a deployment descriptor, first you declare that a bean is a CMT bean, and then you specify a transaction attribute for each method of that bean that requires an attribute.

12.4.1 Specifying the transaction type for a bean

For each bean in a deployment descriptor, you need to specify whether it is going to use a bean-managed transaction or a container-managed transaction. For entity beans it is always a container-managed transaction (CMT). For other two kinds, you specify the type of transaction by using the `<transaction-type>` element in the `<enterprise-beans>` part of the deployment descriptor, as shown here:

```
<ejb-jar>
 <enterprise-beans>
    <session>
       <ejb-name> FortuneCookieBean </ejb-name>
         ...
       <transaction-type> Container </transaction-type>    ⟵   Replace Container
         ...                                                    with Bean for BMT
    </session>
 </enterprise-beans>
    <assembly-descriptor>
     ...
    </assembly-descriptor>
     ...
</ejb-jar>
```

Because an entity bean always uses CMT, the `<transaction-type>` element is not supported by `<entity>`. In other words, you do not declare the transaction type for an entity bean; it is assumed to be container managed.

Once you declared a bean as a CMT bean, you can specify the transaction attributes for its methods that require attributes.

12.4.2 Specifying the transaction attribute for a bean method

After you have declared the bean as CMT in the `<enterprise-beans>` section of the deployment descriptor, you specify the transaction attributes for its methods in the `<assembly-descriptor>` section of the deployment descriptor. The three techniques for specifying transaction attributes for methods are discussed next.

Individual specifications

In this technique, you specify a transaction attribute for a method by specifically naming the method. Here is an example:

```
<ejb-jar>
   <enterprise-beans>
     ...
   </enterprise-beans>
```

```
<assembly-descriptor>
  <container-transaction>
   <method>
    <ejb-name> FortuneCookieBean </ejb-name>
    <method-name> getFortune </method-name>
   </method>
   <trans-attribute> RequiresNew </trans-attribute>          ⊲─── Append more
  </container-transaction>                                          <method>
</assembly-descriptor>                                              elements here
  ...
</ejb-jar>
```

In order to mark multiple methods with the same attribute, you can list all the methods in the same `<container-transaction>` element by using one `<method>` element for each method followed by only one `<trans-attribute>` element for all the methods. If you want to specify a different attribute for a method, you can do that in a separate `<container-transaction>` element.

What if you want to assign different attributes to different versions of an overloaded method? Let's see how you can do that.

Distinguishing between overloaded methods

If you use the technique just described, all the overloaded versions of a method will get the same transaction attribute. To distinguish between the two versions of an overloaded method, you include the parameters in the `<method-param>` element, as shown here:

```
<container-transaction>
    <method>
       <ejb-name> FortuneCookieBean </ejb-name>
       <method-name> getFortune </method-name>
       <method-params>
         <method-param> int </method-param>          ⊲─┐
         <method-param> String </method-param>          │ Two parameters
       <method-params>                                   │ marked
    </method>                                            │ Mandatory
       <trans-attribute> Mandatory </trans-attribute>  ⊲─┘
</container-transaction>
<container-transaction>
    <method>
       <ejb-name> FortuneCookieBean </ejb-name>
       <method-name> getFortune </method-name>
       <method-params>                                 ⊲─┐
          <method-param> String </method-param>          │ One parameter
       <method-params>                                   │ marked Never
    </method>                                            │
    <trans-attribute> Never </trans-attribute>         ⊲─┘
</container-transaction>
```

What happens if you don't specify an attribute for a method that you were supposed to? Let's explore this next.

Defining a default attribute

If there is a method in the bean for which you were supposed to specify a transaction attribute but you did not, it will be marked with a default attribute. But you must define the default attribute as shown here:

```
<container-transaction>
   <method>
    <ejb-name> FortuneCookieBean </ejb-name>
    <method-name> * </method-name>
   </method>
    <trans-attribute> RequiresNew </trans-attribute>
</container-transaction>
```

The wildcard * specifies that all methods of the FortuneCookieBean be marked with RequiresNew. However, any specification by method name will override this specification. Therefore, any method that has not been assigned an attribute explicitly will be left with the default attribute.

When transactions involve data in memory that's related to data in the database, it is important to keep the two synchronized. We explore the transaction synchronization issue next.

12.5   TRANSACTION SYNCHRONIZATION

To maintain data consistency during a transaction, it is important that the bean and the database stay synchronized. Entity beans interact with the database, and they have method calls such as ejbLoad() and ejbStore() that the container calls to facilitate the synchronization of the bean data with the database data. For example, just before committing a transaction, the container calls ejbStore() to give the bean a chance to update its persistent state before it is written into the database. Session beans usually use entity beans in order to deal with the data in the database. However, it is possible for a session bean to interact with the database directly. In that case, the CMT entity bean will need some methods that will help the container keep the bean synchronized, but a session bean does not have the ejbStore() and ejbLoad() methods. Note that the issue exists only in a CMT session bean, because in a BMT session bean, you will code when the transaction starts and when it ends. And the issue exists only for a stateful session bean, because a stateless session bean has to end the transaction before the method in which it started ends, so the container will not get the opportunity to call a synchronization method such as ejbStore() on a stateless session bean. To help the container keep a CMT stateful session bean synchronized, EJB offers the javax.ejb.SessionSynchronization interface shown in figure 12.3. It provides three methods whose function and scope are summarized in table 12.4: afterBegin(), beforeCompletion(), and afterCompletion().

These methods are the callback methods that the container calls to tell the bean when a transaction starts, when it is about to complete, and when it has completed.

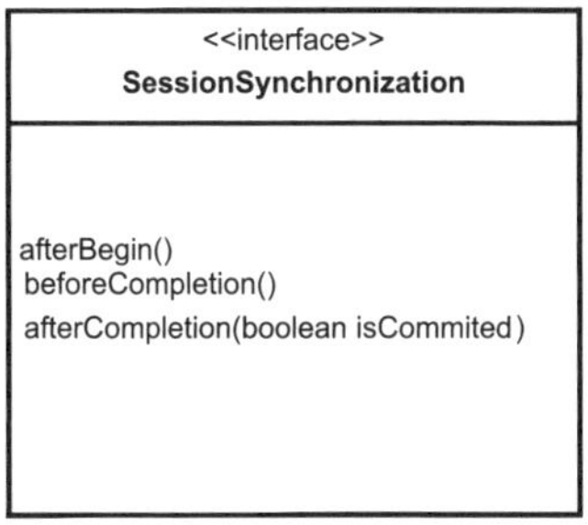

```
          <<interface>>
      SessionSynchronization


  afterBegin()
  beforeCompletion()
  afterCompletion(boolean isCommited)
```

Figure 12.3
Methods in the `javax.ejb.`
`SessionSynchronization` interface.
These methods are used by the
container to keep a stateful CMT session
bean synchronized with the database.

So, the `SessionSynchronization` interface is helpful when your problem is well represented by a session bean (for example, it's a process), and you want the session bean to interact with the database directly, that is, not through an entity bean. The functionalities and scopes of the methods in the `SessionSynchronization` interface are summarized in table 12.4.

Table 12.4 The synchronization methods offered by the `SessionSynchronization` interface for a stateful session bean. The functions and scopes of the methods are summarized.

Method			
When Is It Called?	Typical Work You Will Do	Permission for Context Info	Permission for Access
`afterBegin()`			
Before the first method in a transaction is invoked.	Load the data from the database.	You are allowed to call all methods on the SessionContext to get a reference to bean's home interface or component interface, to get a caller's security information, to mark the transaction to roll back, or to find out if the transaction is marked for rollback.	You can have access to a bean's JNDI context, a resource manager, or another bean.
`beforeCompletion()`			
Immediately before committing a transaction, but after all the tasks of the transaction have been completed.	Last chance to update the database with fresh data or to mark the transaction for rollback by calling `setRollbackOnly()`.	Still in the transaction. Same permissions as for `afterBegin()`.	Still in the transaction. Same permissions as for `afterBegin()`.
`afterCompletion()`			
After the transaction is ended (committed or rolled back). Passing an argument indicating a success or a failure to commit.	Do whatever you have to do to deal with the aftermath of the transaction. By now you know whether the transaction has been committed or rolled back.	Not in the transaction anymore. So you *cannot* do transaction-related things, such as mark the transaction to roll back or find out whether the transaction is marked for rollback.	Cannot access resource managers or other beans. Can access the JNDI context.

ALERT Only stateful session beans, and not stateless session beans, implement the `SessionSynchronization` interface. Furthermore, in order for a stateful session bean to implement this interface, the bean must be a CMT bean.

The methods of a session bean that implements the `SessionSynchronization` interface can be assigned only one of the following transaction attributes: Requires, Required, or Mandatory. These are the only transaction attributes that guarantee that whenever a method is called, it will run in a transaction. Otherwise, it would be possible to execute a bean's method without a transaction, and the container would not call a synchronization method.

The three most important takeaways from this chapter are

- Beans can have either bean-managed transaction (BMT) demarcation coded by the bean developer or container-managed transaction (CMT) demarcation specified by the transaction attributes declared in the deployment descriptor.

- Transaction-related methods come from two interfaces: `UserTransaction`, which is used only by BMT beans, and `EJBContext`, which contains methods for both BMT and CMT beans.

- There are specific methods for each bean flavor for which the transaction attributes must be specified for a CMT bean.

12.6   SUMMARY

EJB offers transaction management for distributed enterprise applications. Lower-level management is always done by the container, while for higher-level management the bean provider has a choice for marking the boundaries of a transaction (called demarcation): container-managed transaction (CMT) demarcation or bean-managed transaction (BMT) demarcation. CMT demarcation is facilitated through transaction attributes defined by the bean provider or the application assembler in the deployment descriptor. There are methods in a session, an entity, and a message-driven bean for which transaction attributes must be specified if the bean is a CMT bean. A session bean supports all six transaction attributes, an entity bean supports only the three attributes that require a transaction, and a message-driven bean supports only two transaction attributes: Required and NotSupported.

Generally speaking, a method can end without completing a transaction, that is, the transaction can propagate across methods. However, in a stateless session bean and in a message-driven bean, you must complete the transaction before the end of the method. Transactions can propagate out of a BMT bean but not into a BMT bean. Also, in a BMT bean, you must not start a new transaction before completing the current one. A BMT bean cannot invoke the `getRollbackOnly()` or `setRollbackOnly()` methods; it invokes `getStatus()` instead. When a bean's method throws a system exception on the container, the container logs the exception, automatically rolls back the current transaction, and discards the bean instance.

Both session beans and message-driven beans can use CMT or BMT demarcation, but entity beans can use only CMT demarcation. This implies that an entity bean cannot use any method from the `UserTransaction` interface because this interface is meant only for BMT beans. When a CMT bean marks a transaction for rollback by using `setRollbackOnly()`, the container must not commit.

As you have seen, a transaction can propagate through methods. There is another thing that can propagate not only from method to method but also from a bean to the container and from the container all the way to the client: an *exception*, which carries the news when something bad happens in a running application. We will explore exceptions in the next chapter.

Comprehend

- Whether the bean is a BMT bean or a CMT bean by looking at a code fragment
- How to specify transaction attributes for methods, inside the deployment descriptor
- Possible and impossible scenarios of sequences of method calls with a transaction attribute assigned to each method

Look out

- If you start a transaction in a method of a stateless session bean or a message-driven bean, you must complete it before the method ends.
- You cannot have nested transactions in a BMT bean.
- Since entity beans always use CMT demarcation, they cannot use the `UserTransaction` interface, because only BMT beans can use the `UserTransaction` interface.
- A message-driven bean can use only two transaction attributes: NotSupported and Required.
- Transaction attributes may be specified either by the bean provider or by the application assembler, but only for CMT beans.
- There may be a combination of BMT and CMT beans in the same deployment descriptor, but a given bean must have either a BMT or a CMT demarcation, but not both.
- In a BMT bean, you can call `setRollbackOnly()` only from within a transaction, that is, between the begin and commit calls.
- In a CMT bean, you can call `setRollbackOnly()` and `getRollbackOnly()` only from within a method with one of these attributes: Mandatory, Required, RequiresNew.
- When an instance in a transaction throws a system exception, the container kills the instance and rolls back the transaction.

Memorize

- The names and functionalities of the methods in the User-Transaction and EJBContext interfaces and whether a BMT bean, a CMT bean, or both can use a given method
- The transaction attributes and what they stand for
- The method names from different bean flavors for which the transaction attributes must be specified

Review questions

Some questions may have more than one correct answer. Choose all that apply.

1. Which of the following statements are true about an EJB transaction in a BMT demarcation?
    a. You can use BMT demarcation only for a session bean or a message-driven bean.
    b. You can start a new transaction before ending a previously started transaction.
    c. A stateful session bean must not complete a transaction in the method where it started before the method returns.
    d. A stateless session bean must complete a transaction in the method where it started before the method returns.

2. Which transaction attributes assigned to a method will assure that the method will always run in a transaction, if it does run?
    a. Mandatory
    b. Never
    c. NotSupported
    d. Required
    e. RequiresNew
    f. Supports

3. Which transaction attributes assigned to a method will assure that the method will always run in an unspecified transaction context, if it does run?
    a. Mandatory
    b. Never

c. NotSupported

d. Required

e. RequiresNew

f. Supports

4. Which of the following transaction attributes assigned to a business method will cause the container to throw `java.lang.IllegalStateException` when the method calls `EJBContext.getRollbackOnly`?

a. Mandatory

b. Never

c. NotSupported

d. Required

e. RequiresNew

f. Supports

5. For which of the following beans can you use BMT demarcation?

a. Message-driven beans

b. Stateful session beans

c. Stateless session beans

d. Entity beans

6. Which of the following attributes can be assigned to a message-driven bean?

a. Required

b. RequiresNew

c. Mandatory

d. Never

e. Supports

f. NotSupported

7. Which of the following methods can be called by a BMT bean?

a. `getRollbackOnly()`

b. `setRollbackOnly()`

c. `setTransactionTimeout()`

d. `getStatus()`

e. `rollback()`

8. Which of the following methods can be called by a CMT bean?

a. `getRollbackOnly()`

b. `setRollbackOnly()`

c. `setTransactionTimeout()`

d. `getStatus()`

e. `rollback()`

9. Which of the following methods of an entity bean must be marked with a transaction attribute?

    a. `remove()` method from the `EJBObject` interface

    b. `remove()` methods from the `EJBHome` interface

    c. `getPrimaryKey()` method from the `EJBObject` interface

    d. `findByPrimaryKey()` method from the bean's home interface

    e. `getEJBHome()` method from the `EJBObject` interface

10. A method `ma()` has the attribute Required and it is executing in transaction TA. Consider the following method calls by method `ma()` to other methods:

    a. `ma() -> mb()`. Method `mb()` runs in transaction TA.

    b. `ma() -> mc()`. Method `mc()` runs in its own transaction, TC

    c. `ma() -> md()`. Method `md()` runs in an unspecified transaction context.

    d. `ma() -> me()`. Method `me()` throws an exception.

Select one of the following attributes for each called method above to force the stated behavior:

Required, RequiresNew, Mandatory, Supports, NotSupported, Never.

C H A P T E R   1 3

EJB exceptions

EXAM OBJECTIVES

12.1 Identify correct and incorrect statements or examples about exception handling in EJB.

12.2 Given a list of responsibilities related to exceptions, identify those which are the bean provider's, and those which are the responsibility of the container provider. Be prepared to recognize responsibilities for which neither the bean nor the container provider is responsible.

12.3 Identify correct and incorrect statements or examples about application exceptions and system exceptions in entity beans, session beans, and message-driven beans.

12.4 Given a particular method condition, identify the following: whether an exception will be thrown, the type of exception thrown, the container's action, and the client's view.

12.5 Identify correct and incorrect statements or examples about the client's view of exceptions received from an enterprise bean invocation.

INTRODUCTION

Bad things can happen to a running application. It can run into an error condition caused by incorrect data entered by the user, a problem in accessing a resource, or a bug in the application code, for example. Java has a comprehensive error-trapping and -handling mechanism called *exception handling*. Exceptions are the messengers that carry the bad news inside the world of applications, from method to method, bean to bean, bean to container, and container to client. There are exceptions that you expect, so you prepare your code for their arrival: undesired but expected guests. These are called *checked exceptions* because the compiler checks whether your code is prepared to deal with them. The counterpart of checked exceptions is *unchecked exceptions*, which the compiler does not check. These are the unexpected messengers that catch you unprepared. In EJB, exceptions are classified as application exceptions and system exceptions. All application exceptions are checked exceptions, and most system exceptions are unchecked exceptions.

We will explore how bad news travels from the bean to the container and from the container to the client. Sometimes the news can be so bad that after hearing it the container will kill the messenger and roll back the transaction in which the news was generated; you witnessed this in the last chapter. In other situations, the container will lazily yield to the exception and let it go to the client in its original form. In yet another situation, it will redress the exception before sending it to the client. We will explore precisely when and how these events happen and to whom.

Your goal in this chapter is to understand the standard application and system exceptions in EJB and how they travel all the way from the bean to the client. To accomplish that we will explore three avenues: application exceptions, system exceptions, and the roles the bean provider and the container play.

13.1 EXCEPTIONS IN JAVA

An exception is an error that happens when an application is running. Java offers a comprehensive and flexible system for exception handling. The main benefit of such a system is that it largely automates the process of error handling, which otherwise would need to be coded into each application. (What a waste of resources that would be!) All exceptions are represented by classes organized into a hierarchy tree. Let's take a look at part of that tree.

13.1.1 The exceptions tree in Java

In Java, exceptions are represented by classes organized into a hierarchy tree. A part of this tree is shown in figure 13.1.

The `Throwable` class, which forms the root of the exceptions tree, is the base class of all exceptions in Java. The two subclasses directly derived from `Throwable` are `Error` and `Exception`.

Errors occur in the Java Virtual Machine (JVM) and not in the application itself. Errors generally represent unusual problems from which it is difficult to recover.

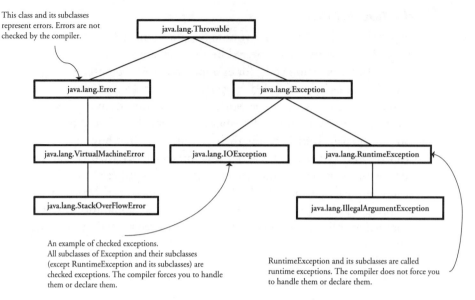

This class and its subclasses represent errors. Errors are not checked by the compiler.

java.lang.Throwable

java.lang.Error

java.lang.Exception

java.lang.VirtualMachineError

java.lang.IOException

java.lang.RuntimeException

java.lang.StackOverFlowError

java.lang.IllegalArgumentException

An example of checked exceptions. All subclasses of Exception and their subclasses (except RuntimeException and its subclasses) are checked exceptions. The compiler forces you to handle them or declare them.

RuntimeException and its subclasses are called runtime exceptions. The compiler does not force you to handle them or declare them.

Figure 13.1 Part of the hierarchy tree of classes representing exceptions in Java. The `Throwable` class forms the root of this tree.

These problems usually originate from the execution environment of the application, for example, running out of memory. Because it is impossible to recover from errors during runtime, programmers are not required to handle them.

Exceptions generally originate from within the application. They may also be related to the way the program interacts with the environment, for example, referring to a nonexistent remote machine. In general, exceptions should be handled in the program. Some examples of exceptions are division by zero, out-of-boundary arrays, and file input/output problems. The `Exception` class has a multitude of subclasses that can be grouped into two categories, as you'll see in the next section.

13.1.2 Checked exceptions and runtime exceptions

Exceptions in Java are classified into two categories: checked exceptions and runtime exceptions.

Checked exceptions

The compiler checks to ensure that your code is prepared for these exceptions, hence the name *checked exceptions*: prepare for unwelcome but expected guests. These exceptions are instances of the `Exception` class or one of its subclasses, excluding the `RuntimeException` branch. Checked exceptions are generally related to how the program interacts with its environment, for example, `URISyntaxException` and `ClassNotFoundException`. The conditions that generate checked exceptions are generally outside the control of your program, and hence they can occur in a correct program. You can anticipate (expect) them, so you must write code to deal with them.

The rule is: when a checked exception is expected, either declare it in the `throws` clause of your method or catch it in the body of your method, or both. In other words, you can throw it without catching it, you can catch it and recover from it, or you can catch it and throw it again.

RuntimeException

Exceptions of type `RuntimeException` generally occur because of program bugs. The programmer is not required to provide code for these exceptions because if the programming were done correctly, these exceptions wouldn't occur. Since the reason for a runtime exception occurring is incorrect code, catching the exception at runtime is not going to help. Besides, it is better to write correct code to prevent runtime exceptions than to write code to catch them. Because the compiler does not check these exceptions, they are also called *unchecked exceptions*. An `Arithmetic-Exception` is an example of a runtime exception. Again, you do not need to declare or catch these exceptions.

After taking this very high-level look at exceptions in Java 2.0 Standard Edition (J2SE), it's time to explore exceptions in EJB.

13.2 EXCEPTIONS IN EJB

The complexity of distributed and transactional applications increases the probability of error and the amount of effort needed to deal with it. In other words, the transactional and distributed nature of the EJB architecture makes support for exception handling in EJB that much more significant.

Not all exceptions in EJB are treated equally. Based on how the container treats exceptions, the exceptions in EJB are grouped into two categories: application exceptions and system exceptions. All application exceptions are checked exceptions, and most system exceptions are unchecked exceptions.

> **NOTE** All application exceptions are checked exceptions. Therefore, when you call another method in your method that can throw an application exception, you must either declare it in the `throws` clause of the calling method or catch it in the body of the calling method or both.

In this section, we explore the standard application exceptions and systems exceptions in EJB.

13.2.1 Standard EJB application exceptions

You saw in the previous section that the root of the exceptions hierarchy tree is the class `Throwable`, which has two direct subclasses: `Error` and `Exception`. Any exception that is a subclass of `Exception`, but not a subclass of `RuntimeException` and not a subclass of `RemoteException`, is an application exception. An application exception is thrown to indicate that the business logic of the application detected a problem. The standard application exceptions in EJB are shown in figure 13.2.

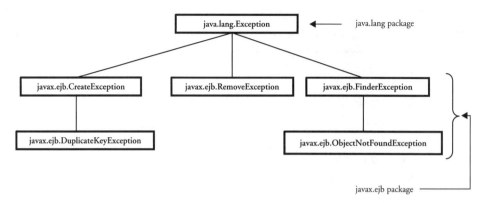

Figure 13.2 Standard application exceptions in EJB. They are subclasses of `Exception` but not subclasses of `RuntimeException` or `RemoteException`.

All five application exceptions (which are subclasses of `java.lang.Exception`) shown in figure 13.2 are in the package `javax.ejb` and are discussed next.

CreateException

A `CreateException` is thrown to indicate that an error has occurred during the process of creating a session bean or entity bean. Both you and the container can throw this exception. For example, if a client called a `create()` method with invalid parameters, you could throw this exception from the `ejbCreate()` or `ejbPost-Create()` method. You must include this exception in the `throws` clause of all the `create()` methods you declare in the home interface of an entity or session bean. You have to include this exception in the `ejbCreate()` and `ejbPostCreate()` methods only if you will possibly throw it from these methods.

In the case of a session bean, a `CreateException` comes from an `ejb-Create()` method, while in the case of an entity bean, it may come from either an `ejbCreate()` or an `ejbPostCreate()` method. If it comes from an `ejbPost-Create()` method, it means the bean has been created but has not been initialized yet. If it comes from the `ejbCreate()` method (of a session or entity bean), it means the bean was never created. You already know the different meanings of the word *create* for session beans and entity beans.

DuplicateKeyException

Being a subclass of `CreateException`, `DuplicateKeyException` is a more specific create exception. It points to the problem of duplicate keys, for example, a request to assign a key to an entity that has already been assigned to another entity.

Either you or the container can throw this exception. A `DuplicateKey-Exception` is thrown only from `ejbCreate()` methods, so you can assume that the entity has not yet been created when this exception is thrown.

FinderException

The container throws the `FinderException` to indicate that something went wrong during the operation requested by a find method invoked by a client. You must include this exception in the `throws` clause of all find methods that you declare in the entity bean's home interface and all the ejbFind (in the case of a bean-managed persistence [BMP] bean) and ejbSelect methods that you declare in the bean class. Recall from chapter 7 that you do not write an ejbFind method in the class of a CMP bean; the container generates this method instead.

ObjectNotFoundException

`ObjectNotFoundException`, a subclass of `FinderException`, is thrown only when a finder method involving a single entity is being invoked and the entity does not exist. The container is responsible for throwing this exception from the ejbFind or ejbSelect methods in the case of a CMP bean, and you throw it in the case of a BMP bean. Recall from chapter 6 that if the return type of a find method is a Collection, you do not throw an exception even if no matching entity is found; instead you return an empty Collection.

RemoveException

`RemoveException` is thrown to indicate an error that happens during an attempt to remove a session or entity bean. For example, if a client invokes the remove method with a primary key as an argument in the case of a session bean, it will cause this exception. It can also occur during an attempt to delete an entity from a database when it does not exist. `RemoveException` does not tell the client conclusively whether or not the entity has been removed before sending the exception. In the case of a session bean, only a client of a stateful session bean can receive this exception because the container creates and removes a stateless session bean without a call from a client.

> **ALERT** A client of a stateless session bean never gets a `RemoveException`. This is because the removal of a stateless session bean is done by the container without any call from the client.

Whenever you call another method from your method that may throw an application exception, you must do at least one of the following:

- Catch the exception in the body of the calling method and recover from it.
- Declare the exception in the `throws` clause of the calling method. In this case, if you don't catch it inside the method, it will simply throw it exactly in the form it receives it. This is called *ducking the exception*. You can also catch it, do something with it, and throw it.

These are the J2SE rules for checked exceptions, and application exceptions are checked exceptions.

Most of the system exceptions in EJB are unchecked exceptions, but not all. Let's explore system exceptions next.

13.2.2 Standard EJB system exceptions

System exceptions are instances of `RuntimeException`, `RemoteException`, or their subclasses. In other words, an exception that is not an application exception is a system exception. These exceptions result from low-level system problems and are problems that a client can't anticipate. However, a system problem may be caused by a programming error. A failure to obtain a database connection or an unexpected `RemoteException` from another bean are examples of these system-level problems.

> **NOTE** All system exceptions are unchecked exceptions except `Remote-Exceptions`, which are checked exceptions. This implies that the remote interfaces should declare them and the client should expect them.

The standard system exceptions that are unchecked exceptions and that are received by local clients are shown in figure 13.3.

The standard system exceptions that are checked exceptions and that are received only by remote clients are shown in figure 13.4.

If a method encounters a runtime exception (`RuntimeException` or any of its subclasses) or an error, it should simply propagate it to the container.

> **NOTE** If a method receives an exception of type `RuntimeException` (or a subclass of it) or an error, the method should throw it exactly as it is received.

A subclass of `RuntimeException` is `EJBException`.

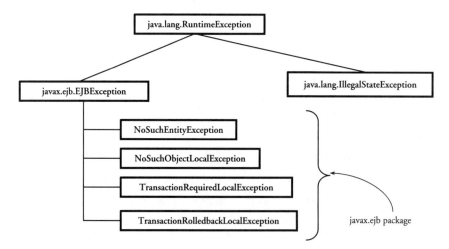

Figure 13.3 `RuntimeException` and its subclasses form a subset of standard system exceptions. These are unchecked exceptions and are thrown back to the bean's local client.

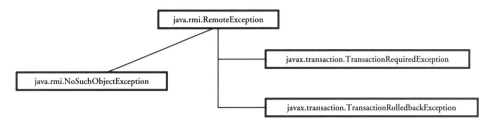

Figure 13.4 `RemoteException` **and its subclasses form a subset of standard system exceptions. These are checked exceptions and are thrown on remote clients.**

EJBException

This exception can be thrown from inside a bean method to tell the container that an exception has happened from which the method cannot recover. If your method receives this exception, just throw it to the container as it is received. If your method encounters a checked exception that the method cannot recover from, you should wrap it in the `EJBException` and throw it to the container. The container can also throw this exception.

> **NOTE** If a method receives a checked exception from which it cannot recover, the method should wrap it inside an `EJBException` and throw it to the container.

Another subclass of `RuntimeException` is `IllegalStateException`. You have met this exception in previous chapters. Let's take another look at it.

IllegalStateException

The container throws `IllegalStateException` when a bean method invokes a method on the context of the bean and it is not allowed to do so. Recall that not all the context methods can be called from all the bean methods. For example, from an `ejbCreate<method>` of an entity bean, you cannot invoke the `getPrimary-Key()` context method, because it's too early for that. Another example would be when you call a transaction-related method such as `getRollbackOnly()` or `set-RollbackOnly()` in the absence of a transaction.

A couple of other exceptions that may look familiar to you from previous chapters are `NoSuchObjectLocalException` and `NoSuchObjectException`. Let's take another look at them.

NoSuchObjectLocalException and NoSuchObjectException

Both of these exceptions occur when a method call is made on an entity that has been removed from the database or on a session bean instance that no longer exists. Under these conditions, the container throws `javax.ejb.NoSuchObjectLocal-Exception` if the call was made by a local client, and it throws `java.rmi.`

`NoSuchObjectException` if the call was made by a remote client. Remember that in the case of a session bean, one of these exceptions will be thrown only if the session bean instance has been removed and not just passivated. If the session bean instance has been passivated, the container will activate it when it is called upon by a client (of course, we are talking about a stateful session bean).

Another subclass of `EJBException` is `NoSuchEntityException`, which we discuss next.

NoSuchEntityException

This exception is thrown by you or the container because `ejbLoad()`, `ejb-Store()`, or a business method was called in response to a call for an entity that has been removed. If this exception makes it to the container, the container will transform it into `NoSuchObjectLocalException` if the client is local or `NoSuchObject-Exception` if the client is remote. In other words, the client never receives an exception called `NoSuchEntityException`.

Next we discuss two pairs of transaction-related exceptions.

TransactionRequiredLocalException and TransactionRequiredException

You learned in chapter 12 that the container will throw an exception if a method with the transaction attribute Mandatory is called by another method without a transaction context. The exception thrown is `TransactionRequiredLocalException` or `TransactionRequiredException`, depending on whether the client is local or remote. The calling method is supposed to make the call to this method only within an existing transaction.

The other pair of transaction-related exceptions relates to the rollback.

TransactionRolledbackLocalException and TransactionRolledbackException

If a client calls a method with a transaction context and the container has to roll back the transaction for reasons other than a bean calling `setRollbackOnly()`, the container sends the client a `TransactionRolledbackLocalException` or a `TransactionRolledbackException`, depending on whether the client is local or remote, respectively. The container may have to roll back, for instance, because a bean throws a system exception.

From the pairs of exceptions discussed above, you should note that when something wrong happens on the EJB server at the system level, a local client will always get an `EJBException` (or any of its subclasses), and a remote client will always get a `RemoteException` (or any of its subclasses). Note that the `RemoteException` (or any of its subclasses) is a system exception but is still a checked exception. If an application exception occurs, the container will always send it to the client exactly as it was thrown.

If an application exception is thrown on the container, the container will send it to the client exactly as it was received. If a system exception is thrown on the container, the container will send an `EJBException` (or a subclass of it) to the client if the client is local and a `RemoteException` (or a subclass of it) if the client is remote.

You know by now that the burden of throwing and handling exceptions is on the bean provider and the container. Let's explore the responsibilities of the bean provider with regard to EJB exceptions.

13.3   BEAN PROVIDER'S RESPONSIBILITIES

It is the bean provider's responsibility to deal with certain exceptions inside the methods that the bean provider writes. An exception may be thrown on the method by another method that was called by this method, or an exception may be created within the current method. The bean provider deals with exceptions by catching and handling them inside the method, throwing them to the container, or both.

Let's see how the bean provider is supposed to deal with application exceptions and system exceptions.

13.3.1   Dealing with application exceptions

You declare application exceptions in the `throws` clauses of the methods of the home and component interfaces of a session bean and an entity bean. They are used to report problem with the business logic and are intended to be handled by the client. So, if you want to throw an application exception from a method in your bean class, you must have declared this exception in the method exposed in the client interface. However, the reverse is not true; that is, if you have declared the exception in the interface, it does not imply that you have to declare it in the bean class; you are required to declare it in your bean class only if you are actually going to throw it. Because a message-driven bean has no client view, you cannot throw an application exception from within a message-driven bean.

If an application exception is thrown on your method, you can recover from the problem that caused the exception or you can rethrow the exception. You can do so either by ducking it or by handling it inside the method body. Let's take a look at both of these approaches.

Ducking the exception

Ducking the exception means to let it keep going without handling it inside the code. If you want to duck an exception thrown on your method, just declare the exception in the `throws` clause and do not catch it inside the method code. An example is shown here:

```
public void getACustomer(String id, String name, String email)
    throws FinderException {
```

```
➥  Context ctx = new InitialContext();
                 Object objref =
                    ➥  ctx.lookup("java:/comp/env/ejb/AnyCustomer");
   CustomerHome home = (CustomerHome)
     ➥  PortableRemoteObject.narrow(objref,    CustomerHome.class);

      // can throw FinderException
      Customer John = home.findByPrimaryKey("11");
}
```

Note that you do not catch the exception here in the method body. So, ducking the exception means telling the messenger of the bad news, "Keep going; I don't want to hear it."

Handling the exception

If you want to handle the exception, declare it in the `throws` clause, and handle it in the `catch` block inside the method code. For an application exception in EJB, the handling must include throwing it to the container (remember, this is on its way to the client!). Why would you throw it to the container from inside the method code rather than just ducking it? Because you may need to do something, such as write a log before throwing it to the container or mark a transaction for rollback. An example is shown here:

```
public void getACustomer(String id, String name, String email)
  ➥  throws FinderException {

 Context ctx = new InitialContext();
            Object objref = ctx.lookup("java:/comp/env/ejb/AnyCustomer");
 CustomerHome home = (CustomerHome)
   ➥  PortableRemoteObject.narrow(objref,    CustomerHome.class);

try{
 Customer John = home.findByPrimaryKey("11");
}catch (FinderException fe){
   System.err.println("Exception: ");
   // Recover from it or rethrow it.
 }
}
```

So, handling an application exception means telling the messenger of the bad news, "Let me hear about it; I might recover from it or let it keep going."

As you already know, EJB offers standard application exceptions. But you can create your own application exceptions, if you are a do-it-yourself kind of person. Let's see how to do it.

Creating your own application exceptions

Now you want to create your own messenger to carry the bad news that might be generated in your code. You can create your own application exceptions and throw them from inside the methods that you write. However, these exceptions must extend `java.lang.Exception` or any of its subclasses except `RuntimeException`. Your application exception must not extend, directly or indirectly, `java.rmi.RemoteException` (or any of its subclasses) either.

So, creating your own application exception means creating a messenger that you can send on a journey to the client if something bad happens. The next question is, what is your responsibility with regard to system exceptions? Let's explore.

13.3.2 Dealing with system exceptions

In EJB, an exception that is not an application exception is a system exception. The bean provider may need to throw system exceptions during the execution of business methods and callback methods. This situation arises when the exception is not expected by the client, in the case of session and entity beans, or when you don't know how to recover from it, for example, in the case of the `onMessage()` method in a message-driven bean where you cannot simply throw an application exception because there is no client to receive it. So, a system exception can be a runtime exception, or it can be a checked exception but you don't know how to recover from it. Both cases are discussed next.

Make it a system exception

If a bean method conducts an operation that causes a checked exception (an exception that is not a subclass of `RuntimeException`) and you don't know how to recover from it, the method code should throw `javax.ejb.EJBException`, which wraps the original exception. We can also talk about checked exceptions that are not declared in the client view, so the client is not expecting them. This is why the original exception is not thrown as it was thrown on your method; it is thrown wrapped inside the system exception, `EJBException`. Since `EJBException` is a runtime exception, you don't need to declare it in the `throws` clause of the method that throws it.

Suppose in your method you do a JNDI lookup on another bean and get the naming exception. You can wrap it inside the `EJBException` and throw it on the container as shown here:

```
public void myMethod() {
  try {
   //Look for another bean
  }catch (javax.naming.NamingException ne) {
  // Wrap this exception inside EJB exception and throw it.
    throw new EJBException(ne);
  }
}
```

With runtime exceptions, however, it's a different story.

Don't touch the runtime exception

If the bean method encounters an error or a runtime exception (RuntimeException or a subclass of it), don't try to catch it; that is, do not use the try-catch block.

> **NOTE** If your method receives an application exception, you may duck it or you may handle it, which means catch it and recover from it or rethrow it. However, if your method catches an application exception that it does not know how to handle, you must wrap it inside the EJBException and throw it.

This sums up your responsibilities with regard to exceptions. Now let's take a look at what the container is supposed to do about exceptions.

13.4 CONTAINER'S RESPONSIBILITIES

The container is on the receiving end of two kinds of exceptions that the bean throws: application exceptions and system exceptions. It sends these exceptions in some form to the client. It can also throw system exceptions of its own such as IllegalStateException on the bean.

13.4.1 Application exceptions

If a bean throws an application exception, the container sends it to the client exactly as it was received. This rule applies to both kinds of application exceptions: the ones that you define (the homemade kind) and the standard EJB application exceptions.

If the bean uses CMT demarcation, and the method was running in a transaction that the container started immediately before the method call, the container will attempt to complete (commit or roll back) the transaction before sending the application exception to the client. If the method has already called setRollbackOnly(), then the container will attempt to roll back the transaction; otherwise it will attempt to commit it. So, the container will not automatically roll back the transaction unless the transaction was already marked for rollback by a call to setRollbackOnly().

> **ALERT** If a bean throws an application exception, the container does not automatically roll back a transaction. For that you need to call the setRollbackOnly() method before the container receives the exception.

Next, let's see what the container's responsibilities are with regard to system exceptions.

13.4.2 System exceptions

A system exception thrown on the container can be an original system exception or a checked exception wrapped in the EJBException. In either case, the container should do the following:

1 Log the exception.
2 Roll back the transaction if the container started one.

3 Discard the bean instance.

4 If the client is remote, send it a `RemoteException`.

5 If the client is local, send it an `EJBException`.

This process is for a CMT bean. For a BMT bean, the steps are the same except for step 2, where the container simply marks any incomplete transaction for rollback. Recall that in a BMT bean, the bean is responsible for completing (committing or rolling back) the transaction.

The three most important takeaways form this chapter are

- Application exceptions and `RemoteExceptions` are checked exceptions.

- System exceptions (except `RemoteExceptions`) are unchecked exceptions.

- The bean provider and the container make the exceptions travel in an orderly manner.

13.5 SUMMARY

EJB offers a comprehensive system for handling exceptions in a distributed and transactional environment. Exceptions in EJB are categorized as application exceptions and system exceptions. All application exceptions are checked exceptions, that is, the compiler checks that your code is prepared for them, and all system exceptions (excluding `RemoteExceptions`) are unchecked exceptions. When a bean throws an application exception to the container, the container throws it to the client exactly as it was received. In this case, the container does not roll back the transaction unless it is marked for rollback by the bean. If a bean throws a system exception on the container, the container kills the bean instance, logs the exception, and rolls back the transaction (for a CMT bean). In this case, the container sends the exception to the client as an `EJB-Exception` if the client is local and a `RemoteException` if the client is remote.

If a bean attempts to invoke a method on its context from a place where it's not supposed to, it will receive an `IllegalStateException` from the container. You cannot make a message-driven bean declare or throw an application exception because it has no client view. Also, the container is not supposed to send `NoSuchEntity-Exception` to the client if it is thrown by a bean method. Instead, it is expected to send the client a more specific exception: `NoSuchObjectException` to the remote client and `NoSuchObjectLocalException` to the local client.

Since EJB is a distributed architecture, the components of the distributed system may be exposed to security threats along their communication lines. We discuss security in EJB in the next chapter.

Comprehend

- Understand how the container handles application exceptions versus system exceptions, and how it handles exceptions going to the local client versus exceptions going to the remote client.
- `RemoteExceptions` go only to remote clients and `EJBExceptions` only to local clients.

Look out

- In the case of an exception, the container will automatically roll back a transaction in only two situations: a `setRollbackOnlyCall()` call was made, or the bean instance threw a system exception.
- Because a message-driven bean does not have a client view, it cannot declare or throw an application exception.
- RemoteException is for a remote client, and it is treated by the client as a checked exception.
- EJBException is for local clients.
- A client of a stateless session bean will never receive a `RemoveException` because the container removes the bean instance without any remove call from the client.
- If a method catches an application exception that it does not know how to handle, for example, it is not declared in the client view or there is no client view as for a message-driven bean, or a bean method performs an operation that produces a checked exception from which it cannot recover, you must wrap the exception in `EJBException` and throw it.

Memorize

- Standard application exceptions, what causes them, and how they travel
- Standard system exceptions, what causes them, and how they travel

Some questions may have more than one correct answer. Choose all that apply.

1. Which of the following are subclasses of `java.rmi.RemoteException`?
   a. `java.rmi.NoSuchObjectException`
   b. `javax.transaction.`
      `TransactionRequiredException`
   c. `javax.ejb.NoSuchEntityException`
   d. `java.lang.IllegalStateException`

2. Which of the following are true about `EJBException`?
   a. If a bean method encounters a `RuntimeException`, it should throw the `EJBException` that wraps the original exception.
   b. If a bean method encounters any unchecked exception, it should throw the `EJBException` that wraps the original exception.
   c. If a bean method encounters any checked exception, it should throw the `EJBException` that wraps the original exception.
   d. If a bean method performs an operation that results in an application exception that it cannot recover from, it should throw the `EJBException` that wraps the original exception.
   e. If a bean method encounters a system exception, it should throw an `EJBException` on the container.

3. Which of the following are true about the container?
   a. If a bean method throws an application exception to the container, the container sends an `EJBException` to the local client.
   b. If a bean method throws a system exception to the container, the container rolls back the transaction in which the exception occurred.
   c. If a bean method throws a system exception to the container, the container sends an `EJBException` to the local client.
   d. If a bean method throws a system exception to the container, the container sends it to the remote client exactly as it was thrown on the container.
   e. If a bean method throws an application exception to the container, the container sends a `RemoteException` to the remote client.

4. Which of the following are true about a `javax.ejb.NoSuchEntityException`?
   a. A remote client will receive this exception.
   b. A local client will receive this exception.

c. A client will never receive this exception.

d. In order to receive this exception, the client must declare it in the `throws` clause.

e. If the container receives this exception, it will discard the bean instance that threw it.

5. Which of the following beans can throw application exceptions?

    a. A session bean with a BMT demarcation

    b. A session bean with a CMT demarcation

    c. An entity bean with a BMT demarcation

    d. An entity bean with a CMT demarcation

    e. A message-driven bean

6. Which of the following are true about an exception that a remote client receives?

    a. The exception can be a `RemoteException`.

    b. The exception can be an `EJBException`.

    c. The exception can be an application exception.

    d. All of the above.

7. If a message-driven bean with a CMT demarcation throws a system exception, which of the following will the container do?

    a. The container will log the exception.

    b. The container will roll back the transaction that it started just before starting the bean method that threw the exception regardless of whether or not the bean called the `setRollbackOnly()` method.

    c. The container will discard the instance that threw the exception.

    d. The container will roll back the transaction only if the bean has invoked `setRollbackOnly()`.

8. If a client receives a `javax.transaction.TransactionRolledbackException`, which of the following may be true about the CMT bean method that threw the exception?

    a. The method is marked with the transaction attribute Mandatory.

    b. The method is marked with the transaction attribute Required.

    c. The method is marked with the transaction attribute Never.

    d. The method is marked with the transaction attribute NotSupported.

9. A remote client invokes a bean method that throws `NoSuchEntity-Exception`. Which of the following exceptions will the client possibly receive?

    a. `NoSuchEntityException`

    b. `NoSuchObjectException`

    c. `RemoteException`

    d. `EJBException`

10. Which of the following are subclasses of `CreateException`?

    a. `DuplicateKeyException`

    b. `NoSuchEntityException`

    c. `IllegalStateException`

    d. `RemoveException`

    e. None of the above

CHAPTER 14

EJB security

EXAM OBJECTIVES

14.1 Identify correct and incorrect statements about the EJB support for security management including security roles, security role references, and method permissions.

14.2 From a list of responsibilities, identify which belong to the application assembler, bean provider, deployer, container provider, or system administrator.

14.3 Given a code listing, determine whether it is a legal and/or appropriate way to programmatically access a caller's security context.

14.4 Given a security-related deployment descriptor tag, identify correct and incorrect statements and/or code related to that tag.

INTRODUCTION

Security management is one of the important services that EJB offers. The low-level security infrastructure in EJB is implemented by the container provider. Security policies are set at deployment time in order to make the beans portable across applications. EJB security boils down to which user has permission to call which method of a bean. Users are defined outside EJB in a specific operational environment (for example, a user named Gurmail Kandola, working on a UNIX machine with username kandola, is a member of user group engineering, has access permission to a MySQL database server, and so on). To the EJB code, a user is represented by an instance of the class `java.security.Principal`. Principals are mapped to security roles, which determine the methods a Principal can access. The application assembler defines the logical security roles, and the deployer maps them to the Principals. A method call from a client may trigger a bean-to-bean chain of calls, as you saw in the previous chapter while exploring transactions. How does security propagate along this chain of calls? How do the various EJB roles split the responsibility for setting security policies? These questions point to some of the important issues that we will explore in this chapter.

Your goal for this chapter is to understand EJB security and how the security assignments and responsibilities flow from method to method and role to role. To accomplish that, we will explore three avenues: declarative and programmatic security in EJB, the flow of responsibilities from role to role in determining security policy, and the flow of security identity within a sequence of method calls.

14.1 IMPLEMENTING SECURITY IN EJB

The security infrastructure in EJB is implemented by the container provider, while the security policies are determined by other EJB roles at deployment and runtime. In this section, we discuss the security requirements presented by the EJB architecture and how they are met. First, we introduce the basic security concepts that you need to grasp in order to comprehend the rest of the material in this chapter.

14.1.1 Understanding basic security concepts

To understand the different features of EJB security and how the various pieces fit together, you need to know what the basic security terms mean. First, we briefly introduce those terms.

Authentication and authorization

Authentication and authorization represent two levels of security on a system, such as a computer system or an application running on a computer. Authentication involves showing your id in order to get into the system, for example, your login and password. Authorization determines what you can and cannot do once you are in the system. For example, first you log on to a file server using authentication, by typing in your login and password. Once you are logged in, you find a set of files that you can only read, another set of files that you can read and change, and yet another set that you cannot even read. This is the authorization part of security. In EJB, authorization means that a client is authorized to call a bean method.

Principals and roles

A Principal is an entity that can be authenticated by a system. It can be, for instance, an end user or an application trying to access another application. In Java, once an entity is authenticated to a system it is represented by an instance of `java.`

`security.Principal`. In EJB, a Principal can be associated with one or more security roles defined by the application assembler.

A security role has a set of permissions assigned to it. A Principal can be mapped to these roles, and then the Principal will have the permissions attached to the role. In other words, a security role is a set of application permissions that can be assigned to a user (or a group of users).

Users and groups

A user is a real person with an account on a system. A group is a collection of users. Either a user or a group can be mapped to a logical security role. In the operational environment, it is the users and groups who use the application, but they live outside of EJB. So, in order to get into the EJB application, they change into Principals and security roles.

> **NOTE** A user of an EJB application lives in a specific operational environment and enters the Java world as a Principal, and the Principal accesses the application by acquiring one or more roles defined within the EJB architecture.

The EJB architecture for distributed and portable enterprise applications has some implications as to how EJB security should look. Let's explore this issue next.

14.1.2 Security in EJB

Implementation of security in any system generally involves two stages: implementing the security infrastructure and allowing an administrator to set and implement security policies on a given system. Keeping this in mind, note that the distributed nature and the portability characteristic of the EJB architecture set the following goals for EJB security:

- Separate the security infrastructure from the business logic of an application, because the bean provider, who is an expert in implementing business logic, may not be a security expert, and some other roles are.
- Remember that EJB applications should be portable across multiple EJB servers, and those servers may possibly be using different security mechanisms.
- Allow security policies to be set at deployment rather than at coding time in order to support portability.

The EJB role responsibilities are determined to meet these goals and requirements. The container provider implements the security infrastructure. The application assembler, the deployer, and the system administrator participate in setting security policies. The EJB spec recommends that the bean provider should neither implement security mechanisms nor hard-code the security policies in the bean's business methods.

Security in EJB is about authorization, for example, who can have access to a certain bean method. The clients of an application exercise certain security roles, and the permission to call methods is assigned to the roles.

14.2　DEFINING THE SECURITY ROLES

It is the deployer's responsibility to deploy the application securely. To do this correctly the deployer needs to know what each business method does in order to determine which user can call it. However, the deployer is not expected to go into the source code. So we have a problem. Here is the solution: the application assembler helps the deployer by providing the security view of an application in the deployment descriptor. The security view contains a set of logical security roles and a set of method permissions for each security role.

The deployment descriptor contains two parts that are related to security: <enterprise-beans>, which is written by the bean provider, and <assembly-descriptor>, which is written by the application assembler. The application assembler defines the security roles in the <assembly-descriptor> part of the deployment descriptor.

The application assembler is responsible for the following:

- Defining each security role using a <security-role> element in the <assembly-descriptor> section of the deployment descriptor.

- Defining the <role-name> element as a subelement of <security-role> to give the security role a name. This step is mandatory.

- Defining the <description> element as a subelement of <security-role> to provide a description for the security role. This step is optional.

A security role applies to all the enterprise beans in the same ejb-jar file. Listing 14.1 shows two security roles defined within the <assembly-descriptor> element.

Listing 14.1　Two security roles named employee and hr-director defined within the `<assembly-descriptor>` element. The `<role-name>` element is the only mandatory element for a `<security-role>`.

```
<assembly-descriptor>
  <security-role>
    <description>
      This role is for any employee of the organization who
      can view only his/her own information.
    </description>
    <role-name> employee </role-name>
  </security-role>

  <security-role>                    Information to
    <description>            ⟵       help the deployer
      This role should only be assigned to the employees who will
      be able to view the information of all the employees and
      change parts of it.
    </description>
    <role-name> hr-director </role-name>    ⟵   Only mandatory
                                                element of security-role
```

```
        </security-role>

</assembly-descriptor>
```

In a given <security-role>, the <role-name> element is the only mandatory element. The <role-name> element is used by the deployer to assign the security role to a user or a group in the actual operational environment. The <description> element is optional and is there to help the deployer understand what this role is before assigning it to an appropriate user or group.

> **NOTE** The role name in the <security-role> element is only logical and does not represent a user or a group in a real operational environment. However, the deployer can map it to a Principal that represents a user in the real operational environment.

Security in EJB is about authorization, namely, permissions to call the bean methods. This is implemented in two steps: granting method permissions to security roles and mapping security roles to Principals, which represent users.

Let's examine how method permissions are defined and granted.

14.3   DEFINING METHOD PERMISSIONS

After defining the security roles, the application assembler can assign method permissions to the roles, that is, the methods of a bean that a user in that role can call. The assembler can assign any of the methods exposed in the component and home interfaces of a bean to a role. We discuss four different techniques for assigning method permissions to a role.

14.3.1   Granting permission to all methods

By using the wildcard *, the application assembler can grant a role permission to all the methods in the home and component interfaces of a bean. An example is shown here:

```
<assembly-descriptor>
  <method-permission>
    <role-name> hr-director </role-name>          ◁─┐  Method permissions
    <method>                                          │  for hr-director
      <ejb-name> EmployeeRecordBean </ejb-name>
      <method-name> * </method-name>
    </method>

    <method>
      <ejb-name> EmployeeProgressBean </ejb-name>
      <method-name> * </method-name>
    </method>
  </method-permission>
</assembly-descriptor>
```

This code means that the role hr-director has been granted permission to call all methods in the home and component interfaces of the beans EmployeeRecordBean and EmployeeProgressBean. In other words, a bean client in the role of hr-director can call any method from the client views of the beans EmployeeRecordBean and EmployeeProgressBean.

This is a sweeping authorization for a role but not an ultimate one. The ultimate authorization would be that any client could call any method of a bean without being checked for authorization, and that is accomplished with the <unchecked> element. The following code fragment means that any method (from the client view) of the bean EmployeeRecordBean can be called by any client unchecked:

```
<method-permission>
  <unchecked/>
  <method>
    <ejb-name> EmployeeRecordBean </ejb-name>
    <method-name> * </method-name>
  </method>
</method-permission>
```

Note that the <unchecked/> element replaces the <role-name> element. A client at runtime is allowed to call a bean method only if the deployer has mapped the Principal associated with the client call to a security role that has permission to call the method, or the method is declared unchecked.

Now you know how a particular role can be allowed to call any method of a bean and how all clients can be allowed to call any method of the bean. Security at this level is fairly loose. You can tighten security further by granting permission at the method level, which we explore next.

14.3.2 Granting permission method by method

The application assembler can allow a role to call a particular method of the home or component interface by naming the method along with naming the bean in the deployment descriptor. An example is shown here:

```
<role-name> hr-director </role-name>
<method>
   <ejb-name> EmployeeRecordBean </ejb-name>
   <method-name> changeEmail </method-name>
</method>
```

In this example, the role hr-director has been granted permission to call the change-Email method of EmployeeRecordBean. If the method changeEmail is overloaded, then the permission will apply to all overloaded versions of the changeEmail() method; in other words, the client in the role of hr-director is permitted to call any version of the overloaded method changeEmail.

If you want to allow the changeEmail method to be called by any client without being checked for authorization, you would again use the <unchecked> element:

```
<method-permission>
    <unchecked/>
    <method>
      <ejb-name> EmployeeRecordBean </ejb-name>
      <method-name> changeEmail </method-name>
    </method>
</method-permission>
```

With the technique discussed in this section, the permission granted for a method would apply to all versions of the overloaded method. What if you want to assign different security to different versions of an overloaded method? The following section shows how to do that.

14.3.3   Distinguishing between overloaded methods

The application assembler can grant permission for specific versions of an overloaded method by naming the method and its arguments. Here is an example:

```
<method-permission>
 <role-name> hr-director </role-name>
    <method>
      <ejb-name> EmployeeRecordBean </ejb-name>
      <method-name> changeEmail </method-name>
      <method-params>
        <method-param> String </method-param>
        <method-param> String </method-param>
      </method-params>
    </method>
</method-permission>
```

This means that the role hr-director is granted permission only to the `changeEmail` method, which has two arguments of type String. What if a method in the home interface has the same name as a method in the component interface, and you want to grant different permissions for both? Let's see how to do that next.

14.3.4   Distinguishing between interfaces

A bean may have two methods with the same name exposed in the home and component interfaces. If the methods need to have different permissions, the application assembler can specify the name of the interface along with the name of the method by using the `<method-intf>` element. For example:

```
<method-permission>
    <role-name> hr-director </role-name>
    <method>
      <ejb-name> EmployeeRecordBean </ejb-name>
      <method-intf> Remote </method-intf>
      <method-name> changeEmail </method-name>
    </method>
</method-permission>
```

The <method-intf> element must be one of the following:

- <method-intf>Home</method-intf>
- <method-intf>Remote</method-intf>
- <method-intf>LocalHome</method-intf>
- <method-intf>Local</method-intf>

These values in the <method-intf> element correspond to the four possible interfaces: the home interface, the remote component interface, the local home interface, and the local component interface, respectively.

Often, one bean will need to call methods on another bean; this way, the original client call may trigger a chain of calls. The question is: what would be the security identity propagating along this chain? The next section explores the answer to this question.

14.4 CONTROLLING THE PROPAGATING SECURITY IDENTITY

A security identity is attached to the client's call to a bean. This means that when a client calls a bean, a caller's Principal is always attached to the call, which you can determine by invoking the getCallerPrincipal() method of the EJBContext. The client's Principal has a security role assigned to it that acts as a security identity of the Principal or the call. Assume that an employee client calls method getPaid() of PaymentBean, and getPaid() calls method getSSN() of RecordBean. The client's Principal and hence the security identity will propagate from getPaid() to getSSN(). Assume that the security role associated with the client's Principal does not allow the client to use getSSN() because this method can be accessed only by the role hr-administrator. In this case, getPaid() will not be able to access get-SSN() because of the security identity propagating with the method call. What if it is necessary for getPaid() to be able to call getSSN(), for example, to verify the identity of the caller? In other words, there will be situations where you want to change the security in a chain of calls, to make it more relaxed or more restrictive. For example, when the client in our example calls getPaid(), and getPaid() in turn calls get-SSN(), we want the call to go through, and in this case, we can do it only by changing the security role going out of PaymentBean into RecordBean to hr-administrator. We can accomplish this by using the <run-as> element within the <security-identity> element in the <enterprise-beans> section of the deployment descriptor. An example follows:

```
<enterprise-beans>
 <entity>
   <ejb-name>PaymentBean</ejb-name>
   ...
   <security-identity>
     <run-as>
      <role-name> hr-administrator </role-name>
```

```
            </run-as>
        </security-identity>
    ...
</entity>
</enterprise-beans>
```

This means that whenever PaymentBean needs to call another bean, it will have the permissions of the hr-administrator security role.

> **ALERT** A bean's `<security-identity>` does not change the security identity of incoming method calls; it is assigned to outgoing method calls.

The methods of PaymentBean will run in the caller's security identity if you don't specify the `<security-identity>` element or if you specify it with the `<use-caller-identity>` element:

```
<enterprise-beans>
 <entity>
  ...
    <ejb-name>PaymentBean</ejb-name>
    ...
    <security-identity>
       <use-caller-identity/>
    </security-identity>
  ...
 </entity>
</enterprise-beans>
```

In this case, when PaymentBean calls a method of RecordBean, it will use the same security identity that it received from its caller.

> **ALERT** Because a message-driven bean (MDB) has no client view, the deployment descriptor should never have `<use-caller-identity>` defined for an MDB. MDBs can use the `<run-as>` element in the `<security-identity>` element.

Note that the `<run-as>` identity applies to a bean as a whole, that is, to all methods of the home and component interfaces of a session and entity bean, to the onMessage() method of an MDB, and to all other bean methods that may come in the chain of calls. It is the responsibility of the application assembler to define the `<security-identity>` element.

Declaring security policies in the deployment descriptor is called *declarative security*, while hard-coding the security policies by the bean provider is called *programmatic security*.

There will be times when you want to disable a method; in other words, no client should be able to call this method regardless of the security identity the client has. Let's explore how to accomplish that.

14.5   DISABLING METHODS

Sometimes you will want to disable a method of an application, so that no client can call the method regardless of what security role is assigned to the Principal representing the client. For example, say that the application offered a discount for a certain period of time by using a method, and now the discount period is over and that method needs to be made inaccessible. To list the methods that cannot be called, the application assembler can use the `<exclude-list>` element as opposed to the `<method-permission>` element in the `<assembly-descriptor>` section of the deployment descriptor. An example code fragment is given here:

```
<exclude-list>
  <description>
    These methods are off limits. No client should be
    allowed to call them.
  </description>
  <method>
    <ejb-name>DiscountBean</ejb-name>
    <method-name> getDiscountForMembers </method-name>
    <method-name> getDiscountForNonMembers </method-name>
  </method>
</exclude-list>
```

What if a method is listed both in `<exclude-list>` and in `<method-permission>`? In that case, `<exclude-list>` will override `<method-permission>` for that method; the deployer must make sure that no client can call the method.

So far, we have explored the roles of the bean deployer and the application assembler in specifying security policies. What kind of role can a bean provider play in determining security policy? We explore this topic next.

14.6   PROGRAMMING SECURITY

The EJB specifications recommend against the bean provider programming security policies. However, there may be situations where you will discover that the declarative security is not flexible enough to satisfy the security needs of an application. In that case you may consider hard-coding security at the cost of portability. Let's begin by identifying the limitations of declarative security that we have discussed in this chapter so far.

14.6.1   Limitations of declarative security

Declarative security supports component-based programming, since you can use the same bean in different security environments by changing the security options at deployment without altering the source code. This makes the bean portable from one security environment to another.

However, declarative security is very simple. For example, it is implemented at the class level. This means that when a role has permission to a method of a class, the role can access that method in all instances of the class. There is no way to limit access to a specific instance by using declarative security. Another situation may be when you want to customize a method depending on which principal is calling the method.

In these and other situations where security policies cannot be implemented using declarative security, you can use programmatic security, but at the cost of portability.

14.6.2 Implementing programmatic security

The EJB spec cautions against implementing programmatic security, that is, hard-coding security in the bean. On the other hand, not all security policies can be implemented declaratively in the deployment descriptor. Therefore, the EJB architecture cautiously offers programmatic access to the caller's security context that partly facilitates the programmatic security option. This is accomplished by giving the bean provider access to the two security-related methods in the EJBContext interface, which you have already seen in previous chapters:

```
public boolean  isCallerInRole(String roleName);
public Principal getCallerPrincipal();
```

The Principal is an instance of the java.security.Principal class, which identifies the caller of the bean. The isCallerInRole(...) method verifies whether the calling Principal is a member of the role specified in the method argument. Calling these methods is also referred to as accessing the security context of the caller. By using these two methods, you can take security implementation to the instance level, while declarative security is only at the class level.

Assume that an employee calls an instance of an entity bean that belongs to that employee. So, in the business method, you can code to check whether the name of the caller is the same as the value of the persistent field, say employeeName, in the bean instance. For example, consider the following code fragment:

```
public void verifyTheEmployee() {
   String employeeName = null;
   Principal p = context.getCallerPrincipal();
    if (p != null) {
     employeeName = p.getName();
   }
 // now that you know the name of the caller, compare it to the
 // value of the appropriate persistent field in the bean. If it
 // does not match, prohibit the caller from doing anything.

  if (employeeName.equals(getEmployeeName())) {
   // everything is fine
  } else {
      // stop this caller.
  }
}
```

Be aware that the getName method on the Principal may not return the user login name. It depends on how the Principal is entered in the real operational environment, and this is done outside of EJB. So, by programming the security, you are tightly coupling the bean with the local operational environment and thereby compromising the portability of the bean.

To verify that the Principal that made the call to the business method of a bean instance is in a specific role, you call the `isCallerInRole(...)` method of the `EJBContext` interface. For example, the following code fragment does this:

```
public boolean checkTheSecurityRole() {
        boolean isRole;
        if (context.isCallerInRole("hr-administrator")) {
                isRole = true;
        } else {
                isRole = false;
        }
        return isRole;
}
```

The hr-administrator refers to a security role that would actually be defined by the application assembler. So, we already have a couple of problems here. First, how will the application assembler, who does not go into the source code, know that the developer has hard-coded a role called hr-administrator into the bean class? Second, two beans in the same ejb-jar file may use different names for security roles that the application assembler wants to treat as one security role. Therefore, we need a link between the role names coded by the bean providers and the logical security roles defined by the application assembler. To facilitate this, the bean provider must declare the hard-coded role names in the deployment descriptor by using the security role references, which we discuss next.

14.6.3   References to security roles

As you noticed in the previous section, the bean provider refers to a security role as hr-administrator in the code. The developer of another bean may refer to this role as hr-manager. It is the responsibility of the bean providers to declare these roles in the `<enterprise-beans>` section of their beans by using the `<security-role-ref>` element. Here is an example:

```
<enterprise-beans>
  ...
  <entity>
   <ejb-name>EmployeeRecordBean</ejb-name>
   ...
    <security-role-ref>
      <description>
          This reference will be linked to an appropriate
          security-role by the application assembler.
      </description>
      <role-name> hr-administrator </role-name>        ⟵  Argument for the
    </security-role-ref>                                    isCallerInRole(... ) method
    ...
```

```
    </entity>
    ...
</enterprise-beans>
```

The `<role-name>` element within the `<security-role-ref>` element specifies the role name that was hard-coded by the bean developer in the bean method.
The application assembler links this hard-coded role to the logical security role by
adding a new element, `<role-link>`, as follows:

```
<enterprise-beans>
  ...
  <entity>
   <ejb-name>EmployeeRecordBean</ejb-name>
   ...
    <security-role-ref>
      <description>
          This reference will be linked to an appropriate
          security-role by the application assembler.
      </description>
      <role-name> hr-administrator </role-name>        ◁─┐  Linking hard-coded
      <role-link> hr-director </role-link>                │  name to security role
    </security-role-ref>
   ...
  </entity>
  ...
</enterprise-beans>
```

> **NOTE**   The `<role-link>` element is defined by the application assembler in the
> `<enterprise-beans>` section of the deployment descriptor. It links the
> hard-coded role to the logical security role defined in the `<assembly-`
> `descriptor>` section of the deployment descriptor.

Throughout the chapter, we have referred to the security responsibilities of the various
EJB roles. Let's summarize them now.

14.7 RESPONSIBILITIES IN IMPLEMENTING EJB SECURITY

The security responsibilities involve implementing security inside an EJB application and mapping it to the actual operational environment in which the application
is running.

14.7.1 Implementing EJB security

The container provider implements the security infrastructure. The security policies
are set at deployment and runtime. This makes the beans reusable across applications
and the applications portable across multiple EJB servers that might be using different
security mechanisms. When one method calls another method, it is the responsibility
of the container to allow the bean provider to have access to the caller's security context from within the bean instances. The container does so by implementing two

methods and exposing them for the bean provider in the `EJBContext` interface: `getCallerPrincipal()` and `isCallerInRole()`.

Although not encouraged by the EJB specifications, the bean provider can implement programmatic security in situations where declarative security is unable to offer what the business logic demands. The bean provider can use the methods `get-CallerPrincipal()` and `isCallerInRole()` in coding the security. However, you must declare any hard-coded role in the `<security-role-ref>` element in the `<enterprise-beans>` section of the deployment descriptor.

The application assembler defines the logical security roles by using the `<security-role>` element in the `<assembly-descriptor>` section of the deployment descriptor. The application assembler also assigns method permissions to the roles by using the `<method-permission>` element in the `<assembly-descriptor>` section of the deployment descriptor and links the hard-coded roles to the appropriate logical security role by adding the `<role-link>` element within the `<security-role-ref>` element defined by the bean provider.

It is the responsibility of the deployer to deploy the application security in the actual operational environment.

14.7.2 Deploying EJB security

The deployer must ensure that the assembled application will be secure after it is deployed in the actual operational environment. The deployer's job is to map the security view specified by the application assembler to the mechanisms and policies of the security domain in the operational environment. To accomplish this, the deployer performs these tasks:

- Assigns the security domain and Principal realm to an EJB application. Multiple Principal realms, such as employees and customers, can exist within the same security domain.

- Maps the principals (users or groups of users) to the security roles in the EJB application.

- Configures the principal delegation for inner component calls, that is, the propagation of security identity along a change of calls. This involves following the instructions provided by elements such as `<run-as>` and `<use-caller-identity>`.

- Secures the resource manager's access.

- Assigns permissions for the methods for which the application assembler did not define permissions, or unchecks these methods.

The exam does not expect you to know how the deployer's tasks are actually accomplished, because most of them (those related to mapping with the operational environment) are done outside the realm of EJB and in a vendor-specific way. But you do need to know what those tasks are.

The three most important takeaways from this chapter are

- High-level EJB security mapped to the operational environment at deployment time falls into two categories: programmatic security and declarative security.
- By default, the security identity of the Principal propagates in a chain of method calls unless it is changed with the security element <run-as>.
- The application assembler defines the logical security roles.

14.8   SUMMARY

Security management is an important feature of EJB servers, which saves the bean provider from coding the security infrastructure inside the application and makes EJB applications portable across different EJB servers. Although the security infrastructure is built into the container, security policies can be set at deployment time. Security policies basically determine which client can call which method of a bean. A user defined by a system administrator outside EJB is represented in Java by an instance of the java.security.Principal class. A security role associated with a Principal determines which methods of a bean can be invoked by the client represented by that Principal. The application assembler defines the logical security roles by using the <security-role> element in the <assembly-descriptor> section of the deployment descriptor. A logical security role is mapped to real users and groups by the deployer.

The application assembler grants a security role the permissions to call certain methods by using the <method-permission> element in the <assembly-descriptor> section of the deployment descriptor. Also, the application assembler can make a method available to all clients by using the <unchecked> element. The deployer must make sure that the method permissions are set for each bean method that can potentially be called by a client. If the application assembler did not specify the permissions to a method, the deployer must do so.

A method call from a client may trigger a chain of bean-to-bean calls. By default, the security identity associated with the client's Principal will propagate through these calls. However, the application assembler can change it using the <run-as> element for a bean. Although the EJB spec discourages using programmatic security, the bean provider can hard-code the security to meet a security need of the business logic that cannot be met by using declarative security. In this case the bean provider must declare the security role names used in the code in <security-role-ref> elements. The application assembler links these to logical security roles by using the <role-link> element.

Comprehend

- How the security assignments by different roles are linked with each other, for example, how `<security-role-ref>` specified by the bean developer is linked to the `<security-role>` specified by the application assembler through `<role-link>`
- How the security identity propagates in a chain of method calls

Look out

- A bean's `<security-identity>` does not change the security identity of incoming method calls; it is assigned to outgoing method calls.
- Because a message-driven bean has no client, a deployment descriptor should never have `<use-caller-identity>` defined for a message-driven bean. You can certainly use the `<run-as>` element in the `<security-identity>` element for a message-driven bean.
- The `<role-link>` element in the deployment descriptor is defined by the application assembler to link the `<security-role-ref>` to `<security-role>`.

Memorize

- The security-related elements defined in the deployment descriptor

Review questions

Some questions may have more than one correct answer. Choose all that apply.

1. Which element in the deployment descriptor is used to specify that any client can access a set of methods?
   a. `<exclude-list>`
   b. `<unchecked>`
   c. `<checked>`
   d. `<security-role>`

2. Which EJB role implements the security infrastructure?
   a. The container provider
   b. The bean provider

c. The system administrator

d. The application assembler

e. The deployer

3. Which EJB role typically sets the security policies for an EJB application?

    a. The container provider

    b. The bean provider

    c. The system administrator

    d. The application assembler

    e. The deployer

4. Which of the following security-related elements are defined by the bean developer in the deployment descriptor?

    a. `<security-role>`

    b. `<security-role-ref>`

    c. `<role-link>`

    d. `<role-name>`

    e. None of the above

5. Which of the following are true about declarative EJB security?

    a. It is not possible to distinguish different versions of an overloaded method.

    b. You can specify different permissions for a method in different instances of a bean.

    c. Permissions specified for a method of a bean apply to that method in all instances of the bean.

    d. It is possible to specify different permissions for a method in the home interface from a method with the same name in the component interface.

    e. The `<security-identity>` element cannot be defined for a message-driven bean.

6. Which of the following are correct statements about EJB security?

    a. If a method is included in both the `<exclude-list>` element and the `<method-permission>` element, the `<method-permission>` element overrides the `<exclude-list>` element for that method.

    b. The `<run-as>` element is defined to specify the security role for all methods in a bean.

    c. The `<exclude-list>` element is used to list the methods that no client can call.

    d. The `<use-caller-identity>` element can be defined for the `onMessage()` method of a message-driven bean.

7. Which of the following elements can be defined in the <enterprise-beans> section of the deployment descriptor?

    a. <security-role>

    b. <security-role-ref>

    c. <role-link>

    d. <security-identity>

    e. <method-permission>

8. Which of the following elements can be defined in the <assembly-descriptor> section of the deployment descriptor?

    a. <security-role>

    b. <security-role-ref>

    c. <role-link>

    d. <security-identity>

    e. <method-permission>

9. In a stateful session bean, a call to the getCallerPrincipal() method gets the IllegalStateException. This call can possibly be made from which of the following methods?

    a. ejbActivate()

    b. ejbPassivate()

    c. ejbRemove()

    d. setSessionContext()

    e. ejbCreate()

10. In a CMP entity bean, a call to the getCallerPrincipal() method gets the IllegalStateException. This call can possibly be made from which of the following methods?

    a. ejbActivate()

    b. ejbPassivate()

    c. ejbStore()

    d. setEntityContext()

    e. ejbLoad()

A P P E N D I X   A

Installing and running RI J2SDKEE 1.3

INTRODUCTION

The purpose of this appendix is to get you started with assembling beans into applications, deploying the application, and executing the application. As you know by now, EJB is part of J2EE. You will use the reference implementation (RI) from Sun for J2EE 1.3. We will show you exactly what software you need to install, how to set up the development environment, and how to create and deploy the application. J2EE 1.3 supports the following operating systems: Solaris 7/8, Linux, and Windows (NT 4.0, 2000 Professional, and XP). The development environment in this appendix is for Windows XP, but the procedure on other platforms is very similar.

A.1   INSTALLING THE REQUIRED JAVA SOFTWARE

You need to install the following Java software:

- Java 2 SDK Standard Edition (J2SE) 1.3. You should have no problem with a higher version of J2SE, but the EJB spec guarantees support for J2SE 1.3 only.
- Java 2 SDK Enterprise Edition (J2EE) 1.3.

You can download the required Java software from the Sun web site. You will need to do a bit of navigation through the wordy pages before you get to the package that you want to download. Be patient but careful. To be specific, do the following:

- If you already have J2SE 1.3 running on your system, skip this step. Otherwise, download J2SE 1.3.1_x from the Sun web site: http://www.java.sun.com/j2se. Click the Old Releases link, and download the appropriate EXE file (for Windows). Double-click the file, and specify the root directory for installation when the installer asks for it.

- J2SE must be installed before this step. Download J2SDKEE 1.3.1_x from the Sun web site: http://www.java.sun.com/j2ee. Click the J2EE 1.3 link, and download the appropriate EXE file (for Windows). Double-click the file, and specify the root directory for installation when the installer asks for it.

Installing J2SDKEE installs the EJB 2.0-compliant J2EE server and some tools, such as deployment and cleanup tools. You need J2SE 1.3 to develop and execute J2EE/EJB applications and to run the J2EE server.

By installing the required software, you have set up part of the development environment. The remaining part is the development environment variables that we discuss next.

A.2   SETTING UP THE DEVELOPMENT ENVIRONMENT VARIABLES

In order for the J2EE server (along with the tools) to run, it is crucial to set up the following four environment variables correctly: JAVA_HOME, J2EE_HOME, PATH, and CLASSPATH. These variables are shown in table A.1.

Table A.1   The environment variables that you need to set. The Example column assumes that the root directories where you installed J2SE and J2SDKEE are c:\jdk1.3.1_11 and c:\j2sdkee1.3.1 on the Windows OS.

Variable Name	Description	Example on Windows
JAVA_HOME	The root directory for J2SE installation.	Set JAVA_HOME=c:\jdk1.3.1_11
J2EE_HOME	The root directory for J2SDKEE installation.	Set J2EE_HOME=c:\j2sdkee1.3.1
PATH	Add the bin directories for J2SE and J2SDKEE to the PATH variable.	Set PATH=%PATH%;%JAVA_HOME%\bin;%J2EE_HOME%\bin
CLASSPATH	Used by the compiler to find .class files. Add the j2ee.jar file to the value of this variable.	Set CLASSPATH =.;%J2EE_HOME%\lib\j2ee.jar

Now that you have set up the environment variables, you are ready to develop, deploy, and execute a simple EJB application.

A.3 DEVELOPING, DEPLOYING, AND EXECUTING AN EJB APPLICATION

In this exercise, we walk you through the process of testing the FortuneBean bean, whose code is presented in chapter 2 and also available on the Manning web site at http://www.manning.com/sanghera. You will use the J2EE server and the deployment tool that you just installed by installing J2SDKEE 1.3. First let's set up the directory structure.

A.3.1 Setting up the directory structure

From the Manning web site, copy the ejbworkshop folder to the hard disk of your computer. We will assume that you copied the folder to the C: drive. The directory structure looks like the one shown in figure A.1.

The ~ejbworkshop\utils directory contains the setejb_env.bat file used to set up the environment variables in this example, and the ~ejbworkshop/projects/src/fortunebean directory contains the Java files for the FortuneBean bean and the interfaces that we discussed in chapter 2. Additional directories and files will be generated automatically as you go through this exercise.

It's time to compile the bean code.

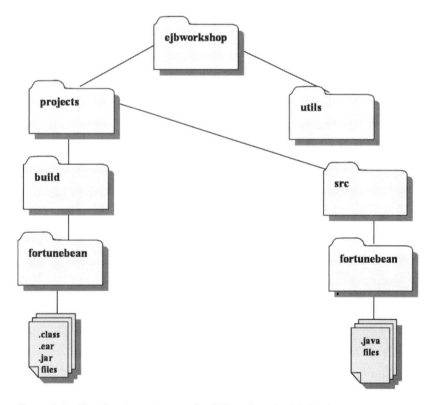

Figure A.1   The directory structure for EJB projects in this book

A.3.2   Compiling the bean code

As shown in figure A.2, change your directory to c:\ejbworkshop\projects. Then issue the `javac` command with the option to place the resulting .class files in the c:\ejb-workshop\projects\build\fortunebean directory.

Now that you have the compiled bean class and the interfaces, it's time to use the reference implementation to assemble and deploy the EJB application from these classes.

Figure A.2   Change your directory to c:\ejbworkshop\projects.

A.3.3   Starting and stopping the J2EE server

To launch the J2EE server, open a terminal window on your computer and type the following at the command prompt:

```
j2ee -verbose
```

Although not required, the `verbose` option is useful for debugging. The output of this command is shown in figure A.3.

```
C:\ejbworkshop\projects\src>j2ee -verbose
J2EE server listen port: 1050
Naming service started:1050
Binding DataSource, name = jdbc/EstoreDB, url = jdbc:cloudscape:rmi:CloudscapeDB;create=true
Binding DataSource, name = jdbc/DB2, url = jdbc:cloudscape:rmi:CloudscapeDB;create=true
Binding DataSource, name = jdbc/Cloudscape, url = jdbc:cloudscape:rmi:CloudscapeDB;create=true
Binding DataSource, name = jdbc/InventoryDB, url = jdbc:cloudscape:rmi:CloudscapeDB;create=true
Binding DataSource, name = jdbc/DB1, url = jdbc:cloudscape:rmi:CloudscapeDB;create=true
Binding DataSource, name = jdbc/XACloudscape, url = jdbc/XACloudscape__xa
Binding DataSource, name = jdbc/XACloudscape__xa, dataSource = COM.cloudscape.core.RemoteXaDataSour
@53c6a3
Starting JMS service...
Initialization complete - waiting for client requests
Binding: < JMS Destination : jms/Queue , javax.jms.Queue >
Binding: < JMS Destination : jms/Topic , javax.jms.Topic >
Binding: < JMS Cnx Factory : jms/QueueConnectionFactory , Queue , No properties >
Binding: < JMS Cnx Factory : QueueConnectionFactory , Queue , No properties >
Binding: < JMS Cnx Factory : TopicConnectionFactory , Topic , No properties >
Binding: < JMS Cnx Factory : jms/TopicConnectionFactory , Topic , No properties >
Starting web service at port: 8000
Starting secure web service at port: 7000
J2EE SDK/1.3.1
Starting web service at port: 9191
J2EE SDK/1.3.1
Loading jar:/c:/j2sdkee1.3.1/repository/PaulSanghera/applications/ConverterApp1080772510544Server.j
Loading jar:/c:/j2sdkee1.3.1/repository/PaulSanghera/applications/AdviceAppli1080589449131Server.jar
Loading jar:/c:/j2sdkee1.3.1/repository/PaulSanghera/applications/ConverterApp2108077/1769228Server.
r
Loading jar:/c:/j2sdkee1.3.1/repository/PaulSanghera/applications/AdviceApp1080848413509Server.jar
J2EE server startup complete.
```

Figure A.3   Output from the J2EE server startup

To stop the server, type the following command:

```
j2ee -stop
```

You may need to open another terminal window to issue this command if the command prompt is not available on the window where you started the server.

In the next section, you will use the deploy tool to create and deploy the EJB application. If something goes wrong in the process, or if you make changes to the application and want to redeploy, you should take the following steps:

1 Un-deploy the current application.

2 Exit from the deploy tool.

3 Stop the J2EE server.

4 Run the cleanup tool by typing `cleanup` at the command prompt.

5 Restart the J2EE server and then restart the deploy tool.

6 Deploy the application.

A.3.4 Creating the application

If it's not already running, start the J2EE server as shown in the previous section. The next step is to start the deploytool utility, which has two modes: command line and GUI. The instructions in this appendix refer to the GUI version. To start the deploytool GUI, open a terminal window and type the command `deploytool`, as shown in figure A.4.

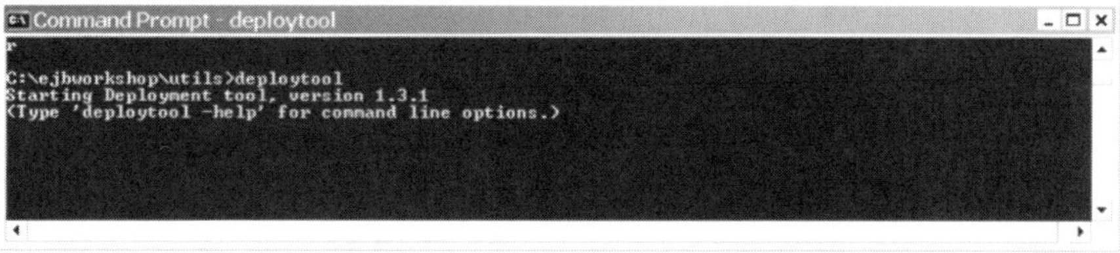

Figure A.4 Start the deploytool utility at a command prompt.

The Application Deployment Tool screen shown in figure A.5 appears. You will work with this window throughout the exercise. Sometimes it will create subwindows, and eventually you will come back to it. The first thing you are going to do is create the application.

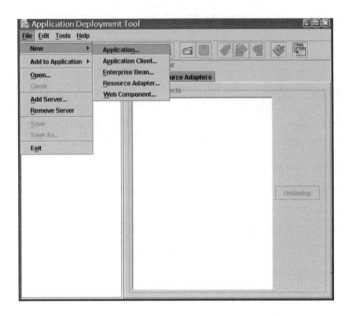

Figure A.5
Output of the
`deploytool`
command

On this screen do the following:

1 Select File > New > Application.

2 Click on Application.

You are presented with the New Application screen shown in figure A.6; the Application Deployment Tool screen remains in the background.

Figure A.6
The New Application
screen

On the New Application screen, do the following:

1 In the Application File Name field, enter the full path to the application directory followed by the application name, for example, c:\ejbworkshop\projects\FortuneApp.

2 Click OK.

3 Confirm that the file FortuneApp.ear appears in the directory c:\ejbworkshop\projects.

This sends you back to the main Application Deployment Tool screen, which now looks like figure A.7.

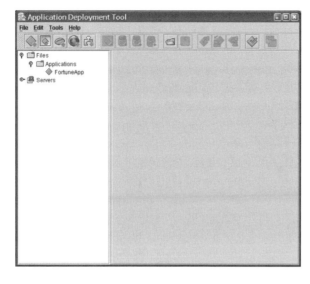

**Figure A.7
The Application
Deployment Tool screen
after creating the
application FortuneApp.
Notice the appearance of
FortuneApp under
Applications in the left
section of the screen.**

If you click the FortuneApp icon, some information about the application appears in the right-hand section of the screen: the location of the .ear file and the META-INF directory icon. There is little in the application just yet.

Our goal is to deploy the bean within the application. To do that, we first need to put the bean into a JAR file and create a deployment descriptor. Let's do that next.

A.3.5   Creating the JAR file and the deployment descriptor

Currently you are at the screen shown in figure A.7. To start the bean wizard, do the following:

1 Select File > New > Enterprise Bean, as shown in figure A.8.

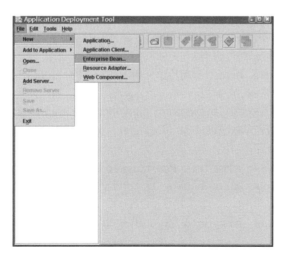

**Figure A.8
Select File > New >
Enterprise Bean to
start the bean wizard.**

2 Click Enterprise Bean.

3 The New Enterprise Bean Wizard is displayed, as shown in figure A.9.

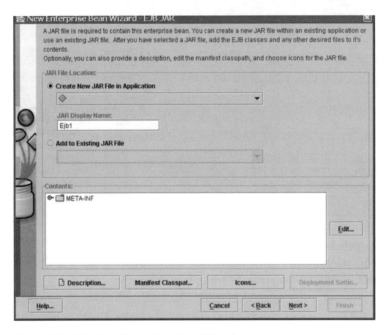

Figure A.9   The New Enterprise Bean Wizard screen

You are going to use this wizard to perform the following tasks: create the JAR file for the bean and put the bean class and the two interfaces into the JAR file. In the New Enterprise Bean Wizard screen, do the following:

1 Click the Create New JAR File in Application radio button.

2 In the combo box, select FortuneApp.

3 In the JAR Display Name field, enter FortuneJAR.

4 Click Edit. You will then see the Edit Contents of FortuneJAR screen, shown in figure A.10.

5 Under Starting Directory, browse to c:\ejbworkshop\projects\build\fortunebean.

6 In the tree under Available Files, locate the .class files for the bean and the related interfaces.

7 Select the following .class files: `Fortune.class`, `FortuneBean.class`, and `FortuneHome.class`. Now the screen looks like the one shown in figure A.11.

8 Click Add to add these three .class files to the bottom box: Contents of FortuneJAR.

9 Click OK.

Figure A.10 The Edit Contents of FortuneJAR screen lets you select the classes that will go into the JAR file.

Figure A.11 The Edit Contents screen after you select the contents for the JAR file

You have added three .class files to the JAR file, and now you are back to the New Enterprise Bean Wizard screen shown in figure A.12.

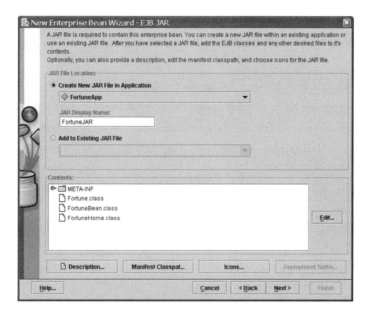

**Figure A.12
The .class files
that you added
to the JAR file**

Now you need to enter the information about the bean that the tool will use to create the deployment descriptor. To proceed, click Next and you will see the screen shown in figure A.13.

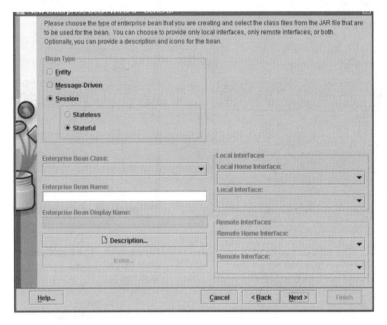

Figure A.13   Enter the bean information for the deployment descriptor.

In this screen, do the following:

1. Under Bean Type, click the Session radio button.
2. Under Session, click the Stateless radio button.
3. In the Enterprise Bean Class combo box, select FortuneBean.
4. In the Enterprise Bean Display Name field, enter FortuneBean.
5. In the Remote Home Interface combo box, select FortuneHome.
6. In the Remote Interface combo box, select Fortune. The screen now looks like the one shown in figure A.14.
7. Click Next. You don't need to change anything on the screen that appears.
8. Click Finish.

You are now back to the main Application Deployment Tool screen shown in figure A.15.

Based on the information you entered, the tool creates the deployment descriptor, which says that it is a stateless session bean, the bean class is FortuneBean, the bean remote component interface is Fortune, and the bean remote home interface is FortuneHome, and so on.

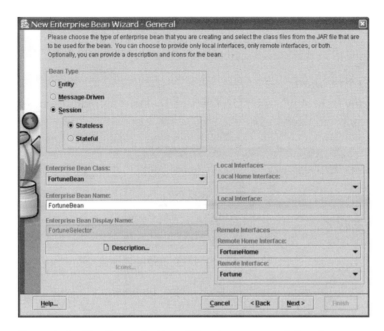

Figure A.14   The Enterprise Bean Wizard screen containing the bean information. The tool will use this information to create the deployment descriptor.

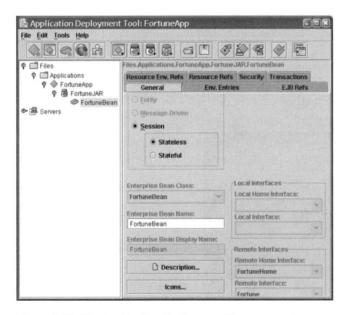

Figure A.15   The Application Deployment Tool screen after you created the JAR file and the deployment descriptor

Congratulations! You have created the JAR file, put the bean-related .class files into the JAR file, and created the deployment descriptor. Now it's time to deploy the bean into the application that you created.

A.3.6 Deploying the bean

You are already at the Application Deployment Tool screen. In this screen select Tools > Deploy, as shown in figure A.16.

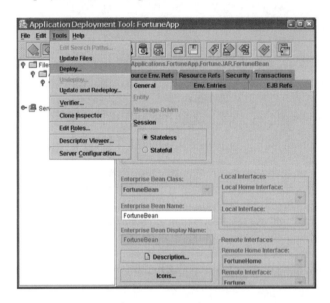

Figure A.16
In the Application
Deployment Tool
screen select
Tools > Deploy.

Clicking Deploy brings up the Deploy FortuneApp – Introduction screen shown in figure A.17. This screen lets you create a JAR file that contains the stub files used by the client to make method calls on the bean. To accomplish this, do the following:

Figure A.17
The Deploy FortuneApp
screen lets you create the JAR
file that will contain the stub
classes needed by the client in
order to access the bean.

1 Select Return Client Jar.

2 Click Next

You will then see the JNDI Names screen shown in figure A.18. You will use this screen to give a JNDI name to your bean. This is the name that will be used in the client code for JNDI lookup for the bean. To accomplish this, do the following:

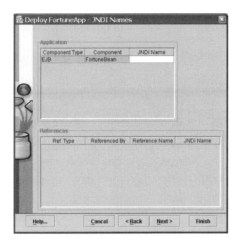

Figure A.18
The JNDI Names screen

1 In the JNDI Name field, type `FortuneSelector` (this is the name we use in the client code).

2 Click Finish.

The Deployment Progress screen shown in figure A.19 will appear. Watch the progress on this screen, and click OK when the deployment completes. In the left section of the Application Deployment Tool window, click Servers > localhost, and you will see your application. Click the application, and you will see the Undeploy tab.

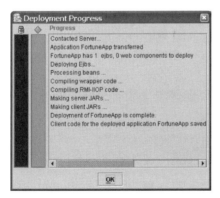

Figure A.19
The Deployment Progress screen

Congratulations! You have successfully deployed your application. Now it's time to run it.

A.4　EXECUTING YOUR EJB APPLICATION

To execute and test your application, you need to package and run the application client. In this section, we explain how to do that.

A.4.1　Packaging the application client

Use the Application Deployment Tool screen to start the New Application Client Wizard: select File > New > Application Client. The wizard displays the Introduction screen. Read the information about the wizard's features and click Next. The JAR File Contents screen appears. Perform the following tasks on this screen:

1 In the combo box, select FortuneApp.

2 Click Edit. The Edit Contents screen is displayed.

3 In the tree under Available Files, locate the directory where your client .class file, FortuneClient.class, is. Select the FortuneClient.class file.

4 Click Add. The file appears in the bottom section of the screen.

5 Click OK.

6 Click Next.

7 In the General screen, perform the following steps:

  a Select FortuneClient in the Main Class combo box.

  b Verify that the entry in the Display Name field is FortuneClient.

  c Select Container-Managed Authentication in the Callback Handler Class combo box.

  d Click Next.

  e Click Finish.

A.4.2　Running the application client

To run the application client, perform the following steps:

1 Confirm that the FortuneApp.ear and FortuneAppClient.jar files exist in the directory c:\ejbworkshop\projects or in another directory depending on your setup.

2 Make sure the FortuneAppClient.jar file is in the CLASSPATH.

3 Issue the following command:

```
runclient -client FortuneApp.ear -name FortuneClient -textauth
```

Make sure the FortuneApp.ear and FortuneClient.class files are in the path.

4 You will be asked to log in. Enter guest for the user name and guest123 for the password.

5 The output is shown in figure A.20.

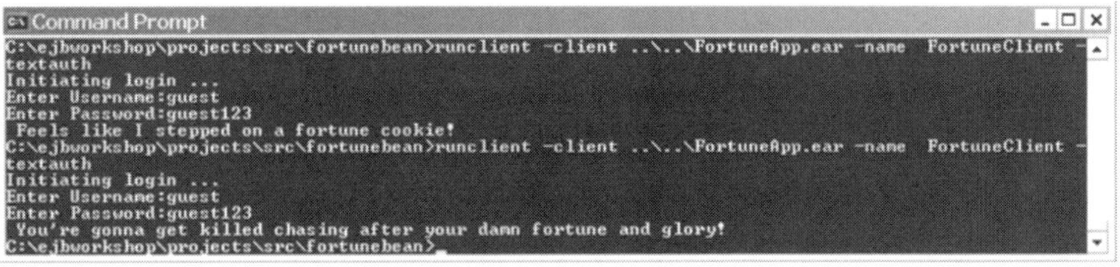

Figure A.20 Output from running the client program, FortuneClient

As a result of the client call, the container invoked the business method on the bean class, which randomly selected a statement and returned it. Now that you have a very simple example running, you can make changes to the business method, add more methods, and modify the client to call those methods. Play with it.

A P P E N D I X   B

An introduction to XML

LEARNING OBJECTIVES

- Understand the similarities and differences between HTML and XML
- Understand the structure of XML: elements and attributes
- Understand document type definitions (DTD)

INTRODUCTION

EJB uses Extensible Markup Language (XML) to write and interpret the documents called deployment descriptors. XML is a markup language standardized by the World Wide Web Consortium (W3C). Its main features and uses are as follows:

- XML facilitates building dynamic web pages by separating the data from the style elements of the document.

- As the name Extensible Markup Language suggests, you can define your own tags. This means you can create your own HTML-like markup language, for example, a language called MusicML, which may contain tags such as `<music>`, `<song>`, `<genre>`, `<artist>`, and `<album>`.

- XML allows you to store data in text files. Applications can exchange data through XML files.

- Data is stored in an XML file by using tags that you can name appropriately, and XML offers a hierarchy of tags, namely, a parent-child relationship between tags. This facilitates a powerful way of writing files containing self-explanatory data with a sophisticated structure.

- Because of its ability to store data, XML is also used to write configuration files for applications, such as the deployment descriptors used with EJB.

In the next section, we will explore how documents are written in XML.

B.1 *XML IN A NUTSHELL*

An XML document is composed of elements. An element, in turn, consists of an opening tag, the corresponding closing tag, and everything between the opening tag and the closing tag. The contents of an element may be another element, character data, or both. The tags defining the elements may contain attributes, just like the tags in HTML.

Let's begin exploring XML by examining the XML elements.

B.1.1 XML elements

An XML document contains elements; you can think of elements as the atoms of an XML document. When you are using XML for storing data, each element can represent a data item, and the hierarchy of elements can be used to represent the relationship between different data items. An element consists of an opening tag, the corresponding closing tag, and everything between the opening tag and the closing tag. For example, consider the following simple element:

```
<name>
     Immanuel Kant
</name>
```

In this example, the element name has the opening and closing tags <name> and </name> and it contains character data: Immanuel Kant. Tags can contain data, another element, or both. Now, consider the following example:

```
<employee>
  <name>
     Immanuel Kant
  </name>
</employee>
```

Notice that the employee element contains another element: name. The element name is called the *child* of employee, and employee is called the *parent* element of name. The hierarchical nature of XML is what allows it to store data with a sophisticated structure. Also, notice the principle of last-open, first-close at work: the tag <name> was opened after opening the <employee> tag and hence is closed before closing the <employee> tag. For example, the following code is invalid:

```
<employee>
 <name>
     Immanuel Kant
</employee>
</name>
```

In addition to parent and child, there is another hierarchy-related term called *sibling*, which refers to the elements at the same level of the hierarchy. For example, in the following the name and address elements are siblings because both are the children of the element employee:

```
<employee>
  <name>
     Immanuel Kant
  </name>
  <address>
     The LogicLand
  </address>
</employee>
```

Furthermore, it's important to know that multiple elements may have the same name. For example, the following code is perfectly valid:

```
<PhilosophyInc>
  <employee>
     <name> Immanuel Kant <name/>
 </employee>
<employee>
  <name> Jean-Paul Sartre </name>
 </employee>
</PhilosophyInc>
```

Note the appearance of the element employee twice, once with the name value Immanuel Kant, the other with the name value Jean-Paul Sartre, and it is perfectly valid.

There are two more syntax-related points about elements that you should know:

- Unlike the tags in HTML, the tags in XML are case-sensitive; or example, <employee>, <Employee>, and <EMPLOYEE> are three different tags.

- In HTML, there are some tags such as <br> that don't have a corresponding closing tag. In XML, each element must have an opening tag and a corresponding closing tag. The name of the closing tag is identical to that of the opening tag preceded by a forward slash (/). For elements that do not contain anything, you can use the shorthand empty tag syntax: for example, <name/> instead of <name></name>.

Just like in HTML, an element may be further specified by using attributes.

B.1.2   XML attributes

Although not required, an element may have one or more attributes that hold extra information about the element. An attribute is a name-value pair associated with an element in order to describe one of its characteristics. For example:

```
<employee employeeID="420">
    <name> Immanuel Kant </name>
</employee>
```

The `employeeID` is an attribute of the `employee` element and its value represents the employee's id number.

An element may have more than one attribute, and the syntax is shown here:

```
<elementName  attr1="value1" attr2="value2" attr3="value3">
  Containment goes here
</elementName>
```

Sometimes you may have to struggle with the issue of whether a data item should be entered into the file as an element or as an attribute. For example, it is perfectly valid to enter the `name` information as an attribute and not as an element, as follows:

```
<employee ID="420" status="temp" name="Immanuel Kant">
    Contents here
</employee>
```

You may ask how you can know whether a given data item should be represented by an attribute or an element. In order to decide, you must know the differences between attributes and elements, as presented in table B.1.

Table B.1   Comparison of the characteristics of elements and attributes

Characteristic	Element	Attribute
Content	Content of an element is displayed if it is a document	Content not displayed
Hierarchy	May have children	Cannot have children
Metadata (information about data)	May have further metadata	Cannot have further metadata
Extensibility	Very extensible	Not extensible

When you have to make a choice between using an element or an attribute, the rule of thumb is that an element is used to represent data, while an attribute is used to represent metadata (information about data). Metadata is not extensible: it may not have structure. Otherwise, it is probably data and not metadata. If you think a data item may be extended further in the hierarchy, do not use an attribute to represent it.

Next, we present a very simple example of an XML file.

B.1.3   A complete example

We have already explored the syntax of elements and attributes. The overall syntax of a complete XML document can be understood by studying listing B.1 for the file employees.xml.

Listing B.1   employees.xml

```
<?xml version="1.0" standalone="no"?>
<!DOCTYPE PhilosophyInc SYSTEM "PhilosophyInc.dtd">
<PhilosophyInc>
  <employee employeeID="420" status="temp" >
    <name> Immanuel Kant </name>
  </employee>
  <employee employeeID="101" status="permanent" >
    <name> Jean-Paul Sartre </name>
  </employee>
</PhilosophyInc>
```

Note the following in listing B.1:

- The first line indicates that this file conforms to the XML 1.0 specifications.

- In the first line, `standalone="no"` means that this is not a standalone document because it points to another document, PhilosophyInc.dtd. We will talk about DTDs in the next section.

- In the second line, the term `SYSTEM` means that the DTD file is stored on the local system/network.

- The second line also specifies the root element `PhilosophyInc`. Each XML document must have one and only one root element, and all other elements must be contained within the root element.

You have learned that XML offers you complete freedom to define elements and the relationships among them. This is not magic. Applications interpret these elements and their relationships using special programs called XML parsers and processors. These parsers may also use the DTD file associated with an XML file in order to validate the XML file.

The employees.xml file presented in this section points to a DTD file, Philosophy-Inc.dtd. We explore this type of document next.

B.2   DOCUMENT TYPE DEFINITIONS

As you learned earlier in this chapter, XML offers you complete freedom for naming elements and defining the hierarchy of elements. However, in reality, within your organization you will be using XML for a certain kind of business and would like to set up some kind of organization-wide standard. Document type definitions (DTDs) presented in a file let you do exactly that. Writing a DTD file is equivalent to defining your own markup language, such as MusicML if your organization deals with some aspect of the music business.

A DTD contains a list of components, such as tags and attributes, of the markup language and the rules that relate the components to each other. For example, a DTD may specify that a new language, MusicML, contains the root element `music` and exactly seven genre elements with the names `alternative`, `pop`, `hip-hop`, `rock`, `folk`, `country`, and `easy-listening`. Further, it defines a rule that these genres are child elements of the root element `music`. In the following sections we explore how to define the rules for elements and attributes in a DTD.

B.2.1 Specifying elements in a DTD

In a DTD, you can specify the following aspects of an element:

- The name of the element
- The relationship of the element with another element, for example, which elements are allowed as children of this element
- Whether the element is required or optional
- Whether the element can be used in an XML file only once, or whether it can be used only in a particular order with other elements

Let's see how an element is specified in a DTD.

Specifying elements

The syntax for specifying an element in a DTD is shown here:

```
<!ELEMENT ElementName ContentType>
```

For example, an element with the name `PhilosophyVille`, which may have any content (data or element or both), will be declared as follows:

```
<!ELEMENT PhilosophyVille ANY>
```

An element declaration begins with `<!ELEMENT` and ends with the character `>`. Note that the case-sensitivity rule for tags also applies to `ELEMENT`. The content type `ANY` is also case sensitive and it means that the element `PhilosophyVille` may contain one or more elements or character data or both. The other possible content for an element is `PCDATA`, declared as follows:

```
<!ELEMENT  name  (#PCDATA)>
```

The keyword `PCDATA` means parsed character data, that is, character data that does not have any child element. The following line in an XML file would be valid for this DTD directive because the `name` element contains only character data:

```
<name> Immanuel Kant </name>
```

The following `name` element in an XML file would not be valid against the above DTD directive because it contains a child element, `firstName`:

```
<name>
  <firstName>  Immanuel </firstName>
</name>
```

Instead of having parsed character data, an element may have a structure, that is, it may have child elements. We explore next how to specify the structure of an element in a DTD.

Specifying element structure

When in a DTD you declare an element with content type ANY, you are still in the absolute freedom zone inside that element. In other words, that element can contain elements with any name, any data, and any hierarchy. However, you could have restricted this freedom by declaring the list of child elements instead. For example, the following declaration in a DTD means that the employee element must contain three child elements: exactly one child element called name, exactly one child element called email, and exactly one child element called address, and in this order:

```
<!ELEMENT employee (name, email, address)>
```

For example, the appearance of email within the employee element in an XML file before name or after address would be invalid, and the appearance of email twice to enter two email addresses for an employee would be invalid, too. What if you want to use an element more than once; for example, you want to enter more than one employee or more than one email addresses of an employee? You can allow multiple entries for an element by appending one of the following characters to the child element's name in DTD: + for one or more entries, * for zero or more entries, or ? for zero or one entry. For example, the following declaration means that the employee element must have one or more email elements and exactly one name and one address element:

```
<!ELEMENT employee (name, email+, address)>
```

All of the child elements must be declared following their appearances in a list, for example:

```
<!ELEMENT employee (name, email+, address)>
<!ELEMENT name (#PCDATA)>
<!ELEMENT email (#PCDATA)>
<!ELEMENT address (#PCDATA)>
```

Of course, we could have allowed any of the child elements to have children, as shown here:

```
<!ELEMENT address (street, city, state)>
<!ELEMENT street (#PCDATA)>
<!ELEMENT city (#PCDATA)>
<!ELEMENT state(#PCDATA)>
```

Just like in HTML, the tags in XML may have attributes, too. Next, we explore how to specify attributes for an element in a DTD.

B.2.2 Specifying attributes in DTD

An attribute contains information about an element in an XML file. Although it's not part of the content of the element, an attribute is a great way of passing information (such as an id) about the element to the application.

Declaring attributes

If an element in an XML file is to have an attribute, it must be declared in the DTD to which the XML file conforms. Declaring an attribute requires that you include the name of the attribute, the name of the element to which it belongs, the attribute type, and optionally its default value. The syntax for declaring an attribute in a DTD file is shown here:

```
<!ATTLIST elementName attributeName
    attributeType attributeDefaultValue>
```

For example, consider the following declaration in a DTD:

```
<!ATTLIST employee status    CDATA    "temp">
```

This means the `employee` element has an attribute named `status` whose type is CDATA (character data) and its default value is temp. If the XML file does not specify the value for this attribute, the default value will be assumed. Next, we discuss the attribute types.

Attribute types

The CDATA attribute type used in the previous example is the most common attribute type. All the valid attribute types are listed in table B.2.

Table B.2   Valid attribute types in XML

Attribute Type	Meaning
CDATA	Character data: plain text without elements.
Enumerated	A list of possible values from which exactly one value must be selected.
ID	The value for this attribute must be unique and not shared by any other attribute of type ID in the document; i.e., it uniquely identifies the element in the document.
IDREF	The value of this attribute refers an attribute of type ID.
IDREFS	A list of IDREFs.
ENTITY	The name of an entity declared in the DTD. An entity refers to a source of data external to the XML file.
ENTITIES	A list of entities.

continued on next page

Table B.2 Valid attribute types in XML *(continued)*

Attribute Type	Meaning
NMTOKEN	The value of this attribute is a valid XML name: it must begin with a letter or an underscore followed by characters that may include letters, digits, underscores, hyphens, and periods.
NMTOKENS	A list of valid XML names.
NOTATION	The name of a notation declared in the DTD. A notation helps to identify the format of non-XML data.

Nine of these types are constants used in the attributeType field, while the Enumerated type presents a list of possible types out of which one must be selected, for example:

```
<!ATTLIST email visible (TRUE | FALSE) "TRUE">
```

This means the value of the attribute visible associated with the element email can be set to either TRUE or FALSE in an XML document; if not set, the default value is TRUE. The application that uses the XML file will show the email address if the attribute value is TRUE and will hide the email address if the value is FALSE. Note that it's still the application that has to interpret the value and take the appropriate action.

In addition to specifying a default value, you can specify several constraints on the value of an attribute. We discuss this topic next.

Attribute values

In addition to defining the attribute types, you can put various requirements on the values of the attributes. You already know how to specify a default value for an attribute. If you don't want to specify a default value, you can require that a value be specified for an attribute in the XML file:

```
<!ATTLIST employee employeeID CDATA #REQUIRED>
```

This constraint is useful when there is no viable default value. Omitting the employeeID attribute in the XML document will make the document invalid; an XML parser/processor will return the error. A weaker alternative to the #REQUIRED keyword is the keyword IMPLIED:

```
<!ATTLIST employee status CDATA #IMPLIED>
```

In this case, if the attribute status is omitted in the XML file, the parser will inform the XML application that no value for this attribute is available, but the XML file will not be deemed invalid. Another useful constraint available for the attribute value is implemented with the keyword #FIXED. It is used when the attribute contains global information that must not be changed. The following example shows the syntax for this constraint:

```
<!ATTLIST employee CompanyName CDATA #FIXED "PhilosophyVille Inc">
```

This means that if you don't include the CompanyName attribute in the XML file, the default value will be used, but if you do include it, you must specify the name, PhilosophyVille Inc, as a value of the attribute.

In the next section, we combine the XML concepts discussed so far into a complete example.

B.2.3   Putting it all together

Listing B.2 shows a complete DTD file. The keyword DOCTYPE is used to declare the root element PhilosophyInc, and the rest of the declarations are embraced in an opening brace and the corresponding closing brace.

Listing B.2   The employees.dtd file

```
<?xml version="1.0" encoding="UTF-8"?>
<!-- PhilosophyInc where the philosophers work -->
<?xml version="1.0"?>
<!-- Declare elements -->
<!ELEMENT PhilosophyInc (companyName, employee*)>
<!ELEMENT companyName (#PCDATA)>
<!ELEMENT employee (name, email+, address*)>
<!ELEMENT name   (#PCDATA)>
<!ELEMENT email (#PCDATA)>
<!ELEMENT address (street, city, state)>
<!ELEMENT street (#PCDATA)>
<!ELEMENT city (#PCDATA)>
<!ELEMENT state(#PCDATA)>
<!ATTLIST employee employeeID CDATA #REQUIRED status CDATA "temp">
```

Note that according to the DTD, the element employee can contain as children one or more email elements and zero or more address elements. An XML file that conforms to this DTD is shown in listing B.3.

Listing B.3   The employees.xml file, which validates against employees.dtd

```
<?xml version="1.0" standalone="no"?>
<!-- This xml file conforms to the dtd employees.dtd -->

<!DOCTYPE PhilosophyInc SYSTEM "PhilosophyInc.dtd">
<PhilosophyInc>
     <companyName>Philosophy Company</companyName>
  <employee employeeID="420" status="temp" >
    <name> Immanuel Kant </name>
    <email> kant@kant.com </email>
    <address>
       <street>1600 Pennsylvania Ave</street>
       <city>Washington</city>
       <state>D.C.</state>
    </address>
  </employee>
```

```
  <employee ID="101" status="permanent">
    <name>Jean-Paul Sartre</name>
    <email>sartre@sartre.com</email>
    <email>jean@sartre.com</email>
  </employee>
</PhilosophyInc>
```

Note that both an XML document and a DTD can contain comments using the following syntax:

```
<!--   Comments go here  -->
```

B.3 FURTHER EXPLORATION

To make you feel comfortable with the XML used in this book, we have only scratched the surface of XML. You should be able to understand the elements, attributes, and the element hierarchy. In case you want to learn more about XML, we list below two of an unlimited number of available resources:

- The W3C web site: http://www.w3.org/XML/
- *J2EE and XML Development*, by Kurt A. Gabrick and David B. Weiss (Manning Publications, 2002)

A sample deployment descriptor file

In this appendix we present a complete deployment descriptor file, ejb-jar.xml. Throughout the book, we have explained various elements of the deployment descriptor that you need to know for the exam, one piece at a time. Here we combine all those pieces into one file in order to present a unified picture:

```xml
<?xml version="1.0"?>
<!DOCTYPE ejb-jar
  PUBLIC "-//Sun Microsystems, Inc.//DTD Enterprise JavaBeans
  2.0//EN" "http://java.sun.com/dtd/ejb-jar_2_0.dtd">
<ejb-jar>
 <enterprise-beans>
  <entity>
   <display-name>OrderBean</display-name>
   <ejb-name>OrderBean</ejb-name>
   <local-home>OrderLocalHome</local-home>
   <local>OrderLocal</local>
   <ejb-class>OrderBean</ejb-class>
   <persistence-type>Container</persistence-type>
   <prim-key-class>java.lang.String</prim-key-class>
   <reentrant>False</reentrant>
   <cmp-version>2.x</cmp-version>
   <abstract-schema-name>OrderSchema</abstract-schema-name>
   <cmp-field>
    <description>description goes here</description>
    <field-name>orderID</field-name>
```

```xml
    </cmp-field>
    <cmp-field>
     <description>description goes here</description>
     <field-name>totalAmount</field-name>
    </cmp-field>
    <cmp-field>
     <description>description goes here</description>
     <field-name>orderStatus</field-name>
    </cmp-field>
    <cmp-field>
     <description>description goes here</description>
     <field-name>orderDate</field-name>
    </cmp-field>
    <primkey-field>orderID</primkey-field>
    <security-identity>
     <description>description goes here</description>
     <use-caller-identity/>
    </security-identity>
    <query>
     <query-method>
         <method-name>ejbSelectGetAllOrders()</method-name>
         <method-params/>
     </query-method>
     <ejb-ql>
       SELECT OBJECT (o) FROM OrderSchema  o
     </ejb-ql>
    </query>
   </entity>
   <entity>
    <display-name>CustomerBean</display-name>
    <ejb-name>CustomerBean</ejb-name>
    <local-home>CustomerLocalHome</local-home>
    <local>CustomerLocal</local>
    <ejb-class>CustomerBean</ejb-class>
    <persistence-type>Container</persistence-type>
    <prim-key-class>java.lang.String</prim-key-class>
    <reentrant>False</reentrant>
    <cmp-version>2.x</cmp-version>
    <abstract-schema-name>CustomerSchema</abstract-schema-name>
    <cmp-field>
     <description>description goes here</description>
     <field-name>customerID</field-name>
    </cmp-field>
    <cmp-field>
     <description>description goes here</description>
     <field-name>name</field-name>
    </cmp-field>
    <cmp-field>
     <description>description goes here</description>
     <field-name>age</field-name>
    </cmp-field>
    <cmp-field>
```

```
     <description>description goes here</description>
     <field-name>email</field-name>
    </cmp-field>
    <cmp-field>
     <description>description goes here</description>
     <field-name>member</field-name>
    </cmp-field>
    <primkey-field>customerID</primkey-field>
    <security-identity>
     <description>description goes here</description>
     <use-caller-identity/>
    </security-identity>
  </entity>
 </enterprise-beans>

 <relationships>
  <ejb-relation>
   <ejb-relationship-role>
    <ejb-relationship-role-name>
       CustomerBean
    </ejb-relationship-role-name>
    <multiplicity>One</multiplicity>
    <relationship-role-source>
     <ejb-name>CustomerBean</ejb-name>
    </relationship-role-source>
    <cmr-field>
     <cmr-field-name>orders</cmr-field-name>
     <cmr-field-type>java.util.Collection</cmr-field-type>
    </cmr-field>
   </ejb-relationship-role>
   <ejb-relationship-role>
    <ejb-relationship-role-name>
       OrderBean
    </ejb-relationship-role-name>
    <multiplicity>Many</multiplicity>
    <cascade-delete />
    <relationship-role-source>
     <ejb-name>OrderBean</ejb-name>
    </relationship-role-source>
    <cmr-field>
     <cmr-field-name>customer</cmr-field-name>
    </cmr-field>
   </ejb-relationship-role>
  </ejb-relation>
 </relationships>

 <assembly-descriptor>
   <security-role>
      <description>
       This role is for any employee of the organization who
       can view only his/her own information.
      </description>
```

```
      <role-name> employee <role-name>
  </security-role>
  <security-role>
    <description>
      This role should be assigned only to the employees who
      will be able to view the information of all the
      customers and change parts of it.
    </description>
    <role-name> customer-service-director <role-name>
  </security-role>
  <method-permission>
   <role-name>customer-service-director</role-name>
    <method>
      <ejb-name>CustomerBean</ejb-name>
      <method-name>*</method-name>
    </method>
    <method>
     <ejb-name>OrderBean</ejb-name>
      <method-name>*</method-name>
    </method>
  </method-permission>
  <container-transaction>
   <method>
    <ejb-name>OrderBean</ejb-name>
    <method-name>submitOrder</method-name>
   </method>
   <trans-attribute>RequiresNew</trans-attribute>
  </container-transaction>
 </assembly-descriptor>

</ejb-jar>
```

A P P E N D I X   D

Review questions and answers

Some questions will have more than one correct answer. Choose all that apply.

CHAPTER 2—OVERVIEW OF ENTERPRISE JAVABEANS

1. You have a J2EE application in which the programmer did not follow the programming restrictions listed in the EJB specification. This means that the application will surely not function properly.

    a. True
    b. False

Answer: B
The application may still function properly; however, your application may not be very portable if you did not follow the programming restrictions. The purpose of the programming restrictions is to ensure the portability of the bean.

2. Which of the following files go into the ejb-jar file delivered by the bean provider?

    a. The bean's class files
    b. The bean's interface files

c. The EJBObject class generated by the container that would be needed to interrupt the client calls

d. The deployment descriptor file ejb.xml

Answer: A, B

The ejb-jar file includes the bean class files and their home and component interfaces. It also includes the deployment descriptor file whose name must be ejb-jar.xml and not ejb.xml.

3. The name of the deployment descriptor file must be:

a. ejb-jar.xml
b. deployment.xml
c. ejb.xml
d. Any filename with the extension .xml

Answer: A

The deployment descriptor must be stored with the name ejb-jar.xml in the META-INF directory.

4. The name of the ejb-jar file must be ejb-jar.xml.

a. True
b. False

Answer: B

The name of the deployment descriptor file stored in the ejb-jar file must be ejb-jar.xml.

5. The EJB container offers which of the following services?

a. Security management
b. Transaction management
c. Load balancing
d. Fault tolerance

Answer: A, B

The distributed nature of EJB architecture allows for load balancing and fault tolerance, but the spec does not require the container to offer these services.

6. Which of the following kinds of beans would survive a server crash?

a. Entity beans
b. Stateless session beans
c. Stateful session beans
d. Message-driven beans

Answer. A

An entity bean survives a server crash because the entity that an entity bean represents lives in persistent storage. When the server is restarted, the container can always find a bean instance to represent that entity.

7. Which of the following are true about an enterprise bean according to the EJB 2.0 spec?

    a. A bean cannot use `java.net.Socket`.
    b. A bean instance variable cannot be declared static and final.
    c. A bean cannot listen on a socket as a server.
    d. A bean cannot use the `java.io` package.
    e. A bean cannot use `this` in the body of a class method.

Answer: C, D

The bean can use the client socket but not the server socket. The bean must not use read/write static fields; it's allowed to use read only (final) static fields. The bean must not pass `this` in the argument of the method or as a result of the method.

8. As a bean provider, you can take it for granted that the EJB container will provide which of the following services?

    a. Clustering
    b. Load balancing
    c. Distributed transaction management
    d. Support for JSP and servlets
    e. Generate classes that implement the home and component interfaces of a bean

Answer: C, E

The EJB container is not required to offer clustering, load balancing, or support for JSP and servlets.

9. As a bean provider, you can take for granted that the EJB container will provide which of the following APIs?

    a. JNDI
    b. JMX
    c. JXTA
    d. JAXP
    e. JINI

Answer: A, D

JMX, JXTA, and JINI are not required of the container.

10. Which of the following roles are responsible for making sure that all the declared EJB references in the deployment descriptor are bound to the homes of the enterprise beans that exist in the operational environment?

    a. Application assembler
    b. Container provider
    c. Bean provider
    d. System administrator
    e. Deployer

Answer: E

The deployer maps the logical environment of the application with the real operational environment.

11. Which of the following are true about the ejb-jar file?

    a. The ejb-jar file is a contract between the application assembler and the system administrator.
    b. The ejb-jar file is a contract between the application assembler and the deployer.
    c. The ejb-jar file is a contract between the bean provider and the application assembler.
    d. The ejb jar file must have the name ejb-jar.xml.
    e. The ejb-jar file must contain only one deployment descriptor.

Answer: B, C, E

The system administrator has nothing to do with the ejb-jar file. It is the deployment descriptor file and not the ejb-jar file that must have the name ejb-jar.xml.

12. Which of the following deployment descriptor elements will the bean provider use to declare a bean reference that the bean provider is using to get access to the home of an enterprise bean?

    a. `<env-entry>`
    b. `<ejb-ref>`
    c. `<resource-ref>`
    d. `<ejb-link>`

Answer: B

The `<resource-ref>` element is used to declare a resource manager connection factory reference, while the `<ejb-ref>` element is used to declare a bean reference that the bean provider is using to get access to the home of an enterprise bean.

13. Which of the following are valid entries in the deployment descriptor?

    a.   `<env-entry-type> java.lang.Boolean</env-entry-type>`
    b.   `<env-entry-type> int </env-entry-type>`
    c.   `<env-entry-type> short </env-entry-type>`
    d.   `<env-entry-type> java.lang.Character</env-entry-type>`
    e.   `<env-entry-type> char </env-entry-type>`

Answer: A, D

The value of the `<env-entry-type>` element must be a wrapper type (Boolean, Byte, Character, Double, Float, Integer, Short) or a String.

14. In your bean code you do a JNDI lookup on a JDBC connection by the following code fragment:

```
InitialContext ctx = new InitialContext();
DataSource dsrc = (DataSource)ctx.lookup("java:comp/env/jdbc/dis-
countDB");
Connection con = dsrc.getConnection();
```

Which of the following are correct entries in the `<resource-ref-name>` element in the deployment descriptor?

    a.   `java:comp/env/jdbc/discountDB`
    b.   `env/jdbc/discountDB`
    c.   `jdbc/discountDB`
    d.   `discountDB`
    e.   All of the above

Answer: C

The name entered as the value of the `<resource-ref-name>` element is relative to the basic JNDI environment context: `java:comp/env/`.

CHAPTER 3—CLIENT VIEW OF A SESSION BEAN

1. Suppose Lottery is a reference to the component interface of a stateless session bean named LotteryBean. Which of the following are valid methods that a bean provider may put in the home interface of LotteryBean?

    a.   `create()`
    b.   `create(String id)`
    c.   `createSuperLotto(int number)`
    d.   `CreateMiniLotto()`
    e.   `NewLotto(float amount)`

Answer: A

You can declare only one `create()` method in the home interface of a stateless session bean, and it must be a no-argument method.

2. Suppose Lottery is a reference to the component interface of a stateful session bean named LotteryBean. Which of the following are valid methods that a bean provider may put in the home interface of LotteryBean?

    a. `create()`
    b. `create(String id)`
    c. `createSuperLotto(int number)`
    d. `CreateMiniLotto()`
    e. `NewLotto(float amount)`

Answer: A, B, C

In the home interface of a stateful session bean you can declare one or more create methods with or without arguments. They can also be of the form `create` `<METHOD>` as in option C. Option D would be the correct answer if the C in Create were lowercase.

3. Which of the following statements are true about locating or using the home interface of a session bean?

    a. Once acquired, the home interface can be used only once.
    b. Each instance of a session bean has its own EJBHome object.
    c. The InitialContext must be narrowed before it can be used to get the home interface.
    d. Only remote clients need to get the home interface; local clients can get to the component interface directly.
    e. The local client can use the home interface to remove the bean instance.
    F. None of the above.

Answer: F

All bean instances of a given type share the EJBHome object, and it is not the Initial-Context but the reference to the home interface that is narrowed. Local clients also need the home interface to get to the component interface.

4. Which of the following statements are true about the remote component interface of a session bean?

    a. All methods in the remote home interface and the remote component interface declare to throw `javax.ejb.RemoteException`.
    b. All methods in the remote home interface and the remote component interface declare to throw `java.rmi.RemoteException`.

c. A client locates the remote component interface from JNDI and then narrows it before invoking methods on it.
d. A remote client can use the method `remove(Object key)` from the home interface to remove a stateful session bean instance.
e. A handle for an EJBObject reference may be obtained from the remote home interface.

Answer: B
The `RemoteException` is in the package `java.rmi`. It is not the remote component interface that is narrowed; it is the remote home interface. Session beans don't have a key, so you cannot delete them by using keys. The `getHandle()` method that returns a handle to the EJBObject reference is in the remote component interface and not in the remote home interface.

5. Which of the following statements are true about a remote client that wants to remove a session bean?

   a. The client can remove the session bean by invoking a no-argument `remove()` method on the remote home interface.
   b. The client can remove the session bean by invoking a no-argument `remove()` method on the remote component interface.
   c. The client can remove the session bean by invoking the `remove()` method with the object handle as an argument on the remote home interface.
   d. The client can remove the session bean by invoking the `remove()` method with the object handle as an argument on the remote component interface.

Answer: B, C
The home interface does not have a no-argument `remove()` method; only the component interface does. The only remove method the remote component interface has is the no-argument `remove()` method.

6. Which of the following statements are true about a session bean client?

   a. A local client can remove the bean by invoking a method on the home interface.
   b. Only a remote client can use the `remove()` method in the component interface.
   c. A stateful session bean is created by the container when the client invokes a `create()` method on the home interface.
   d. A create call from a client on a stateless session bean may not result in creating any instance of the bean. The container can create stateless session bean instances before any call from the client.
   e. A remove call from a client on a stateless session bean instance results in removing the instance.

Answer: C, D
The local home interface has only one remove method, and a session bean client cannot call it because it takes a key as an argument. However, the local component interface does have the no-argument remove() method, which can be used by the local client. The creation or removal of stateless session bean instances is not associated with the create() and remove() calls from a client.

7. Which of the following are true about using the isIdentical() method of the session bean component interface?

   a. Comparing two EJB Objects given out by the same home of a stateless session bean will always return true.
   b. Comparing two EJB Objects given out by the same home of a stateful session bean will always return true.
   c. You can use the equals(...) method instead of isIdentical() if you wish.
   d. Comparing two EJB Objects given out by two different homes of stateless session beans will always return false.

Answer: A, D
Two EJB Objects of two stateful session bean instances are not equal, while two EJB Objects of two stateless session bean instances belonging to the same home are always equal. The results of using the equals(...) method for comparing EJB Objects are not guaranteed to be correct.

8. Assuming L and R are the local and remote clients for session bean B, which of the following are true statements?

   a. L can pass its reference for B as a return value of a method call from R.
   b. R can pass its reference for B as a parameter in a method call to L.
   c. L cannot call methods on R. Doesn't this depend on what R actually is, and where it is located?
   d. L cannot call methods on B.

Answer: B, C
The local client, of course, can call the bean methods, but it cannot pass the local interface reference to the remote client.

9. Which of the following statements are true about session beans?

   a. You must declare a no-argument create() method both in the home interface and the component interface of a stateless session bean.
   b. You must write a no-argument remove() method in both the remote home interface and the remote component interface of a session bean.

c. A stateless session bean does not need a `create()` method because the container creates the stateless session bean instances without any call from the client.

d. None of the above.

Answer: D

You are required to put a no-argument `create()` method in the home interface (not the component interface) of a stateless session bean and one or more create or `create <METHOD>` methods in the home interface of a stateful session bean. The no-argument `remove()` method is inherited from the `EJBObject` interface, which is implemented only by the remote component interface and not the remote home interface.

10. Which of the following are the bean provider's responsibility in the case of a session bean?

a. To declare the no-argument `create()` method in the home interface of a stateless session bean

b. To declare the no-argument `remove()` method in the home interface

c. To write the component interface for the session bean

d. To implement the methods of the `EJBObject` interface

e. To make sure the business methods declared in the component interface are neither final nor static

Answer: A, C, E

The no-argument `remove()` method is inherited from the `EJBObject` interface, which is implemented only by the remote component interface and not the remote home interface. The methods of the `EJBObject` interface are implemented by the container.

CHAPTER 4—BIRTH OF A SESSION BEAN

1. Which of the following interfaces are implemented by the bean provider?

a. `javax.ejb.SessionBean`
b. `javax.ejb.SessionContext`
c. `javax.ejb.EJBContext`
d. `javax.ejb.EnterpriseBean`
e. `javax.ejb.EJBObject`
F. `javax.ejb.EJBHome`

Answer: A

There is no such interface as `EnterpriseBean`. All other interfaces mentioned here except `SessionBean` are implemented by the container.

2. Which of the following are correct statements about a session bean class?

    a. It extends the interface `SessionBean`.
    b. It is written by the bean provider.
    c. Its business method must not throw `RemoteException`.
    d. It can have a `finalize()` method.
    e. It implements `SessionContext`.

Answer: B, C
You do not extend an interface; you implement it. You never put a `finalize()` method in your bean class because if you do, it cannot be extended to write helper classes. `SessionContext` is implemented by the container, not by the bean class.

3. Which of the following show the correct sequence in which the methods would be invoked in the process of creating a session bean instance?

    a. `newInstance(), ejbCreate(), setSessionContext()`
    b. `newInstance(), getSessionContext(), ejbCreate()`
    c. `newInstance(), setSessionContext(), ejbCreate()`
    d. `setSessionContext(), newInstance(), ejbCreate()`
    e. `ejbCreate(), newInstance(), setSessionContext()`
    F. `ejbCreate(), setSessionContext(), newInstance()`

Answer: C
The container creates an instance, invokes the `setSessionContext()` method on it to give it a context, and then calls the `ejbCreateMethod()`.

4. Which of the following statements are true about a stateful session bean?

    a. An `ejbRemove()` call from the container removes the bean instance and puts it out for the garbage collector.
    b. An `ejbCreate()` call is made by the container only when a client invokes a create method.
    c. You can get the security information about a client from inside the `ejbCreate()` method.
    d. The container will call the `setSessionContext()` method only once.
    e. All of the above.

Answer: E
The `setSessionContext()` method will be called only once regardless of whether it is a stateful or a stateless session bean. Options A, B, and C are true only about a stateful and not a stateless session bean.

5. Which of the following statements are true about a stateless session bean?

   a. An ejbRemove() call from the container removes the bean instance and puts it out for the garbage collector.
   b. An ejbCreate call is made by the container only when a client invokes a create method.
   c. You can get the security information about a client from inside the ejbCreate() method.
   d. The container will call the setSessionContext() method only once.
   e. All of the above.

Answer: D

The setSessionContext() method will be called only once regardless of whether it is a stateful or a stateless session bean. Options A, B, and C are true only about a stateful and not a stateless session bean.

6. Which of the following statements are correct about a session bean whose class contains the following method? public void ejbCreate(String id){}

   a. It is a stateless session bean.
   b. The home interface of the bean has the method create(String id) declared in it.
   c. It is a stateful session bean.
   d. The component interface of the bean has the method ejbCreate(String id) declared in it.
   e. None of the above.

Answer: B, C

Only a stateful session bean and not a stateless session bean can have a create method with arguments. An ejbCreate<method> in the bean class corresponds to a create<method> in the home interface.

7. For a session bean, which of the following are the container's responsibilities?

   a. Call ejbCreate().
   b. Implement javax.ejb.SessionBean.
   c. Implement javax.ejb.EJBContext.
   d. Implement ejbRemove().
   e. Implement setSessionContext().

Answer: A, C

The ejbCreate methods are implemented in the bean class by the bean provider. The SessionBean interface, which includes the methods setSessionContext() and ejbRemove(), is also implemented by the bean provider in the bean class.

8. Which of the following statements are true about a business method implemented in the session bean class and declared in the component interface?

   a. The method must declare `RemoteException` in the bean class if the method is exposed in a remote interface.
   b. If the method definition declares an application exception in the interface, it must do so in the class as well.
   c. The method must not be declared final or static.
   d. The method must not begin with `ejb`.
   e. You cannot have overloaded methods.

Answer: C, D
You never declare `RemoteException` in the bean class. Who will get the exception? The container, not the remote client. You need to declare an application exception in the class method only if you are actually going to throw it: the standard Java rule. You can always have overloaded methods in Java.

9. From which of the following methods can you call the `isCallerInRole()` method of the SessionContext?

   a. `setSessionContext()`
   b. `ejbCreate()` method of a stateless session bean
   c. `ejbCreate()` method of a stateful session bean
   d. None of the above

Answer: C
The container can create an instance of a stateless session bean (and hence call the `ejbCreate()` method) without any create call from a client. Therefore, you cannot call the `isCallerInRole()` method from the `ejbCreate()` method of a stateless session bean. Also, the caller information is not available when the container calls the `setSessionContext()` method.

10. Which of the following exceptions are thrown if a bean instance makes a prohibited method call to its session context?

   a. `java.lang.IllegalStateException`
   b. `java.rmi.RemoteException`
   c. `javax.ejb.IllegalMethodCall`
   d. `javax.ejb.NoSuchMethodException`
   e. `javax.ejb.NoSuchObjectException`

Answer: A
Which session method you can call depends on in which state of its lifecycle the bean instance is.

CHAPTER 5—LIFECYCLE OF A SESSION BEAN

1. Which of the following methods can be called from the code of a stateless session bean's client?

   a. `ejbCreate()`
   b. `remove()`
   c. `create()`
   d. `ejbRemove()`
   e. `createDiscount()`

Answer: B, C
The methods beginning with the prefix `ejb` are not directly accessible to the client. The only create method exposed to the client of a stateless session bean is the no-argument `create()` method.

2. Which of the following methods can be invoked by the container on the stateless session bean?

   a. `ejbCreate()`
   b. `remove()`
   c. `create()`
   d. `ejbRemove()`
   e. `createDiscount()`

Answer: A, D
The create and remove methods are called by the client, and the corresponding ejb-Create and ejbRemove methods are called by the container.

3. Which of the following methods belong to the `SessionBean` interface?

   a. `ejbCreate()`
   b. `ejbActivate()`
   c. `create()`
   d. `setSessionContext()`
   e. `getRollbackOnly()`

Answer: B, D
The ejbCreate methods do not belong to the `SessionBean` interface; you have to implement them: an ejbCreate method corresponding to each create method in the home interface. The `getRollbackOnly()` method belongs to the `EJB-Context` interface.

4. Which of the following methods belong to the `SessionContext` interface, directly or by inheritance?

   a. `ejbCreate()`
   b. `ejbActivate()`
   c. `create()`
   d. `setSessionContext()`
   e. `getRollbackOnly()`
   F. `getEJBHome()`

Answer: E, F
`SessionContext` gets the `getEJBHome()` and `getRollbackOnly()` methods by inheritance from the `EJBContext` interface.

5. Which of the following lists presents the correct sequence in which the listed methods would be executed in the lifecycle of a stateful session bean?

   a. `ejbCreate()`, `setSessionContext()`, `ejbActivate()`, `ejbPassivate()`
   b. `ejbCreate()`, `ejbActivate()`, `ejbPassivate`, `setSessionContext()`
   c. `setSessionContext()`, `ejbCreate()`, `ejbPassivate()`, `ejbActivate()`
   d. `setSessionContext()`, `ejbCreate()`, `ejbActivate()`, `ejbPassivate()`
   e. `ejbActivate()`, `ejbCreate()`, `setSessionContext()`, `ejbPassivate()`

Answer: C
Instantiating the bean and setting its context followed by invoking the `ejbCreate()` method must happen before calling any other method on the bean instance. The `ejbActivate()` method is called only after `ejbPassivate()` because only a passivated bean can be activated.

6. In which of the following cases will the container remove a session bean instance without invoking the `ejbRemove()` method?

   a. The bean instance throws a system exception.
   b. The bean instance in a passive state times out.
   c. The bean instance in the method ready state times out.
   d. The bean instance calls a prohibited method of its session context.
   e. The client invokes the method `remove()`.

Answer: A, B

The only situations where a bean instance is removed without executing ejbRemove are when the bean instance throws a system exception and when the bean instance times out while in the passive state and the server crashes.

7. Which of the following statements show what happens when a client invokes a session bean instance that does not exist?

    a. `javax.ejb.NoSuchObjectLocalException` for the local client
    b. `javax.ejb.NoSuchObjectException` for the remote client
    c. `javax.ejb.RemoveException`
    d. `javax.ejb.ObjectNotFoundException`
    e. `java.rmi.NoSuchObjectException` for the remote client

Answer: A, E

`NoSuchObjectLocalException` is thrown to the local client and it is in the `javax.ejb` package, while `NoSuchObjectException` is thrown to the remote client and it is in the `java.rmi` package.

8. Which of the following statements are true about the lifecycle of a session bean?

    a. Only a stateful session bean, and not a stateless session bean, in a transaction can be passivated.
    b. The client cannot invoke a `create()` or `remove()` call on a stateless session bean.
    c. Only a stateful session bean can be activated or passivated.
    d. The container will invoke an `ejbRemove()` call on a stateful session bean only in response to a `remove()` call from the client.
    e. Two clients may end up using the same stateless session bean instance, one after the other.

Answer: C, E

A stateless session bean has no passive state, and a stateful session bean cannot be passivated while in a transaction. The home interfaces of both stateless and stateful session beans can have the no-argument create method, and they both have the `remove()` methods.

9. Which of the following are valid declarations for the business methods in the class of a session bean?

    a. `public void ejbSetDiscount(float number);`
    b. `public void setDiscount(float number) throws RemoteException;`

c. `public static void setDiscount(float number);`
d. `public void setDiscount();`

Answer: D

The business methods must not have the prefix `ejb`, must not throw `Remote-Exception`, and must not be static or final.

10. From which of the following methods can't a stateful session bean access the methods of another bean?

a. `ejbRemove()`
b. `ejbPassivate()`
c. `setSessionContext()`
d. `ejbCreate()`
e. None of the above

Answer: C

The only access-related things a bean instance can do in the `setSession-Context()` method are to get a reference to its home and an access to its JNDI environment.

CHAPTER 6—CLIENT VIEW OF AN ENTITY BEAN

1. Which of the following statements are true about the entity bean's remote home interface?

a. Both the `create()` and `remove()` methods are declared in the interface by the bean developer.
b. Both the `create()` and `remove()` methods are inherited from `javax.ejb.EJBHome`.
c. The `create()` method is declared by the bean developer, and the `remove()` methods are inherited from `javax.ejb.EJBHome`.
d. The `remove()` methods are declared by the developer, and the `create()` method is inherited from `javax.ejb.EJBHome`.
e. The bean provider must provide the `create()` method.

Answer: C

The create methods in an entity bean's remote home interface are optional, and if declared, they are declared by the bean developer, as opposed to the remove methods, which are inherited from the `EJBHome` interface.

2. The developer is required to put which of the following methods in the entity bean home interface?

   a. `create()` and `findByPrimaryKey()` methods
   b. One or more `create()` methods
   c. One or more business methods
   d. Only one method, `findByPrimaryKey()`

Answer: D

You are required to put only one method in the entity bean's home interface: `findByPrimaryKey()`. You can also declare `create()` and (home) business methods in the home interface, but you are not required to do so.

3. Which of the following are illegal names for the business methods defined in an entity bean home interface?

   a. `findAllCustomers(...)`
   b. `removeTheCustomer(...)`
   c. `createCustomer(...)`
   d. `create()`
   e. `retrieveCustData(...)`

Answer: A, B, C, D

You cannot start the name of a business method with the prefix `find`, `remove`, or `create` in order to avoid conflict with the find, remove, and create methods.

4. How many create methods can you declare in the entity bean home interface?

   a. One or more
   b. Zero or more
   c. Exactly one
   d. Zero

Answer: B

The create methods in an entity bean home interface are optional. You can declare zero or more of them.

5. How many find methods can you declare in the entity bean home interface?

   a. One or more
   b. Zero or more
   c. Exactly one
   d. Zero

Answer: A

You are required to declare at least one find method in the entity bean home interface: `findByPrimaryKey()`.

6. Consider an entity bean with `Customer` as its remote component interface and `CustomerHome` as its remote home interface. Which of the following are legal method declarations in the home interface?

   a. `public CustomerHome findCustomerByEmail(String email);`
   b. `public Customer findCustomerByEmail(String email);`
   c. `public Customer findCustomerByEmail(String email)`
       `throws FinderException, RemoteException;`
   d. `public Customer findCustomerByEmail(String email)`
       `throws FinderException;`
   e. `public String findCustomerByEmail(String email) throws`
       `FinderException, RemoteException;`

Answer: C

The return type of a find method in remote home interface must be a remote component interface (or a collection of it), and it must throw a finder exception and a remote exception.

7. Consider an entity bean with `Customer` as its local component interface and `CustomerHome` as its local home interface. Which of the following are legal method declarations in the home interface?

   a. `public CustomerHome findCustomerByEmail(String email);`
   b. `public Customer findCustomerByEmail(String email);`
   c. `public Customer findCustomerByEmail(String email)`
       `throws FinderException, RemoteException;`
   d. `public Customer findCustomerByEmail(String email)`
       `throws FinderException;`
   e. `public String findCustomerByEmail(String email) throws`
       `FinderException, RemoteException;`

Answer: D

The return type of a find method in a local home interface must be a local component interface (or a collection of it), and it must throw a finder exception and not a remote exception.

8. Which of the following are the valid ways a client can get a reference to the remote component interface of an entity bean representing a specific entity?

    a. Call a create method
    b. Call a find method
    c. Obtain a reference from the handle
    d. Call `getBeanReference()`
    e. Obtain the reference as a parameter in a method call

Answer: A, B, C, E
There is no standard method named getBeanReference in the home interface to get a reference to the remote component interface.

9. A client calls a finder method whose return type is a Collection of references to the remote interface of an entity bean. Assume no match for that entity is found. Which of the following will be the result of this call?

    a. `ObjectNotFoundException`.
    b. An empty Collection will be returned.
    c. An entity would be created and a reference to that entity would be returned.
    d. `EntityNotFoundException`.

Answer: B
If no entity is found in the database, a call to a single-entity finder method will result in `ObjectNotFoundException`, while a call to a multiple-entity finder will simply return an empty Collection, and there will be no exception.

10. Which of the following are true statements about what happens when a `remove()` method is called using the component interface of an entity bean representing a specific entity in the database?

    a. The entity bean instance is deleted.
    b. The entity in the database is deleted.
    c. Both the entity and the entity bean instance survive, but that entity bean instance does not represent that entity anymore.
    d. Nothing happens; the container simply ignores the call.

Answer: B
The `remove()` call to an entity bean deletes the entity in the database, and the bean instance representing that entity goes back into the pool.

CHAPTER 7—BIRTH OF AN ENTITY BEAN

1. Consider two references, customerOne and customerTwo, to the component interface `Customer` of an entity bean. What is the correct way to find out if the two references refer to the same bean instance?

    a. `customerOne == customerTwo`
    b. `customerOne.equals(customerTwo)`
    c. `customerOne.isIdentical(customerTwo)`
    d. All of the above

Answer: C

The component interface references are compared by using the `isIdentical()` method, while the primary keys are compared by using the `equals()` method.

2. Consider an entity bean whose primary key is defined by two fields, courseID and teacherID, in a class named `CoursePK`. The key class is specified in the deployment descriptor with the following code fragment:

```
<prim-key-class> CoursePK </prim-key-class>
<primkey-field> courseID </primkey-field>
<primkey-field> teacherID </primkey-field>
```

Which of the following are valid statements about this code fragment?

    a. This is valid only for a BMP bean.
    b. This is valid only for a CMP bean.
    c. This is valid for both CMP and BMP beans.
    d. This is an invalid specification of the primary key in the deployment descriptor.

Answer: D

You never use the `<primkey-field>` element when the key is composed of multiple fields. You write the primary key class and mention its name in the deployment descriptor using the `<prim-key-class>` element.

3. Which of the following methods are allowed to be invoked from within the method `setEntityContext()`?

    a. `getEJBHome()`
    b. `getEJBLocalHome()`
    c. `getEJBObject()`
    d. `getPrimaryKey()`

Answer: A, B

When the container calls the `setEntityContext()` method, the bean instance has only its home and a JNDI context.

4. Which of the following statements are true about a CMP entity bean?

    a. You cannot write JDBC code in the bean class to make a connection and send queries to any database.

    b. You cannot write JDBC code in the bean class to change the values of virtual persistent fields of your bean.

    c. You can write JDBC code and get connected to any database you want.

    d. You can write JDBC code to read the virtual persistent fields, but you cannot change their values.

Answer: B

Even in a CMP bean you can write code to directly connect to the database. However, you cannot manage the persistent fields from your bean class.

5. Which of the following are not legal method declarations in a CMP entity bean class to set the value of a persistent field?

    a. `public abstract String setEmail(String email);`
    b. `public void setEmail(String email);`
    c. `public abstract void setEmail(String email);`
    d. `public abstract void SetEmail(String email);`

Answer: A, B, D

The name of a setter method should begin with a prefix set with lowercase s, it must be declared abstract, and its return type must be void.

6. Which two of the following are a legal pair of getter and setter accessor methods declared in a CMP entity bean class to set and get the values of a persistent field?

    a. `public abstract void setID(int id);`
    b. `public abstract String getID();`
    c. `public abstract Object getID();`
    d. `public abstract int getID();`

Answer: A, D

The return type of a get method and the argument type of the corresponding set method must match each other.

7. How many `ejbPostCreate()` methods can a CMP bean class have?

    a. Zero or more
    b. One or more
    c. One only
    d. Zero only
    e. Zero or one only

Answer: A

Each `ejbPostCreate()` method corresponds to a `create()` method in the home interface, and the home interface of an entity bean can have zero or more create methods.

8. Which methods of the `EntityContext` interface can be called from within an `ejbCreate<method>` of an entity bean class?

   a. `getEJBObject()`
   b. `getPrimaryKey()`
   c. `getEJBHome()`
   d. `getRollbackOnly()`
   e. `getUserTransaction()`

Answer: C, D

When the ejbCreate method is called, the bean instance does not have an EJBObject and a primary key assigned to it yet. Because an entity bean is a CMT bean, it can never call the `getUserTransaction()` method.

9. Which methods of the `EntityContext` interface can be called from within an `ejbPostCreate<method>` of an entity bean class?

   a. `getEJBObject()`
   b. `getPrimaryKey()`
   c. `getEJBHome()`
   d. `getRollbackOnly()`
   e. `getUserTransaction()`

Answer: A, B, C, D

By the time ejbPostCreate method is called, the instance has access to everything it needs; it has acquired its full beanhood. However, being a CMT bean, an entity bean can never call the `getUserTransaction()` method.

10. Which of the following statements about the entity bean are true?

   a. All entity bean instances of the same type (say CustomerBean) have the same Home, that is, an instance of an object that implements the home interface of this bean.
   b. A specific entity bean instance can be accessed by only one client at a time.
   c. If two clients wanted to access the same entity in the database concurrently, the container would make two entity bean instances to represent that entity.
   d. If two clients wanted to access the same entity in the database concurrently, the container would make one entity bean to represent that entity, and the two clients would get their own references to the same EJBObject corresponding to that one entity bean instance.

Answer: A, D

Entity beans support concurrent access by multiple clients, and entity beans instances of the same bean type (say CustomerBean) have the same EJBHome, but each instance has its own EJBObject.

CHAPTER 8—LIFECYCLE OF AN ENTITY BEAN

1. Which of the following statements are true about the method `ejbFindBy-PrimaryKey("25")`?

   a. It can be invoked only on a bean instance in the pooled state.
   b. It can be invoked only on a bean instance in the ready state.
   c. It can be invoked on a bean instance that is either in the ready state or in the pooled state.
   d. It can be invoked only on a bean instance that is representing the entity with the primary key 25.
   e. By the time the results of the method invocation are returned to the client, the entity with the primary key 25 if found is associated with a bean instance.

Answer: A

The find methods are invoked on instances in the pool where no instance represents a specific entity.

2. In a CMP bean, what should the bean provider do about the ejbFind methods?

   a. Declare them as public and abstract.
   b. Declare then as private and abstract.
   c. Declare them as public.
   d. Declare them as private.
   e. Not declare them at all.

Answer: E

In a CMP entity bean, you do not implement the ejbFind methods; the container does that.

3. When an `ejbCreate<method>` method is invoked, what other methods must the container invoke?

   a. `ejbActivate()`
   b. `ejbStore()`
   c. `ejbFindByPrimaryKey()`
   d. `ejbPostCreate()`

Answer: D

The container must invoke `ejbPostCreate()` for each `ejbCreate()` method, and it must invoke ejbLoad after loading the data to the bean. The `ejbFindBy-PrimaryKey()` method is invoked in the pooled state and is not associated with the `ejbCreate()` method. The `ejbStore()` method is invoked before the `ejb-Passivate()` and `ejbRemove()` methods.

4. Consider the method `getUserTransaction()` of the interface `Entity-Context`. From which methods of an entity bean class can this method be called?

    a. `ejbCreate<method>`
    b. Home business methods
    c. Business methods exposed in the component interface
    d. `ejbStore()`
    e. None of the above

Answer: E

Entity beans are CMT beans, and only BMT beans can call `getUserTransaction()`.

5. Which of the following does an entity bean instance have in the ready state?

    a. It has an EntityContext assigned to it.
    b. It has a primary key assigned to its context.
    c. It has an EJBObject.
    d. Its EJBObject has a primary key assigned to it.
    e. None of the above.

Answer: A, B, C, D

In the ready state a bean instance has everything it needs. It is in its full beanhood.

6. Which of the following methods, invoked on an entity bean, are always associated with a state change in the bean's lifecycle?

    a. `setEntityContext(…)`
    b. `ejbLoad()`
    c. `ejbPassivate()`
    d. `ejbRemove()`
    e. `ejbSelect()`

Answer: A, C, D

The `ejbLoad()` method can be called anytime by the container to refresh the bean's state. It does not always have to be associated with the state change.

7. Which of the following are the legal method declarations for an entity bean class?

    a. `public static Collection ejbHomeListCustomers()`
    b. `public Collection ejbHomeListCustomers() throws RemoteException`
    c. `public Collection ejbHomeListCustomers()`
    d. `public Collection ejbHomelistCustomers()`
    e. `public Collection EJBHomeListCustomers()`

Answer: C

A method in the class must not throw `RemoteException`, it must not be static, and the home business methods must start with the prefix `ejbHome` followed by the `<method>` name with first letter uppercased. No class method should throw `RemoteException`.

8. Which of the following methods can be invoked on the EntityContext from inside the `ejbActivate()` method of an entity bean class?

    a. `getPrimaryKey()`
    b. `getCallerPrincipal()`
    c. `getRollbackOnly()`
    d. `getEJBObject()`
    e. `isCallerInRole()`

Answer: A, D

The `ejbActivate()` method runs in an unspecified transactional context, and so no transaction related information is available. The instance does not have the entity data loaded into it yet, no client business call is being served, and so no client information (getCallerPrincipal) is available.

9. Which of the following actions can you achieve by invoking an appropriate method on the EntityContext from inside the `ejbPassivate()` method of an entity bean class?

    a. Get the primary key
    b. Get security information about the client
    c. Mark a transaction for rollback
    d. Call another bean's method
    e. Access the JNDI environment of the bean

Answer: A, E

The `ejbPassivate()` method has the same access as the `ejbActivate()` method.

10. Which of the following actions can you achieve by invoking an appropriate method on the EntityContext from inside the `ejbStore()` method of an entity bean class?

    a. Get the primary key
    b. Get security information about the client
    c. Mark a transaction for rollback
    d. Call another bean's method
    e. Access the JNDI environment of the bean

Answer: A, B, C, D, E
The container calls the `ejbStore()` method to give the bean provider (who wrote the code) a chance to update the persistent state of the bean instance. During the `ejbStore()` execution the transaction context still exists. So the `ejbStore()` method can access anything that a business method in the ready state can access.

CHAPTER 9—ENTITY BEAN RELATIONSHIPS

1. Which of the following are the responsibilities of a bean provider for an entity bean using container-managed persistence and container-managed relationships?

    a. The bean provider must define the CMR fields in the deployment descriptor.
    b. The bean provider must declare the get and set methods in the bean class.
    c. The bean provider must implement the get and set methods in the bean class.
    d. The bean provider must declare the CMR fields as variables in the bean class.
    e. None of the above.

Answer: A, B
The CMR fields are not declared as variables in the bean class; instead you declare the corresponding get and set accessor methods in the bean class that the container implements.

2. Which of the following statements are true about an entity bean that has a bidirectional container-managed relationship with another bean?

    a. The bean must have a local component interface.
    b. The bean must have a remote component interface.
    c. The return type of the get method for its CMR field must be RMI-IIOP compatible.
    d. The get method return type may be java.util.List.
    e. The bean should have only a local component interface and no remote interface.

Answer: A

In order to become a target for a relationship a bean must have a local component interface, which is the return type of the get method corresponding to a CMR field. It may have remote interfaces as well, but they are not required.

3. Which of the following are possibly valid tags in defining the type of a CMR field in a deployment descriptor?

    a. `<cmr-field-type> java.util.List </cmr-field-type>`
    b. `<cmr-field-type> java.util.Map </cmr-field-type>`
    c. `<cmr-field-type> java.util.Collection </cmr-field-type>`
    d. `<cmr-field-type> java.util.Set </cmr-field-type>`
    e. `<cmr-field> java.util.Collection</cmr-field>`

Answer: C, D

The valid tag is `<cmr-field-type>`, which is specified when the return of the corresponding get method is a collection, and its valid values are java.util.Collection and java.util.Set.

4. Which of the following are valid declarations for the get method corresponding to the CMR field order where the CMR field points to the Order bean that has the remote component interface `Order` and the local component interface `OrderLocal`?

    a. `public abstract Order getOrder();`
    b. `public abstract OrderLocal getOrder();`
    c. `private abstract Order getOrder();`
    d. `private abstract OrderLocal getOrder();`
    e. `public abstract OrderLocal getOrders();`

Answer: B

The name of the get method corresponding to a CMR field is the CMR field name with the first letter uppercased and preceded by the prefix `get`, and the return type is the local component interface of the target bean.

5. Which of the following statements are true about an entity bean that uses container-managed persistence and relationships?

    a. It can have a relationship that involves only one other bean.
    b. It can have a relationship that involves many other beans.
    c. It can have a relationship with only a session bean.
    d. Its class must be declared abstract by the bean provider.

Answer: A, D

There are only two entity bean types that can be involved in a given relationship, such as CustomerBean and OrderBean. Of course, many instances can be involved. The bean class has a pair of abstract get and set methods corresponding to each CMR field; therefore, the class must be declared abstract.

6. Which of the following deployment descriptor elements are used to declare the name of a CMR field?

   a. `<cmr-field> teacher </cmr-field>`
   b. `< cmr-field-name> teacher </cmr-field-name>`
   c. `<field-name> teacher </field-name>`
   d. `<field-name> Teacher </field-name>`
   e. `<cmr-name> teacher </cmr-name>`

Answer: B

The name of the deployment descriptor element used to specify the name of a CMR field is `<cmr-field-name>`.

7. Which of the following statements are true for an entity bean that uses a container to manage its persistence and relationships?

   a. The type of a CMP field is determined from the corresponding get and set methods.
   b. The type of a CMR field is determined from the corresponding get and set methods.
   c. The type of a CMP field is declared in the deployment descriptor.
   d. The type of a CMR field must be declared in the deployment descriptor if it is a Collection.
   e. The type of a CMP or CMR field is declared inside the bean class in the form of a variable declaration.

Answer: A, D

The type of a CMP field is not declared in the deployment descriptor. The container figures out the type from the return type of the corresponding get and set methods. This is also true for a single-valued CMR field. However, if the CMR field is a Collection, its type must be declared in the deployment descriptor whose legal value can be java.util.Collection or java.util.Set.

8. Which of the following statements are true about the relationships between entity beans that use container-managed persistence?

   a. The relationship can be only bidirectional.
   b. The relationship can be only unidirectional.

c. The relationship may be one-to-one, one-to-many, or many-to-many.

d. Only two bean instances at maximum may be involved in a relationship.

Answer: C

The relationships can be one-to-one, one-to-many, or many-to-many.

9. Consider the following lines in the deployment descriptor:

```
1. <ejb-relationship-role>
2.    <ejb-relationship-role-name>
3.         OrderBean
4.     </ejb-relationship-role-name>
5.    <multiplicity>Many</multiplicity>
6.    <cascade-delete/>
7.    <relationship-role-source>
8.    <ejb-name>OrderBean</ejb-name>
9.    </relationship-role-source>
10.    <cmr-field>
11.       <cmr-field-name>
12.            customer
13.       </cmr-field-name>
14.    </cmr-field>
15. </ejb-relationship-role>
```

Line 6 in the above listing means which of the following?

a. If a customer is deleted, all the orders related to that customer will be deleted.

b. If a customer is deleted, all the orders related to all the customers will be deleted.

c. If an order is deleted, the customer related to the order will also be deleted.

d. If all the orders related to a customer are deleted, the customer will be deleted too.

Answer: A

Because OrderBean has a multiplicity of many, the element `<cascade-delete/>` means that if a customer is deleted, all the orders corresponding to that customer will be deleted.

10. Consider the following relationship between two beans, Order and BackupOrder:

o1 ↔ b1
o2 ↔ b2

where o1 and o2 represent the instances of the Order bean and b1 and b2 represent the instances of the BackupOrder bean, and the relationship shown is one-to-one. Now the following code is executed:

```
b1.setOrder(b2.getOrder())
```

After the execution of this code, which of the following will be true?

a. o1.getBackupOrder() == null
b. o2.getBackupOrder == null
c. b1.getOrder() == null
d. b2.getOrder() == null
e. None of the above

Answer: A, D

The relationship of o2 is moved from b2 to b1. Because b1 can have a relationship with only one instance of Order, its relationship with o1 is overwritten by its relationship with o2. So the only relationship that exists now is between o2 and b1. In other words, o2 and b1 have a relationship, and o1 and b2 do not.

CHAPTER 10—EJB QUERY LANGUAGE

In the following questions, assume that OrderSchema and CustomerSchema are the abstract schemas for the beans OrderBean and CustomerBean, respectively.

1. Which of the following are valid EJB QL queries?

a. SELECT OBJECT (o)
   FROM OrderSchema o
b. SELECT OBJECT (o.totalAmount)
   FROM OrderSchema o
c. SELECT o FROM OrderSchema o
d. SELECT o.totalAmount
   FROM OrderSchema o

Answer: A, D

The keyword OBJECT is used in the SELECT clause only when the return type is the abstract schema type.

2. Which of the following are valid EJB QL queries?

a. SELECT OBJECT (o) FROM OrderSchema o
   WHERE o.customer > 30
b. SELECT OBJECT o.customer
   FROM OrderSchema o
c. SELECT OBJECT (o) FROM OrderSchema o
   WHERE o.customer.member = TRUE
d. SELECT OBJECT (c)
   FROM CustomerSchema c
   WHERE c.orders.orderStatus = 'pending'

Answer: C

The customer is not a CMP field, so you cannot compare it with a value such as 30. The keyword OBJECT is used in the SELECT clause only when the return type is the abstract schema type. The path c.orders.orderStatus is invalid because orders is a Collection.

3. Which of the following are a valid use of a WHERE clause in EJB QL?

    a. WHERE o.totalAmount > 100
    b. WHERE o.totalAmount == 100
    c. WHERE o.totalAmount != 100
    d. WHERE o.totalAmount <> 100
    e. WHERE o.totalAmount = 100

Answer: A, D, E

The operator for equals in EJB QL is = and not ==, and the operator for not equal is <> and not !=.

4. Consider the following expression:

    o.totalAmount BETWEEN 100.00 AND 500.00

    This expression may be replaced by which of the following expressions in order to produce the same result?

    a. o.totalAmount < 500.00
        AND o.totalAmount > 100.00
    b. o.totalAmount <= 500.00
        AND o.totalAmount >= 100.00
    c. o.totalAmount <= 500.00
        AND o.totalAmount > 100.00
    d. o.totalAmount < 500.00
        AND o.totalAmount >= 100.00

Answer: B

The BETWEEN expression is inclusive, which means 100.00 and 500.00 are included in the select range.

5. Consider the following expression:

    o.totalAmount NOT BETWEEN 100.00 AND 500.00

    This expression may be replaced by which of the following expressions in order to produce the same result?

a.   o.totalAmount > 500.00
       OR o.totalAmount < 100.00
b.   o.totalAmount >= 500.00
       OR o.totalAmount <= 100.00
c.   o.totalAmount >= 500.00
       OR o.totalAmount < 100.00
d.   o.totalAmount > 500.00
       OR o.totalAmount <= 100.00

Answer: A

The NOT BETWEEN expression is inclusive, which means 100.00 and 500.00 are not included in the select range.

6.   In EJB 2.0, EJB QL queries are written for which of the following methods?

     a.   The get and set methods corresponding to the CMP fields
     b.   The find methods
     c.   The ejbSelect methods
     d.   The create methods
     e.   The remove methods

Answer: B, C

The EJB QL queries are associated with the find and ejbSelect methods.

CHAPTER 11 — MESSAGE-DRIVEN BEANS

1.   Which of the following methods will the compiler expect you to implement in an MDB class?

     a.   ejbRemove()
     b.   onMessage()
     c.   setMessageDrivenContext()
     d.   ejbCreate()

Answer: A, B, C

These methods come from the interfaces that the bean class implements. The ejbCreate() method does not come from any interface.

2.   If an MDB bean instance invokes the method getEJBLocalHome() on the context of the bean instance, what will be the result?

     a.   You will not be able to compile the code.
     b.   A reference to the local home interface of the bean will be returned.
     c.   A handle to the local home interface of the bean instance will be returned.
     d.   The container will throw the exception java.lang.IllegalStateException.

Answer: D

You cannot invoke the getEJBLocalHome method on the bean context because the bean has no client view.

3. Which of the following are valid statements about a message-driven bean?

    a. A message-driven bean can have only a local home interface.
    b. The identity of a message-driven bean is hidden from the client.
    c. You can invoke the getEJBLocalHome() method on the bean's context from inside the onMessage() method.
    d. The container invokes the ejbActivate() method on the bean instance before invoking the onMessage() method.

Answer: B

An MDB does not have a client view, and it does not have the ejbActivate() container callback.

4. Which of the following interfaces must be implemented, directly or indirectly, in a message-driven bean class?

    a. javax.ejb.MessageDrivenContext
    b. javax.ejb.MessageDrivenBean
    c. javax.jms.MessageListener
    d. javax.jms.MessageProducer
    e. javax.jms.MessageConsumer

Answer: B, C

The MDB class implements the MessageDrivenBean and MessageListener interfaces, and the container implements the MessageDrivenContext interface. The bean does not implement any interface from JMS except the Message-Listener.

5. Consider two message-driven beans: MarketingService and BusinessService. Both beans have subscribed to a Topic destination, CustomerInfo. A message arrives at the Topic destination. Which of the following can happen?

    a. Only one instance of MarketingService and one instance of BusinessService will receive the message.
    b. Multiple instances of MarketingService and BusinessService will receive the message.
    c. Only one instance either from MarketingService or from BusinessService will receive the message.
    d. All the instances of MarketingService and BusinessService will receive the message.

Answer: A

Only one instance of a given type gets the message. Only one type can be associated with a Queue, while multiple types can be associated with a Topic.

6. Consider that method `A()` in an application sends a message; in response the method `onMessage()` of an MDB is called. The `onMessage()` method invokes another method, `B()`. Method `B()` throws an application (checked) exception. Which of the following are the correct ways to deal with this exception in the `onMessage()` method?

    a. Throw the exception back to method `A()`.
    b. Handle the exception inside the method `onMessage()`.
    c. Throw the exception back to the container.
    d. Throw `RemoteException`.

Answer: B

You cannot throw an application (checked) exception from inside the `onMessage()` method because the bean has no client. The `onMessage()` method will handle the application exception thrown on it, which means to either recover from it or wrap it in `javax.ejb.EJBException` and throw it. The MDB should never throw `RemoteException`.

7. Which of the following show the correct sequence of methods invoked on an MDB during its lifecycle?

    a. `newInstance()`, `ejbCreate()`, `setMessageDrivenContext()`, `onMessage()`, `ejbRemove()`
    b. `onMessage()`, `ejbCreate()`, `ejbRemove()`
    c. `newInstance()`, `setMessageDrivenContext()`, `ejbCreate()`, `onMessage()`, `ejbRemove()`
    d. `setMessageDrivenContext()`, `ejbCreate()`, `onMessage()`

Answer: C, D

The container instantiates the bean by calling `newInstance()`, and gives it a context by invoking `setMessageDrivenContext()` on it. Following this, the container calls the `ejbCreate()` method. The `ejbRemove()` method is called at the end in order to put the instance back to the does not exist state.

8. Which of the following are true statements about an MDB associated with a Queue?

    a. Only one instance from the pool of an MDB type can process a message at a given time.
    b. Multiple instances from the pool of an MDB type can process messages at the same time.

c. One instance can handle only one message at a time.

d. A message will go to only one bean instance.

Answer: B, C, D

While more than one bean instance can work at a time processing different messages, a given instance can process only one message at a time. A message in a Queue goes to only one instance.

9. From which of the following methods can a message-driven bean with a BMT demarcation get a reference to the transaction?

   a. `ejbCreate()`

   b. `ejbRemove()`

   c. `onMessage()`

   d. `setEJBMessageDrivenContext()`

Answer: A, B, C

It cannot get a reference to a transaction in the `setEJBMessageDriven-Context()` method because the transaction cannot possibly exist when this method is called.

10. From which of the following methods can a message-driven bean with a CMT demarcation invoke methods on another bean?

   a. `ejbCreate()`

   b. `ejbRemove()`

   c. `onMessage()`

   d. `setEJBMessageDrivenContext()`

Answer: C

The bean has access to other beans only from the `onMessage()` methods. All the other methods shown here are called during the transition between the two states does not exist and pooled.

CHAPTER 12—EJB TRANSACTIONS

1. Which of the following statements are true about an EJB transaction in a BMT demarcation?

   a. You can use a BMT demarcation only for a session bean or a message-driven bean.

   b. You can start a new transaction before ending a previously started transaction.

   c. A stateful session bean must not complete a transaction in the method where it started before the method returns.

   d. A stateless session bean must complete a transaction in the method where it started before the method returns.

Answer: A, D

Entity beans can be only CMT beans and not BMT. In a stateless session bean and a message-driven bean, if you start a transaction in a method, you must end it before the method completes.

2. Which transaction attributes assigned to a method will assure that the method will always run in a transaction, if it does run?

   a. Mandatory
   b. Never
   c. NotSupported
   d. Required
   e. RequiresNew
   F. Supports

Answer: A, D, E

A method with the Never attribute, if it runs, runs with an unspecified context, while a method with the NotSupported attribute also always runs in an unspecified context. A method with the Supports attribute runs in the transaction in which it is called, and it runs with an unspecified transaction context if it is called without a transaction context.

3. Which transaction attributes assigned to a method will assure that the method will always run in an unspecified transaction context, if it does run?

   a. Mandatory
   b. Never
   c. NotSupported
   d. Required
   e. RequiresNew
   F. Supports

Answer: B, C

If a method with the Never attribute is called within a context, it throws an exception, and if it is called without a transaction, it runs in an unspecified transaction context. A method with the NotSupported attribute always runs in an unspecified transaction context.

4. Which of the following transaction attributes assigned to a business method will cause the container to throw `java.lang.IllegalStateException` when the method calls `EJBContext.getRollbackOnly`?

   a. Mandatory
   b. Never

c. NotSupported

d. Required

e. RequiresNew

F. Supports

Answer: B, C, F

A method with Never, NotSupported, or Supports usually runs in an unspecified context.

5. For which of the following beans can you use BMT demarcation?

    a. Message-driven beans

    b. Stateful session beans

    c. Stateless session beans

    d. Entity beans

Answer: A, B, C

Entity beans always use CMT demarcation.

6. Which of the following attributes can be assigned to a message-driven bean?

    a. Required

    b. RequiresNew

    c. Mandatory

    d. Never

    e. Supports

    F. NotSupported

Answer: A, F

You can assign only the Required or NotSupported attribute to a method of a message-driven bean.

7. Which of the following methods can be called by a BMT bean?

    a. `getRollbackOnly()`

    b. `setRollbackOnly()`

    c. `setTransactionTimeout()`

    d. `getStatus()`

    e. `rollback()`

Answer: B, C, D, E

A BMT bean can call any method from the `UserTransaction` interface, but there are two methods in the `EJBContext` interface that it cannot call: `getRollbackOnly()` and `setRollbackOnly()`. The `UserTransaction` interface also has `setRollbackOnly()`, but it does not have `getRollbackOnly()`.

8. Which of the following methods can be called by a CMT bean?

   a. `getRollbackOnly()`
   b. `setRollbackOnly()`
   c. `setTransactionTimeout()`
   d. `getStatus()`
   e. `rollback()`

Answer: A, B
A CMT bean can call only methods that exist in the `EJBContext` interface. It cannot call methods from the `UserTransaction` interface.

9. Which of the following methods of an entity bean must be marked with a transaction attribute?

   a. `remove()` method from the `EJBObject` interface
   b. `remove()` methods from the `EJBHome` interface
   c. `getPrimaryKey()` method from the `EJBObject` interface
   d. `findByPrimaryKey()` method from the bean's home interface
   e. `getEJBHome()` method from the `EJBObject` interface

Answer: A, B, D
The `getPrimaryKey()` method from the `EJBObject` interface and the `getEJBHome()` method from the `EJBObject` interface are not required to be marked.

10. A method `ma()` has the attribute Required and it is executing in transaction Ta. Consider the following method calls by method `ma()` to other methods:

   a. `ma() -> mb()`. Method `mb()` runs in transaction TA.
   b. `ma() -> mc()`. Method `mc()` runs in its own transaction, TC.
   c. `ma() -> md()`. Method `md()` runs in an unspecified transaction context.
   d. `ma() -> me()`. Method `me()` throws an exception.

Select one of the following attributes for each called method above to force the stated behavior: Required, RequiresNew, Mandatory, Supports, NotSupported, Never.
Answer:

   a. Required or Mandatory
   b. RequiresNew
   c. NotSupported
   d. Never

CHAPTER 13—EJB EXCEPTIONS

1. Which of the following are subclasses of `java.rmi.RemoteException`?

    a. `java.rmi.NoSuchObjectException`
    b. `javax.transaction.TransactionRequiredException`
    c. `javax.ejb.NoSuchEntityException`
    d. `java.lang.IllegalStateException`

Answer: A, B
`IllegalStateException` is a subclass of `RuntimeException`, and `NoSuch-EntityException` is a subclass of `EJBException`.

2. Which of the following are true about `EJBException`?

    a. If a bean method encounters a `RuntimeException`, it should throw an `EJBException` that wraps the original exception.
    b. If a bean method encounters any unchecked exception, it should throw an `EJBException` that wraps the original exception.
    c. If a bean method encounters any checked exception, it should throw an `EJBException` that wraps the original exception.
    d. If a bean method performs an operation that results in a checked exception that it cannot recover from, it should throw the `EJBException` that wraps the original exception.
    e. If a bean method encounters a system exception, it should throw an `EJBException` on the container.

Answer: D
System exceptions are remote exceptions or runtime exceptions. If a method encounters a runtime exception (`RuntimeException` or any of its subclasses) or an error, it should simply propagate it to the container. If a method receives a checked exception (that the client is not expecting) from which it cannot recover, the method should wrap it inside an `EJBException` and throw it to the container.

3. Which of the following are true about the container?

    a. If a bean method throws an application exception to the container, the container sends an `EJBException` to the local client.
    b. If a bean method throws a system exception to the container, the container rolls back the transaction in which the exception occurred.
    c. If a bean method throws a system exception to the container, the container sends an `EJBException` to the local client.

d.   If a bean method throws a system exception to the container, the container sends it to the remote client exactly as it was thrown on the container.

e.   If a bean method throws an application exception to the container, the container sends a RemoteException to the remote client.

Answer: B, C

If a bean throws an application exception, the container sends it to the client exactly as it was received. If a bean throws a system exception on the container, the container sends it to the client in the form of a RemoteException if the client is remote and in the form of an EJBException if the client is local.

4.   Which of the following are true about a javax.ejb.NoSuchEntity-Exception?

a.   A remote client will receive this exception.

b.   A local client will receive this exception.

c.   A client will never receive this exception.

d.   In order to receive this exception, the client must declare it in the throws clause.

e.   If the container receives this exception, it will discard the bean instance that threw it.

Answer: C, E

The container will transform NoSuchEntityException into NoSuchObject-LocalException if the client is local or NoSuchObjectException if the client is remote. Because it is a system exception, any bean instance that throws it on the container gets killed.

5.   Which of the following beans can throw application exceptions?

a.   A session bean with a BMT demarcation

b.   A session bean with a CMT demarcation

c.   An entity bean with a BMT demarcation

d.   An entity bean with a CMT demarcation

e.   A message-driven bean

Answer: A, B, C, D

A message-driven bean cannot throw an application exception because it has no client view.

6.   Which of the following are true about an exception that a remote client receives?

a.   The exception can be a RemoteException.

b.   The exception can be an EJBException.

c. The exception can be an application exception.
d. All of the above.

Answer: A, C
Only local clients get an `EJBException`.

7. If a message-driven bean with a CMT demarcation throws a system exception, which of the following will the container do?

   a. The container will log the exception.
   b. The container will roll back the transaction that it started just before starting the bean method that threw the exception regardless of whether or not the bean called the `setRollbackOnly()` method.
   c. The container will discard the instance that threw the exception.
   d. The container will roll back the transaction only if the bean has invoked `setRollbackOnly()`.

Answer: A, B, C
The container needs a `setRollbackOnly()` call for an application exception before it can roll back the transaction. For a system exception, it does not care whether the `setRollbackOnly()` call was made or not; it rolls back the transaction anyway.

8. If a client receives a `javax.transaction.TransactionRolledback-Exception`, which of the following may be true about the CMT bean method that threw the exception?

   a. The method is marked with the transaction attribute Mandatory.
   b. The method is marked with the transaction attribute Required.
   c. The method is marked with the transaction attribute Never.
   d. The method is marked with the transaction attribute NotSupported.

Answer: A, B
If a client receives a transaction rolled back exception, it must have made the call in a transaction.

9. A remote client invokes a bean method that throws `NoSuchEntity-Exception`. Which of the following exceptions will the client possibly receive?

   a. `NoSuchEntityException`
   b. `NoSuchObjectException`
   c. `RemoteException`
   d. `EJBException`

Answer: B

The container will transform `NoSuchEntityException` into `NoSuchObject-LocalException` if the client is local or `NoSuchObjectException` if the client is remote. The remote client may get `RemoteException`, but not `EJBException`, for other reasons.

10. Which of the following are subclasses of `CreateException`?

    a. `DuplicateKeyException`
    b. `NoSuchEntityException`
    c. `IllegalStateException`
    d. `RemoveException`
    e. None of the above

Answer: A

`DuplicateKeyException` is a subclass of `CreateException`. `RemoveException` is a subclass of `Exception`, and the other two are system exceptions.

CHAPTER 14 — EJB SECURITY

1. Which element in the deployment descriptor is used to specify that any client can access a set of methods?

    a. `<exclude-list>`
    b. `<unchecked>`
    c. `<checked>`
    d. `<security-role>`

Answer: B

You use the `<unchecked/>` element instead of the `<role-name>` element inside the `<method-permission>` element and before the `<method>` element in order to give any client access to the method.

2. Which EJB roles implement the security infrastructure?

    a. The container provider
    b. The bean provider
    c. The system administrator
    d. The application assembler
    e. The deployer

Answer: A

The security infrastructure is implemented by the container provider, while the security policies are determined largely by the application assembler and the deployer.

3. Which EJB role typically sets the security policies for an EJB application?

    a. The container provider
    b. The bean provider
    c. The system administrator
    d. The application assembler
    e. The deployer

Answer: D, E
The security policies are determined largely by the application assembler and the deployer.

4. Which of the following security-related elements are defined by the bean developer in the deployment descriptor?

    a. `<security-role>`
    b. `<security-role-ref>`
    c. `<role-link>`
    d. `<role-name>`
    e. None of the above

Answer: B
The hard-coded security role name is listed in the `<security-role-ref>` element by the bean provider, and the application assembler uses the `<role-link>` element to link this role to the logical security role defined in the element `<security-role>`.

5. Which of the following are true about declarative EJB security?

    a. It is not possible to distinguish different versions of an overloaded method.
    b. You can specify different permissions for a method in different instances of a bean.
    c. Permissions specified for a method of a bean apply to that method in all instances of the bean.
    d. It is possible to specify different permissions for a method in the home interface from a method with the same name in the component interface.
    e. The `<security-identity>` element cannot be defined for a message-driven bean.

Answer: C, D
You can distinguish interfaces by specifying the `<method-intf>` element, and you can distinguish the different versions of an overloaded method by using the `<method-params>` element. You can define the `<security-identity>` element for an MDB, but you cannot specify `<use-caller-identity/>` for an MDB because an MDB does not have a client.

6. Which of the following are correct statements about EJB security?

    a. If a method is included in both the `<exclude-list>` element and the `<method-permission>` element, the `<method-permission>` element overrides the `<exclude-list>` element for that method.

    b. The `<run-as>` element is defined to specify the security role for all methods in a bean.

    c. The `<exclude-list>` element is used to list the methods that no client can call.

    d. The `<use-caller-identity>` element can be defined for the `onMessage()` method of a message-driven bean.

Answer: B, C

The `<exclude-list>` element overrides the `<method-permission>` element. You cannot define the `<use-caller-identity>` element for the `onMessage()` method because an MDB does not have a client.

7. Which of the following elements can be defined in the `<enterprise-beans>` section of the deployment descriptor?

    a. `<security-role>`
    b. `<security-role-ref>`
    c. `<role-link>`
    d. `<security-identity>`
    e. `<method-permission>`

Answer: B, C, D

The `<security-role>` and `<method-permission>` elements are defined in the `<assembly-descriptor>` section of the deployment descriptor.

8. Which of the following elements can be defined in the `<assembly-descriptor>` section of the deployment descriptor?

    a. `<security-role>`
    b. `<security-role-ref>`
    c. `<role-link>`
    d. `<security-identity>`
    e. `<method-permission>`

Answer: A, E

The application assembler defines the logical security roles in the `<assembly-descriptor>` section of the deployment descriptor. The `<security-identity>` element is defined in the `<enterprise-beans>` section of the deployment descriptor, where the hard-coded roles are also defined and linked to the logical security roles.

9. In a stateful session bean, a call to the `getCallerPrincipal()` method gets the `IllegalStateException`. This call can possibly be made from which of the following methods?

    a. `ejbActivate()`
    b. `ejbPassivate()`
    c. `ejbRemove()`
    d. `setSessionContext()`
    e. `ejbCreate()`

Answer: D
When the `ejbCreate()`, `ejbRemove()`, `ejbActivate()`, or `ejbPassivate()` method of a stateful session bean is executed, the bean has a client. So out of the listed methods, only from the `setSessionContext()` method will a call to `getCallerPrincipal()` generate `IllegalStateException`.

10. In a CMP entity bean, a call to the `getCallerPrincipal()` method gets the `IllegalStateException`. This call can possibly be made from which of the following methods?

    a. `ejbActivate()`
    b. `ejbPassivate()`
    c. `ejbStore()`
    d. `setEntityContext()`
    e. `ejbLoad()`

Answer: A, B, D
Activation and passivation in an entity bean are different from in a session bean: they are a transition between the pooled state and the method-ready state. When these methods are being executed, no client security information is available.

Exam Quick Prep

This appendix provides Quick Preparation Notes, a recap of all the important concepts that are covered in the exam objectives, courtesy Whizlabs Software Pvt. Ltd. (www.whizlabs.com). Developed comprehensively, these points will help you brush through key areas in one go with ease and retain them until you take the exam, helping you answer the questions correctly. You should go through this appendix one more time the day before you take the exam.

We have grouped the information according to the exam objectives provided by Sun. Therefore, the numbering of the objectives corresponds to the numbering given to the objectives on Sun's web site. The objectives are listed with the chapters in which they are discussed. However, since the first chapter of the book does not correspond to any of the exam objectives, the objectives start at chapter 2.

CHAPTER 2—OVERVIEW OF ENTERPRISE JAVABEANS

(Objectives 1.1–1.5, 13.1–13.3)

1.1 *Identify the use, benefits, and characteristics of Enterprise JavaBeans technology, for version 2.0 of the EJB specification.*

Important concepts	Exam tips
✧ There are three different types of EJB: session, entity, and message-driven beans. Furthermore, session beans come in two flavors: stateless and stateful.	EJB does not guarantee load balancing, fail-over, or clustering.
✧ EJB containers provide such services as transaction, security, concurrency, networking, resource management, persistence, and messaging. This allows the EJB developer to concentrate on the business logic.	The local client view is provided for entity and session beans by defining local home and component interfaces.
✧ As of version 2.0, EJB supports the local client view and efficient access to beans from local clients.	Since message-driven beans (MDBs) do not present any interfaces, they do not have a client view.
✧ EJB supports container-managed persistence (CMP) and container-managed relationships (CMR).	

1.2 *Identify EJB 2.0 container requirements.*

Important concepts	Exam tips
✧ All EJB 2.0-compliant containers must provide the following APIs: • Java 2 Platform Standard Edition 1.3 (J2SE 1.3) • EJB 2.0 Standard Extension • JDBC 2.0 Standard Extension (support for row sets only) • JNDI 1.2 Standard Extension • JTA 1.0.1 Standard Extension (UserTransaction interface only) • JMS 1.0.2 Standard Extension • JavaMail 1.1 Standard Extension (for sending mail only) • JAXP 1.0	EJB 2.0-compliant containers are not required to provide the following APIs: • Java Servlet • JavaServer Pages • Java Cryptography Extensions (JCE) • J2SE 1.4 or higher

1.3 *Identify correct and incorrect statements or examples about EJB programming restrictions.*

Important concepts	Exam tips
✧ All static member fields in a bean must also be declared final.	Using client sockets is allowed in EJB; however, listening on a ServerSocket is not allowed.

continued on next page

Important concepts	Exam tips

✧ The bean *must* not
   • Use the AWT or Swing package to output information
   • Access files and directories in the file system
   • Use java.net.ServerSocket for listening and accepting network connections
   • Use the Reflection API to obtain information about declared members of classes
   • Create or obtain the classloader
   • Create or set a security manager
   • Contain code that stops the Java Virtual Machine (JVM)
   • Change the input, output, or error streams
   • Manage threads or ThreadGroups
   • Obtain security policy information for a particular code source
   • Load any native library
   • Define a new class in an existing package
   • Pass `this` as an argument or method result
	Read/write static fields are not allowed in EJB, so static fields can be used only with the `final` keyword.

1.4 *Match EJB roles with the corresponding description of the role's responsibilities, where the description may include deployment descriptor information.*

Important concepts	Exam tips

✧ An enterprise bean provider is responsible for
   • Creating the Java classes that implement the enterprise bean's business methods
   • Defining the bean's home and component interfaces for session and entity beans
   • Adding information about the bean in the deployment descriptor
	The bean provider develops the business logic for the bean, specifies the EJB QL queries for the query methods, and declares names used in the code for the environment properties, other beans, and security role references.

✧ An application assembler is responsible for
   • Combining enterprise beans into larger deployable application units
   • Inserting the application assembly instructions into the deployment descriptors
	The application assembler packs all the beans and other application components into a single ejb-jar file for the application and customizes the properties, security roles, and transaction behavior at the application level.

✧ A deployer is responsible for
   • Deploying the enterprise beans contained in the ejb-jar files in a specific EJB server and container
   • Mapping the security roles defined by the application assembler to the user groups and accounts that exist in the operational environment
   • Generating the additional container-specific classes and interfaces that enable the container to manage the enterprise beans at runtime
	The deployer customizes the application to work in a specific operational environment and ensures that all the required information has been provided in the deployment descriptor.

continued on next page

Important concepts	Exam tips

✧ A container/server provider is responsible for
   • Providing the deployment tools needed for deploying enterprise beans
   • Providing runtime support for the deployed enterprise bean instances
   • Versioning the installed enterprise bean components
 	
✧ A system administrator is responsible for
   • Configuring and administrating the enterprise's computing and networking infrastructure that includes the EJB server and container	

1.5 *Given a list, identify which are requirements for an EJB-jar file.*

Important concepts	Exam tips

✧ The ejb-jar file *must* contain
   • The enterprise bean class
   • The home and component interfaces for session and entity beans
   • The primary key class (only for entity beans)
   • All classes needed by the classes and interfaces listed in the previous three points, except Java system classes
	The ejb-jar file *must not* contain the stubs of the `EJBHome` and `EJBObject` interfaces.

✧ The deployment descriptor must be named ejb-jar.xml and must be in the META-INF directory.	The ejb-jar file is not required to contain the manifest file for the beans.

13.1 *Identify correct and incorrect statements or examples about an enterprise bean's environment JNDI naming.*

Important concepts	Exam tips
✧ The enterprise bean environment can be accessed by instantiating javax.naming.InitialContext and looking up subcontexts of the java:comp/env JNDI context.	The bean cannot change the value of the environment entry at runtime.
✧ Each enterprise bean defines its own set of environment entries.	Each deployment of the bean results in the creation of a distinct home, so the environment entries can have different values for each deployment.
✧ All bean instances within the same home share the same environment entries.	

13.2 *Identify correct and incorrect statements about the purpose and/or use of the deployment descriptor elements for environment entries, ejb references, and resource manager connection factory references, including whether a given code listing is appropriate and correct with respect to a particular deployment descriptor element.*

Important concepts	Exam tips
✧ Environment entries are declared by using the `<env-entry>` deployment descriptor element.	The value of `<ejb-ref-type>` can only be Session or Entity. Message-driven beans cannot be looked up using JNDI since they do not have client view interfaces. Instead, a client locates the destination attached with a message-driven bean by using the JNDI lookup.
✧ Environment entries can be either of type java.lang. String or one of the primitive wrapper class types (specified in the `<env-entry-type>` deployment descriptor element).	The value of the `<ejb-link>` element must be the same as the value of the `<ejb-name>` element in the referenced bean. The referenced bean can be in any deployment descriptor in the application.
✧ Environment entry values can be specified by using the `<env-entry-value>` element of the deployment descriptor.	
✧ The environment entry values must satisfy the following requirements: • The value must be a valid string for the constructor of the specified type. • The value of an entry whose type is java.lang.Character must be a single character.	
✧ EJB references are used to allow the bean provider to refer to the home interface of other enterprise beans (sort of an import statement).	
✧ Local EJB references are declared by using `<ejb-local-ref>` elements in the deployment descriptor.	
✧ Remote EJB references are declared by using `<ejb-ref>` elements in the deployment descriptor.	
✧ Both `<ejb-local-ref>` and `<ejb-ref>` contain the following elements: • `<ejb-ref-name>`: Specifies the name under which the bean is accessible in JNDI, for example, ejb/SomeSessionBean • `<ejb-ref-type>`: Specifies whether the bean is a session or entity bean	

continued on next page

Important concepts	**Exam tips**

◇ Local EJB references also contain the following deployment descriptor elements:
- `<local-home>`: Specifies the local home interface of the bean
- `<local>`: Specifies the local component interface of the bean

◇ Remote EJB references also contain the following deployment descriptor elements:
- `<home>`: Specifies the remote home interface of the bean
- `<remote>`: Specifies the remote component interface of the bean

◇ The `<ejb-link>` deployment descriptor element is specified to link the `<ejb-ref>` or `<ejb-local-ref>` element with the `<entity>` or `<session>` element that describes the referenced bean.

◇ A resource manager connection factory is an object that the bean provider must use to create connections to resource managers; for example, javax.sql.DataSource is a factory for java.sql.Connection.

◇ The `<resource-ref>` deployment descriptor element is used to declare a new resource manager connection factory reference. This element contains the following subelements:
- `<res-ref-name>`: Specifies the name under which the resource manager is accessible in JNDI, for example, jdbc/SomeDataSource
- `<res-type>`: Specifies the resource manager type, for example, javax.sql.DataSource
- `<res-sharing-scope>`: Specifies whether connections obtained from a resource manager connection factory are shareable or not. Possible values are
- Shareable
- Unshareable (default)
- `<res-auth>`: Specifies which authentication approach is used for connecting to the resource manager connection factory. Possible values are
- Application: The bean programmatically signs on to the resource manager.
- Container: The container signs on to the resource manager on behalf of the bean.

◇ Resource environment references describe administered objects that can be retrieved and used by the bean provider.

continued on next page

Important concepts	Exam tips

❖ The `<resource-env-ref>` deployment descriptor element is used to declare a new resource environment reference. This element contains the following ones:
  • `<resource-env-ref-name>`: Specifies the name under which the resource is accessible in JNDI, for example, jms/SomeQueue
  • `<resource-env-ref-type>`: Specifies the Java type of the resource, for example, javax.jms.Queue
 	
❖ Examples of administered resources are
  • A JMS destination (a javax.jms.Queue or javax.jms.Topic)
  • A JDBC connection
 	
❖ It is important to distinguish between resource manager connection factories references and resource environment references. Factories are used to create connections to resource managers, while resources are the existing connections that can be reused.	

13.3 *Given a list of responsibilities, identify which belong to the deployer, bean provider, application assembler, container provider, system administrator, or any combination.*

Important concepts	Exam tips
❖ Environment entry values can be specified by the bean provider, application assembler, or deployer by using the `<env-entry-value>` element of the deployment descriptor.	If the value of the `<res-auth>` element is set to Container, the deployer is responsible for providing the sign-on information for the resource manager.
❖ The bean provider declares `<ejb-ref>` and `<ejb-local-ref>` elements in the deployment descriptor to declare EJB references.	Although the values for the `<env-entry-value>` element may be filled by the bean provider or application assembler, the deployer must ensure that all the `<env-entry-value>` elements contain legal values.
❖ The application assembler specifies the `<ejb-link>` deployment descriptor element to link the declared EJB reference with the referenced bean.	
❖ The bean provider uses the `<resource-env-ref>` deployment descriptor element to declare a new resource environment reference.	
❖ The bean provider uses the `<resource-ref>` deployment descriptor element to declare a new resource manager connection factory reference.	
❖ The deployer binds the resource manager connection factory references to the actual resource manager connection factories, which are configured in the container.	

CHAPTER 3—CLIENT VIEW OF A SESSION BEAN

(Objectives 2.1–2.2)

2.1 *Identify correct and incorrect statements or examples about the client view of a session bean's local and remote home interfaces, including the code used by a client to locate a session bean's home interface.*

Important concepts	Exam tips
✧ The remote home interface of a session bean must implement javax.ejb.EJBHome.	The remote client view of beans is location-independent, but this is not true for local clients.
✧ The local home interface of a session bean must implement javax.ejb.EJBLocalHome.	The arguments and results of the methods of the local interface and local home interface are passed by reference, while for remote interfaces, they are passed by value.
✧ The code for locating the home interface of a remote session bean, say sb, is ```\n Context ctx = new InitialContext();\n Object obj = ctx.lookup("java:comp/env/ejb/sb");\n SessionBeanHome sbHome =\n (SessionBeanHome)javax.rmi.PortableRemoteObject.narrow(obj,\n SessionBeanHome.class);\n```	If a client tries to invoke remove(Object primaryKey) on the home interface of a (local or remote) session bean, javax.ejb.RemoveException is thrown by the EJB container because session beans do not have client-accessible primary keys.
✧ The code for locating the home interface of a local session bean is ```\n Context ctx = new InitialContext();\n Object obj = ctx.lookup("java:comp/env/ejb/sb");\n SessionBeanLocalHome sbHome = (SessionBeanLocalHome) obj;\n``` (Note the absence of narrowing.)	Local clients cannot remove session beans through the home interface, since the Handle object is only for remote beans.
✧ The remote home interface of a session bean allows you to • Create a new session object • Remove an existing session object • Retrieve the javax.ejb.EJBMetaData interface for the session bean • Obtain a handle for the remote home interface of the session bean	
✧ The local home interface of a session bean allows you to create a new session object.	

continued on next page

Important concepts	Exam tips

◇ In order to create a session bean, clients can call any `create<METHOD>()` method of the home interface.

◇ The home interface of stateless session beans must have only one no-argument `create()` method, while that of stateful beans must have one or more `create <METHOD>()` methods with different argument lists.

◇ The create methods of the home interface of a session bean
  - May throw any application exception
  - Must throw `javax.ejb.CreateException`
  - Must throw `java.rmi.RemoteException` (only for remote session beans)

◇ An existing session bean can be removed by invoking `remove(Handle handle)` on the session bean's home interface (only for remote session beans).

2.2 *Identify correct and incorrect statements or examples about the client view of a session bean's local and remote component interfaces.*

Important concepts	Exam tips
◇ The remote interface of a session bean must implement javax.ejb.EJBObject.	To test the equality of beans, always use the `isIdentical()` method; the behavior of the equals method is not defined in this case.
◇ The local interface of a session bean must implement javax. ejb.EJBLocalObject.	`RemoteException` is not thrown by methods declared in the local home and component interfaces.

◇ An existing session bean can be removed by invoking `remove()` on the session bean's component interface.

◇ The component interface of a session bean allows you to
  - Invoke business methods
  - Get the home interface of the session bean
  - Test the equality of the session bean with another session bean
  - Remove the session bean
  - Retrieve the session bean's handle (only for remote session beans)

◇ Since session beans do not have client-accessible primary keys, invoking `getPrimaryKey()` on the component interface of a session bean results in
  - `java.rmi.RemoteException` being thrown to remote clients
  - `javax.ejb.EJBException` being thrown to local clients

continued on next page

Important concepts	Exam tips
◇ Since session beans hide their identity, their home interfaces must not define any finder methods.	
◇ Two different stateful session bean instances, for example, sb1 and sb2, created from the same home always have different identities; that is, `sb1.isIdentical(sb2)` must return `false`.	
◇ Two different stateless session beans, for example, sb1 and sb2, created from the same home always have the same identity; that is, `sb1.isIdentical(sb2)` must return `true`.	

CHAPTER 4—BIRTH OF A SESSION BEAN
(Objectives 3.1, 3.3–3.6, 4.2)

3.1 *Identify correct and incorrect statements or examples about session beans, including conversational state, the SessionBean interface, and create methods.*

Important concepts	Exam tips
◇ All session beans must implement the `SessionBean` interface, which includes the following lifecycle-related methods for the bean: • `void ejbActivate()` • `void ejbPassivate()` • `void ejbRemove()` • `void setSessionContext(SessionContext ctx)`	In the case of stateless session beans, the home interface will contain only one no-argument `create()` method. This is because stateless beans do not retain state across multiple method calls.
◇ The home of a session bean must have at least one `create<METHOD>` method, which is invoked by the client to create the bean.	A call to the `create<METHOD>` method in the home will be delegated to the matching `ejbCreate<METHOD>` method in the bean.

3.3 *Identify the interface and method for each of the following: Retrieve the session bean's remote home interface, Retrieve the session bean's local component interface, Determine if the session bean's caller has a particular role, Allow the instance to mark the current transaction as a rollback, Retrieve the UserTransaction interface, Prepare the instance for re-use following passivation, Release resources prior to removal, Identify the invoker of the bean instance's component interface, Be notified that a new transaction has begun, Be notified that the current transaction has completed.*

Important concepts	Exam tips
✧ All session beans receive a reference to a `javax.ejb.SessionContext` interface when they are created.	Stateless session beans must not implement the `SessionSynchronization` interface since they do not maintain the client state across invocations.
✧ `SessionContext` extends the `EJBContext` interface.	BMT session beans must not implement the `SessionSynchronization` interface since they manage the transactions themselves and hence do not need to be notified.
✧ The following methods can be invoked on `SessionContext` (SessionContext defines only the getEJBObject and getEJBLocalObject methods. All the other methods are inherited from EJBContext): • `getEJBHome()` and `getEJBLocalHome()`: Retrieve the remote and local home interfaces of the session bean • `getEJBObject()` and `getEJBLocalObject()`: Retrieve the remote and local component interfaces of the session bean • `getCallerPrincipal()`: Retrieves the javax.security.Principal object associated with the caller • `isCallerInRole(String role)`: Tests whether the caller has been assigned the role given in the argument • `getRollbackOnly()`: Tests whether the transaction has been marked for rollback (only for CMT session beans) • `setRollbackOnly()`: Marks the current transaction for rollback (only for CMT session beans) • `getUserTransaction()`: Retrieves a javax.transaction.UserTransaction object for bean-managed transaction demarcation (only for BMT session beans)	The `getRollbackOnly()` and `setRollbackOnly()` methods of the Session-Context interface must be used only in the methods that execute in the context of a transaction.
✧ Stateful session beans may optionally implement the `javax.ejb.SessionSynchronization` interface in order to be notified when transaction management–related methods are performed by the container. This interface defines the following callbacks: • `afterBegin()`: Invoked when a new transaction has begun • `beforeCompletion()`: Invoked just before completing the current transaction	

continued on next page

Important concepts	Exam tips

◇ `afterCompletion(boolean committed)`: Invoked after the transaction has completed. The status (successfully committed or not) is passed in as the argument.

3.4 *Match correct descriptions about purpose and function with which session bean type they apply to: stateless, stateful, or both.*

Important concepts	Exam tips
◇ Stateful session beans can be activated and passivated. Stateless session beans cannot be activated and passivated since they do not maintain client state across multiple method calls.	Any stateless session bean instance can be used by any client, since stateless session beans do not store any client-specific data.
◇ The creation and removal of a stateful session bean are initiated by the client, but the life of a stateless session bean is entirely managed by the container.	
◇ Stateless session beans support instance pooling, while stateful beans do not.	
◇ Stateless session beans can have instance variables, but they cannot preserve the variable values across method calls.	

3.5 *Given a list of responsibilities related to session beans, identify those which are the responsibility of the session bean provider, and those which are the responsibility of the EJB container provider.*

Important concepts	Exam tips
◇ The session bean provider is responsible for providing the following class files: • Session bean class • Session bean's remote interface and remote home interface, if the session bean provides a remote client view • Session bean's local interface and local home interface, if the session bean provides a local client view	The bean can have either a remote client view or a local client view, or both. So, the bean provider has to provide one of the following combinations: • Local home and local component interfaces • Remote home and remote component interfaces • Both of the above
◇ The container provider provides the deployment tools, which are responsible for generating the following: • Session EJBHome class • Session EJBObject class • Session EJBLocalHome class • Session EJBLocalObject class	

3.6 *Given a list of requirements, identify those which are the requirements for a session bean class, remote component interface, remote home interface, create methods, business methods, local component interface, local home interface.*

Important concepts	Exam tips

❖ The session bean class must
  • Implement the `javax.ejb.SessionBean` interface
  • Be public
  • Not be final or abstract
  • Have one public constructor with no arguments
  • Not define any `finalize()` method
	A create method in the home interface returns the component interface, while the corresponding ejbCreate method in the bean class returns `void`.

❖ Implement the business methods of the component interface and the `ejbCreate<METHOD>()` methods corresponding to the `create<METHOD>` methods of the home interface	The methods defined in the bean class must not throw `RemoteException`.
❖ A stateful session bean's home interface must define one or more `create<METHOD>(…)` methods. For each `create<METHOD>()` method, there must be one matching `ejbCreate<METHOD>()` method in the session bean class.	
❖ A stateless session bean class must have one and only one create method, it must not take any arguments, and it must be called `ejbCreate()` (no suffix!).	

❖ The `ejbCreate<METHOD>()` methods must
  • Have `ejbCreate` as a prefix followed by the name of the corresponding create method in the home interface
  • Be public
  • Not be final or static
  • Have a return type of `void`
  • Have arguments whose types are legal RMI-IIOP types if there is a corresponding create method in the remote home interface
  • Declare to throw `javax.ejb.CreateException` and any application exceptions	

4.2 *Given a list of methods of a stateful or stateless session bean class, define which of the following operations can be performed from each of those methods: SessionContext interface methods, UserTransaction methods, JNDI access to java:comp/env environment naming context, resource manager access and other enterprise bean access.*

Important concepts	Exam tips

✧ The only operations that can be performed in every method of a BMT or CMT (stateful or stateless) session bean are
  • `getEJBHome()` and/or `getEJBLocalHome()`
  • JNDI access to java:comp/env
	A stateless session bean cannot call `getCallerPrincipal()` and `isCallerInRole()` methods in ejb-Create, because there is no client associated with the stateless bean's creation.

✧ The following methods of a CMT stateful session bean execute in an unspecified transaction context:
  • `setSessionContext()`
  • `ejbCreate<METHOD>()`
  • `ejbRemove()`
  • `ejbActivate()`
  • `ejbPassivate()`
	Stateless session beans cannot access resource managers and enterprise beans from the `ejbCreate()` and `ejbRemove()` methods because the container does not have a meaningful transaction context at that time.

✧ The following methods of a stateless session bean execute in an unspecified security context:
  • `setSessionContext()`
  • `ejbCreate()`
  • `ejbRemove()`
	Resource manager access is not allowed from the constructor, `setSession-Context()`, and `afterCompletion()` methods in a stateful session bean.

CHAPTER 5—LIFECYCLE OF A SESSION BEAN
(Objectives 4.1–4.3, 3.2)

4.1 *Identify correct and incorrect statements or examples about the lifecycle of a stateful or stateless session bean instance.*

Important concepts	Exam tips
✧ The creation/removal of a stateful session bean is the responsibility of the client; that is, the client must invoke a create method on the home interface or a remove method on the home or component interface in order to create/remove the stateful session bean.	Stateful session beans are never passivated while in a transaction.
✧ The creation/removal of a stateless session bean is not the responsibility of the client; that is, even if the client invokes the single create method on the home interface or a remove method on the home or component interface, the stateless session bean might not be created/removed as a result of the call. The EJB container can create and remove sessionless bean instances without any call from the client.	If a bean times out while in passivated state, it is simply removed without activation, and it does not get an `ejbRemove()` call

continued on next page

Important concepts	Exam tips

✧ Stateful session beans can be removed
  • By the container without a call from the client, after a specific timeout period
  • By the container when a client invokes a `remove()` method on the home or component interface	

4.2 *Given a list of methods of a stateful or stateless session bean class, define which of the following operations can be performed from each of those methods: SessionContext interface methods, UserTransaction methods, JNDI access to java:comp/env environment naming context, resource manager access and other enterprise bean access.*

Important concepts	Exam tips

✧ The only operations that can be performed in every method of a BMT or CMT (stateful or stateless) session bean are
  • `getEJBHome()` and/or `getEJBLocalHome()`
  • JNDI access to java:comp/env
	A stateless session bean cannot call `getCallerPrincipal()` and `isCallerInRole()` methods in ejb-Create, because there is no client associated with the stateless bean's creation.

✧ The following methods of a CMT stateful session bean execute in an unspecified transaction context:
  • `setSessionContext()`
  • `ejbCreate<METHOD>()`
  • `ejbRemove()`
  • `ejbActivate()`
  • `ejbPassivate()`
	Stateless session beans cannot access resource managers and enterprise beans from the `ejbCreate()` and `ejbRemove()` methods because the container does not have a meaningful transaction context at that time.

✧ The following methods of a stateless session bean execute in an unspecified security context:
  • `setSessionContext()`
  • `ejbCreate()`
  • `ejbRemove()`
	Resource manager access is not allowed from the constructor, `setSession-Context()`, and `afterCompletion()` methods in a stateful session bean.

4.3 *Given a list of scenarios, identify which will result in an ejbRemove method not being called on a bean instance.*

Important concepts	Exam tips

✧ The container might not invoke the `ejbRemove()` method in any of the following cases:
  • A crash of the EJB container
  • When a system exception is thrown from any instance methods
  • When the session bean times out while it is in the passivated state
	The bean will get an `ejbRemove()` call if the client calls the `remove()` method or the bean times out while in the method ready state.

3.2 *Identify the use of, and the behavior of, the ejbPassivate method in a session bean, including the responsibilities of both the container and the bean provider.*

Important concepts	Exam tips
✧ Passivation is a technique to save the bean's conversational state to a persistent medium when the client is inactive between calls, in the case of stateful session beans.	All open resources, such as open sockets, must be closed in the `ejbPassivate()` method and reopened in the `ejbActivate()` method.
✧ When the bean is about to be passivated, the `ejbPassivate()` method is invoked.	
✧ The bean provider must ensure that the ejbPassivate method leaves the instance fields ready to be serialized by the container.	
✧ The following special types are persisted during passivation, if stored in nontransient fields: • Objects whose runtime type implements, directly or indirectly, the `java.io.Serializable` interface • `null` • Reference to the remote or local home and component interfaces • Reference to the SessionContext object • Reference to the JNDI Environment Naming Context (ENC) • Reference to a `javax.transaction.UserTransaction` interface • Reference to a resource manager connection factory	
✧ The container may passivate a session bean instance only when the instance is not in a transaction.	
✧ The container may destroy a session bean instance if the instance does not meet the requirements for serialization after ejbPassivate.	

CHAPTER 6—CLIENT VIEW OF AN ENTITY BEAN
(Objectives 5.1–5.4)

5.1 *Identify correct and incorrect statements or examples about the client of an entity bean's local and remote home interface, including view the code used to locate an entity bean's home interface, and the home interface methods provided to the client.*

Important concepts	Exam tips
✧ The remote home interface of an entity bean must implement javax.ejb.EJBHome.	Home business methods are used for performing operations that are not specific to an entity.

continued on next page

Important concepts	Exam tips
✧ The local home interface of an entity bean must implement javax.ejb.EJBLocalHome.	The `PortableRemoteObject.narrow()` method is required only for the remote home interface and not for the local home interface.

✧ The code for locating the home interface of an entity bean by a remote client is

```
Context ctx = new InitialContext();
Object obj = ctx.lookup("java:comp/env/ejb/
eb");
EntityBeanHome ebHome =
(EntityBeanHome)javax.rmi.PortableRemoteOb-
ject.narrow(obj,
EntityBeanHome.class);
```

✧ The code for locating the home interface of an entity bean by a local client is

```
Context ctx = new InitialContext();
Object obj = ctx.lookup("java:comp/env/ejb/
eb");
EntityBeanLocalHome ebHome = (EntityBean-
LocalHome) obj;
```

✧ (Note the absence of narrowing.)

✧ The home interface of an entity bean allows a client to
- Create a new entity
- Find an existing entity
- Remove an existing entity
- Execute a home business methodRetrieve the `javax.ejb.EJBMetaData` interface for the entity bean (only for remote entity beans)
- Obtain a handle for the remote home interface of the entity bean (only for remote entity beans)

✧ In order to create an entity, clients can call any `create<METHOD>()` method of the home interface.

✧ An existing entity can be removed by invoking any of the following methods:
- `remove()` on the entity bean's component interface
- `remove(Object primaryKey)` on the entity bean's home interface
- `remove(Handle handle)` on the entity bean's home interface (only for remote entity beans)

5.2 *Identify correct and incorrect statements or examples about the client view of an entity bean's local component interface (EJBLocalObject).*

Important concepts	Exam tips
✧ The local interface of an entity bean must implement javax.ejb.EJBLocalObject. ✧ The component interface of an entity bean allows you to • Invoke business methods • Get the home interface of the entity bean • Test the equality of the entity bean with another entity bean • Remove the entity • Retrieve the entity bean's handle (only for remote entity beans) • Retrieve the entity bean's primary key	More than one client can access the same entity bean instance concurrently.

5.3 *Identify correct and incorrect statements or examples about the client view of an entity bean's remote component interface (EJBObject).*

Important concepts	Exam tips
✧ The remote interface of an entity bean must implement the javax.ejb.EJBObject interface. ✧ The getHandle() method of the remote component interface returns the javax.ejb.Handle object for the entity bean. ✧ The Handle object is serializable; it can be held beyond the life of a client process by serializing the handle to the database.	The remote interface reference can be obtained from the handle of the entity bean. The getEJBObject() method of the Handle interface returns the EJB object represented by this handle.

5.4 *Identify the use, syntax, and behavior of the following entity bean home method types for CMP: finder methods, create methods, remove methods, and home methods.*

Important concepts	Exam tips
✧ The create methods of the home interface of an entity bean • May throw any application exception • Must throw javax.ejb.CreateException • Must throw java.rmi.RemoteException (only for remote interfaces)	There can be zero or more create methods; it is legal to have one without arguments.

continued on next page

Important concepts	Exam tips
❖ Finder methods must be prefixed with find and must throw javax.ejb.FinderException. In addition, java.rmi.RemoteException must be declared in the finder methods of the remote home interface.	It is optional for the entity bean to have create() methods; however, the findByPrimaryKey() method is mandatory.
❖ The local or remote home interface of an entity bean must include the findByPrimaryKey() method.	The return type of the create method is the component interface of the bean. The finder methods return either the component interface or a collection of those.
❖ The (local or remote) home interface of an entity bean may define business methods that do not pertain to a specific entity bean instance. They are called home business methods, and their name must not start with create, find, or remove.	

CHAPTER 7 — BIRTH OF AN ENTITY BEAN
(Objectives 6.1, 6.6, 8.1–8.2)

6.1 *Identify correct and incorrect statements or examples about the entity bean provider's view and programming contract for CMP, including the requirements for a CMP entity bean.*

Important concepts	Exam tips
❖ Container-managed persistence (CMP) provides a separation between the entity bean class and its persistent representation.	Accessor methods and collection classes for CMR fields must not be exposed through remote interfaces.
❖ A CMP entity bean can have container-managed relationships (CMR) with other CMP entity beans.	Local interface types must not be exposed through remote interfaces.
❖ An abstract persistence schema is the set of XML elements in the deployment descriptor, which describes the CMP and CMR fields.	

❖ The CMP programming contract specifies that
  • The CMP entity bean class is abstract.
  • CMP fields are not defined in the bean class.
  • The CMP and CMR fields must be specified in the deployment descriptor using the cmp-field and cmr-field elements, respectively.
  • Accessor methods are defined for the CMP and CMR fields.
  • Accessor methods are public and abstract, named with the first letter of the name of the cmp-field or cmr-field in uppercase and prefixed by get or set.	

continued on next page

Important concepts	Exam tips
✧ The accessor methods for a container-managed relationship field must be defined in terms of the local interface of the related entity bean.	

6.6 *Identify the interface(s) and methods a CMP entity bean must and must not implement.*

Important concepts	Exam tips

✧ The entity bean class must
  • Implement the `javax.ejb.EntityBean` interface
  • Be public and abstract
  • Not be final
  • Have one public constructor with no arguments
  • Not define any `finalize()` method
  • Implement the business methods of the component interface
  • Implement the `ejbCreate<METHOD>()` and `ejbPostCreate<METHOD>()` methods corresponding to `create<METHOD>()` methods in the home interface
  • Implement the `ejbHome<METHOD>()` methods
  • Declare abstract get/set accessor methods for the bean's abstract persistence schema
 	
✧ The `ejbCreate<METHOD>()` methods must
  • Have `ejbCreate` as a prefix
  • Be public
  • Not be final or static
  • Declare their return type as the primary key class
  • Have arguments whose types are legal RMI-IIOP types if there is a corresponding create method in the remote home interface
  • Correspond to one `create<METHOD>()` method in the home interface
  • Declare to throw `javax.ejb.CreateException` and any application exceptions
 	
✧ The `ejbPostCreate<METHOD>()` methods must
  • Have `ejbPostCreate` as a prefix
  • Be public
  • Not be static
  • Declare their return type as void
  • Declare to throw `javax.ejb.CreateException` and any application exceptions
 	
✧ The `ejbHome<METHOD>()` methods must
  • Have `ejbHome` as a prefix
  • Be public
  • Not be final or static
  • Have arguments and return values whose types are legal RMI-IIOP types
  • Correspond to one business method of the home interface
  • Throw any application exceptions
  • Not throw `java.rmi.RemoteException`
	The bean class does not need to implement the component interface in its signatures. It may do that, but this is not recommended. However, you do need to implement the methods of the component interface in the body of the class.

continued on next page

Important concepts	Exam tips

❖ The ejbSelect<METHOD>() methods must
  - Have ejbSelect as a prefix
  - Be public and abstract
  - Declare to throw javax.ejb.FinderException and any applica-
    tion exceptions

❖ The business methods must
  - Not start with the prefix ejb
  - Be public
  - Not be final or static
  - Have arguments and return values whose types are legal RMI-IIOP
    types if they are exposed in the bean's remote interface
  - Define any application exceptions

8.1 *From a list of behaviors, match them with the appropriate EntityContext method*
responsible for that behavior.

Important concepts	Exam tips
❖ All entity beans receive a reference to a javax.ejb. EntityContext interface when the container calls the setEntityContext(...) method after instantiating them.	The only method that the EntityContext interface has and the SessionContext interface does not have is getPrimaryKey.
❖ EntityContext extends the EJBContext interface.	EntityContext inherits the getUserTransaction() method from the EJBContext interface, but this method cannot be called by entity beans, since entity beans do not support bean-managed transactions (BMT).
❖ The following methods can be invoked on EntityContext. (EntityContext defines only the getPrimaryKey, getEJBObject, and getEJBLocalObject methods. All the other methods are inherited from EJBContext.) • getEJBHome() and getEJBLocalHome(): Retrieve the remote and local home interfaces of the entity bean • getEJBObject() and getEJBLocalObject(): Retrieve the remote and local component interfaces of the entity bean • getPrimaryKey(): Retrieves the primary key of the entity bean • getCallerPrincipal(): Retrieves the javax. security.Principal object associated with the caller • isCallerInRole(String role): Tests whether the caller has been assigned the role given in the argument • getRollbackOnly(): Tests whether the transaction has been marked for rollback • setRollbackOnly(): Marks the current transaction for rollback	

8.2 *Identify correct and incorrect statements or examples about an entity bean's primary key and object identity.*

Important concepts	Exam tips

✧ Primary keys of entity beans come in two flavors:
  • A key that maps to a single field in the entity bean class (single-field key)
  • A key that maps to multiple fields in the entity bean class (compound key)
	The primary key must be a legal value type in RMI-IIOP.

✧ A single-field primary key is specified by the bean provider in the `<primkey-field>` element of the deployment descriptor.	The primary key class must provide suitable implementation of the `hashCode()` and equals methods.

✧ A compound primary key class of an entity bean must
  • Be public and must have a public constructor with no parameters
  • Declare only public member fields whose names must be a subset of the names of the container-managed fields declared in the deployment descriptor
	If the bean provider uses java.lang. Object as the value for the `<prim-key-class>` element, it is the deployer's responsibility to choose the primary key type at deployment time.

✧ If you, the bean provider, do not know the type of the primary key in advance (for example, when deployment-specific keys must be used), you must use java.lang.Object in the `<prim-key-class>` element of the deployment descriptor and as the argument of the `findByPrimaryKey()` method.	
✧ The value of a primary key of an entity bean instance must not be changed after it has been set; otherwise, a `java.lang.IllegalStateException` is thrown by the EJB container.	
✧ The primary key is usually set in the `ejbCreate<METHOD>()` method, that is, before the entity bean can participate in a relationship.	

CHAPTER 8—LIFECYCLE OF AN ENTITY BEAN
(Objectives 7.1–7.3)

7.1 *Identify correct and incorrect statements or examples about the lifecycle of a CMP entity bean.*

Important concepts	Exam tips
✧ The bean instance moves from the does not exist state to the pooled state with the invocation of the bean class constructor followed by the `setEntityContext(…)` method.	When associated with `ejbPassivate()`, the `ejbStore()` method is always invoked before the `ejbPassivate()` method is called.

continued on next page

Important concepts	Exam tips
✧ The bean instance can move from the pooled to the ready state either through the `ejbCreate<METHOD>()` and `ejbPostCreate<METHOD>()` methods or through the `ejbActivate()` method.	When associated with `ejbActivate()`, the `ejbLoad()` method is always invoked after the `ejbActivate()` method is called.
✧ The bean instance moves from the ready state to the pooled state through the `ejbRemove()` method or the `ejbPassivate()` method.	The `ejbSelect()` methods are for the bean's private use only; they are not invoked by clients.
✧ The bean instance moves from the pooled state to the does not exist state through the invocation of the `unsetEntityContext()` method.	
✧ The `ejbFind()` and `ejbHome()` methods can be invoked on the bean instance while the bean instance is in the pooled state.	
✧ The `ejbLoad()` method is called after synchronizing the state of an enterprise bean instance with the entity in the database.	
✧ The `ejbStore()` method is invoked before the container synchronizes the entity in the database with the state of the enterprise bean instance.	
✧ The `ejbSelect()` methods may be invoked by home business methods while the bean is in the pooled state or by entity-specific business methods while the bean is in the ready state.	

7.2 *From a list, identify the purpose, behavior, and responsibilities of the bean provider for a CMP entity bean, including but not limited to: setEntityContext, unsetEntityContext, ejbCreate, ejbPostCreate, ejbActivate, ejbPassivate, ejbRemove, ejbLoad, ejbStore, ejbFind, ejbHome, and ejbSelect.*

Important concepts	Exam tips
✧ The bean provider is responsible for • Using the `setEntityContext()` method to allocate any resources that are to be held by the instance for its lifetime • Using the `unsetEntityContext()` method to free any resources that are held by the instance • Using the `ejbCreate()` method to initialize the instance in this method from the input arguments • Returning `null` from the implementation of the `ejbCreate()` method • Using the `ejbPostCreate<METHOD>()` method to set the values of cmr-fields • Using the `ejbActivate()` method to acquire additional resources that the bean needs while it is in the ready state • Using the `ejbPassivate()` method to release the resources that the bean acquired during the `ejbActivate()` methodUsing the `ejbRemove()` method for anything to be done before the entity is removed from the database • Defining `ejbSelect()` methods as abstract methods	The values of cmr-fields of the entity bean may not be set in the `ejbCreate()` method since the bean identity is not available there.
	The ejbFind methods are not written by the bean provider but are generated by the container. Bean identity is not available in the ejbHome methods because they are invoked on beans in the pooled state.

7.3 *From a list, identify the responsibility of the container for a CMP entity bean, including but not limited to: setEntityContext, unsetEntityContext, ejbCreate, ejbPostCreate, ejbActivate, ejbPassivate, ejbRemove, ejbLoad, ejbStore, ejbFind, ejbHome, and ejbSelect.*

Important concepts	Exam tips
✧ The container is responsible for • Passing the EntityContext object reference to the setEntityContext method • Invoking the setEntityContext method after creating the bean instance and before adding it to the pool • Invoking the `unsetEntityContext()` method to reduce the number of instances in the pool • Invoking the `ejbCreate()` method when a client invokes a matching `create()` method on the entity bean's home interface • Establishing the primary key of the entity before invoking the ejbPostCreate method. Note that it is still the responsibility of the bean provider to establish the values of all the fields that make up the key before the end of the ejbCreate method. • Invoking the corresponding ejbHome method when the client calls the home method • Generating implementations of the ejbSelect methods and ejbFind methods • Invoking the ejbFind method on an instance when a client invokes a matching `find()` method on the bean home	The container must not reuse a bean instance after invoking the `unset-EntityContext()` method on it.
	The `setEntityContext()`, `ejbPassivate()`, `ejbActivate()`, and `unsetEntityContext()` methods execute in an unspecified transaction context. The `ejbLoad()` and `ejbStore()` methods may be invoked by the container any number of times and in any order during the life of the instance.

CHAPTER 9—ENTITY BEAN RELATIONSHIPS

(Objectives 6.2–6.5)

6.2 *Identify correct and incorrect statements or examples about persistent relationships, remove protocols, and about the abstract schema type, of a CMP entity bean.*

Important concepts	Exam tips
✧ Container-managed relationships are defined in terms of the local interfaces of the related entity beans.	`<cascade-delete>` can be specified only for entity beans that are in a relationship with another entity bean whose multiplicity is One.
✧ An entity bean that does not have a local interface can have only unidirectional relationships from itself to the other entity bean; that is, it can have one or more instances of the related bean but not vice versa.	The remote interface of a bean is not allowed to expose its CMR fields, but a local interface can do so because relationships are defined only for colocated beans.
✧ The Collection interfaces that must be supported by the EJB container for container-managed relationships fields are `java.util.Collection` and `java.util.Set`.	A CMP entity bean type can have relationships with many bean types at the same time.
✧ The container-managed relationship fields must be set in the `ejbPostCreate<METHOD>()` method and not in the `ejbCreate<METHOD>()` method.	
✧ Entity beans that participate in a relationship should be defined in the same deployment descriptor.	
✧ Entities can be removed • By using the `<cascade-delete>` element in the deployment descriptor • By invoking a remove method on the home or component interface	

6.3 *Identify correct and incorrect statements or examples about the rules and semantics for relationship assignment, and relationship updating, in a CMP bean.*

Important concepts	Exam tips
✧ Relationships may be one-to-one, one-to-many, or many-to-many—either bidirectional or unidirectional.	The identity of the collection object referenced by a cmr-field does not change when a set accessor method is executed.
✧ When assignment operations are performed on container-managed relationships, referential integrity is maintained.	After many-to-many relationships are assigned, the Collection objects referenced by the cmr-fields are not shared, but the objects contained in the Collections are.

continued on next page

Important concepts	Exam tips
✧ In the case of a one-to-one relationship, assigning an instance from a cmr-field in one instance to a cmr-field of the same relationship type in another instance effectively moves the object, and the value of the cmr-field in the first instance is set to `null`.	
✧ In the case of a one-to-many relationship, if a collection of entity objects is assigned from a cmr-field in one instance to a cmr-field of the same relationship type in another instance, the objects in the collection are effectively moved.	
✧ In the case of a many-to-many relationship, if the value of a cmr-field is assigned to a cmr-field of the same relationship type in another instance, the objects in the collection of the first instance are assigned as the contents of the cmr-field of the second instance.	

6.4 *Match the name with a description of purpose or functionality, for each of the following deployment descriptor elements: ejb-name, abstract-schema-name, ejb-relation, ejb-relationship-role, cmr-field, cmr-field-type, and relationship-role-source.*

Important concepts	Exam tips
✧ The `<abstract-schema-name>` element specifies the name of the type to be used as the type of an entity bean in an EJB QL query.	In a unidirectional relationship, the cmr-field element is specified only for the bean that is the source of the relationship and not for the target bean.
✧ The relationships are defined in the `<relationships>` section of the deployment descriptor.	The ejb-name and abstract-schema-name must be unique within the ejb-jar file.
✧ Within the `<relationships>` element, each entity-to-entity relationship is defined in a separate `<ejb-relation>` element.	
✧ Every `<ejb-relation>` element has two `<ejb-relationship-role>` subelements, one for each related bean type.	
✧ Each relationship role refers to an entity bean by means of an `<ejb-name>` subelement contained in the `<relationship-role-source>` element.	
✧ The `<multiplicity>` element describes the multiplicity of the role that participates in a relation. Its value can be One or Many.	
✧ In a relationship, if one bean maintains a reference to the other bean, the reference is declared using the cmr-field element.	

continued on next page

Important concepts	Exam tips
✧ When the relationship is of type one-to-many or many-to-many, it is necessary to use `<cmr-field-type>` to specify which collection class (`java.util.Collection` or `java.util.Set`) to use for the cmr-field.	

6.5 *Identify correctly implemented deployment descriptor elements for a CMP bean (including container-managed relationships).*

Important concepts	Exam tips
✧ An `<ejb-relation>` element contains a description, an optional `<ejb-relation-name>` element, and exactly two relationship role declarations defined by the `<ejb-relationship-role>` elements. The name of the relationship, if specified, is unique within the ejb-jar file.	CMP fields are defined within the `<entity>` element of the deployment descriptor, while CMR fields are defined within the `<relationships>` element.
	The `<relationship-role-source>` element has to be specified for both the beans in the relationship and not just for the bean that maintains a reference to the other.

CHAPTER 10 — EJB QUERY LANGUAGE
(Objectives 9.1–9.3)

9.1 *Identify correct and incorrect syntax for an EJB QL query including the SELECT, FROM, and WHERE clauses.*

Important concepts	Exam tips
✧ The `SELECT` and `FROM` clauses are mandatory in an EJB QL query. The `WHERE` clause is optional.	Legal identifiers for identification variables must satisfy the same rules as for normal Java identifiers.
✧ Abstract schema names (`<abstract-schema-name>`) are used to specify the name of the abstract schema type of entity beans, for use in EJB QL queries.	EJB QL queries are case-insensitive.
✧ The keyword `DISTINCT` removes all duplicates from the result set. This means that the corresponding finder method might return java.util.Set instead of java.util.Collection.	The keyword `AS` is optional in a `FROM` clause.
✧ The `FROM` clause is used to declare identification variables (separated by commas), such as Collection member declarations or range variable declarations. Identification variables cannot be declared in any other clause.	

continued on next page

Important concepts	Exam tips

◇ An identification variable can be anything as long as
  - It is not the same as a reserved EJB QL identifier.
  - It does not have the same name as an `<abstract-schema-name>`.
  - It does not have the same name as an `<ejb-name>`.

◇ The keyword `IN` is used to declare Collection member declarations, as in `FROM Person p, IN(p.addresses) AS addr`.

◇ Path expressions allow one to navigate over container-managed persistent fields and container-managed relationship fields, as in `p.addr.street` (`addr` is a CMR field of `p` and `street` is a CMP field of `addr`).

◇ The `WHERE` clause is used to restrict the results of a query by means of conditional expressions that select only appropriate objects.

◇ String literals are of type String, integer literals are of type Long, floating-point literals are of type Double, and boolean literals take the values TRUE and FALSE.

◇ Input parameters to EJB QL queries can be denoted by using the character `?` followed by an integer starting from `1` (`?1`, `?4`, and so on).

9.2 *Identify correct and incorrect statements or examples about the purpose and use of EJB QI.*

Important concepts	Exam tips
◇ EJB QL queries are defined in the `<ejb-ql>` deployment descriptor element.	EJB QL queries cannot be used to insert or update database records.

◇ EJB QL queries are
  • Defined in terms of the abstract persistent schema of the entity beans
  • Portable across databases and data schemas
	EJB QL queries can navigate over one or more CMR fields to end at either a CMR or a CMP field.

◇ EJB QL queries are used to specify how finder (`ejbFind<METHOD>()` and `ejb-Select<METHOD>()`) methods should be implemented by the EJB container.	

9.3 *Identify correct and incorrect conditional expressions, between expressions, in expressions, like expressions, and comparison expressions.*

Important concepts	Exam tips
❖ BETWEEN expressions allow defining a range of values to be returned by the query.	Two NULL values are not considered to be equal.
❖ LIKE expressions allow comparing a value with a given pattern. In the pattern string, % stands for any sequence of characters, and _ represents a single character.	The BETWEEN expression may be used only on numeric primitives and their wrappers.
❖ IS EMPTY expressions allow testing whether a Collection is empty or not.	
❖ MEMBER OF expressions allow testing whether a given parameter or identification variable is a member of a given Collection.	
❖ IN expressions test for membership in a list of literal string values.	

CHAPTER 11—MESSAGE-DRIVEN BEANS
(Objectives 10.1–10.4)

10.1 *Identify correct and incorrect statements or examples about the client view of a message-driven bean, and the lifecycle of a message-driven bean.*

Important concepts	Exam tips
❖ Message-driven beans don't have any client view; that is, they don't have any home or component interfaces, local or remote.	The lifetime of an MDB is controlled by the container, not by the client.
❖ Similar to stateless session beans, message-driven beans do not maintain a conversational state.	MDB instances do not maintain state, but they can contain instance variables.
❖ Message-driven beans consume messages asynchronously from a JMS destination (javax.jms.Queue or javax.jms.Topic). In the future, other messaging middleware might be supported.	

❖ The code for locating the destination from which a message-driven bean consumes a message is
`Context ctx = new InitialContext();`
`Queue someQueue = (javax.jms.Queue)`
`ctx.lookup("java:comp/env/jms/someQueue");`	

continued on next page

Important concepts	Exam tips

❖ A message-driven bean class must implement the `javax.ejb.MessageDrivenBean` interface. As a result, the following methods must be implemented by the bean class:
  - `setMessageDrivenContext(MessageDrivenContext mdc)`: Invoked by the container when the bean is created in order to pass it a reference to its context
  - `ejbRemove()`: Invoked by the container when the bean is about to be removed

❖ A message-driven bean class must implement the `javax.jms.MessageListener` interface. As a result, the following method must be implemented by the bean class:
  - `onMessage(Message msg)`: Invoked by the container when a message has been received and must be handled

❖ All message-driven beans receive a reference to a `javax.ejb.MessageDrivenContext` interface when the container calls the `setMessageDrivenContext()` method after instantiating the bean.

❖ A message-driven bean is associated with a JMS destination by using the `<message-driven-destination>` element in the deployment descriptor.

❖ The container might delete an MDB instance without invoking the `ejbRemove()` method in any of the following cases:
  - A crash of the EJB container
  - A system exception is thrown from any instance methods

❖ The only context/access–related operation that can be performed in all methods of a BMT or CMT message-driven bean is JNDI access to java:comp/env.

❖ The following methods of a CMT message-driven bean execute in an unspecified transaction context:
  - `setMessageDrivenContext()`
  - `ejbCreate()`
  - `ejbRemove()`

10.2 *Identify the interface(s) and methods a JMS Messaged-Driven bean must implement.*

Important concepts	Exam tips
✧ A message-driven bean class must implement the `javax.ejb.MessageDrivenBean` interface. As a result, the following methods must be implemented by the bean class: • `setMessageDrivenContext(MessageDriven-Context mdc)`: Invoked by the container when the bean is created in order to pass it a reference to its context • `ejbRemove()`: Invoked by the container when the bean is about to be removed	None of the methods defined in the MDB throw application exceptions or `RemoteException`, since there are no clients.
✧ A message-driven bean class must implement the `javax.jms.MessageListener` interface. As a result, the following method must be implemented by the bean class: • `onMessage(Message msg)`: Invoked by the container when a message has been received and must be handled	The bean class must have no-argument `ejbCreate()` and `ejbRemove()` methods.
✧ The message-driven bean class must • Be public • Not be final or abstract • Have one public constructor with no arguments • Not define any `finalize()` method	The `onMessage()` method must have a single argument of type javax.jms.Message.
✧ The `ejbCreate()` method must • Be named ejbCreate • Be public • Not be final or static • Have a return type void • Have no arguments • Not throw any application exceptions	
✧ The `ejbRemove()` method must • Be named ejbRemove • Be public • Not be final or static • Have a return type void • Have no arguments • Not throw any application exceptions	
✧ The `onMessage()` method must • Be public • Not be final or static • Have a return type void • Have a single argument of type javax.jms.Message • Not throw any application exceptions	

10.3 *Identify the use and behavior of the MessageDrivenContext interface methods.*

Important concepts	Exam tips
✧ All message-driven beans receive a reference to a `javax.ejb.MessageDrivenContext` interface when the container calls the `setMessageDrivenContext()` method on the MDB instance. `MessageDrivenContext` extends the `EJBContext` interface.	The message-driven context remains associated with the instance for the lifetime of the instance.
✧ The following methods can be invoked on `MessageDrivenContext`. (`MessageDrivenContext` does not define any new methods. All the methods are inherited from `EJBContext`.) • `getEJBHome()` and `getEJBLocalHome()`: Message-driven beans must not call these methods because they do not have home interfaces. • `getCallerPrincipal()` and `isCallerInRole(String role)`: Message-driven beans must not call these methods because they do not have clients. • `getRollbackOnly()`: Tests whether the transaction has been marked for rollback (only for CMT message-driven beans) • `setRollbackOnly()`: Marks the current transaction for rollback (only for CMT message-driven beans) • `getUserTransaction()`: Retrieves a javax.transaction.UserTransaction object for bean-managed transaction demarcation (only for BMT message-driven beans)	The MDB has no clients; hence, a bean instance cannot call client-related methods in the `MessageDrivenContext`.

10.4 *From a list, identify the responsibility of the bean provider, and the responsibility of the container provider for a message-driven bean.*

Important concepts	Exam tips
✧ The message-driven bean provider is responsible for • Writing the message-driven bean class • Indicating in the acknowledge-mode deployment descriptor element whether JMS AUTO_ACKNOWLEDGE semantics or DUPS_OK_ACKNOWLEDGE semantics should apply. This is only for BMT beans.	The container does not guarantee that messages are received in the same order in which they are sent by the client, the JMS producer.
✧ The container provider • Is responsible for managing the message-driven bean instances at runtime • Must ensure that only one thread is executing an instance at any given time • Must support the deployment of a message-driven bean as the consumer of a JMS queue or a durable subscription • Must follow the rules with respect to transaction scoping, security checking, and exception handling • Is responsible for the generation of additional classes when the message-driven bean is deployed	If the transaction of an MDB using container-managed transactions is rolled back, the message handling is rolled back by the container.

CHAPTER 12—EJB TRANSACTIONS

(Objectives 11.1–11.4)

11.1 *Identify correct and incorrect statements or examples about EJB transactions, including bean-managed transaction demarcation, and container-managed transaction demarcation.*

Important concepts	Exam tips

◇ There are two different transaction management techniques:
  • Bean-managed transaction (BMT) demarcation
  • Container-managed transaction (CMT) demarcation
	The EJB 2.0 specification supports flat transactions; that is, it does not allow nested transactions.

◇ BMT beans use the `javax.transaction.UserTransaction` interface in order to demarcate transactions. Entity beans cannot use bean-managed transaction demarcation; that is, there are no BMT entity beans.	Session and message-driven beans can use both CMT and BMT (but not at the same time), while entity beans must use only CMT.
◇ CMT beans rely on the container for everything related to transaction management.	
◇ The only valid transaction attributes for message-driven beans are Required and NotSupported. The use of other transaction attributes is not meaningful for message-driven beans because there can be no preexisting transaction context (RequiresNew, Supports) and no client to handle exceptions (Mandatory, Never).	

◇ The `javax.transaction.UserTransaction` interface can be obtained by
  • Invoking `getUserTransaction()` on the EJBContext object of the bean
  • Looking up java:comp/UserTransaction through JNDI	

◇ The `javax.transaction.UserTransaction` interface provides the following features to BMT beans:
  • `begin()` for starting a transaction
  • `commit()` for committing a transaction
  • `rollback()` for rolling back a current transaction
  • `getStatus()` for retrieving the current status of the running transaction
  • `setRollbackOnly()` for marking the current transaction for rollback	

◇ The `javax.ejb.EJBContext` interface is extended by the `SessionContext`, `EntityContext`, and `MessageDrivenContext` interfaces. EJBContext provides the following methods to CMT beans:
  • `getRollbackOnly()` for retrieving whether the current transaction has been marked for rollback or not
  • `setRollbackOnly()` for marking the current transaction for rollback	

continued on next page

Important concepts	Exam tips
✧ The methods of the previous point can be invoked only by methods with the following transaction attributes (`java.lang.IllegalStateException` is thrown otherwise): • Required • RequiresNew • Mandatory	
✧ BMT stateful session beans can start a transaction in one method and terminate it in another method.	
✧ BMT stateless session beans must start and terminate a transaction within the same method.	
✧ BMT message-driven beans must commit the current transaction before the end of the `onMessage()` method.	
✧ The `javax.ejb.SessionSynchronization` interface is intended for CMT stateful session beans that wish to be informed when the container performs transaction management operations.	

11.2 *Identify correct and incorrect statements about the Application Assembler's responsibilities, including the use of deployment descriptor elements related to transactions, and the identification of the methods of a particular bean type for which a transaction attribute must be specified.*

Important concepts	Exam tips
✧ In order to specify whether a session or message-driven bean uses bean-managed or container-managed transaction demarcation, the bean provider uses the `<transaction-type>` element in the deployment descriptor and specifies, respectively, Bean or Container as the value of that element.	For a message-driven bean, the transaction attribute must be specified for the bean's onMessage method. All other methods are called with an unspecified transaction context.
✧ The application assembler is responsible for assigning transaction attributes to methods of CMT beans in the `<container-transaction>` element in the deployment descriptor.	Transaction attributes must not be specified for the methods of a session bean's home interface.
✧ The application assembler must specify transaction attributes either for all the methods or for none. In the latter case, the deployer will be in charge of assigning transaction attributes to methods.	
✧ Entity beans with EJB 2.0 container-managed persistence should use only the following transaction attributes (the bean will not be portable if it uses other transaction attributes): • Required • RequiresNew • Mandatory	

continued on next page

Important concepts	Exam tips

✧ The following methods always execute within an unspecified transaction context:
- Methods with the following transaction attributes
- NotSupported
- Never
- Supports (when the client calls the method without a transaction context)
- `ejbCreate<METHOD>()`, `ejbRemove()`, `ejbActivate()`, and `ejbPassivate()` methods of a CMT session bean
- `ejbCreate()` and `ejbRemove()` methods of a CMT message-driven bean

11.3 *Given a list of transaction behaviors, match them with the appropriate transaction attribute.*

Important concepts	Exam tips
✧ The application assembler uses transaction attributes in the deployment descriptor to specify the transaction management or how the container must manage transactions.	Only Mandatory and Never might throw exceptions if the transaction context does not satisfy their requirements.

✧ The transaction attributes are
- Required: A transaction must exist in order to run the method. If there are none, a new transaction is created by the container.
- RequiresNew: The method must run in a new transaction (created by the container) even if a client transaction exists.
- Supports: The method will run in an unspecified transaction context if no transaction exists and in the client transaction if one exists.
- NotSupported: The method will run in an unspecified transaction context in every case. An existing client transaction will be put on hold until the method returns.
- Mandatory: A transaction must exist in order for the method to execute. If none exists, `javax.transaction.TransactionRequiredException` is thrown to remote clients and `javax.ejb.TransactionRequiredLocalException` is thrown to local clients.
- Never: No transaction must exist in order for the method to execute. If one exists, `java.rmi.RemoteException` is thrown to remote clients and `javax.ejb.EJBException` is thrown to local clients.

11.4 *Given a list of responsibilities, identify those which are the container's with respect to transactions, including the handling of getRollbackOnly, setRollbackOnly, getUserTransaction, SessionSynchronization callbacks, for both container and bean-managed transactions.*

Important concepts	Exam tips
◇ The bean provider uses the `UserTransaction` interface to demarcate transactions.	The `afterBegin()` method of the `SessionSynchronization` interface is called on the bean instance before any business method is executed as part of the transaction.
◇ The container ensures that an instance that starts a transaction completes the transaction before it starts a new transaction.	The container may not call the `beforeCompletion()` method of the `SessionSynchronization` interface, if the transaction has been marked for rollback.
◇ `SessionSynchronization` callbacks are made by the container to inform the bean instance of the transaction events; this is applicable only in the case of CMT beans.	

CHAPTER 13 — EJB EXCEPTIONS

(Objectives 12.1–12.5)

12.1 *Identify correct and incorrect statements or examples about exception handling in EJB.*

Important concepts	Exam tips
◇ The EJB 2.0 specification distinguishes two different kinds of exceptions: • System exceptions: subtypes of `java.lang.RuntimeException`, `java.rmi.RemoteException` • Application exceptions: subtypes of `java.lang.Exception` that are not subtypes of `java.lang.RuntimeException`	An application exception class must not be defined as a subclass of `RuntimeException` or `RemoteException`.
◇ The following exceptions are standard application exceptions: • `javax.ejb.CreateException` • `javax.ejb.DuplicateKeyException` • `javax.ejb.FinderException` • `javax.ejb.ObjectNotFoundException` • `javax.ejb.RemoveException`	An application exception thrown by an enterprise bean instance should be reported to the client by the container, as it is.

continued on next page

Important concepts	Exam tips
✧ The following exceptions are system exceptions: • `java.lang.RuntimeException` • `java.rmi.RemoteException` • `java.rmi.NoSuchObjectException` • `javax.ejb.EJBException` • `javax.ejb.NoSuchEntityException` • `javax.transaction.TransactionRolledbackException` • `javax.ejb.TransactionRolledbackLocalException` • `javax.transaction.TransactionRequiredException` • `javax.ejb.TransactionRequiredLocalException`	All unchecked exceptions and `RemoteException` come under the category of system exceptions, although the client has to prepare for (expect) `RemoteException`.

12.2 *Given a list of responsibilities related to exceptions, identify those which are the bean provider's, and those which are the responsibility of the container provider. Be prepared to recognize responsibilities for which neither the bean nor the container provider is responsible.*

Important concepts	Exam tips
✧ If the bean method runs in the context of the caller's transaction • When an application exception is thrown by the bean instance, the container rethrows the exception to the client as it is.	For a bean method running in unspecified transaction context, any system exceptions thrown by bean methods are logged and the bean is discarded.
✧ For other exceptions, the exception is logged and marked for rollback, and the instance is discarded. The container throws `TransactionRolledbackException` to remote clients and `TransactionRolledbackLocalException` to local clients.	
✧ If the bean method runs in the context of a new transaction started • For an application exception, if the instance called `setRollbackOnly()`, then the container rolls back the transaction and rethrows the exception. Otherwise, the container attempts to commit the transaction and then rethrows the exception. • When other exceptions are logged, the transaction is rolled back and bean instance is discarded. `RemoteException` is thrown by the container to remote clients and `EJBException` to local clients.	
✧ If a system exception is thrown • If the exception is a subtype of `java.lang.RuntimeException`, the bean provider in the bean class code must propagate it to the container as it is. • If the exception is a checked exception or error, the bean provider in the bean class code must wrap it in a `javax.ejb.EJBException` and throw it to the container.	

12.3 *Identify correct and incorrect statements or examples about application exceptions and system exceptions in entity beans, session beans, and message-driven beans.*

Important concepts	Exam tips
✧ When an application exception is thrown (only from session or entity bean classes), the current transaction (if any) is not automatically rolled back by the container.	Stateless session beans never receive `RemoveException`.
✧ When an application exception is thrown (only from session or entity bean classes), the executing bean is not automatically discarded.	Message-driven bean methods never throw application exceptions.
✧ Application exceptions are always passed on to the client as they are received by the container. If the container started the transaction (if the transaction attribute value is Required or RequiresNew), the container attempts to commit the transaction if `getRollbackOnly()` returns `false` and rolls it back otherwise.	
✧ If a system exception is thrown, the container will always perform all of the following: • Log the exception for audit purposes • Mark the current transaction (if one exists) for rollback • Discard the bean instance • Release the managed resources	

12.4 *Given a particular method condition, identify the following: whether an exception will be thrown, the type of exception thrown, the container's action, and the client's view.*

Important concepts	Exam tips
✧ If a system exception is thrown from a bean method and the client started the transaction (only for session and entity beans with a transaction attribute value of Required, Mandatory, or Supports), the container will throw a `javax.transaction.Transaction-RolledbackException` to remote clients and a `javax.ejb.TransactionRolledback-LocalException` to local clients.	A `java.rmi.RemoteException` will be thrown by the container to remote clients and a `javax.ejb.EJBException` to local clients if a system exception is thrown from a bean method and any of the following are true: • The bean is a BMT session or message-driven bean. • The exception was thrown from a method executing in an unspecified transaction context (NotSupported, Never, or Supports). • The exception was thrown from a method executing within a container-initiated transaction (Required or RequiresNew.

continued on next page

Important concepts	Exam tips
✧ If a method with the Mandatory transaction attribute is invoked by a client within an unspecified transaction context, the container will throw a `javax.transaction.TransactionRequiredException` if the client is remote and `javax.ejb.TransactionRequiredLocalException` if the client is local.	
✧ If a method with the Never transaction attribute is invoked by a client within a transaction, the container will throw a `java.rmi.RemoteException` if the client is remote and `javax.ejb.EJBException` if the client is local.	

12.5 *Identify correct and incorrect statements or examples about the client's view of exceptions received from an enterprise bean invocation.*

Important concepts	Exam tips
✧ A client that is an enterprise bean with container-managed transaction demarcation can use the `EJBContext.getRollbackOnly()` method to test whether the transaction has been marked for rollback.	If a client attempts to invoke a stateful session object that was removed, the Container will throw `java.rmi.NoSuchObjectException` to remote clients or `javax.ejb.NoSuchObjectLocalException` to local clients.
✧ A client that is an enterprise bean with bean-managed transaction demarcation, and other client types, can use the `UserTransaction.getStatus()` method to obtain the status of the transaction.	Local clients can receive any of the following exceptions: • Any application exception • `javax.ejb.TransactionRolledback-LocalException` • `javax.ejb.EJBException`
✧ If a client program receives an application exception, the client can continue calling the enterprise bean.	Remote clients can receive any of the following exceptions: • Any application exception • `javax.transaction.TransactionRolledback-Exception` • `java.rmi.RemoteException`

CHAPTER 14—EJB SECURITY
(Objectives 14.1–14.4)

14.1 *Identify correct and incorrect statements about the EJB support for security management including security roles, security role references, and method permissions.*

Important concepts	Exam tips
✧ Security management in EJB can be declarative or programmatic.	Security role references are local to the bean in which they are declared; that is, they are not shared between bean types.
✧ Security management in EJB can be declarative or programmatic.	A method permission consists of one or more methods that can be invoked by one or more security roles.
✧ All security roles referred to in the code are declared as security role references by using the deployment descriptor element called `<security-role-ref>`.	A security role may appear in several method permissions; that is, a security role may be allowed to execute different groups of methods.
✧ Logical security roles are declared using the `<security-role>` element. The security role references are mapped to these roles using the `<role-link>` element.	
✧ Method permissions can be specified for security roles, which allow only the users belonging to those roles to access the given methods.	

14.2 *From a list of responsibilities, identify which belong to the application assembler, bean provider, deployer, container provider, or system administrator.*

Important concepts	Exam tips

✧ The bean provider is responsible for
  • Declaring security role references (`<security-role-ref>` in the deployment descriptor)
  • Invoking `getCallerPrincipal()` or `isCallerInRole()` on the EJB context to access the caller's security context
	The EJB container must never return `null` from `getCallerPrincipal()` by ensuring that all enterprise bean method invocations received through the home and component interfaces are associated with a valid Principal.

continued on next page

continued on next page

✧ The application assembler is responsible for
  • Declaring security roles (<security-role> in the deployment descriptor) and linking them (by using <role-link>) with the security role references defined by the bean provider
  • Declaring method permissions for each security role, that is, for assigning group of methods to security roles of the application
  • Specifying that certain methods may be invoked without any authorization checking, by using the <unchecked> element instead of a set of roles in a <method-permission> element
  • Specifying that certain methods should never be called, by using the <exclude-list> element in the deployment descriptor
  • Specifying whether the caller's security identity (<use-caller-identity> in the deployment descriptor) or a specific run-as security identity (<run-as> in the deployment descriptor) should be used for the execution of the methods of an enterprise bean

✧ The deployer is responsible for
  • Mapping the security view (security roles, method permission, and so on) that was specified by the application assembler to the mechanisms and policies used by the security domain in the operational environment in which the application is deployed
  • Assigning Principals and/or groups of Principals (users, user groups, and so on) to the security roles (<security-role> in the deployment descriptor)
  • Performing any tasks that have not been performed by the application assembler and/or bean provider
  • Changing any value provided by the bean provider and/or application assembler in order to adapt the security policy to the operational environment

✧ The EJB container provider
  • Must provide adequate deployment tools for allowing the deployer to map the security information in the deployment descriptor to the security management mechanisms used in the target operational environment
  • Must provide a security domain and principal realms to the enterprise beans
  • Must provide access to the caller's security context via the getCallerPrincipal() and isCallerInRole() methods of EJBContext
  • Is responsible for providing secure access to resource managers
  • Is responsible for enforcing the security policies defined by the deployer
  • Must throw java.rmi.RemoteException to a remote client and javax.ejb.EJBException to a local client if the client tries to invoke a method without the necessary permissions (<method-permission> in the deployment descriptor)

✧ The system administrator is responsible for creating/removing user accounts and adding/removing users from user groups.

14.3 *Given a code listing, determine whether it is a legal and/or appropriate way to programmatically access a caller's security context.*

Important concepts	Exam tips
❖ The security role references declared using the `<security-role-ref>` element are used as arguments of the `isCallerInRole()` method.	If the `isCallerInRole()` or `getCallerPrincipal()` method is invoked when no security context exists, `java.lang.IllegalStateException` is thrown at runtime.
❖ `getCallerPrincipal()` always returns the java.security.Principal object that represents the caller of the bean *and not* the java.security.Principal object that represents the run-as security identity of the bean.	
❖ `isCallerInRole()` allows the bean provider to make sure that only a certain role can execute a given portion of the code.	

14.4 *Given a security-related deployment descriptor tag, identify correct and incorrect statements and/or code related to that tag.*

Important concepts	Exam tips
❖ If a method is marked as `<unchecked>`, the security permissions are not checked before the method is invoked.	If both `<unchecked>` and security roles are declared in a method permission element, `<unchecked>` has priority.
❖ The `<security-identity>` element specifies whether the caller's security identity is to be used for the execution of the methods of the enterprise bean or whether a specific `<run-as>` identity is to be used. The `<use-caller-identity>` element or the `<run-as>` element must be specified for this.	The `<use-caller-identity>` element cannot be used with message-driven beans since they do not have a calling client.
❖ The `<use-caller-identity>` element is used to specify that an enterprise bean will execute under the caller's identity; that is, the bean will always execute using the same Principal that was used to invoke the bean method.	The `<run-as>` identity applies to the bean as a whole, that is, to all the methods of the enterprise bean's home and component interfaces.
❖ The `<run-as>` element defines a run-as identity, which is used as the bean's identity when it tries to invoke methods on other beans; that is, the bean will execute using a Principal that is different from that which was used to invoke the bean methods.	

index

MORE TITLES FROM MANNING

SCWCD Exam Study Kit: Second Edition
 by Hanumant Deshmukn, Jignesh Malavia
  and Mathew Scarpino
 ISBN: 1-932394-38-9
 560 pages, $49.95
 May 2005

SWT/JFace in Action
 by Mathew Scarpino, Stephen Holder, Stan-
  ford Ng and Laurent Mihalkovic
 ISBN: 1-932394-27-3
 496 pages, $44.95
 November 2004

For ordering information on these and other Manning titles,
go to www.manning.com

MORE TITLES FROM MANNING

Hibernate in Action
    by Christian Bauer and Gavin King
    ISBN: 1-932394-15-X
    400 pages, $44.95
    August 2004

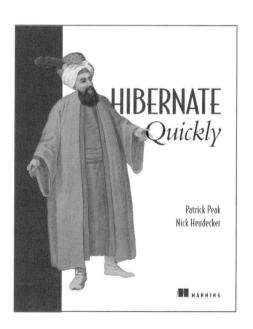

Hibernate Quickly
    by Patrick Peak and Nick Heudecker
    ISBN: 1-932394-41-9
    220 pages, $34.95
    June 2005

For ordering information on these and other Manning titles,
go to www.manning.com

MORE TITLES FROM MANNING

Spring in Action
  by Craig Walls and Ryan Breidenbach
  ISBN: 1-932394-35-4
  472 pages, $44.95
  February 2005

Eclipse in Action: A Guide for Java Developers,
Second Edition
  by David Gallardo, Ed Burnette,
    Robert McGovern
  ISBN: 1-932394-55-9
  570 pages, $44.95
  September 2005

For ordering information on these and other Manning titles,
go to www.manning.com

MORE TITLES FROM MANNING

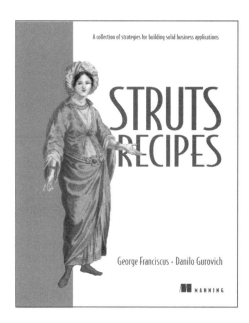

Struts Recipes
   by George Franciscus and Danilo Gurovich
   ISBN: 1-932394-24-9
   520 pages, $44.95
   December 2004

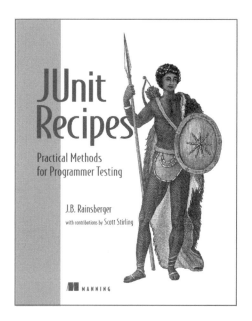

JUnit Recipes
   by J.B. Rainsberger
       with Scott Sterling
   ISBN: 1-932394-23-0
   752 pages, $44.95
   July 2004

For ordering information on these and other Manning titles,
go to www.manning.com

MORE TITLES FROM MANNING

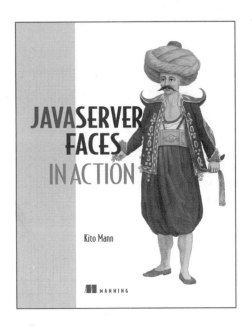

JavaServer Faces in Action
 by Kito Mann
 ISBN: 1-932394-12-5
 744 pages, $49.95
 October 2004

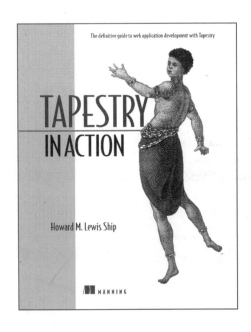

Tapestry in Action
 by Howard M. Lewis Ship
 ISBN: 1-932394-11-7
 5801 pages, $44.95
 March 2004